THE RECEPTION OF GRIMMS' FAIRY TALES

THE RECEPTION OF GRIMMS' FAIRY TALES

Responses, Reactions, Revisions

Edited by Donald Haase

Wayne State University Press   Detroit

Library of Congress Cataloging-in-Publication Data

The Reception of Grimms' Fairy tales : responses, reactions, revisions
    / edited by Donald Haase.
        p.   cm.
    Includes index.
    ISBN 0–8143–2207–7 (alk. paper)
    1. Kinder- und Hausmärchen.   2. Grimm, Wilhelm, 1786–1859—
Criticism and interpretation.   3. Grimm, Jacob, 1785–1863—
Criticism and interpretation.   4. Fairy tales—Germany—History and
criticism.   I. Haase, Donald.
PT921.R4   1993
398.21′0943—dc20   92–47394

Designer: Mary Primeau

Jane Yolen's ''The Brothers Grimm and Sister Jane'' © Jane Yolen.

Jane Yolen's ''Toads'' © June 1989. Published with permission of the author and her agent, Curtis Brown, Ltd.

Angela Carter's ''Ashputtle: or, The Mother's Ghost'' first appeared in *Merveilles & contes*, vol. 1, no. 2, December 1987. Published with the author's permission.

Maria Tatar's ''Wilhelm Grimm/Maurice Sendak: *Dear Mili* and the Literary Culture of Childhood'' from *Off with Their Heads* (Princeton: Princeton University Press, 1992). Reprinted with permission.

Contents

Contents

Acknowledgments

The idea for this volume grew out of work I did with two Summer Seminars for School Teachers sponsored by the National Endowment for the Humanities. I am grateful to the participants in those Seminars for that initial stimulus. I am also grateful for support provided by a National Endowment for the Humanities Travel to Collections Grant and a research grant from the German Academic Exchange Service. My own institution, Wayne State University, significantly encouraged this work with a Career Development Chair and a Graduate Research Assistant. I want also to acknowledge the assistance of the Brüder Grimm-Museum in Kassel, especially Dr. Bernhard Lauer and Ursula Lange-Lieberknecht. Thanks are also due to my research assistant, Randy Schantz.

Introduction

Donald Haase

Hansel and Gretel are alive and well
And they're living in Berlin
She is a cocktail waitress
He had a part in a Fassbinder film
And they sit around at night now
Drinking schnapps and gin . . .

—Laurie Anderson, "The Dream Before"

AS A BOOK, Grimms' *Fairy Tales* has been with us not even two hundred years. Nonetheless, the tales' world-wide reception and popularity have given them the venerable aura of longevity. Explanations for this longevity have conventionally been one-dimensional generalizations about some universal quality residing within the tales themselves. The tales endure, we are told, because they are timeless, true, or good. Publishers in particular echo each other on the back covers of their editions by proclaiming that Grimms' classic stories are "ageless tales of myth and magic" (Hunt) or that they contain "ageless magic and mythology" (Manheim). Similarly, some attribute the tales' apparently timeless appeal to universal moral and aesthetic values. During the sesquicentennial of the first publication of Grimms' collection, the prolific Grimm scholar Wilhelm Schoof used the book's longevity and international reception to defend it against the moral and aesthetic criticism of its earliest detractors. After all, Schoof concludes in a remarkable non sequitur, "a book that has endured for one and one-half centuries and entered the consciousness of many peoples cannot be bad'' (335).

Laurie Anderson's image of a late twentieth-century urban Hansel and Gretel reminds us that the reception of Grimms' fairy tales is not so simple a matter. Hansel and Gretel—along with other fairy-tale characters—may live on, but they do not always play the parts given them by the Grimms. Conventional explanations of the fairy tale's longevity no longer suffice to account for these unconventional roles. Proclamations of the tales' ''ageless magic'' might help sell the stories, and affirmations of their universal moral and aesthetic ''goodness'' might be edifying, but sentimental hype hardly explains why Hansel and Gretel ''sit around at night now drinking schnapps and gin.''

The facts of the tales' reception paint a much more problematic and multifaceted picture. For one, we cannot ignore the irony that the Grimms collected and published their book of tales because they believed the stories were dying out. The times, they thought, were not conducive to the survival of these ''timeless'' tales. So it would seem that the stories were allowed to survive not because they were ageless, but because they were not.

A second problematic irony is that when we speak of the reception of Grimms' fairy tales, we are frequently not actually talking about the Grimms' book itself, but about the responses, reactions, and revisions it has provoked. The contradiction is summed up beautifully on the dust jacket of Jack Zipes's important translation of *The Complete Fairy Tales of the Brothers Grimm:* ''Enchanting, brimming with the wonder and magic of *once upon a time,* the fairy tales of the Brothers Grimm are the special stories of childhood that stay with us throughout our lives. But most Americans know them only secondhand, in adaptations that greatly reduce the tales' power to touch our emotions and intrigue our imaginations.'' Grimms' tales, according to this, can impact us profoundly in childhood and become an enduring part of our lives without our having known them at all. Strong magic indeed. Yet, the magic here is in the publisher's sales pitch. If secondhand adaptations and retellings have usurped the place of Grimms' own texts and do constitute our primary experience, then we can no longer speak of the longevity of Grimms' tales, but at best of their reincarnation. Just how firsthand the reception of Grimms' tales is, to what extent they have ''entered the consciousness of many peoples'' directly or in some mediated or altered form, is a significant question.

Put somewhat differently, the question is actually "What constitutes the Grimm text?" The Grimm Brothers themselves gave us a model in which the concept of the text is significantly expanded. In their collection, the text of an individual tale is firmly embedded in an extended context that influences how we respond to the stories. The collection's title, its dedication and prefaces, each tale's position in the collection and editorial development, and the Grimms' annotations have all been used to understand the significance of the tales and have thus acted as a textual frame.[1] Similarly, in subsequent editions and translations the titles, illustrations, prefaces, forewords, afterwords, notes, parallel texts, and even the publisher's dust jacket copy have become part of the text by attempting to frame the tales in a certain way and direct our responses. All sorts of what Gérard Genette calls paratexts have become part of our experience of the Grimm text, complicating the question of reception in manifold ways.

The problem of textuality and reception raises still other questions. Do we "know" Grimms' fairy tales when we read them in translation? Translations, after all, can give us widely divergent experiences of the same Grimm original, which is why we have seen the production of so many new English editions in the last two decades.[2] Do retellings, adaptations, and variants make up in any way our experience of Grimms' fairy tales? Many adaptations deliberately revise well-known tales and thus depend on the recipient's ability to perceive intertextual relationships. Those of us who teach Grimms' tales, however, know how common it is for the process to be reversed. Better acquainted with "secondhand" versions, students respond and react to Grimms' stories against the background of these other fairy-tale experiences—particularly the Disney experience.

As Disney's animated fairy tales remind us, the medium of adaptation adds yet another dimension to the issue of reception. Grimms' book has been transformed by the most diverse media, including oral storytelling, literature, illustration and graphic arts, audio recording, radio, television, animation, cinema, and electronic video. Reception becomes a much more difficult and differentiated question once we get beyond Schoof's idea of a "good book," which ignores the thematic and formal consequences of adaptation, not to mention the role of economics in the reception of Grimms' tales.[3]

Whatever reincarnations might account for the ongoing reception of Grimms' stories, it is important to recognize that not all responses are positive. There has never been a seamless tradition of positive Grimm reception. In fact, since their first publication, as Schoof's belated defense indicates, the Grimms' stories have frequently elicited negative reactions, including rejection and critical revision. Challenges to Grimms' canonical collection of fairy tales continue, in fact, to this day.

The history of Grimm reception, then, is not the simple success story of a good book that has been widely accepted because of its moral and aesthetic appeal. The reception of Grimms' *Fairy Tales* is a much more dynamic process characterized by diversity and dissonance. It is a multifaceted process involving the production, institutionalization, definition, acceptance, rejection, transformation, revision, and interpretation of a protean book of stories that emerged over the course of the Grimms' adult lifetime. This volume seeks to illuminate the reception of Grimms' fairy tales by exploring some of the diversity and dynamics of that reception in the responses, reactions, and revisions the tales have elicited in Western Europe and North America.

Siegfried Neumann's essay reviews the genesis of Grimms' collection and establishes that the reception of their tales begins with the brothers' own reception of the folk tradition. Their work as editors and collectors has significantly influenced the course of fairy-tale reception to this day. By framing the stories with their own mythic understanding of the folktale, minimizing the importance of the individual storyteller in their annotations, and idealizing the storyteller in their preface, the Grimms established a context that has encouraged the view of fairy tales as transcendent and timeless. Their consciously limited selection of tales from the often bawdy oral tradition and their idealized aesthetic re-creation of the folktale have skewed our sense of the folk tradition and shaped our expectations of the fairy tale generally. So normative are the Grimms' scholarship and tales, that their own reception of the fairy tale continues to give shape to folklore scholarship and even to an object of that scholarship—the repertoire and style of contemporary oral storytellers.

The Grimms' normative influence on folklore studies is confirmed in specific detail by Ines Köhler-Zülch, who examines the reception of the Grimms' work by their nineteenth-century disciple Heinrich Pröhle. In adopting the Grimms' methods and editorial style, Pröhle helped establish their collection and their editorial methods as authoritative. And in doing that he helped define the way in which scholars would receive and transmit folk materials. Pröhle's reception of Grimms' *Fairy Tales,* then, facilitated the institutionalization of the Grimms' work, which has affected both the nature and the interpretation of the folk texts passed on by scholars.

The Grimms' editorial methods also had reverberations outside of Germany. This is documented in part by Brian Alderson, who is interested in the linguistic transaction that takes place when an oral genre is published in written form. The crucial issue for Alderson, however, is the additional language transaction and transformation that occur when Grimms' texts are translated into another language. Alderson investigates how English translators of Grimms' stories responded to the original German tales with their own translations. Working in the golden age of English children's literature and responding to the stylistic dictates of that market, English translators failed to reproduce the vigor and oral register of Grimms' stories. Nonetheless, Grimms' first English translator, Edgar Taylor—although he could not transcend the formality of written English diction—was able to render the tales so that they appealed to English readers. In the form of Taylor's *German Popular Stories* (1823–26), Grimms' *Kinder- und Hausmärchen* impacted English folklore studies and children's literature alike, attesting to their enthusiastic reception abroad. But the translators' failure to replicate in English the authentic voice of the German text reveals that the received and accepted text—the "book" that has "entered into the consciousness" of English readers—was something significantly other than the Grimms'. And Alderson's conclusion that each generation may have need of its own translation underlines the elusive nature of the Grimm text, especially in foreign cultures, and the recipients' role in determining the legitimate shape of that text.

While Edgar Taylor's translation, with all its faults, achieved remarkable success abroad, the Grimms' own book—the actual *Kinder- und Hausmärchen*—had a much different reception at home. The common myth that the collection achieved nearly immediate public success is debunked by Ruth Bottigheimer, who documents for the first time that Germans embraced Grimms' *Fairy Tales* only late in the nineteenth century and only under certain social, political, and economic conditions. Her work here elaborates on an argument she has made elsewhere that Grimms' incorporation of folk values in their

13

tales at first did not match the tastes of their middle-class readers, who only later developed the nostalgic taste that made them increasingly receptive to the Grimms' collection ("From Gold to Guilt"). Drawing on all the available evidence, Bottigheimer establishes that before and during the copyright period the fairy-tale market was dominated by Ludwig Bechstein, who finally lost ground to the Grimms near the turn of the century, when the copyright on the Grimms' tales expired and the interests of the middle-class reading public shifted. Once the tales were established in the educational system and became aligned with the nationalistic ideology of German politics, they quickly achieved canonical status in public consciousness. Despite attempts by occupation forces to suppress the tales following World War II, and despite critical attacks from the radical left, publishers and consumers continue to give the tales a dominant place in the contemporary marketplace.

Because of its canonical status, the Grimm fairy tale has easily overshadowed other fairy tale traditions, which are in their own way critical reactions to the Grimm genre. In her essay, "Trivial Pursuit? Women Deconstructing the Grimmian Model in the *Kaffeterkreis*," Shawn Jarvis focuses on a less well-received tradition of fairy-tale discourse and advances it as an alternative model to the Grimm tradition. Jarvis draws special attention to the fairy tales produced in mid-nineteenth-century Germany in the female literary circle known as the *Kaffeterkreis*. Focusing on Gisela von Arnim's tale "The Rose Cloud," Jarvis demonstrates how the story deconstructs the restrictive Grimm model of silent and passive women and replaces it with one that empowers females with speech and active intelligence. "The Rose Cloud" represents for Jarvis a larger but neglected tradition of fairy-tale writing by females that offers us even today new ways of thinking about writing fairy tales and living in society—ways that are obscured in a culture that prizes Grimms' tales above all others.

Feminist criticism is a significant and controversial component of the contemporary reception of Grimms' tales. The issue is a complex one, to be sure. Many readers reject the feminist critique of patriarchal values in Grimms' stories, and feminists themselves disagree about the tales' depiction of women.[4] Jarvis's work illuminates the issue by revealing how some nineteenth-century German women actually responded to Grimms' stories. The juxtaposition of Gisela von Arnim's contemporary response to Grimms' models is a compelling confirmation of the feminist critique, for it demonstrates how, at least in the case of the intellectually active *Kaffeterkreis,* perceptive young women raised on Grimms' stories responded to them by proposing alternative tales.

To study the response of nineteenth-century readers to Grimms' tales—to know how they understood and reacted to the stories—is a problematic undertaking, especially when it comes to youthful recipients. Lacking access to the immediate response, we are left to make inferences from reconstructed experiences or from indirect accounts. The work that has already been done in this area is quite tentative and preliminary. Gerhard Heilfurth, for instance, has documented that Grimms' fairy tales were a staple in the Karl Marx family and a special favorite of Marx's daughter Eleanor; but more precise insights into the nature of the response are elusive. August Nitschke has drawn on autobiographical accounts from the sixteenth to the nineteenth centuries to draw interesting conclusions about the ways in which children responded to fairy tales, but these accounts are in large measure later recollections of childhood responses. As the essay by Jarvis demonstrates, writers who react to Grimms' stories with revised narratives and characterizations offer us the opportunity to understand more precisely how specific readers received the original tales. Jarvis's study of a fairy-tale composition by a young woman raised and educated in the Grimm tradition gives us a direct insight into her response to that tradition.

In his essay on Friedrich Nietzsche's "Little Brier Rose," Richard Perkins discovers another nineteenth-century reaction to the Grimms that constitutes still another reversal of the Grimm model composed by a mature adolescent. Nietzsche's adolescent lyric adaptation of "Brier Rose" (No. 50) is an appropriation of the fairy tale by the emerging philosopher and fits into the context of his later philosophy and critique of Western culture. Perkins's analysis of Nietzsche's "Brier Rose" poem and his discovery of allusions to specific Grimm tales in Nietzsche's mature philosophical writings reveal Nietzsche's dissatisfaction with the Grimm model. Unlike Gisela von Arnim, who deconstructed the norms of patriarchal power in Grimms' tales, Nietzsche inverted the tales in order to reverse the effeminate and senile weakness that he believed they elicited in European culture. This inversion of the Grimm model was intended to break the spell of Romantic, nationalistic, democratic, and optimistic illusions, and—through the regeneration of the old model—bring forth redeemed works of heroism and genius. So while Nietzsche despises the fairy tale for its foolish, often

15

mercenary, utopianism and for its fearful depiction of power, his own revisionary use of the genre and of the Grimms' tales in particular reaffirms its strong appeal, as well as its power to regenerate and transform culture. Such an ambivalent reaction to the fairy tale—characterized by both rejection and reappropriation—is not atypical of the reception of Grimms' tales generally.

In the twentieth century Grimms' tales have been frequently reappropriated and revised for the modern world. In earlier work Wolfgang Mieder has shown how lyrical and media adaptations of Grimms' stories constitute anti–fairy tales that act as social and cultural commentaries by treating the optimistic, utopian elements of the Grimm model with irreverence, irony, and satire. His essay here shows how modern German writers have reappropriated Grimms' stories in trenchant aphorisms that belong to the anti–fairy tale tradition. The conviction behind these aphoristic revisions is that fairy tales must be made relevant to modern readers by juxtaposing the Grimms' utopian world to the sociopolitical reality of today. In terms of reception, the strategy is one that simultaneously challenges and draws attention to the Grimms' stories.

Challenges to Grimms' tales on a large scale have been especially common since the reign of National Socialism, when the abuse of the Grimms' work provoked serious reconsideration of the fairy tales' social, political, and pedagogical role. Jack Zipes discusses the struggle over Grimms' tales in the two postwar Germanys by focusing on the ways in which writers have used short prose narratives to challenge and re-create the form and ideology of fairy tales. Completed as the Federal Republic of Germany and the former German Democratic Republic were reuniting, Zipes's essay explores how the debate over fairy tales emerged in the postwar era and took shape against the background of the two Germanys' common cultural history and new sociopolitical structures. Zipes's analysis of this postwar reception reveals the centrality of Grimms' fairy tales to the cultural identity of both Germanys and the role the stories have played, and very likely will continue to play, in the redefinition of German cultural ideology.

The fairy tale as a means of cultural control also occupies the attention of Maria Tatar, who explores the link between fairy-tale reception and children's literary culture. Tatar's essay revolves around Maurice Sendak's response to the "recently discovered" tale by Wilhelm Grimm, "Dear Mili," which Sendak spent three years illustrating. Tatar questions the contradiction between Sendak's explicit disdain for moral didacticism in children's literature and his overwhelmingly positive response to this didactic tale about salvation through death. Sendak embraces "Dear Mili," she concludes, because it reflects the artist's *adult* obsession with his own childhood experiences—especially his preoccupation with death. What comes to light through this analysis of Grimm's tale and Sendak's response is the inevitable role of the adult's perspective in the production and reception of children's literature. If Grimms' tales have become a children's classic, then that is so because adults—not children—have raised them to that status. With nearly unqualified control over what gets published, marketed, purchased, read, and canonized, adults privilege works such as the Grimms' because they reflect adult reconstructions of childhood experience, which may or may not find a commensurate response in children. Because children's own needs and experiences remain ultimately unknowable to us, the adult's sense of how children respond to fairy tales will define which stories have a place in children's literary culture.

This difference between the institutionalized response to fairy tales and the response of actual recipients is the subject of my own essay in this volume. While scholars may theorize about what constitutes an acceptably informed or responsible reading of Grimms' tales, this form of institutional control has its limits. It is certainly useful and legitimate to undertake interpretations that seek to reconstruct a tale's historical intentions and meaning, and to expect that such readings will be informed and productively constrained by appropriate evidence. The unresolved controversies of fairy-tale scholarship, however, suggest how diverse even "responsible" interpretations can be. Indeed, the textual characteristics of the Grimm fairy tale resist a definitive reconstruction of "original" meaning and even invite contradictory responses. Moreover, text-focused fairy-tale interpretation cannot tell us how fairy tales actually operate in the diverse contexts of reception, where the recipient's subjective disposition contributes to the individual response. Without attention to readers' responses to fairy tales, we will have theories, but no documented understanding, of how Grimms' fairy tales actually become meaningful in their reception.

Kay Stone's essay moves us towards such an understanding by exploring the reception of Grimms' tale by contemporary North American storytellers. Stone's research is based on the performers' responses to questions about the place of Grimms' tales in their repertoires; she draws, too, on her own experiences as a storyteller. In investigating how storytellers understand their own transformation of Grimms' written texts into oral performance, Stone confirms the Grimms' significant influence on the shape of contemporary oral narratives (thus following the direction indicated by Siegfried Neumann in his essay). Beyond that, however, what Stone learns about the performers' selection and personal re-creation of Grimms' stories reveals how the tales appeal to the tellers for diverse personal reasons. Yet, in their public re-creations, the performers and their stories seem to transcend personal involvement and connect with their listeners, who find a resonance in the storytellers' re-creations.

The storyteller's personal re-creation of the fairy tale for an audience has something in common with the scholar's interpretive work, which also retells—or at least reformulates—the story for others. As a mediator of the tale in one of its variations, the scholar-interpreter represents the tale so that it can more explicitly be seen to reflect his or her own understanding. While objectivity appears to lie at the heart of this scholarly representation, its true source is the critic's personal response. Jacques Barchilon, a French-born scholar known particularly for his work on Perrault, reflects in his essay on his own response to Grimms' tales. Barchilon's response develops in the context of his French cultural heritage, so Grimms' stories initially take on meaning for him as they mirror the tales of Perrault. As a French reader coming to the tales as an adult, Barchilon acknowledges that his experience will necessarily be different from that of Germans who assimilated Grimms' stories as children. Barchilon emphasizes, too, that as a scholar he is compelled to search consciously for meaning, to interpret, which is "the soul of folk and fairy tale appreciation." Still, one senses that Barchilon only grudgingly accepts the necessity of the critic's self-conscious interpretive response. This may explain his ultimate attraction to psychoanalytic and aesthetic interpretations, which only objectify what are at heart very subjective responses: the fairy tale's resonance in our unconscious and the reader's ambivalent response to the fairy tale's supernatural realm.

These personal reflections on a scholar's response to Grimms' fairy tales are followed by the invited responses of four very different creative artists who have been influenced by Grimms' collection. The storyteller and author Jane Yolen (one of Kay Stone's respondents) relates

18

how three of Grimms' tales have been for her "life myths." She recounts not only how these favorite tales of childhood have helped shape her own literary work, but also how they prefigured concerns in her adult life—from the peace movement to the women's movement, and her life as a writer.

The Canadian author Margaret Atwood remembers how a mail-order book of Grimms' *Fairy Tales* became the most significant literary memory of her childhood, despite the anxious reservations of her parents, who were surprised by the book's frightening contents. Atwood's reflections not only confirm the pervasive reincarnations of Grimms' tales in her fiction, they also illuminate the unpredictable responses of individual readers. Atwood, the author of *A Handmaid's Tale,* dismisses the charges of sexism in Grimms' book by pointing out that the courageous, spell-casting women she remembers from "her" book of tales taught her the power of the word.

Like both Yolen and Atwood, artist-illustrator Trina Schart Hyman counts Grimms' fairy tales not only among the best-remembered stories of childhood, but also as a significant influence on her creative life as an adult. For Hyman, in fact, they were also a way of life that she compares to a religion. The details she recounts about her childhood and her illustrations help us understand not only Hyman's art, but also the way in which fairy tales can shape someone's perception and experience of the world. The intensity of Hyman's relationship to the Grimms—and the ironic humor evident in her description of it—give us, I think, important insights into how her fairy-tale illustrations might be understood. Complaints about the predictability of her fairy-tale illustrations, for example, overlook the ironic touches in her work, such as the partially hidden couple making love in the bushes in Hyman's *Sleeping Beauty.*[5]

When asked to write about their personal responses to fairy tales, Yolen, Atwood, and Hyman all produced autobiographical narratives about their childhood discovery of Grimms' *Fairy Tales.* The British writer Angela Carter, known for her remarkable fairy-tale adaptations, responded with a fairy tale. Her response, an adaptation of Grimms' "Cinderella," or "Ashputtle" (No. 21), is appropriate here not only because it is the last acknowledged response to the Grimms by Carter, who died recently at only fifty-one, but also because her fictional revision helps mark the broad parameters of reception. Carter's "Ashputtle" can be taken as an epilogue, linking scholarly and fictional representations of Grimms' tales, and bringing us back to Laurie Anderson's Hansel and Gretel, who introduced these essays.

The pieces in this volume move chronologically, dealing first with the Grimms' preparation of their collection for a nineteenth-century audience and finally with the contemporary re-creation of "Cinderella" for readers in the late twentieth century. They also move along a continuum of response. They begin with a scholar's historical account and end in confession and fictional re-creation by creative artists. In doing so the contributions to this volume represent, however incompletely, the breadth and diversity of response. If the longevity of Grimms' fairy tales can be explained, then it seems to me we must account for that endurance on the basis of the tales' flexibility—their openness to diverse responses, reactions, and revisions.

While we have the Grimms to thank for giving us the classical tales, it has been a host of storytellers, editors, publishers, translators, writers, adaptors, artists, scholars, teachers, and readers who have kept them alive in the most diverse, often truncated, sometimes but for the name nearly unrecognizable forms. If Hansel and Gretel are still living in Berlin, acting in movies and serving cocktails, it is because they have left the forest and their father's home, and assumed new identities. Character players with a high recognition factor, they allowed themselves to be re-created for the twentieth century as they will be re-created for the twenty-first.

The Brothers Grimm themselves have joined their fictional characters and also been re-created for the twentieth century. Scholars re-create them regularly, of course, every time we advance new representations of the brothers' life and work. Among the Grimms' more explicitly fictional reincarnations, one expresses well the premise behind this present collection. In his horror novel *Shadowland*, the contemporary American writer Peter Straub revives the Brothers Grimm and endows them with a consciousness of their tales' wonderfully terrifying depth. In search of meaning behind a forbidden door, the novel's main character Tom Flanagan discovers the brothers Jakob and Wilhelm, who speak to him cryptically about their lives and stories, and also about Shadowland. As the brothers depart, Tom presses them for answers:

> Both brothers laughed, and blew out the candles on their desks.
> "I have another question," Tom said into the lively blackness.

"Ask the stories, child," said a departing voice.
A flurry of quiet rustling, then silence: Tom knew they were gone.
"But they never give the same answers," he said to the black room.
(225–26)

Indeed, Grimms' fairy tales never do give the same answers, which is why they endure. What keeps Hansel and Gretel, and even Jacob and Wilhelm, alive is not their moral character, not what they contain, but the potential they have to play whatever roles are given them, to have meaning conferred upon them, to give an answer to whoever asks the question. It is their protean nature, their many voices, their ability to mirror whatever it is we wish to see, that continually invite our responses and demand our reactions.

Notes

1. See Haase, "The Sleeping Script," where I argue for the thematic, and therefore textual, connection between Grimms' preface and "Brier Rose" (No. 50).

2. I am referring particularly to Alderson, Luke, Manheim, and Zipes.

3. On these various issues, see Bottigheimer, "Iconographic Continuity"; Dégh; Haase, "Gold into Straw"; Hearne; Jerrendorf; Mieder; Ockel; Sahr; and Zipes, *Trials and Tribulations.*

4. See, for example, Marcia Lieberman's response to Alison Lurie's argument that classical fairy tales should appeal to feminists. Jack Zipes discusses both critical and fictional feminist responses to the fairy tale in his introduction to *Don't Bet on the Prince,* while Kay Stone usefully categorizes the diverse approaches feminist scholars have taken to the fairy tale.

5. See Zipes's critique of Hyman's illustrated retelling of Grimms' "Brier Rose," *The Sleeping Beauty (The Brothers Grimm* 159–61). Details such as the amorous couple in *The Sleeping Beauty* are, unfortunately, more easily discerned in Hyman's original works than they are in the mass-produced publications. It is ironic that Hyman, who is charged with predictably romanticized illustrations, has been criticized by school officials in Culver City, California, for portraying a red-nosed, wine-imbibing grandmother in her *Little Red Riding Hood.* Apparently too unconventional for these readers, Hyman's book has been removed from the state's list of recommended reading for young children ("Little Red Riding Hootch").

Donald Haase

Works Cited

Alderson, Brian, trans. *Popular Folk Tales.* By the Brothers Grimm. Garden City, NY: Doubleday, 1978.

Anderson, Laurie. "The Dream Before." *Strange Angels.* Audiotape. Warner Bros., 25900-4, 1989. (*Collected Videos.* Warner Reprise Video, 1990.)

Bottigheimer, Ruth B. "From Gold to Guilt: The Forces Which Reshaped *Grimms' Tales.*" McGlathery 192–204.

———. "Iconographic Continuity in Illustrations of 'The Goose Girl' (KHM 89)." *Children's Literature* 13 (1985): 49–71.

Dégh, Linda. "What Did the Grimm Brothers Give to and Take from the Folk?" McGlathery 66–90.

Genette, Gérard. *Seuils.* Paris: Seuil, 1987.

Grimm, Wilhelm. *Dear Mili.* Trans. Ralph Manheim. Illus. Maurice Sendak. New York: Farrar, Straus & Giroux, 1988.

Haase, Donald. "Gold into Straw: Fairy Tale Movies for Children and the Culture Industry." *The Lion and the Unicorn* 12.2 (1988): 193–207.

———. "The Sleeping Script: Memory and Forgetting in Grimms' Romantic Fairy Tale (KHM 50)." *Merveilles & contes* 4 (1990): 167–76.

Hearne, Betsy. "Booking the Brothers Grimm: Art, Adaptations, and Economics." *Book Research Quarterly* 2.4 (1986–87). Rpt. in McGlathery 220–33.

Heilfurth, Gerhard. "Ein Lesefund: Grimms Märchen in der Familie von Karl Marx." *Brüder Grimm Gedenken* 7 (1987): 243–45.

Hunt, Margaret, trans. *The Complete Grimm's Fairy Tales.* Rev. James Stern. 1944. New York: Pantheon, 1972.

Hyman, Trina Schart, illus. *Little Red Riding Hood.* New York: Holiday House, 1983.

———, illus. *The Sleeping Beauty.* Boston: Little, Brown, 1977.

Jerrendorf, Marion. "Grimms Märchen in Medien: Aspekte verschiedener Erscheinungsformen in Hörfunk, Fernsehen and Theater." Diss. U Tübingen, 1985.

Lieberman, Marcia. " 'Some Day My Prince Will Come': Female Acculturation through the Fairy Tale." *College English* 34 (1972): 383–95.

"Little Red Riding Hootch." *Time* 4 June 1990: 57.

Luke, David, trans. *Selected Tales.* By Jacob and Wilhelm Grimm. Harmondsworth: Penguin, 1982.

Lurie, Alison. "Fairy Tale Liberation." *New York Review of Books* 17 Dec. 1970: 42–44.

Manheim, Ralph, trans. *Grimms' Tales for Young and Old: The Complete Stories.* New York: Anchor Press/Doubleday, 1977.

McGlathery, James M., ed. *The Brothers Grimm and Folktale.* Urbana: U of Illinois P, 1988.

Mieder, Wolfgang. "Grimm Variations: From Fairy Tales to Modern Anti-Fairy Tales." *Tradition and Innovation in Folk Literature.* Hanover: UP of New England, 1987. 1–44. (Rev. and rpt. in *Germanic Review* 62 [1987]: 90–102.)

Nitschke, August. "The Importance of Fairy Tales in German Families before the Grimms." McGlathery 164–77.

Ockel, Eberhard. "Märchen erzählen: Kritische Analyse von Beispielen der akustischen Vermarktung." *Muttersprache* 96 (1986): 13–32.

Sahr, Michael. "Zur Wirkung von Märchen: Eine medienvergleichende Betrachtung zum Grimmschen Märchen: Der alte Sultan." *Das gute Jugendbuch* 27 (1977): 67–75. Rpt. in *Kinderliteratur und Rezeption: Beiträge der Kinderliteraturforschung zur literaturwissenschaftlichen Pragmatik.* Ed. Bettina Hurrelmann. Baltmannsweiler: Schneider, 1980. 351–65.

Schoof, Wilhelm. "150 Jahre 'Kinder- und Hausmärchen': Die Grimmschen Märchen im Urteil der Zeitgenossen." *Wirkendes Wort* 12 (1962): 331–35.

Stone, Kay F. "Feminist Approaches to the Interpretation of Fairy Tales." *Fairy Tales and Society: Illusion, Allusion, and Paradigm.* Ed. Ruth B. Bottigheimer. Philadelphia: U of Pennsylvania P, 1986. 229–36.

Straub, Peter. *Shadowland.* 1980. New York: Berkley Books, 1981.

Zipes, Jack. *The Brothers Grimm: From Enchanted Forests to the Modern World.* New York: Routledge, 1988.

———, trans. *The Complete Fairy Tales of the Brothers Grimm.* New York: Bantam, 1987.

———. Introduction. *Don't Bet on the Prince: Contemporary Feminist Fairy Tales in North America and England.* New York: Methuen, 1986. 1–36.

———. *The Trials and Tribulations of Little Red Riding Hood: Versions of the Tale in Sociocultural Context.* South Hadley, MA: Bergin & Garvey. 1983.

The Brothers Grimm as Collectors and Editors of German Folktales

Siegfried Neumann

T HE NAMES OF Jacob and Wilhelm Grimm inevitably evoke thoughts of Grimms' *Fairy Tales*. In the form given them by Wilhelm in the last edition he produced in 1857, the *Kinder- und Hausmärchen* have been printed so often and become so widely known that this book constitutes in public consciousness the ultimate achievement linked with the name Grimm. In fact, none of their works occupied the brothers—at least Wilhelm—over so long a period as the collecting, editing, and annotating of the fairy tales. Spanning almost fifty years, this work represents in terms of duration alone the "work of a lifetime." And, indeed, fairy tale research seems to be the one area of their work in which the Grimms not only achieved the strongest resonance, but also in which they determined with particular clarity the course of future research.[1] So in essence the *Kinder- und Hausmärchen* are still the standard source work on which our knowledge of the German folktale is based;[2] and even in the folkloric research of other countries one can still find today traces of the Grimms' influence.[3]

Assessments of the Brothers Grimm as collectors and students of the fairy tale, however, run the risk of focusing on the final form of the *Kinder- und Hausmärchen* and its success. In doing so, one all too easily overlooks the fact that the collection represents basically an early work. When Jacob and Wilhelm began to devote themselves intensively to German folk literature in 1805, they were not yet scholars but only twenty-year-old university students who were reacting to newly experienced stimuli. Their teacher in Marburg, the legal historian Friedrich Karl von Savigny, had awakened their inclination for historical studies and steered their interest towards "Old Germanic" literature. And Clemens Brentano, one of the leaders of the Heidelberg Romantic circle, had won the brothers over and enlisted them in his search for surviving forms of traditional folk poetry, which he planned to publish.[4]

There were certainly models for these efforts, such as Johann Karl August Musäus—however problematic his *Volksmährchen der Deutschen* (1782–86) appeared even to his contemporaries. And above all there was the example of Johann Gottfried Herder, whose high assessment of the song (*Lied*) and fairy tale as the poetry of the folk was echoed by the Romantic movement.[5] This echo is especially evident in Clemens Brentano and Achim von Arnim's folk song collection *Des Knaben Wunderhorn* (1806–08), to which the Brothers Grimm themselves had already contributed.

A corresponding fairy-tale collection was supposed to follow *Des Knaben Wunderhorn,* and the fairy-tale narratives that the Grimms excerpted from old books or transcribed from friends in the Wild and Hassenpflug families in Kassel during and after 1807 were intended solely for Brentano's projected publication. But already in a letter to Arnim on 19 October 1807, Brentano writes that he had found the brothers "after two years of long, diligent and very rigorous study, so erudite and so rich in notes, experiences, and the most varied perspectives regarding all romantic poetry" that he was "shocked" "at their modesty concerning the treasures" they possessed. They were working, he writes, "in order one day to write a proper history of German poetry" (Steig, *Achim von Arnim und Clemens Brentano* 224). Nonetheless in 1810 the Grimms sent Brentano their fairy-tale notes upon his request—but not, of course, without first having their own copies made. And in 1811, when Brentano still had made no arrangements for his projected fairy-tale book, they conceived the plan of preparing their own, for which the copies would serve as a starting point.

At this time, under the influence of Napoleon's foreign rule, the Brothers Grimm not only sought "in the history of German literature and language consolation and refreshment . . . from the enemy's high spirits," as Jacob formulated it retrospectively in 1841 (*Kleinere Schriften* 546); they also felt that by collecting and publishing surviving forms of "Old Germanic" literature and folk poetry they were fostering national self-reflection. Like Herder, from whom the Romantic movement borrowed the concept of natural poetry (*Naturpoesie*), the Grimms also saw in folk poetry—in the songs, fairy tales, and legends of the common people—the original source of poetry and the echo of ancient literature. And in this context they understood "folk poetry" largely in an ethnic sense—as the poetry of Germans, Poles, and so on (*Geschichte der deutschen Volksdichtung* 91). At the same time the Grimms viewed fairy tales as belonging "to those poetic works whose content had most purely and powerfully preserved the essence of early epic poetry" (Ginschel 250). As Wilhelm emphasized already in 1811: "These fairy tales deserve better attention than they have so far received, not only because of their poetry, which has its own loveliness and gives to everyone who heard them as a child a golden moral and a happy memory for life; but also because they belong to our national poetry, since it can be shown that they have lived throughout several centuries among the folk" (*Altdänische Heldenlieder* xxvi–xxvii). And writing of the fairy-tale book he had prepared in collaboration with Wilhelm, Jacob observed: "I would not have found any pleasure in working on it if I were not of the belief that it could become to the most serious and oldest people, as well as to me, important for poetry, mythology, and history."[6] And in 1860 he emphasized explicitly that he had "immediately recognized the value of these traditional forms for mythology" and had therefore "insisted vigorously on the faithfulness of the collection and rejected embellishments."[7]

But what about this "faithfulness"? The fairy-tale manuscripts originally intended for Brentano, which were preserved among his unpublished papers, range from mere notes to relatively complete texts. And these exhibit certain individual differences. Fairy tales in the original manuscript taken down by Jacob are in most cases texts characterized by concise language and which in part only outline a tale's subject. Wilhelm's transcriptions, on the other hand, constitute tales with a more polished content and smoother narration. But for publication even these had to be shaped and polished as narratives. To what extent this was or was not also true of the subsequent sketches specifically intended for their own book of fairy tales we do not know, because these manuscripts were not preserved. However, the revision of the original manuscript for the first edition reveals that the Grimms, who were novices at such literary activity, largely followed their models, so that hardly any stylistic differences are discernable between texts edited by Jacob and Wilhelm (Rölleke; Ginschel 222–24). When the preface to the first volume of the *Kinder- und Hausmärchen* in 1812 states that "no details have been added or embellished or changed" (XVIII; trans. in Tatar 210), that applies only to the content, but not to the linguistic appearance of the printed fairy-tale texts.

Nevertheless, the brothers were in fact intent upon tales issuing genuinely from the oral folk tradition and considered it important that such tales be recorded in their own right. Consequently, they often provided the same tale type in two or three versions, sometimes even under the same heading, as with Nos. 20, 32, and 36. This alleged faithfulness to the sources (even if they were only limitedly accessible) constitutes for the brothers a primary scientific concern, as suggested in the quoted statements from Jacob. This is corroborated as well by the following facts: (1) the Grimms preferred stories from oral sources to texts with a literary character (so that part of their literary excerpts in the original manuscript were not printed along with the other pieces); (2) besides the most diverse kinds of fairy tales and comical tales (*Schwänke*), the brothers also included in their edition legends, tall tales, and horror stories, among which were thematically uninteresting or poorly told pieces;[8] (3) the Grimms gave their book a programmatic preface and scholarly notes. At the same time, the *Kinder- und Hausmärchen* were naturally supposed to make these stories available to wider circles, as indicated already by the title. And here pedagogical factors played a role, for the book was supposed to become a "manual of education"— "ein eigentliches Erziehungsbuch" (*Kinder- und Hausmärchen: 1812 und 1815* 2: VIII). But because of the problematic content and awkward narrative style of certain texts, as critics noted, such an effect was apparently not possible. As a consequence the nine hundred copies of the first volume seemed for some years to be almost unmarketable.[9]

On the basis of the criticism their book received, against which the Grimms defended themselves and which they privately had to acknowledge, they apparently imposed a different standard for the selection and revision of tales for the projected second volume. This standard was defined by two widely praised tales from the first volume that had come from Philipp Otto Runge: "The Fisherman and His Wife" (No. 19) and "The Juniper Tree" (No. 47). With these texts as their models, the Grimms themselves developed an ideal fairy-tale form that in the end could be produced only by talented storytellers or retellers and could find its counterpart only in artistically shaped texts. They found both in the intellectually active bourgeois and aristocratic circles in which they moved. Particularly in enlisting the aristocratic Haxthausen family of Westphalia as tale collectors and informants, and in discovering the *Märchenfrau* Dorothea Viehmann from Niederzwehren near Kassel, the Grimms became the beneficiaries of a string of aesthetically pleasing fairy tales. Moreover, the tales in Westphalian dialect and those of Viehmann appear to be directly transcribed from the oral narration. That the tales in the second volume of 1815 (with thirty-three of seventy texts from the Haxthausen family and fifteen from Viehmann) were as a rule better told than those in the first volume was very substantially related to the greater storytelling talent of the new sources. But Wilhelm, who for the most part attended to the editing of the newly collected material, seems to have also exercised a stronger editorial hand wherever his experience with the first volume suggested it might be necessary. "You have," wrote Arnim to Wilhelm after receiving the second volume on 10 February 1815, "genially collected, and have sometimes right genially helped, which of course you don't mention to Jacob; but you should have done it even more often" (Steig, *Achim von Arnim und Jacob und Wilhelm Grimm* 319). The preface and notes demonstrate that the Grimms adhered to the scientific intentions they had applied to the first volume, but this time the emphasis lay visibly on the presentation of a more appealing text, which was aimed at larger groups of readers. Nonetheless, the second volume sold as poorly as the first (Schoof 27; Grimm, *Kinder- und Hausmärchen: 1819* 2: 541–43).

Therefore, in the course of being prepared for the second edition of 1819, Grimms' collection underwent an extensive revision. Twenty-seven of the texts contained in the first volume and seven of those in the second were deleted, either because they no longer met the aesthetic demands of the Grimms or because they were otherwise questionable (e.g., due to their cruelty). Eighteen texts of the first edition were merged with newly collected variants of specific tales or so substantially changed by other thematic or formal revisions that virtually new texts resulted. And forty-five texts, revised in varying degrees, were incorporated as new texts in the collection, which now grew to 170 tales.[10] Thus resulted almost by half a new book of fairy tales; and in it Wilhelm Grimm's poetically atuned stylizing—his unique fairy-tale voice—became distinct for the first time. Consistent with this development, the heavily expanded annotations were relegated in 1822 to their own separate volume, which addressed itself especially to readers with a specialized scholarly interest (Grimm, *Kinder- und Hausmärchen: 1819* 2: 548, 556–64).

But popular success came first in 1825 with the Small Edition of the *Kinder- und Hausmärchen*, which was conceived primarily for children and included fifty selected texts and seven engravings. This edition smoothed the way for the reception of the large edition, which Wilhelm sought continuously with every new edition to enrich through the addition of new or better fairy-tale texts. Up until the seventh and final edition of 1857, Wilhelm not only adopted new stories from other contemporary collections (e.g., Nos. 171–72 from Mecklenburg, Nos. 181 and 186 from Oberlausitz, Nos. 184–85 and 188–89 from Bavaria); he also replaced weak texts with better narrated variants of the same tales, which accordingly appeared under new titles (e.g., No. 101 "Der Bärenhäuter" instead of "Der Teufel Grünrock," No. 107 "Die beiden Wanderer" instead of "Die Krähen," No. 136 "Der Eisenhans" instead of "De wilde Mann," etc.).

Simultaneously Wilhelm further honed the texts stylistically from edition to edition. The opening lines of "The Frog King" (No. 1) serve as a good example. The first edition of 1812 reads:

> Es war einmal eine Königstochter, die ging hinaus in den Wald und setzte sich an einen kühlen Brunnen. Sie hatte eine goldene Kugel, die war ihr liebstes Spielwerk, die warf sie in die Höhe und fing sie wieder in der Luft und hatte ihre Lust daran. (*Kinder- und Hausmärchen: 1812 und 1815* 1: 1)

> Once upon a time there was a king's daughter who went into the forest and sat down at a cool well. She had a golden ball that was her favorite toy. She would throw it up and catch it in the air and was amused by this.

The second edition of 1819 already shows distinct changes, which aim at greater concreteness:

> Es war einmal eine Königstochter, die wußte nicht was sie anfangen sollte vor langer Weile. Da nahm sie eine goldene Kugel, womit sie

schon oft gespielt hatte und ging hinaus in den Wald. Mitten in dem
Wald aber war ein reiner, kühler Brunnen, dabei setzte sie sich nieder,
warf die Kugel in die Höhe, fing sie wieder, und das war ihr so ein Spielwerk. *(Kinder- und Hausmärchen: 1819* 1: 9)

Once upon a time there was a king's daughter who was so bored she
didn't know what to do. So she took a golden ball that she often played
with and went into the forest. Now in the middle of the forest there was
a clear, cool well and she sat down next to it, threw the ball into the air,
and she would play this way.

In the last edition edited by Wilhelm from 1857, the scene has been so
thoroughly painted that it can nearly stand alone:

In den alten Zeiten, wo das Wünschen noch geholfen hat, lebte ein
König, dessen Töchter waren alle schön, aber die jüngste war so schön,
daß die Sonne selber, die doch so vieles gesehen hat, sich verwunderte,
sooft sie ihr ins Gesicht schien. Nahe bei dem Schlosse des Königs lag
ein großer dunkler Wald, und in dem Walde unter einer alten Linde war
ein Brunnen; wenn nun der Tag recht heiß war, so ging das Königskind
hinaus in den Wald und setzte sich an den Rand des kühlen Brunnens;
und wenn sie Langeweile hatte, so nahm sie eine goldene Kugel, warf
sie in die Höhe und fing sie wieder; und das war ihr liebstes Spielwerk.
(Kinder- und Hausmärchen: Ausgabe letzter Hand 1: 29)

In olden times, when wishing still helped, there lived a king whose
daughters were all beautiful, but the youngest was so beautiful that the
sun itself, which had seen so many things, was always filled with amaze-
ment each time it cast its rays upon her face. Now, there was a great dark
forest near the king's castle, and in this forest, beneath an old linden
tree, was a well. Whenever the days were very hot, the king's daughter
would go into the forest and sit down by the edge of the cool well. If she
became bored, she would take her golden ball, throw it into the air, and
catch it. More than anything else she loved playing with this ball. (Trans.
in Zipes 2)

The Grimm fairy-tale style is fully developed here. But what also
clearly emerges is Wilhelm's manner and art of narration, which
seek—in this case to the extreme—to plumb the fairy-tale events down
to their very details. One can respond to the result in two ways—by
lamenting the loss of the folktale's simplicity, or by welcoming the poetic enrichment.[11] In any case, these examples clearly demonstrate the
growth of an aesthetically oriented attitude.

The orientation towards fairy tales as linguistic-artistic survivals is certainly also one of the reasons that the Grimms did not turn their attention more closely to those who told these fairy tales. Moreover, in viewing folk literature as natural poetry (*Naturpoesie*), the Grimms were inclined to view their informants less as individual storytellers than as oral sources. If they nonetheless described their best storyteller in the preface to the second volume, that was done largely from this very perspective. Dorothea Viehmann, a "peasant woman" who told "genuine Hessian tales," as the preface claims (in reality she was a tailor's wife from a Huguenot family), corresponded to the Grimms' image of an ideal tale teller from the simple folk, among whom they expected to find the guardians of the oral storytelling tradition: "Devotion to tradition is far stronger among people who always adhere to the same way of life than we (who tend to want to change) can understand" (*Kinder- und Hausmärchen: 1812 und 1815* 2: V–VI; trans. in Tatar 212). Also in the letters of the Haxthausen family there is talk of trips into the surrounding villages "to gather from the mouths of the old rural population the tales, folk songs, and children's songs that still live" (Schoof 38, 74, 81, 95). However, we know little about storytellers who came from the working classes of the population. On the other hand, the fact that Grimms' informants belonged above all to the educated classes and to the aristocracy does not at all mean that their tales reflect principally the tradition as it existed in these social circles. Yet vast areas of oral folktale tradition remained inevitably unknown to the Grimms; and vulgar stories, which even then made up a large part of the popular tradition, were very likely consciously overlooked in the course of collecting. Consequently, on the basis of sources alone, the popular tradition is only partially represented in Grimms' collection— even if one takes into account that the repertoire of oral tales established in the middle-class homes of Kassel or among the Haxthausens depended largely on the folk tradition or found its motifs reflected in it. [12]

The Brothers Grimm themselves apparently did not consider this manner of transmission to be a shortcoming. Already in the preface to the first volume we find the idea that although fairy tales are "never fixed and always changing from one region to another, from one teller to another, they still preserve a stable core" (*Kinder- und Hausmärchen: 1812 und 1815* 1: XIII; trans. in Tatar 208). In this respect the Grimms saw all their informants as well as themselves as links in a

31

chain of storytellers, each having a certain right to retell the tales in his or her own way. At the same time, whenever faced with several versions of the same tale, Wilhelm endeavored in each case to give the best one in terms of content and narrative. And when he thought it possible to expand or to "improve" this version with another transmission, he would do it—convinced that in this way the "genuine" folktale could be reconstructed. In doing so—as the 1856 volume of annotations attests—he had no inhibitions about blending texts from Hesse, Westphalia, and Mecklenburg, or from an older written tradition and recent oral tradition. He was concerned above all with a text's inner coherence and the completeness of individual motifs. Further revision focused on conforming the tale's content to childlike understanding, portraying the tale's characters (they were supposed to be as vivid as possible), and attempting to animate the depictions through direct speech, linguistic expressions, verses, and so forth (Ginschel 215–17). All this spoke to a concern already expressed in the second volume of the first edition: "The aim of our collection was not just to serve the cause of the history of poetry: it was also our intention that the poetry living in it be effective" (*Kinder- und Hausmärchen: 1812 und 1815* 2: XIII; trans. in Tatar 214). Through his textual revisions, however, Wilhelm—despite all his efforts to reconstruct the "genuine" voice of the folk—increasingly endowed the fairy tales with a poetic art form of his own making. In other words, the Grimms' original striving to record the oral tradition was gradually replaced (at least from our contemporary perspective) by literary principles: "Despite loving fidelity towards the folk tradition, the Brothers Grimm created from it a work of literature" (Berendsohn 26).

Consequently, the final edition of 1857 can be used only in a limited way if one seeks to discover clues in the tales' content that point to their origin in the contemporary folk tradition. This edition contains in large measure very beautiful fairy tales, which are by the same token Grimms' own versions and in which some elements of social criticism have been deleted in order not to offend the groups of readers the Grimms were addressing. For example, in the first published version of the tale "Godfather Death" (1812, No. 44), the poor man answers the "good Lord" with these words: " 'I don't want you to be godfather! You give to the rich and let the poor go hungry.' With that he left him standing there and went on" (*Kinder- und Hausmärchen: 1812 und 1815* 1: 193). In later editions, however, this commentary follows:

32

"The man said that because he did not know how wisely God distributes wealth and poverty" (*Kinder- und Hausmärchen: 1819* 1: 153; trans. in Zipes 161). With that interpolation, the original message of this passage is fundamentally changed and turned into its opposite (Steinitz). On the other hand, a tale such as "The Tablecloth, the Knapsack, the Cannon Hat, and the Horn" (1812, No. 37), which was told to the Grimms by the retired dragoon Johann Friedrich Krause and in which the king and his royal household are ultimately massacred, was replaced in the second edition by a variant in which the same events are even more drastically depicted (No. 54).

To be sure, the tales printed in the first edition, which were repeatedly recorded at the beginning of the nineteenth century, clearly reveal that it was primarily young women of the bourgeoisie and aristocracy who supplied the Grimms with these stories. Their tales, especially those like "Cinderella" (No. 21), "Brier Rose" (No. 50), and "Snow White" (No. 53), which are favorites among later generations of children, depict the fate of young girls, whose lives are miraculously fulfilled through love for a prince. But in the case of the tailor's wife Dorothea Viehmann, it is not only an outstanding storyteller who speaks, but also a representative of the simple folk. One needs only to read her tale "The Clever Farmer's Daughter" (1815, No. 8),[13] whose plot is embedded in critical depictions of the social milieu that show the feudal lords' oppression of peasants. Here, as in Viehmann's tale of the battle of the animals (1815, No. 16),[14] the victory of the weak over the strong is painted with obvious engagement. And it is hardly coincidental that the impoverished old dragoon Krause should tell the tale of the faithful dog Old Sultan, whose master threatens to destroy him in his old age now that his useful days are over (1812, No. 48). So the Grimms' collection does contain features in which one can recognize directly the views of the oppressed, the "voice of the folk." And in some cases these traces survive even into the last edition of 1857.

In sum: With a remarkable feel for the nature of folk literature, the Brothers Grimm collected as much of the oral narrative tradition and documented it as "faithfully" and as comprehensively as was possible for them under the existing conditions. The *Kinder- und Hausmärchen* became a world-wide success "because here for the first time significant national and international traditions of the intellectual culture from the broadest spectrum of the folk appeared elevated to the level and clothed in the language of 'belles lettres,' without their content or message having been decisively altered" (*Geschichte der deutschen Volksdichtung* 90).

What distinguished the Grimm collection most clearly of all from its precursors was the wealth and diversity of the tales it presented.[15] Even the first edition of the *Kinder- und Hausmärchen* of 1812–15 included nearly the complete stock of tale types that have been found subsequent to the Grimms in the folk traditions of the various German regions. That makes the Grimms' collection even to this day *the* book of German fairy tales. And the brothers were not content just to reproduce the texts; in the volumes of commentary published both in 1822 and 1856,[16] they also attempted to place each fairy tale, comical tale (*Schwank*), and legend in the context of German and non-German oral narrative traditions. From these volumes of commentary and the important work of Bolte and Polívka that they generated, there runs a straight line to the tale type and motif indices as well as to the comparative oral narrative research of recent decades.[17] In this respect the Brothers Grimm can be regarded without question as the fathers of international folktale research. Even much of what they documented, as it were, in passing has had a stimulating effect. For example, the brief characterization of Dorothea Viehmann in the second volume of the *Kinder- und Hausmärchen* in 1815 became the starting point for worldwide narrator research (Dégh, *Märchen* 47–65; Lüthi 83–105).

But above all, ever since the Grimms folktales have been collected in nearly all regions of the earth. And for this purpose collectors have increasingly made use of tape recordings, which capture the exact wording of a spoken narration. Modern folk narrative research demands unconditional authenticity in recording from informants, whereas this was still not possible for the Grimms. Yet in their work one observes at least the demand for authenticity—for instance, in Jacob's *Circular* of 1815, where he writes: "It is above all important that these objects be recorded faithfully and accurately, without make-up or accessories, from the mouths of the tellers, when feasible in and with their very own words, with the greatest exactitude and detail; and whatever might be gotten in the living regional dialect would therefore be doubly valuable, although even sketchy fragments are not to be rejected." Whoever follows these principles in collecting oral materials circulating today is still well advised. Of course, narrative research is no longer just interested in the narrated material itself, but also in the narrator and audience, in the context and motivation of the narrative event, and in the role of storytelling in the intellectual and cultural life of people today.[18] In this respect we have achieved so far only limited results that—in the distant wake of the Grimms—urgently need further study and elaboration.[19]

Whoever conducts oral narrative research today—especially in German-speaking regions—will repeatedly hear tales, particularly fairy tales, that directly or indirectly go back to the Grimms' collection. In those instances, good storytellers—even when they use dialect to retell what they have read—strive to stay as close as possible to the published model. For it is generally expected of contemporary storytellers to retell fairy tales "properly"—that is, in the "Grimm version." But one can readily observe that storytellers of an impulsive or imaginative nature, despite their acknowledged debt to this source, break away from the original and endow the Grimms' tales with innovations in content and a different linguistic guise.[20] In both cases we are faced with the distinct reverse influence of the Grimms' collection on the oral folktale itself—in other words, the reception of Grimms' tales by the oral tradition. This is a phenomenon that deserves the special attention of scholars of oral narrative.[21]

Notes

This contribution is based on the author's articles "Zur Entstehung und zum Charakter der Grimmschen 'Kinder- und Hausmärchen': Bemerkungen aus volkskundlicher Sicht," *Jacob und Wilhelm Grimm: Vorträge anläßlich der 200. Wiederkehr ihrer Geburtstage,* Sitzungsberichte der Akademie der Wissenschaften der DDR: Gesellschaftswissenschaften, 1985, 6/G (Berlin: Akademie-Verlag, 1986) 55–64; and "Die Brüder Grimm als Sammler und Herausgeber deutscher Volksmärchen," *Die Brüder Grimm: Beiträge zu ihrem Schaffen,* ed. Kreisheimatmuseum Haldensleben and Die Stadt- und Bezirksbibliothek "Wilhelm Weitling" (Magdeburg: Druckhaus Haldensleben, 1988) 36–45. Translated by Donald Haase.

1. Denecke 63–87; Woeller, "Die Bedeutung der Brüder Grimm"; and Bolte and Polívka. See also the bibliographical references that follow.
2. This is the case even though the folkloric content of the collection has been critically examined for years. See, for example, Schoof; Karl Schmidt;

Woeller, "Der soziale Gehalt"; and Grimm, *Kinder- und Hausmärchen: Ausgabe letzter Hand*.

3. See Briggs; Gašparíková; Horák; Leitinger; Michaelis-Jena; Nişcov; Ortutay; Peeters; Pomeranceva; Pulmer; Leopold Schmidt; Ziel, "A.N. Afanas'evs Märchensammlung"; Ziel, "Wirkungen."

4. On the intellectual and ideological development of the Brothers Grimm, see Stern 4–14.

5. See Jahn; Arnold; and Benz.

6. Jacob's letter of 28 Jan. 1813 to Arnim (Steig, *Achim von Arnim und Jacob und Wilhelm Grimm* 271).

7. Jacob's letter of 18 Feb. 1860 to Franz Pfeiffer ("Zur Geschichte der deutschen Philologie" 249).

8. An itemized and somewhat original overview of the generic diversity is given by Berendsohn 33–127.

9. Lemmer 107–16; Grimm, *Kinder- und Hausmärchen: 1819* 2: 536; and Ginschel 230–31.

10. Here again twenty-nine contributions came from the Haxthausens and eighteen from Dorothea Viehmann.

11. See, respectively, Panzer 1: xlii–xlvii; and Grimm, *Kinder- und Hausmärchen: 1819* 2: 570.

12. See the overview of Grimms' contributors and informants compiled by Heinz Rölleke in Grimm, *Kinder- und Hausmärchen: Ausgabe letzter Hand* 3: 559–74.

13. In the second and subsequent editions this tale appeared, with few changes, as No. 94.

14. In the second and subsequent editions this tale appeared, with few changes, as No. 102.

15. See Wesselski; and Neumann, *Es war einmal*.

16. The 1856 volume is vol. 3 of Grimm, *Kinder- und Hausmärchen: Ausgabe letzter Hand*.

17. See the monographs published in the series *Folklore Fellows Communications;* and the progressively appearing volumes of the *Enzyklopädie des Märchens*. English-speaking readers can find more information about this important latter work in Uther.

18. See Strobach et al. 5–26; and Neumann, "Volkserzählung heute."

19. For the former German Democratic Republic see Neumann, "Volkserzähler unserer Tage in Mecklenburg"; *Ein mecklenburgischer Volkserzähler; Eine mecklenburgische Märchenfrau;* "Mecklenburgische Erzähler"; as well as Eichler.

20. See Neumann, *Eine mecklenburgische Märchenfrau* 31–40.

21. See Ranke; Dégh, "Grimm Brothers"; and Neumann, *Mecklenburgische Volksmärchen* 35. (See below, in this book, the essay by Kay Stone on Grimms' tales as told by contemporary North American storytellers.—ED.)

Works Cited

Altdänische Heldenlieder, Balladen und Märchen. Trans. Wilhelm Grimm. Heidelberg: Mohr und Zimmer, 1811.

Arnold, Günter. "Herders Projekt einer Märchensammlung." *Jahrbuch für Volkskunde und Kulturgeschichte* 27 (1984): 99–106.

Benz, Richard. *Märchen-Dichtung der Romantiker: Mit einer Vorgeschichte.* Gotha: Perthes, 1908.

Berendsohn, Walter A. *Grundformen volkstümlicher Erzählerkunst in den Kinder- und Hausmärchen der Brüder Grimm.* Hamburg: Gente, 1921.

Bolte, Johannes, and Georg Polívka. *Anmerkungen zu den Kinder- und Hausmärchen der Brüder Grimm.* 5 vols. Leipzig: Dieterich, 1913–32.

Briggs, Katharine M. "The Influence of the Brothers Grimm in England." *Brüder Grimm Gedenken* 1 (1963): 511–24.

Dégh, Linda. *Märchen, Erzähler und Erzählgemeinschaft.* Trans. Johanna Till. Berlin: Akademie-Verlag, 1962.

———. "What Did the Grimm Brothers Give to and Take from the Folk?" *The Brothers Grimm and Folktale.* Ed. James M. McGlathery. Urbana: U of Illinois P, 1988. 66–90.

Denecke, Ludwig. *Jacob Grimm und sein Bruder Wilhelm.* Stuttgart: Metzler, 1971.

Eichler, Ingrid. *Sächsische Märchen und Geschichten—erzählt von Otto Vogel.* Berlin: Akademie-Verlag, 1971.

Enzyklopädie des Märchens. Ed. Kurt Ranke. Vols. 1 ff. Berlin: De Gruyter, 1975–.

Folklore Fellows Communications. Vols. 1 ff. Helsinki: Soumalainen Tiedeakatemia, 1910–.

Fraenger, Wilhelm, and Wolfgang Steinitz, eds. *Jacob Grimm zur 100. Wiederkehr seines Todestages: Festschrift des Instituts für deutsche Volkskunde.* Berlin: Akademie-Verlag, 1963.

Gašparíková, Viera. "Die Folkloreprosa in der Slowakei im zweiten Drittel des 19. Jahrhunderts unter dem Blickwinkel des Werkes der Brüder Grimm." *Brüder Grimm Gedenken* 8 (1988): 240–50.

Geschichte der deutschen Volksdichtung. Ed. Hermann Strobach. Berlin: Akademie-Verlag, 1981.

Ginschel, Gunhild. *Der junge Jacob Grimm: 1805–1819.* Berlin: Akademie-Verlag, 1967.

Grimm, Brothers. *Kinder- und Hausmärchen: Ausgabe letzter Hand mit den Originalanmerkungen der Brüder Grimm.* Ed. Heinz Rölleke. 3 vols. Stuttgart: Reclam, 1980.

———. *Kinder- und Hausmärchen gesammelt durch die Brüder Grimm: Vergrößerter Nachdruck der zweibändigen Erstausgabe von 1812 und 1815.* Ed.

Heinz Rölleke and Ulrike Marquardt. 2 vols. and suppl. Göttingen: Vandenhoeck & Ruprecht, 1986.

———. *Kinder- und Hausmärchen: Nach der 2. vermehrten und verbesserten
Auflage von 1819*. Ed. Heinz Rölleke. 2 vols. Cologne: Diederichs, 1982.

Grimm, Jacob. *Circular wegen Aufsammlung der Volkspoesie*. Wien, 1815. Ed.
Ludwig Denecke. Afterword by Kurt Ranke. Kassel: Brüder Grimm-
Museum, 1968.

———. *Kleinere Schriften*. Vol. 8. Ed. Eduard Ippel. Gütersloh: Bertelsmann,
1890.

Horák, Jiří. "Jacob Grimm und die slawische Volkskunde." Fraenger and
Steinitz 11–70.

Jahn, Erwin. "Die *Volksmärchen der Deutschen* von Johann Karl August Musäus." Diss. U of Leipzig, 1914.

Leitinger, Doris. "Die Wirkung von Jacob Grimm auf die Slaven, insbesondere
auf die Russen." *Brüder Grimm Gedenken* 2 (1975): 66–130.

Lemmer, Manfred, ed. *Grimms Märchen in ursprünglicher Gestalt*. Leipzig:
Insel, 1963.

Lüthi, Max. *Märchen*. 7th ed. Stuttgart: Metzler, 1979.

Michaelis-Jena, Ruth. "Die schottischen Beziehungen der Brüder Grimm."
Brüder Grimm Gedenken 2 (1975): 334–42.

Neumann, Siegfried Armin. *Es war einmal . . . Volksmärchen aus fünf Jahr-
hunderten*. 2 vols. Rostock: Hinstorf, 1982.

———. "Mecklenburgische Erzähler der Gegenwart und ihre Märchen."
*Märchen in unserer Zeit: Zu Erscheinungsformen eines populären Erzähl-
genres*. Ed. Hans-Jörg Uther. Munich: Diederichs, 1990. 102–14.

———. *Eine mecklenburgische Märchenfrau: Bertha Peters erzählt Märchen,
Schwänke und Geschichten*. Berlin: Akademie-Verlag, 1974.

———. *Mecklenburgische Volksmärchen*. Berlin: Akademie-Verlag, 1971.

———. *Ein mecklenburgischer Volkserzähler: Die Geschichten des August
Rust*. 2nd ed. Berlin: Akademie-Verlag, 1970.

———. "Volkserzähler unserer Tage in Mecklenburg: Bemerkungen zur
Erzähler-Forschung in der Gegenwart." *Deutsches Jahrbuch für Volkskunde*
15 (1969): 31-49.

———. "Volkserzählung heute: Bemerkungen zu Existenzbedingungen und
Daseinsformen der Volksdichtung in der Gegenwart." *Jahrbuch für Volkskunde und Kulturgeschichte* 23 (1980): 92–102.

Nişcov, Viorica. "Über den Widerhall der volkskundlichen Beschäftigung der
Brüder Grimm in Rumänien." *Brüder Grimm Gedenken* 2 (1975): 146–67.

Ortutay, Gyula. "Jacob Grimm und die ungarische Folkloristik." Fraenger and
Steinitz 169–89.

Panzer, Friedrich, ed. *Die Kinder- und Hausmärchen der Brüder Grimm in
ihrer Urgestalt*. 2 vols. Munich: Beck, 1913.

Peeters, Karel C. "Der Einfluß der Brüder Grimm und ihrer Nachfolger auf die Volkskunde in Flandern." *Brüder Grimm Gedenken* 1 (1963): 405–20.

Pomeranceva, Erna. "A.N. Afanas'ev und die Brüder Grimm." Fraenger and Steinitz 94–103.

Pulmer, Karin. "Zur Rezeption der Grimmschen Märchen in Dänemark." *Brüder Grimm Gedenken* 8 (1988): 181–203.

Ranke, Kurt. "Der Einfluß der Grimmschen Kinder- und Hausmärchen auf das volkstümliche deutsche Erzählgut." *Papers of the International Congress of European and Western Ethnology, Stockholm 1951*. Ed. Sigurd Erixon. Stockholm: International Commission of Folk Arts and Folklore, 1956. 126–35.

Rölleke, Heinz, ed. *Die älteste Märchensammlung der Brüder Grimm: Synopse der handschriftlichen Urfassung von 1810 und der Erstdrucke von 1812*. Cology/Geneva: Fondation Martin Bodmer, 1975.

Schmidt, Karl. *Die Entwicklung der Grimmschen Kinder- und Hausmärchen seit der Urhandschrift*. Halle: Niemeyer, 1932.

Schmidt, Leopold. "Die Brüder Grimm und der Entwicklungsgang der österreichischen Volkskunde." *Brüder Grimm Gedenken* 1 (1963): 309–31.

Schoof, Wilhelm. "Zur Entstehungsgeschichte der Grimmschen Märchen." *Hessische Blätter für Volkskunde* 29 (1930): 1–118.

Steig, Reinhold. *Achim von Arnim und Clemens Brentano*. Stuttgart: Cotta, 1894.

———. *Achim von Arnim und Jacob und Wilhelm Grimm*. Stuttgart: Cotta, 1904.

Steinitz, Wolfgang. "Lied und Märchen als Stimme des Volkes." *Deutsches Jahrbuch für Volkskunde* 2 (1956): 11–32.

Stern, Leo. *Der geistige und politische Standort von Jacob Grimm in der deutschen Geschichte*. Berlin: Akademie-Verlag, 1963.

Strobach, Hermann, et al. *Deutsche Volksdichtung: Eine Einführung*. Leipzig: Reclam, 1979.

Tatar, Maria. *The Hard Facts of the Grimms' Fairy Tales*. Princeton: Princeton UP, 1987.

Uther, Hans-Jörg. "The Encyclopedia of the Folktale." *Fairy Tales and Society: Illusion, Allusion, and Paradigm*. Ed. Ruth B. Bottigheimer. Philadelphia: U of Pennsylvania P, 1986. 187–93.

Wesselski, Albert. *Deutsche Märchen vor Grimm*. 2 vols. 2nd ed. Brünn: Rohrer, 1942.

Woeller, Waltraud. "Die Bedeutung der Brüder Grimm für die Märchen- und Sagenforschung." *Wissenschaftliche Zeitschrift der Humboldt-Universität zu Berlin*. Gesellschafts- und sprachwissenschaftliche Reihe 14 (1965): 507–14.

———. "Der soziale Gehalt und die soziale Funktion der deutschen Volksmärchen." *Wissenschaftliche Zeitschrift der Humboldt-Universität zu*

Berlin. Gesellschafts- und sprachwissenschaftliche Reihe 10 (1961): 395–459; 11 (1962): 281–307.

Ziel, Wulfhild. "A.N. Afanas'evs Märchensammlung 'Narodnye russkie skazki' (1855–1863)—geplant nach dem Vorbild der 'Kinder- und Hausmärchen' der Brüder Grimm: Beispiele ausführlicher Anmerkungen, in denen auf Jacob und Wilhelm Grimm verwiesen wird." *Brüder Grimm Gedenken* 8 (1988): 204–21.

———. "Wirkungen von Jacob und Wilhelm Grimm auf die Sammlung russischer Volksbilderbogen 'Russkie narodnye kartinki' von Dmitrij Aleksandrovič Rovinskij (St. Petersburg 1881)." *Brüder Grimm Gedenken* 9 (1990): 171–83.

Zipes, Jack, trans. *The Complete Fairy Tales of the Brothers Grimm.* New York: Bantam, 1987.

"Zur Geschichte der deutschen Philologie. I: Briefe von Jacob Grimm." *Germania: Vierteljahrsschrift für deutsche Alterthumskunde* 11 (1866): 239–56.

Heinrich Pröhle: A Successor
to the Brothers Grimm

Ines Köhler-Zülch

IN THE MIDDLE of the nineteenth century two books of fairy tales were on their way to becoming best-sellers in German-speaking regions: the *Kinder- und Hausmärchen* of the Brothers Grimm and Ludwig Bechstein's *Deutsches Märchenbuch*. First published in 1845, Bechstein's work had already entered its twelfth edition by 1853 as *Ludwig Bechstein's Märchenbuch* with illustrations by Ludwig Richter. In contrast, by that same year, the Small Edition of Grimms' *Kinder- und Hausmärchen*, which was first published in 1825, had appeared in nine editions, while the Large Edition, originally published in 1812–15, had entered only its sixth edition in 1850. Yet, despite the comparatively larger and more rapid initial success of Bechstein's collection, beyond German-speaking areas and in the scholarly world, the Grimms' tales have been consistently out in front, a fact to which this volume of essays itself bears witness.

Initially, the popularity of Grimms' collection is not to be attributed solely to the work itself, but must be viewed in the context of the complete works of the brothers Jacob and Wilhelm Grimm. Their activity as collectors and editors, their folkloristic, linguistic, juridical, and religious scholarship, which they themselves viewed as interrelated areas of study, made them authorities whose intentions and scholarship also benefited their folktale collection in various ways.[1] The Grimms' call for continued collecting and editing of folk traditions produced in its own right a significant multiplication effect for the *Kinder- und Hausmärchen:* The pioneering deed of the young Grimms at the beginning of the nineteenth century was to successfully fend off resistance and assert folk traditions as a serious object of research, so that by the middle of the century the collecting of folklore had already become fairly well established.[2] Beginning in the 1840s there was an increase in projects to collect and edit folk traditions "in the spirit of the Grimms,"[3] and the basic standard for these collections were predominantly Jacob and Wilhelm Grimms' *Kinder- und Hausmärchen* and *Deutsche Sagen.* In this essay I would like to introduce one of the Grimms' followers as a collector and editor—Heinrich Pröhle.

In 1852 Pröhle writes, not quite true to the facts but representative of the contemporary opinion: "Until a year ago there were only two collections corresponding to our conception of a fairy-tale edition: Grimms' and Bechstein's" ("Gebräuche und Aberglauben" 581). He also refers to newly published collections of folktales and announces one of his own. Even though Pröhle was acquainted with contemporary collectors, had corresponded with some of them, and used their work for purposes of comparison in his own collections, it is the Brothers Grimm who appeared again and again in his works as authorities and initiators, not only in respect to their fairy-tale collection, but also in respect to their other works, especially Jacob's *Deutsche Mythologie.*[4] Pröhle acknowledged Jacob Grimm as his teacher in *Rheinlands schönste Sagen und Geschichten* (viii) and dedicated his dissertation about Mt. Brocken's various names and legends to him,[5] while he dedicated his *Märchen für die Jugend* to Wilhelm. Moreover, we know from Jacob and Wilhelm Grimms' letters to Pröhle that he sent the brothers not only his publications but also other materials for their research (Gürtler and Leitzmann 112–14, 214–20).

Who was Heinrich Pröhle, and what were his main activities? Here are some key biographical facts: He was born the son of a pastor on 4 June 1822 near Neuhaldensleben. He studied from 1843 to 1845 in Halle, but after difficulties resulting from his fraternity (*Burschenschaft*) activities, he moved to Berlin, where he became Jacob Grimm's student. He travelled, partly by foot, to southern Germany and Austria-Hungary. In 1848 he began working as a journalist and professional writer. In 1850 he hiked cross-country and stayed for longer periods in the Harz Mountains, where he resided from 1853 to 1857 near Wernigerode. He graduated in 1855 with a doctorate and from 1859 to 1890 taught at a Berlin secondary school. He died on 28 May 1895 in Berlin (Grosse; Pröhle, *Geschichte*).

Characterized by the encyclopedias of his time as an "extraordinarily active" author (Stern 279), Pröhle was truly prolific. He not only wrote books about literary, religious, and cultural history, but also compiled and edited legends besides publishing his own collections of folklore. Moreover, he authored literary works of his own[6] and published articles in the most diverse magazines. Those articles, which are still not systematically collected, also served to improve his poor financial situation (Grosse 348).

Pröhle's forte was not his literary or critical writing, but his activity as a folklorist, as a 1929 biography devoted to him observes: "His literary and pedagogical essays are rightly forgotten; his novels, novellas, and poems no longer pleasing to us today. What has survived him and will have lasting worth, are his collections of customs and legends from the Harz region" (Grosse 342). And as far as folklorists are concerned, Pröhle was already distinguished in an obituary as "The Harz Legend and Fairy-tale Man" (Weinhold 330).

In his works dedicated to folklore, on the other hand, there is no doubt that Pröhle's strength lay in his practical activity as a collector and not in the area of theory and systematics. He tended to be sketchy, essayistic, and anecdotal. His dissertation received a devastating critique from Wilhelm Mannhardt, and when Wilhelm Grimm—anticipating the Aarne-Thompson catalog of tale types or at least the work of Bolte and Polívka—suggested to Pröhle that someone might "want to take on a tedious but very useful task," namely producing a catalog of German fairy tales with German and international variants, Pröhle seems not to have been responsive.[7]

Pröhle's major work as collector and editor of folk narrative traditions took place in the early 1850s. At that time the gathering of folk traditions in German-speaking regions occurred under specific scholarly and political conditions—to name but the appearance of Jacob Grimm's *Deutsche Mythologie* (1835), the failed 1848 Revolution, and its aftermath. The interplay of scientific (i.e., mythological), political (i.e., national), and pedagogical interests also left its mark on Pröhle's work (Schenda; Gerndt, "Volkssagen"). Seldom, wrote Pröhle, has "a prophecy been so brilliantly fulfilled as has the conjecture that Wilhelm Grimm voiced during the stormy times of 1848 on the occasion of a new edition of the *Kinder- und Hausmärchen*, that namely these storms would in no way diminish the diligence of those who collected folk traditions, but on the contrary would strengthen and vivify it. How it came about that since those fateful days many a dear soul has fled to the bosom of the folk, is only all too clear" ("Gebräuche und Aberglauben" 580). So political frustration over the failure of a united German nation to emerge led to intensive research of folk traditions.[8] The use of folklore as a means of strengthening national consciousness was not a phenomenon limited to the nineteenth century or to German-speaking countries; however, it was possible to use it in this way only after folklore had become an acceptable subject of study.

In 1819 the Grimms had stated in the foreword to the second edition of their tales that their collection should not only avail the history of poetry and mythology but also serve as an educational reader.[9] Similarly, Pröhle stressed in his editions of fairy tales and legends that he wished to contribute to both mythology and pedagogy.[10] In this context his invocation of the Grimms as authorities in specific roles is clear: Wilhelm functioned as a "shield" in pedagogical discussions, Jacob in mythological argumentation. It should be remembered that according to his assertion the reconstruction of old (i.e., pre-Christian) beliefs can be facilitated by studying not only legends (although according to Pröhle much more directly so) but also fairy tales. These are, of course, the Grimms' well-known "tiny fragments of a burst gemstone," "the vestiges of a belief that reaches back into most ancient times" (*Kinder und Hausmärchen*, 6th ed., 1: LXVII; also *Kinder- und Hausmärchen: Ausgabe letzter Hand* 3: 409 [421]).

Pröhle collected principally in the Harz, a mountain range in central Germany. Its highest peak, the Brocken (1142 meters), which was the subject of Pröhle's dissertation, has also been called Blocksberg since the sixteenth century and is known in both the oral and written traditions as the stage for the witches' sabbats on Walpurgis Night. Pröhle's limitation to a single region is not a result of petty patriotic narrow-mindedness, but rather corresponds to the Grimms' notion that collections should be organized regionally, which in turn derives from ideas and experiences of Clemens Brentano (Jacob Grimm, *Circular;* Ginschel 273). Thus, research into folk traditions of the Harz is conceived as part of a topical apprehension of the German-language area. Moreover, according to Pröhle, collecting requires the investigator's intimate knowledge of the field. This means, for example, that the collector should have an active (and not simply a passive) knowledge of the local dialect (*Deutsche Sagen* x). Pröhle held fast to these premises and was readily praised by scholars such as Wilhelm Grimm and Wilhelm Mannhardt.[11]

In collecting regional materials Pröhle proceeded differently than did the Grimms, who "at no time went across the countryside collecting fairy tales" (Grimm, *Kinder- und Hausmärchen: Ausgabe letzter Hand* 3: 600), but who rather had their raconteurs come most often to them, or who received contributions directly from their circle of friends and acquaintances. Moreover, in comparison to other collectors of his time, Pröhle appears to have been an exception and further distinguishes himself by an extraordinary effusiveness about his field methods and experiences.[12]

To establish field contacts, Pröhle visited the city hall in the mining town Zellerfeld on paydays, followed court cases, allowed people to accost him or to beg from him, and eagerly accepted invitations to private homes. He even became a godfather, albeit, as he noted, surely only because of the christening-gift, as shortly thereafter he saw his godchild among a group of immigrants on their way to America. Later he boarded for a longer period in Lerbach, a small village in the Upper Harz, and took a room at an inn where many wagoners and foresters called. He participated in the life of the inn, and people came to him to tell stories. Some raconteurs he met on his tours, like his primary informant, "a man called Bertram," of whom Pröhle reports age, family status, occupation, and the origins of his story repertoire. He writes, moreover, that Bertram had offered himself as his factotum for a trifling reward and that his interest in folk traditions and his insight were so great, "that since his own memories have been exhausted, he is incessantly thinking about leading other storytellers to me, and as a rule he has chosen well" (*Kinder- und Volksmärchen* XVIII). If it is tempting at first to regard the much-praised Bertram as the image of a model narrator such as Frau Viehmann in Grimms' collection (unlike this old female storyteller, however, Bertram is in the "prime of manhood"), he is also to be considered from another point of view, namely as a "good informant," as "practically the researcher's colleague."[13]

45

Pröhle openly discusses some methodological procedures, such as the question of paying informants and the problem of false information. He also recommends that collectors of legends not let their informants know whether the collector himself actually believes in them. Although he cannot be expected to offer a methodical reflection on the conditions of fieldwork, some of his statements are worth mentioning. For example, he observes that it would only be possible for a stranger "to make, as it were, the people themselves an object of study in the same way and haste as I did" (*Harzbilder* 2); and he remarks, "Whenever you penetrate their circles, you do so as a thoughtless collector, who leaves behind no gift for their hospitality" ("Aus dem Tagebuch" XXX).

Pröhle's cognitive interest is evident, and the corresponding methods he recommends in his guidelines for collecting legends are rigorous (*Feldgarben*). For example, according to Pröhle, it is up to the collector to decide who should tell a tale and what kind of story it should be. But Pröhle himself does not appear to have always followed his own guidelines, and sometimes gives information that does not strictly pertain to his field of research. In his accounts of visits in the spinning-rooms, there is no mention of mythical fairy tales; instead he tells of card playing and of an illegal travelling Thuringian merchant of medicines. He notes repeatedly that people told him life stories instead of fairy tales and legends; he draws attention to the current fashion among young people to write drinking songs and to copy them down in notebooks; and he comments on the general economic situation.

Even when Pröhle did depart from his guidelines and more often than not acted as a journalist and travel author, he proceeded nonetheless as a collector with a scientific purpose, who felt committed to the norms of his time and to what he considered valid scientific precepts. And here again we see the Grimms' enormous standardizing influence. They created with the *Kinder- und Hausmärchen* and *Deutsche Sagen* a canon, from which they had consciously and unconsciously excluded large classes of oral narrative traditions. Their conception of the childlike purity and innocence of fairy tales, especially evident in the discussion with Achim von Arnim about the tale "The Wedding of Mrs. Fox" (Ginschel 251–54), and their conviction that the vestiges of antiquity could be found in fairy tales and legends, had a lasting effect on the following generation of collectors. Pröhle writes of the German folktales as "innocent flights [*Spiele*] of the imagination with that true and sincere naiveté, with that pure, childlike nature" which stand in

46

contrast to those "oriental fairy tales slanted for the youth particularly in Germany."[14] And he recommends in collecting legends that tellers of personally experienced ghost stories should be suppressed.[15] This means that selection already takes place during the act of collecting. The editing signified yet another filter.[16] Although some of the ghost stories escaped this scrupulous attention, they were eventually eliminated whenever possible in the second edition.[17]

How did Pröhle deal with the material that he collected? The only remark he makes concerning the recording of tales is one observation in his first scholarly collection, *Kinder- und Volksmärchen*. There he notes tersely that he had recorded many fairy tales as literally as possible but had transcribed them into High German at his desk (X). In contrast, he discusses the processes of adaptation relatively often and in detail. His explanation that he repeatedly revised the fairy tales after recording them is not at all disguised or apologetic but appears actually to be obligatory (X). The discussion of the appropriate styles of both fairy tales and legends seems to be a matter of course in other contemporary collections as well. The "tone," which the Grimms adopted, Pröhle found impossible to imitate,

> since it rests plainly on a perfect command of all the facets of language. . . . Because of the attention which Wilhelm Grimm devoted to the collection, hardly any line remained without import in the course of the numerous editions, and it [the collection] contains a wealth of insights into the microcosm of house and home and nature, which one would seek mostly in vain among our academic narrators [Erzählern von Fach]. (X)

The alterations that Wilhelm Grimm—as an *Erzähler von Fach*—undertook from one edition of the *Kinder- und Hausmärchen* to the next did not go unheeded by contemporaries; however, these changes were evaluated in a diametrically opposite way than they are today. The term "Erzähler von Fach" could not be clearer: the collector himself is to be understood as the last narrator before printing. Characterizing the style of other collectors, Pröhle complains that "as a storyteller" Professor Meier should have "struck the tone of the folk poet, as the Grimms do so well" (*Harzsagen: Gesammelt auf dem Oberharz* XXV). Similarly he rejected Bechstein's "historical novelistic style." He therefore deemed it necessary to create, in the *Kinder- und Volksmärchen*, his own tone, according to his familiarity with the north German folk

47

character (*Kinder- und Volksmärchen* XI). In *Märchen für die Jugend* on the other hand, where Pröhle also stressed an appropriate selection process regarding the content, he intended the style "especially for young people and had not wanted to keep it generally folklike" (*Märchen für die Jugend* XV).

Pröhle differentiates, then, between folk and nonfolk styles and even further between the styles of fairy tales and legends. According to him, the presentation of the legend requires a simple tone, and here too he praises the Grimms' great model as unequalled (*Harzsagen: Gesammelt auf dem Oberharz* XXV). Among legend styles he distinguishes yet again, according to whether the text derives from an oral or printed source, the language of the latter being characterized by a somewhat older period (*Harzsagen: Zweite Auflage* 269). Contrarily, "with the language of a legend recorded from the oral tradition, the goal is reached when the reader must say of the majority of items: this is how our people [Volk] think today and also how they express their thoughts" (*Harzsagen: Gesammelt auf dem Oberharz* XXV). Folk tone always involves, then, a staging of orality and folk character. And Pröhle gives even more detailed information about establishing such a tone:

> In the orally collected [nach dem Volksmunde] legends that I recorded in High German, I have strived to lend the language the approximate characteristics that I still heard on the one hand around 1850 from my tale-tellers, who were by background familiar with Low German, and on the other hand that I heard up to 1850 from High German-speakers of some standing, who were born in the last decades of the eighteenth century. In both cases the language was not the same; however, in this book I have sought to take the mid-course. (*Harzsagen: Zweite Auflage* 269)

So ultimately this is not a question of any willful deception on Pröhle's part regarding the authenticity of the text. "Orally collected" (*aus dem Volksmunde*), as it stands in many titles of contemporary collections, means only that the editor asserts that a tale, which circulated orally for a longer period, has in turn been told to him or to a contributor (see Köhler-Zülch and Shojaei Kawan).

As was practice since the Grimms, Pröhle used, besides personally collected items, also submissions from contributors, mostly teachers and ministers, and items received as a result of circulars calling for material, as well as items from written sources. The *Kinder- und Volks-*

märchen contain seventy-eight items, plus three of Pröhle's own "fabrications," as such given in the addenda. Of the seventy-eight items relevant here twenty-three have no annotations whatsoever, and for only thirteen is there a source listed. No single fairy tale is attributed to Pröhle's primary informant Bertram; Pröhle's father is given as the only narrator (*Kinder- und Volksmärchen* No. 73). Of sixty-four items in *Märchen für die Jugend* only sixteen have scholarly notations. And Pröhle thanks three contributors by name, without linking them to the tales they contributed. Likewise, in the volumes of legends not every item receives an annotation; and here too the contributors are acknowledged by their names and the places from which they submitted material, but almost never with connection to their texts. The method is always the same: no source is given for texts of oral origin, in contrast to published sources, which Pröhle cites together with the page number (*Harzsagen: Gesammelt auf dem Oberharz* XXVI).

Not only Pröhle followed this principle; almost all of his contemporaries had practiced it since the Grimms. Adalbert Kuhn and Wilhelm Schwartz differentiate within this system and clarify the reasoning behind it. The "great masses of the people," the "lower classes," are much more reliable informants for Kuhn and Schwartz than the middle and upper classes, with whom subjective interpretations and arbitrary modifications occur. "This is the reason why we always indicated explicitly when a legend was communicated to us by people of the educated classes, whereas it is to be assumed, that where only the label 'oral' is given, the lower classes and usually the lowest were consistently the source" (Kuhn and Schwartz XII).

Pröhle, who knew Kuhn and Schwartz's volume well (see, for example, *Harzsagen: Gesammelt auf dem Oberharz* 242), forgoes all labels such as "oral source" (XXVI). Despite the sociological definition of orality (*Volksmund*), this perspective is bound to the Romantic concept that folk traditions have no individual owner, but are instead common property. Indicating the names of storytellers seemed therefore unnecessary, but places of origin were deemed important. Done as a matter of course and even deemed necessary, the adaptation of "orally" (*aus dem Volksmund*) collected and acquired texts should be seen in this light. And here Wilhelm and Jacob Grimm were of one mind—in contrast to the often circulated opinion of the brothers' differing concepts of adaptation. Even though Jacob Grimm was in favor of extreme textual fidelity in editing monuments of Middle High

49

German, so much so that he spoke out against a normalization of the aural and written forms, he did not extend these principles to the oral transmission of tales (i.e., the *Kinder- und Hausmärchen* and the *Deutsche Sagen*).[18] Together with the conception of the oral tradition as common property, the focus of research determined their method and that of their successors. The focus was on the material (*Stoff*), the content, not on oral narration, the act of performance, itself.[19]

The Grimms had already supplied the model of contaminating variants in order to gain a "more complete" and "purer" version of a tale. While Pröhle scrupulously draws attention to his contaminations in the *Kinder- und Volksmärchen*, in the *Märchen für die Jugend* he simply writes: "It must be noted at least in general that variants of one and the same tale were used very frequently, but always in the most critical manner possible" (224). He makes an exception with two texts, since in these cases he used "independent fairy tales."

Not only had the Grimms' standards set a precedent, but in addition reviewers kept watch over the observance of these norms. In the case of Pröhle's *Märchen für die Jugend* for example, Mannhardt wrote in his review that the value of the individual pieces varied widely: several had very old and characteristic features, and others very obvious traces of the effect of modern literature on the folk (413). So those pieces with ancient characteristics seemed valuable, whereas the contemporary tradition was of no interest for research purposes. Wolf, on the other hand, complained of the *Kinder- und Volksmärchen* that Pröhle "appears to us often to have gone too far with faithfulness, in that he paid too little attention to the agreeableness of the presentation, and the awkwardness, harshness, and roughness, which many pieces show, should have been avoided" (371). Wolf even suggests how this could be remedied. Whether Pröhle's selecting of tales or his numerous statements about adaptation were motivated by such reviews remains to be seen.

According to Wolf in the same review, a more pleasant style would have been conducive to the sale of the book and, in consideration of the increasing sales figures per edition of the Grimms' collection, he is without doubt correct. Wolf considered a wide distribution of Pröhle's collection to be desirable not only because it had a scientific purpose but also because it heightened understanding of oral tradition. And indeed, this parallels the intentions of the *Kinder- und Volksmärchen*. Here Pröhle rejects material from the folk tradition that had been treated in a novella-like manner and complains that fairy tales without "true mythical characteristics are also diluted weekly in our newspapers and served with a not very appetizing sauce [*Senf*]" (*Kinder- und Volksmärchen* XI). Because of this inauthentic presentation of the oral tradition, Pröhle concludes that it is occasionally good "to present material of this kind . . . in purer form in fairy-tale books."

Pröhle argues even more forcefully for the influence of feedback in the case of legends. He rejected vehemently the "newer Harz literature" for tourism, which already had invaded the region.[20] He expresses his disgust for tourism and the "hotel industry" at Kyffhäuser, "which could certainly have some influence on the alteration of a German legend" (*Harzsagen: Zweite Auflage* 267–68; the Holy Roman Emperor Frederick Barbarossa is supposed to sleep in Kyffhäuser until his return). And it was his endeavor that legends be given back to the folk ("Wie sammelt man Volkssagen?" 376). For this reason he arranged his collection of legends topographically, because "otherwise local legends would be returned to individual regions only by nonscientific, general German legend adaptations" (*Harzsagen: Gesammelt auf dem Oberharz* XXVI). According to Pröhle, his collection was supposed to become, "in those places where legends are of local interest, a book for the folk and the home [*Volks- und Hausbuch*]." Is this a transplanting and continuation of the Grimms' ideas about folktales as tales for children and the home?

The Grimms' experience up to 1816 that the fruits of other collectors could hardly be available "until an exemplary collection made clear what disdained and trivial things are involved" (*Deutsche Sagen* 1: XXV) had finally been confirmed. These "disdained and trivial things" became several decades later established instruments of knowledge for comprehending the past and for educating in the present for the future; and both collections by the Brothers Grimm, supported by the *Deutsche Mythologie*, were the guide books for many collectors—including Pröhle.

In conclusion, we can point to the impact of Pröhle's Grimm reception on the Grimms themselves. Not only did Pröhle thoroughly know the *Kinder- und Hausmärchen* and the *Deutsche Sagen* and use them for comparative purposes—in the fifty-five notes to his *Kinder- und Volksmärchen*, for example, he refers to approximately thirty parallels in the Grimms' collection—but Wilhelm Grimm also knew Pröhle's collection very well and included in the final edition of his fairy tales forty references to both the *Kinder- und Volksmärchen* and *Märchen für die Jugend.* Moreover, he adopted "The Moonlight," No. 39 in Pröhle's *Märchen für die Jugend,* as "The Moon," No. 175 in his own collection of fairy tales. The opening of Pröhle's story, "In the land of Schnorrwitz people came too late when the Lord meted out the sun, moon and stars," is retold by Wilhelm Grimm as: "Long ago there was a land where the night was always dark and the sky was spread out over it like a black cloth, because there the moon never rose and no star twinkled in the darkness." So, as in the closing of a circle or perhaps the turning of a spiral, Pröhle's reception of the Grimms' methodological legacy is reciprocated and compounded in Wilhelm Grimm's reception of Pröhle's work.

Notes

Translated by Randy Schantz.

1. On the breadth of Grimms' work see Ludwig Denecke's articles on Jacob Grimm and on Wilhelm Grimm in the *Enzyklopädie des Märchens.*
2. In 1850 Wilhelm Grimm himself wrote in the sixth edition of the tales: "How lonely our collection stood when it first came forth, and what plentiful seed has sprouted since then. People smiled indulgently then about the claim that thoughts and perceptions were contained here, whose beginnings went back into the darkness of antiquity; but now this is hardly ever contradicted. There is a search for fairy tales that recognizes their scientific value" (Grimm, *Kinder und Hausmärchen,* 6th ed., 1: XXVIII; Grimm, *Kinder- und Hausmärchen: Ausgabe letzter Hand* 3: 360 [372]).
3. Rudolf Schenda has found 198 titles of legend publications alone for the period 1850–70. Ursula Mildenberger examines a total of 201 collections of legends, 183 for the period 1830–70, of which approximately half refer to the Grimms. I would like to thank Rudolf Schenda for directing me to pertinent literature.
4. Pröhle writes that his Harz legends were inspired "by the desire for a new collection of Harz legends, which Jacob Grimm expressed in the 2nd edition of the *Deutsche Mythologie*" (*Harzsagen: Gesammelt auf dem Oberharz* xv–xvi; see Grimm, *Deutsche Mythologie* 1: XII [XIV]). He prefaces his *Unterharzische Sagen* only with a motto signed "Jacob Grimm, April 28, 1844" (VII–VIII). The motto constitutes an excerpt from the *Deutsche Mythologie* (1: XI [XIII]–XII [XIV]).

5. "De Bructeri nominibus et de fabulis quae ad eum montem pertinent." See Gürtler and Leitzmann (217) concerning Wilhelm Grimm's mediation with the historian and jurisprudent Friedrich Christoph Dahlmann (then at the University of Bonn), one of the Göttingen Seven (see Denecke, *Jacob Grimm und sein Bruder Wilhelm* 134–37), who like Jacob Grimm not only lost his professorship for protesting against the King of Hannover's violation of the constitution in 1837, but also was ordered to leave the city of Göttingen within three days.

6. Leopold Hirschberg enumerates forty-six titles; see also *Meyers Konversationslexikon* 14 (1896): 258.

7. In a letter from 16 December 1854 (Gürtler and Leitzmann 216). Otherwise it appears that Pröhle tended to utilize the letters and their suggestions. See Wilhelm Grimm's letter to Pröhle of 4 July 1856 about health problems and the publishing of the 1856 volume of annotations to the *Kinder- und Hausmärchen* (Gürtler and Leitzmann 218), and Pröhle's review of the volume (Pröhle, *Feldgarben* 367).

8. Concerning Jacob and Wilhelm Grimms' political engagement, such as their participation in the Germanists' conferences of 1846 in Frankfurt and 1847 in Lübeck, or Jacob Grimm's participation in the constitutional assembly of 1848 in the Paulskirche in Frankfurt, see Denecke, *Jacob Grimm und sein Bruder Wilhelm* 139–42.

9. Pröhle used the sixth edition of the Grimms' *Kinder- und Hausmärchen* (1850), which contained all the collection's forewords from the second edition on, as well as Wilhelm Grimm's exposition on the fairy tale and fairy-tale literature.

10. In modern terminology his *Märchen für die Jugend* is basically an "educational unit." It is worth noting that Pröhle's choice of words often echoes the Grimms'. For example, compare Pröhle's assertion that "these fairy tales too are recognized more and more as very essential nourishment" (*Märchen für die Jugend* XI) with Jacob Grimm's statement concerning "fairy tales and legends that give healthy nourishment to youth and to the folk even to this day" (*Deutsche Mythologie* 1: XIII [XV]).

11. Thus Wilhelm Grimm in a letter to Pröhle 30 April 1855: "I rejoice in your continuing activity in researching customs and traditions of the Harz region. If such work is to be thorough and to have lasting value, it is essential that one be a native, as you are, and be attentive for a long period" (Gürtler and Leitzmann 218). In a collective review of five of Pröhle's works Wilhelm Mannhardt writes: "What a pure gain for science arises when a man who is not unacquainted with antiquarian knowledge and who is familiar through and through with the folklife of a certain region pursues with diligence and love the traditions of just such a delimited region where he is at home" (412).

12. Pröhle voices his opinion in various places: not only in the forewords to his collections, especially to the *Kinder- und Volksmärchen,* but also in "Gebräuche und Aberglauben"; "Eine Pfingstbetrachtung"; "Wie sammelt man Volkssagen?"; and "Aus dem Tagebuch." For analogous details recalling Pröhle see "Methode des Wanderstudiums" and its "Handwerksgeheimnisse" by Pröhle's contemporary Wilhelm Heinrich Riehl (1823–97) and Richard Wossidlo's research report of field experiences of a half century later.

13. In this context see Jeggle's explanations of "Schatzsucherblick" in Romanticism and the appearance of the informant in the scholarly world (16–19), as well as Lindner's studies of the primary informant in the role of travel guide and research assistant (key person) in ethnological research.

14. *Märchen für die Jugend* XIII. See Pröhle, "Die Überlieferungen" 364–65, on fairy tales "which on the other hand were not transmitted into fairy-tale books, probably because of their sordid character," and on other not so "refined," but related tales "which are in German fairy-tale collections." He means here AT 1360C: Old Hildebrand; Grimm No. 95: "Der alte Hildebrand" (in this case a dialect text).

15. "Wie sammelt man Volkssagen?" 375. See also Pröhle, *Harzsagen: Zweite Auflage* 268, where he notes that "mere ghost stories as well as mere fragments of tales" were removed for the second edition of the *Harzsagen.* To be sure, the aversion to ghost stories had a pre-Grimm precedent. Already Otmar, whose *Volcks = Sagen* was a plentiful source for the Grimms' *Deutsche Sagen,* wrote that ghost stories were so lifeless, "they were not worthy of retelling" (55). In Pröhle's discussion of Otmar, whom he valued highly and designated as the originator of German legend research, the various views of the Enlightenment and Romanticism in reference to the legend become evident (*Harzsagen: Gesammelt auf dem Oberharz* XVII–XX).

16. See the reference to similar methods by the Danish collector, editor, and researcher Sven Hersleb Grundtvig in Dollerup et al. 259–60.

17. For example, from the second edition of the *Harzsagen* Pröhle excluded in addition to ghost stories "The Clausthaler Girl in America," an interesting tale given the contemporary wave of immigrants to America, some of whom came from the Harz (*Harzsagen: Gesammelt auf dem Oberharz* 89). In this tale a girl follows her new husband to America, where he rejects her. Subsequently she comes upon a castle, where she sleeps in a bed of the "finest wing feathers" but fears that she has fallen among thieves. However, the castellan marries her, and from then on she always sleeps in a bed of "wing feathers." Immediately associations may be drawn to European magazine articles from the 1950s about dream marriages and luxurious waterbeds in Hollywood.

18. See Ginschel 212–78. Ginschel (221) cites Grimm No. 51, "Foundling," as proof for the surprising similarity between Jacob and Wilhelm Grimm's

stylistic adaptation. This tale served Wilhelm Schoof in his study of the KHM style as an example of Wilhelm Grimm's technique, although it was told by Jacob Grimm.

19. See Gerndt, "Sagen und Sagenforschung." The frequently incomplete citation of a passage from the foreword to the second edition of the Grimms' *Kinder- und Hausmärchen* often leads to misunderstandings about the Grimms' idea of fidelity: "As to the method by which we collected, we were concerned above all with accuracy and truth. We have added nothing from our own resources. . . . That the expression of individual details is largely our own, goes without saying" (Grimm, *Kinder und Hausmärchen*, 6th ed., 1: XV–XVI; *Kinder- und Hausmärchen: Ausgabe letzter Hand* 1: 21).

20. See Schenda and ten Doornkaat 41–50 for the importance of travel literature for the transmission of "folk narratives." Pröhle himself was an editor of Harz guidebooks, such as *Der Harz: Praktisches Handbuch für Reisende.* The Grieben-Führer—Grieben-Guidebooks—rarely permitted detailed discussion of folk traditions (38 and 73–74), but they did make it possible for him to refer to his Harz legends, in which he made reference in return to the Grieben-Führer: "The topographical arrangement of the Harz legends in this edition corresponds to the principal tour, which underlies the travel handbook" (*Harzsagen: Zweite Auflage* 271). See Pröhle, *Heinrich Heine und der Harz* and *Abhandlungen über Goethe, Schiller, Bürger* for Heine's and Goethe's travels through the Harz, including a visit to the Brocken. See Köhler-Zülch.

Works Cited

Denecke, Ludwig. "Grimm, Jacob Ludwig Karl." *Enzyklopädie des Märchens.* Berlin: de Gruyter, 1988. 6: 171–86.

———. "Grimm, Wilhelm Carl." *Enzyklopädie des Märchens.* Berlin: de Gruyter, 1988. 6: 186–95.

———. *Jacob Grimm und sein Bruder Wilhelm.* Stuttgart: Metzler, 1971.

Dollerup, Cay, et al. "The Ontological Status, the Formative Elements, the 'Filters' and Existences of Folktales." *Fabula* 25 (1984): 241–65.

Gerndt, Helge. "Sagen und Sagenforschung im Spannungsfeld von Mündlichkeit und Schriftlichkeit." *Fabula* 29 (1988): 1–20.

———. "Volkssagen: Über den Wandel ihrer zeichenhaften Bedeutung vom 18. Jahrhundert bis heute." *Volkskultur in der Moderne.* Ed. U. Jeggle et al. Reinbek: rowohlts enzyklopädie, 1986. 397–409.

Ginschel, Gudrun. *Der junge Jacob Grimm: 1805–1819.* Berlin: Akademie-Verlag, 1967.

Grimm, Brothers. *Deutsche Sagen.* 2 vols. Berlin: Nicolaische Buchhandlung, 1816–1818.

―――. *Kinder und Hausmärchen.* 6th ed. Göttingen: Dieterichsche Buchhandlung, 1850.

―――. *Kinder- und Hausmärchen: Ausgabe letzter Hand mit den Originalanmerkungen der Brüder Grimm.* Ed. Heinz Rölleke. 3 vols. Stuttgart: Reclam, 1980.

Grimm, Jacob. *Circular wegen Aufsammlung der Volkspoesie.* Wien, 1815. Ed. Ludwig Denecke. Afterword by Kurt Ranke. Kassel: Brüder Grimm-Museum, 1968.

―――. *Deutsche Mythologie.* 4th ed. 3 vols. Ed. Elard Hugo Meyer. Gütersloh/Berlin, 1875–78. Rpt. with intro. by Leopold Kretzenbacher. Graz: Akademische Druck- und Verlagsanstalt, 1968.

Grosse, Walther. "Heinrich Christoph Ferdinand Pröhle." *Mitteldeutsche Lebensbilder.* Magdeburg: Historische Kommission für die Provinz Sachsen und für Anhalt, 1929. 4: 342–53.

Gürtler, Hans, and Albert Leitzmann, eds. *Briefe der Brüder Grimm.* Jena: Frommann, 1923.

Hirschberg, Leopold. *Der Taschengoedeke.* Vol. 2. Munich: Deutscher Taschenbuchverlag, 1970.

Jeggle, Utz. "Zur Geschichte der Feldforschung in der Volkskunde." *Feldforschung: Qualitative Methoden in der Kulturanalyse.* Ed. U.J. Tübinger Vereinigung für Volkskunde e.V. *Schloß* 62 (1984): 11–46.

Köhler-Zülch, Ines. "Die Hexenkarriere eines Berges: Der Brocken alias Blocksberg. Ein Beitrag zur Sagen-, Hexen- und Reiseliteratur." *Festschrift für Maja Bošković-Stulli.* Zagreb, 1993.

Köhler-Zülch, Ines, and Christine Shojaei Kawan. "Les Frères Grimm et leurs contemporains: Quelques reflexions sur l'adaptation des contes traditionnels dans le contexte socio-culturel du XIXᵉ siècle." *D'un conte . . . à l'autre: La variabilité dans la littérature orale.* Paris: Editions du CNRS, 1990. 249–60.

Kuhn, Adalbert, and Wilhelm Schwartz. *Norddeutsche Sagen, Märchen und Gebräuche.* Leipzig: Brockhaus, 1848.

Lindner, Rolf. "Ohne Gewähr: Zur Kulturanalyse des Informanten." *Feldforschung: Qualitative Methoden in der Kulturanalyse.* Ed. Utz Jeggle. Tübinger Vereinigung für Volkskunde e.V. *Schloß* 62 (1984): 59–71.

Mannhardt, Wilhelm. Rev. of Pröhle's dissertation. *Zeitschrift für deutsche Mythologie und Sittenkunde* 3 (1855): 319–21.

―――. Rev. of Pröhle's *Harzbilder* etc. *Zeitschrift für deutsche Mythologie und Sittenkunde* 3 (1855): 411–14.

Mildenberger, Ursula. "Deutschsprachige Sagensammlungen des 19. Jahrhunderts: Ein Beitrag zur Rezeptionsgeschichte der 'Deutschen Sagen' der Brüder Grimm." Ts. U of Munich, 1987.

Otmar [Johann Carl Christoph Nachtigal]. *Volcks = Sagen.* Bremen: Wilmans, 1800.

Pröhle, Heinrich. *Abhandlungen über Goethe, Schiller, Bürger.* Potsdam, 1889.

————. "Arx Hercinia." *Deutsches Museum* 2 (1852): 241–55.

————. *Aus dem Harze: Skizzen und Sagen.* Leipzig: Avenarius und Mendelssohn, 1851.

————. "Aus dem Tagebuch eines deutschen Sammlers." *Deutsches Museum* 15 (1856). Rpt. in Pröhle, *Harzsagen: Zweite Auflage* XV–XLI.

————. *Deutsche Sagen.* Berlin: Frank, 1863.

————. *Feldgarben.* Leipzig: Gräbner, 1859.

————. "Gebräuche und Aberglauben." *Deutsches Museum* 2 (1852): 580–89.

————. *Geschichte der burschenschaftlichen Bewegung unter dem Ministerium Eichhorn insbesondere der hallischen Burschenschaft von 1842–1845.* Berlin: Verlag der Burschenschaftlichen Blätter, 1894.

————. *Der Harz: Praktisches Handbuch für Reisende. Neu bearbeitet.* 22nd ed. Griebens Reise-Bibliothek 2. Berlin: Goldschmidt, 1890.

————. *Harzbilder: Sitten und Gebräuche aus dem Harzgebirge.* Leipzig: Brockhaus, 1855.

————. *Harzsagen: Gesammelt auf dem Oberharz und in der übrigen Gegend von Harzeburg und Goslar bis zur Grafschaft Hohenstein und bis Nordhausen.* Leipzig: Avenarius und Mendelssohn, 1854. New ed. Ed. Will-Erich Peuckert. Göttingen: Schwartz, 1957.

————. *Harzsagen: Zweite Auflage in Einem Bande.* Leipzig: Mendelssohn, 1886.

————. *Heinrich Heine und der Harz.* Harzburg, 1888.

————. *Kinder- und Volksmärchen.* Leipzig: Avenarius und Mendelssohn, 1853. Rpt. with afterword by Helga Stein. Hildesheim: Olms, 1975.

————. *Märchen für die Jugend: Mit einer Abhandlung für Lehrer und Erzieher.* Halle: Buchhandlung des Waisenhauses, 1854.

————. "Eine Pfingstbetrachtung." *Magdeburger Correspondent* 114–15 (1853). Rpt. in Pröhle, *Unterharzische Sagen* 174–82.

————. *Rheinlands schönste Sagen und Geschichten: Für die Jugend bearbeitet.* Berlin: Meidinger, ca. 1886.

————. "Die Überlieferungen in ihren moralischen, ästhetischen und nationalen Beziehungen." Pröhle, *Feldgarben* 353–66.

————. *Unterharzische Sagen.* Aschersleben: Fokke, 1856. Lindlar: Kierdorf, 1979.

————. "Wie sammelt man Volkssagen?" Pröhle, *Feldgarben* 374–76.

Riehl, Wilhelm Heinrich. *Wanderbuch.* 3rd ed. Stuttgart: Cotta, 1892. 3–33.

Schenda, Rudolf. "Mären von deutschen Sagen: Bemerkungen zur Produktion von 'Volkserzählungen' zwischen 1850 und 1870." *Geschichte und Gesellschaft* 9 (1983): 26–48.

Schenda, Rudolf, in collaboration with Hans ten Doornkaat. *Sagenerzähler und Sagensammler der Schweiz: Studien zur Produktion volkstümlicher Geschichte und Geschichten vom 16. bis zum frühen 20. Jahrhundert.* Bern: Haupt, 1988.

Schoof, Wilhelm. "Beiträge zur Stilentwicklung der Grimmschen Märchen." *Zeitschrift für deutsche Philologie* 74 (1955): 424–33.

Stern, Adolf. *Lexikon der deutschen Nationalliteratur.* Leipzig: Bibliographisches Institut, 1882.

Weinhold, Karl. "Heinrich Pröhle †." *Zeitschrift des Vereins für Volkskunde* 5 (1895): 329–30.

Wolf, Johann Wilhelm. Rev. of Pröhle's *Kinder- und Volksmärchen. Zeitschrift für deutsche Mythologie und Sittenkunde* 1 (1853): 370–71.

Wossidlo, Richard. "Über die Technik des Sammelns volkstümlicher Überlieferungen." *Zeitschrift des Vereins für Volkskunde* 16 (1906): 1–24.

The Spoken and the Read: *German Popular Stories* and English Popular Diction

Brian Alderson

WHEN PROFESSOR ELLIS sat down at the academic hearthside and told everyone his "one fairy story too many," he doubtless got the audience participation that he expected. One does not impugn the adventurous exploits of the Two Brothers—to say nothing of all their hangers-on—without preparing for either an offended silence or (which would have been more fun) cries of alarm and disapproval.

By being so provocative, however, Professor Ellis has given a fresh momentum to the always-interesting debate over what divides oral literature from written literature and how the first may be most faithfully represented in the second. He refers tellingly to the gap that exists between the Grimms' statements of method that appear in their first preface (1812) and their second (1819). For where, to begin with, they claimed of their collection that "no particular has been either added through our own poetic recreation, or improved and altered," they subsequently (and silently) changed this to "we have added nothing of our own, have improved no circumstance or trait of the story itself, but have

59

given its content just as we received it; that the expression largely originates with us is self-evident" (trans. in Ellis 13 and 17). In other words, as they built up their experience of editing folktales, they came to realize that it was not so easy to put the *content* of a told story into print in the *diction* of a told story because readers would be confronted by an unfamiliar literary register. (The practicalities of the matter are defended by Heinz Rölleke in his review of *One Fairy Story Too Many* when he remarks that no publisher—and surely no reading public— would have taken on a collection of oral tales reproduced verbatim in 1819, and that if the Grimms had put all their fragmentary and contradictory materials into print, "hätte kein Hahn danach gekräht" [331]— no one would have given a hoot.)

In terms of the controversy, Professor Ellis may well be justified in seeing some "conspiracy" on the Grimms' part to try to cover their back-tracks from the ideals of 1812—and Heinz Rölleke's explanation comes a little late, for surely the Grimms could have taken the readers of their own day a little more into their confidence. What matters though is not imputations of nefarious practice but the barely resolved question of how you can make print convey the timbres of the storyteller's voice. The implications of such an exercise may not have been altogether clear in the heady days when the first preface was formulated, but the shoulder-shrugging "is self-evident" of the second preface may well betoken an acceptance that the consistent preservation of "oral register" was no longer on the agenda.

Nevertheless, the progress of Grimms' *Kinder- und Hausmärchen* from 1819 onwards never saw a complete abandonment of the storyteller's presence, and the collection remains a book of monumental significance, first through the range of quite new narrative themes that it brought into print and second through the stimulus that it gave to a greater awareness of oral modes. So rich a mixture of nursery stories, beast fables, peasant anecdotes, and comic or Romantic tales had never been set out in the vernacular before (Galland's *Arabian Nights* had none of the Grimms' casual variety); and even though important vernacular elements were modified or edited away, the Grimms still presented the world with examples of storytelling methods that were perceptibly different from standard "literary" ones. There is a certain poetic justice in the fact that from 1812 onwards the Grimms' collection preserved, in verbatim enough style, the texts of the two stories that most fully represented the Grimm revolution: "The Fisherman and

His Wife'' (No. 19) and ''The Juniper Tree'' (No. 47). Although they had both been collected before the Grimms started serious work on the *Kinder- und Hausmärchen,* and had both been previously published elsewhere, these tales, with their refinements entangled amongst primitivisms, and with their vigorous dialect speech patterns, showed the potential that the printed word had for catching something of the directness and the unmediated abruptness of the told story. And, of course, Professor Ellis chose not to notice that the Grimms included other dialect stories as their work progressed, although material like ''Gambling Hans'' (No. 82) or ''Going Travelling'' (No. 143) hardly has the narrative power of those two early stories.

Ways forward from such models as these are not difficult to discern for those interested in pursuing German *Volkstümlichkeit;* and indeed, the Grimms themselves pioneered an ever-widening context for the study of popular culture through their philological and their antiquarian studies. *Pace* Professor Ellis, one might even argue that some of Wilhelm's tinkerings with the stories as edition succeeded edition were made with the intention of implanting more of a storytelling voice rather than prettifying by expansion. ''The Frog King'' (No. 1), for instance, opens with commendable directness in the first edition: ''Es war einmal eine Königstochter, die ging hinaus in den Wald und setzte sich an einen kühlen Brunnen'' (''There was once a princess who went out into the forest and sat herself down beside a cool well''; *Kinder- und Hausmärchen: 1812 und 1815* 1: 1). It hardly seems necessary that Wilhelm should replace this in the third edition with a new sentence containing twenty-six more words and four extra subclauses. Nevertheless, by beginning the story thus with the famous and untranslatable ''In den alten Zeiten, wo das Wünschen noch geholfen hat'' he clearly desired to add a trope that was essentially the product of a storytelling, rather than a literary, voice.[1] (Untranslatability is often a good guide in these matters—just look at all those impossible little rhymes that keep turning up in the stories.)

But if we turn to the influence that the arrival of Grimms' collection had upon English *Volkstümlichkeit,* then we are faced with a much sharper division between these two voices, for we are now dealing not simply with the conveyance of a told story into print, but also with the translation of that transaction. The Brothers Grimm, whatever the purity of their motives as the recorders of folktale, are now inescapably given over to the hands of their translators.

61

There is not much doubt that in the second decade of the nineteenth century the climate for a translation of the *Kinder- und Hausmärchen* into English was a favorable one. During the period when the first German editions were appearing, there had been a great upsurge in both the publishing and the public acceptance of traditional tales in England. The most notable signs of this had been the arrival of superior editions of the standard tales of "Mother Goose" and "Mother Bunch," and the playful publication of single tales from these collections as picture books, alongside a new exploitation of native folktale resources. Thus publishers like Benjamin Tabart with his four volumes of *Popular Stories for the Nursery* (1804–09), and John Harris with his handsome editions of Perrault and d'Aulnoy (1817), brought an air of refinement to material that had hitherto subsisted in near-chapbook state. At the same time they were part of a competing body of publishers issuing such attractive (and saleable) picture books as *Jack and the Beanstalk* and *A True History of a Little Old Woman Who Found a Silver Penny*. This last was a versified version of the nursery story of "The Old Woman and Her Pig," and Tabart's edition of 1806 concluded with a four-panel, fold-out panorama that is one of the earliest examples of such a device in an English children's book.

Given this energetic new fashion there is a satisfying appropriateness over the earliest welcome that was given to the Grimms' tales in England. This appeared in 1819 in the body of a review article in the *Quarterly Review,* which had been prompted by the appearance of *Fairy Tales, or the Lilliputian Cabinet,* collected by none other than Benjamin Tabart and published by him in 1818.[2] The author of the *Quarterly* article was Francis Cohen, who changed his name in 1824 and is now better known as the antiquary Sir Francis Palgrave, father of the golden treasurer. Although he spends the first long paragraph of his review in writing about the Tabart volume, he is disappointingly vague in his criticisms and not altogether well informed about the contemporary state of children's-book publishing. What he is really keen to do is to construct a platform from which he can launch a general survey of popular lore and a defense of it as a subject for legitimate study. He rambles along in the leisurely style approved by the *littérateurs* of the period, providing instances of "the vivid imagination of man in the childhood of his race" (92). Then, after four and a half pages, he introduces his main theme:

The most important addition to nursery literature has been effected in Germany, by the diligence of John and William Grimm, two antiquarian brethren of the highest reputation. Under the title of 'Kinder und Hausmärchen' they have published a collection of German popular stories, singular in its kind, both for extent and variety, and from which we have acquired much information.[3]

There then follows a lengthy sequence of excursions into the imaginative and antiquarian hinterland of folklore, where Cohen draws initial examples from the Grimms' collection and uses them to discuss wider folkloristic and comparative interpretations. Impressed as he obviously is with the quite new contribution that the Grimms' work has brought to folklore studies, the "information" that he derives from the collection nevertheless has no connection with narrative processes and has everything to do with probing the contents of these "idle stories" which "boast a higher antiquity than romances and poems of much greater pretensions" (97).

In a similar way, this interpretive urge was also prominent among the motives that led Edgar Taylor to become the first English translator of Grimm with his *German Popular Stories* (1823–26). He knew Francis Cohen (and indeed, in a letter to the Grimms in 1823 he called him "our friend and neighbour" [Hartwig 7]); and before ever he embarked on his translation—or perhaps while he was working on it—he too published some reflections on the nature of folktale. These were embodied in four articles that appeared in Henry Colburn's *New Monthly Magazine and Literary Journal* between 1821 and 1822 under the title "German Popular and Traditionary Literature."

As with the *Quarterly* article, considerable chunks of this four-part essay are given over to either retelling German tales and legends or discussing their relationship with stories from other cultures. Otmar's "Ziegenhirt" (which Taylor put into the second volume of his Grimm collection as "Peter the Goatherd") is, obviously enough, compared with "Rip Van Winkle"; legends of giants and dwarfs are linked to their treatment in Old High German sagas. And when he finally turns to "the beautiful collection of Nursery Literature (chiefly consisting of Fairy Tales) which has lately been edited with so much care by Messrs. Grimm" (148), Taylor is equally preoccupied with finding roots and parallels: "The Jew in the Bush" (No. 110), for instance, and its similarity to the English chapbook "The Frere and the Boye."

The stressing of comparative or anthropological elements in these stories by amateurs like Cohen and Taylor should come as no surprise. After all, at this period (perhaps even today), learned gentlemen—indeed, learned *lawyers*—might appear to be demeaning themselves in writing about "idle stories," and it behooved them to put out a modest display of intellectual paraphernalia to justify their interest. But even from the date of his *New Monthly Magazine* articles Edgar Taylor was also attracted by the benefits that fairy tales might bring to children's reading. In contrast to "the prudery and artificial taste" of the previous century the time had come to "welcome the aera when our children shall be allowed once more to regale themselves with that mild food which will enliven their imaginations, and tempt them on through the thorny paths of education" (146). And with phrases that foreshadow his preface to the first volume of his Grimm translation, he deprecates the "scientific compendiums, lisping botanies, and leading-string mechanics" that have come to obscure "the Delights of Valentine and Orson, the beautiful Magalona, or Fair Rosamond" (147).

As his work on the translation matured, therefore, Taylor steered a tactful course between the interests of those who might see the Grimms' collection as a repository of popular lore, open to scientific study, and those who might find it a lively addition to the gradually emergent body of entertaining children's literature. "The Translators were first induced to compile this little work by the eager relish with which a few of the tales were received by the young friends to whom they were narrated," says Taylor (and his collaborator David Jardine) at the start of *German Popular Stories* in 1823 (1: iii). This is a point that they reiterated when sending a presentation copy to the Brothers Grimm themselves: "In compiling our little volume we had the amusement of some young friends principally in view" (Hartwig 6–7). At the same time, though, they claimed "some little pretensions to literary consideration," whereby they were led to a modest discussion of the mythological background to the tales in their preface, and also to the extensive adoption of the Grimms' historical *Anmerkungen* in their own twenty-page appendix of notes.

In both these functions, however, the translators—or, most probably, just Edgar Taylor—were essentially preoccupied with what the stories had to say. They probe the nature of particular incidents, like the uncertain benevolence of the elves in "The Elves" (No. 39), and they discover analogues in anything from Olaus Magnus to Milton; or they perceive elements in the stories where they are "compelled sometimes to conciliate local feelings and deviate a little from strict translation" (Hartwig 7), making the stories more suitable for a child audience. "Giant" is preferred to "Devil" in No. 29 "to avoid offence"; and the translators admit, "we have not entered into the particulars of the queen's death" in "Snow-drop" (No. 53), although with a proper respect for sources Taylor tends to record such omissions and changes in the notes at the end of the book (1: 236 and 1: 230).

Only at the margins of their commentaries do Taylor and Jardine touch upon the issue of narrative voice. They acknowledge on their title page that the *German Popular Stories* are "collected by M. M. Grimm, from oral tradition"—although Cruikshank's wonderful accompanying illustration shows the storyteller *reading* to his hilarious audience. (This changed in volume 2, where we get a plausible view of *die Märchenfrau* about to spring a few hobgoblins onto her gaping youthful listeners.) In the preface, however, there is no statement of intent equivalent to Jacob Grimm's desire for authenticity, only a general recognition at the start that stories such as these were traditionally— quoting a seventeenth-century source— "'the revivers of drowzy age at midnight'" told to a company around the Christmas fire-block (1: iii– iv). And, again, in the notes there is only the briefest mention here and there of the linguistic features of the tales that are being discussed: the affinity of the Pomeranian dialect of "The Fisherman and his Wife" to Lowland Scots, and English, or Scottish, vernacular equivalents to some of the interpolated rhymes.

With diction thus appearing to have so much less a priority than content, it would not be surprising if this first translation of Grimm attracted the sort of objection that Francis Cohen levelled at Benjamin Tabart's *Fairy Tales*. That collection, he had said, "recals [sic] but faintly the pleasant homeliness of the narrations which used to delight us" and was apparently (he is very unspecific) designed for a public now grown "strangely fastidious" in its taste (91). And indeed, a criticism of that kind was levelled in 1834 by W. J. Thoms, the antiquary to whom we owe the word "folk-lore," when he regretted Taylor's omission of homely expressions, striking incidents, and repetitions in his translation of "The Juniper Tree."[4]

That criticism applies to other stories, too, and can be easily demonstrated in the case of Grimm No. 27. The 1819 German version of that story, translated by Taylor as "The Travelling Musicians," describes the following encounter involving the musicians on the road to Bremen: "Es dauerte nicht lange, so saß da eine Katze auf dem Weg und machte ein gar trübselig Gesicht. 'Nun, was ist dir dann in die Quere gekommen?' sprach der Esel. 'Ei,' antwortete die Katze, 'wer kann da lustig seyn, wenns einem an den Kragen geht?' " (*Kinder- und Hausmärchen: 1819* 1: 103). This is rendered by Taylor as: "They had not gone far before they saw a cat sitting in the middle of the road and making a most rueful face. 'Pray, my good lady,' said the ass, 'what's the matter with you? you look quite out of spirits!' 'Ah me!' said the cat, 'how can one be in good spirits when one's life is in danger?' " (1: 10). Not much critical acumen is needed to see that Taylor has here passed up two splendid opportunities for injecting some English colloquial vigor to match that in the German: "was ist dir dann in die Quere gekommen" and "wenns einem an den Kragen geht." His response has been not only to mistranslate but also to make literary, rather than oral, turns of phrase by using the address "Pray, my good lady" and by breaking up the direct question with the phrase "said the ass."

Such lapses are not easily excusable or explicable. Many translators indeed discover that half the fun of their job is in finding appropriately colorful equivalents for idiosyncratic passages like this. The frequency with which Taylor backs away from such opportunities, though, suggests that he knew what he was doing and that he was after a certain consonance of tone—imposing an edited coherence on the stories that would make his book a unity. After all, there is evidence of editorial forethought running throughout the book, clearly evident in the choice of the opening story accompanied by Cruikshank's narrative frontispiece, and in the grouping together of the animal stories of "Riffraff," "Herr Korbes," and "The Death of the Hen" (Nos. 10, 41, and 80) under the generic—and English—title of "Chanticleer and Partlet."

One can indeed argue that the Grimms—as they themselves recognized—were well served by this translation. For although it is deeply conservative in its response to the originalities of the *Kinder- und Hausmärchen,* and although it is cavalier over the precise matching of words—which the Grimms also recognized—it is nevertheless a version with a proper feeling for the rhythms of English prose. If the Grimms could not finally follow the ideals of a "pure" recording of the storyteller's voice, we can hardly expect their translator—embattled in the "fastidious" climate of 1823—to exceed them. What he did do, over many pages of his book, was to respond naturally to the language of the stories and make them sound as though they had originated in English rather than in German. (His text does not derogate either from its superlative illustrations. Cruikshank's etchings here have long been recognized as one of his greatest achievements; what is less frequently noticed is the aptness of their setting. The coherence of Taylor's text, the typography, the mise-en-page all combine with the illustrations to make *German Popular Stories* one of the most attractive books of its time, and one entirely suited to its humble but revolutionary contents.)

Respect for Taylor's achievement, both in the first volume of his translation and in its successor of 1826, is enhanced when one comes to consider the Grimms' fate in England as the nineteenth century progressed—a fate of which neglect was certainly not to be a part. The two volumes met with a ready response (perhaps because of Cruikshank's pictures as much as Taylor's translation), and they were both reprinted at least twice before 1834. Then, from 1839 onwards, they gained wider circulation in the one-volume form of *Gammer Grethel, or German Fairy Tales and Popular Stories,* which converted Cruikshank's etchings into wood engravings by (probably John) Byfield and added some wood-engraved versions of Ludwig Emil Grimm's illustrations from the German Small Edition of 1825 as well.

At the same time, these stories, either in translation or in their German original, helped to foster the growth of English folklore studies. W. J. Thoms was not alone in seeing the significance of the Grimms' tales, and these along with the Grimms' *Deutsche Sagen* of 1816–18, materially influenced the work of such pioneers as Thomas Keightley and James Orchard Halliwell. They also prompted that sure evidence of general interest: adaptation and exploitation by competitive publishers.

Adaptation—the wholesale reworking of stories that originated in Taylor's volumes—set in very early. By 1825 Messrs. Dean & Munday, the publishers of popular children's books, had put out editions of at least two stories converted into verse and issued as picture books of sixteen leaves apiece. *Unlucky John and His Lump of Silver: A Juvenile Comic Tale* was put into "easy verse" by Madame Leinstein, while *Wishing; or the Fisherman and His Wife: A Juvenile Poem* came from the pen of "a lady" (who may have been Madame Leinstein, too). In both instances the original story has been drastically curtailed and altered following Taylor's original. Unlucky John, for example, is given a lump of silver, as in Taylor, rather than gold, as in the original Grimm No. 83. And the fisherman's wife now seeks universal rather than divine powers:

> She laugh'd, and in her impious pride,
> Besought the fish to yield her soon
> A pow'r, by silken reins to guide
> The evolutions of the moon.

These two Dean & Munday books are the first examples of stories from the *Kinder- und Hausmärchen* being adapted to the purposes of the picture-book market—a process that has now grown beyond the control of even the most sophisticated bibliographic analysis. One of the most interesting of their immediate successors, however, demands attention—partly because it reveals how quickly publishers accepted the playful possibilities of adapting fairy tales and partly because it brings in an acknowledgment of its source.

The story in question is entitled "The Wolf and Seven Kids" (Grimm No. 5), and it appears in a composite volume with the cover title *The Three Bears and Their Stories,* published from 60 Pall Mall, London, by Messrs. Wright in 1841. The book begins with "The Story of the Three Bears" and then leads on to a versified account by the author of how he visited the bears in their cottage. The bears ask him what he will take, but he seeks only enlightenment:

> "Nothing I thank you, friends," I said,
> "I am not hungry, but instead
> Of eating, I shall like to hear
> The story which it would appear,
> Was from that book just now about
> By my young friend to be read out."
> As we sat down I asked to see
> The book, the wee Bear gave it to me—
> And it was German—True, indeed!
> Bears now can every language read,
> And one as easily, we find,
> As the other, when they feel inclined.
> Having returned the book to him—
> Call'd 'Stories by the brothers Grimm'—
> He chose a tale and then began.

There follows (also in verse—nearly 150 years before Roald Dahl) the first separate printing of Grimm No. 5 in English.

Now it is unsurprising—if, by purist standards, unacceptable—to find folktales mauled in this way in the interests of book-making. Publishers and editors, then as now, perceive the original story simply as raw material to be fashioned by author and illustrator alike into an end-product for the market, and the relationship of that end-product to its oral beginnings is hardly likely to matter when even the substance of the narrative is cavalierly treated. (Madame Leinstein's *Unlucky John* is bound to lose fluency when converted into doggerel; but it also loses dramatic point with the omission of the climactic interview with the knife-grinder.)

When one turns to more formal attempts to build upon, or replicate, the Taylor translations, though, one hardly finds a more responsible recognition of the demands of the original and of the need to acknowledge in some way the status of the Grimms' tales as being "from oral tradition." In the sixty years following Edgar Taylor's first volume there were three English translations that have a claim to being serious renderings and that also had wide dissemination and a lengthy published life: the *Household Stories*, "newly translated" by an anonymous figure (who may have been the illustrator E. H. Wehnert) and first published in parts by Addey & Co. in 1852–53; the *Grimm's Fairy Tales*, translated by Mrs. H. B. Paull and illustrated by W. J. Weigand (1868); and the apparently definitive *Grimm's Household Tales* "with the author's notes," translated by Margaret Hunt, with a sixty-six–page introduction by Andrew Lang (1884). Along with Taylor these editions dominated both the British and the American markets for Grimm for many years. Even now the Margaret Hunt translation is widely know in the compendium illustrated by Josef Scharl with slight revisions by James Stern.[5]

The failure of these new translations to make any consistent improvement upon Edgar Taylor's work is manifest. They very often adapt and change their sources without even signalling the fact in the way that Taylor did, and they lack the feeling for English prose that is one of Taylor's claims to acceptance.

Examples of their substantive and linguistic weakness could be chosen from anywhere, but perhaps the plainest demonstration occurs in the passage from "The Bremen Town Musicians," which has already been quoted to show Taylor's shortcomings:

69

Wehnert's (?) translation:

Presently they came to a Cat sitting in the middle of the path with a face like three rainy days! "Now then, old shaver, what has crossed you?" asked the Ass.

"How can one be merry when one's neck has been pinched like mine?" answered the Cat. (1: 133)

Mrs. Paull's translation:

Not long after they saw a cat sitting in the road with a face as dismal as three days of rainy weather.

"Now, what has come across you, old whiskers?" asked the ass.

"How can one be merry when one has a collar on?" said the cat.

Hunt's translation:

Before long they came to a cat, sitting on the path, with a face like three rainy days! "Now then, old shaver, what has gone askew with you?" asked the donkey.

"Who can be merry when his neck is in danger?" answered the cat. (*Grimm's Household Tales* 1: 114)

In each of these examples there is an obvious improvement on Edgar Taylor's translation in terms of completeness. To be sure, these renderings are based on Grimms' final 1857 version and not on the 1819 version used by Taylor. The translators, however, appear on all counts to be more responsive to Grimms' rich language. They have, in the first place, responded to the two new colloquial phrases that Wilhelm Grimm interpolated into the tale after Taylor's translation had appeared: "wie drei Tage Regenwetter" and "alter Bartputzer" (*Kinder- und Hausmärchen: Ausgabe letzter Hand* 1: 161). Moreover, they have confronted the other colloquial turns that Taylor neglected. In no case, however, do they find a convincing English equivalent, nor does their phrasing show any appreciation of the rhythms of English storytelling. Margaret Hunt, in her preface, quotes extensively from the Grimms' own statement of aims, and writes admiringly of the way in which they retained local patois in their *Märchen;* but when she says of her own work, "this is, I believe, the first [translation] which has aimed at presenting them precisely as given by the Brothers Grimm," she is not referring at all to a precise representation of colloquial elements but only to the (not completely) restored contents of the stories (*Grimm's Household Tales* 1: v).

As these lame renderings retained their status, however (and were joined by further renderings not much better), a recognition of the values of "the storytelling voice" did begin to emerge for, at least, the editors of home-grown folktales. Between the 1820s and the 1840s Robert Chambers in Scotland and James Orchard Halliwell in England began to publish traditional rhymes and stories with a more acute perception of what was authentic than had been shown before. Chambers, of course, had a fine precedent for the preservation of local speech patterns in the example of Walter Scott (with whom, as is well known, the Grimms corresponded); Halliwell seems to have been more hampered by genteel traditions. He acknowledges Chambers's *Popular Rhymes of Scotland* (1826) as "the most delightful book of the kind ever published" (52), but when he reprints "The Black Bull of Norway" in his *Popular Rhymes and Nursery Tales* (1849), he wantonly deprives it of its colloquial force. Even when he introduces colorful dialect speech, as in "The Princess of Canterbury," it does not fit comfortably into the literary register of the tale.

Such beginnings held the possibility of development, however, and the shades of Chambers and Halliwell preside cheeringly over the later history of folktale in the nineteenth century: the founding of the Folklore Society in 1878 and, almost adjunct to its scholarly activities, the gathering of the first intelligently edited collection of *English Fairy Tales* by Joseph Jacobs in 1890. As a compiler Jacobs was almost entirely dependent on printed, rather than oral, sources, but he did recognize the need for an oral register. The preface to his *English Fairy Tales* states that "this book is meant to be read aloud, and not merely taken in by the eye" (xi), and Jacobs had in fact a spirited sense of how to make a story sound right. He did, however, in the same preface, invoke the Brothers Grimm to justify his decision to rewrite many of the stories—quoting the words of their manifesto cited above at the outset of this essay—but the purpose of his disclaimer was to excuse his modification of the most "oral" feature of storytelling: the use of dialect. "Children," he said dismissively, "and sometimes those of larger growth, will not read dialect" (x).

That blunt statement may have sounded unduly pessimistic on the other side of the Atlantic. By the time that *English Fairy Tales* was published, there had already been ten years of enthusiastic acclaim throughout the United States (and Britain too, for that matter) for the most remarkable folktale collection to appear since the Grimms'. This was the series of tales published by Joel Chandler Harris in various journals and gathered into book form most notably in *Uncle Remus: His*

Songs and His Sayings (1880) and *Nights with Uncle Remus* (1883). These were the first books to take up the challenge of the first Grimm preface to reproduce stories "as faithfully as possible" (*so rein als möglich* [qtd. in Ellis 13]) and to convey not simply the story but the presence of the storyteller, too.

Wonder at Joel Chandler Harris's achievement is increased rather than diminished when his "amateur status" is taken into account. Although his motives for collecting and printing his "folk-lore of the old plantation" were analogous to those of the Grimms—he wished to make true representation of a neglected art[6]—he made no claim to scholarly or scientific abilities. He collected and printed his stories because he loved them, and (*pace* Joseph Jacobs) he knew that their matter could not be separated from their manner. "The dialect is a part of the legends themselves, and to present them in any other way would be to rob them of everything that gives them vitality," he wrote in his introduction to *Nights with Uncle Remus* (XXVIII); and his determined effort to reproduce in print the very sound of that dialect is one of the most momentous events in folktale history.

One example can perhaps show Harris's kinship with the Grimms (whose work does not seem to have influenced him) and his advance on all those translators who had so little understood the character of storytelling. There is a moment in Grimms' "The Wolf and the Seven Little Kids" when the wolf tries to get into the goat's house. Here is Margaret Hunt:

> It was not long before some one knocked at the house-door and cried, "Open the door, dear children; your mother is here, and has brought something back with her for each of you." But the little kids knew that it was the wolf, by the rough voice; "We will not open the door," cried they, "thou art not our mother. She has a soft, pleasant voice, but thy voice is rough." (*Grimm's Household Tales* 1: 21)

This incident is paralleled in Harris's " 'Cutta Cord-La!' " from *Nights with Uncle Remus,* where Daddy Jack is telling a like tale of attempted deceit. Brer Wolf is trying to get B'er Rabbit's grandmother to eat in return for the time when he and B'er Rabbit had eaten the wolf's grandmother; but B'er Rabbit has hidden his grandmother up a coconut tree. Brer Wolf observes what is going on and then tries to get granny to throw down the rope so that he can get into the tree:

"Wun B'er Rabbit is gone way, Brer Wolf bin-a come back. 'E stan'
by da tree root; 'e holler:
    " '*Granny!— Granny!—O Granny! Jutta cord-la!*'
    "Granny Rabbit hol' 'e head 'pon one side; 'e lissun good. 'E say:
    " 'I bery sorry, me son, you bin hab so bad col'. You' v'ice bin-a
soun' rough, me son.' " (245)

The rhythmic and graphic quality of such language is indisputably an
authentic re-creation of a storytelling voice. It is also indisputably different from what Harris called "the intolerable misrepresentations of
the minstrel stage" (*Uncle Remus* 4). Indeed, Harris's virtuoso abilities
as recorder are particularly evident here since he is giving his story in
the Gullah dialect of the Georgia coast, distinctively different from the
accents of Uncle Remus.

With the emergence of the United States as a pioneering influence in
folklore studies (witness the work of Francis Child on English and Scottish ballad traditions, and the growth of local archives of folklore and
folk song) it is not surprising to find that the first escape that Grimm
translation made from the formality of nineteenth-century diction was
at Milford, New Jersey (via Minnesota). Although it occurred as late as
1936 and in the context of children's-book publishing rather than
through any more scholarly medium, the *Tales from Grimm* "freely
translated and illustrated" by Wanda Gág is, in its way, the first true
successor to the *German Popular Stories* of Taylor and Cruikshank 113
years earlier.

My reasons for saying this are manifold. To some extent they have to
do with Wanda Gág's commitment to the work in hand: she had been
brought up on the stories in the German community of New Ulm, Minnesota ("I spoke no English until I went to school"; *Growing Pains*
xviii); she loved the stories; and she had a clear vision of how they
might be presented in a volume integral with her own folksy drawings.
At the same time she realized that straight translation was not an ideal
procedure—not because of incipient "goriness" (she took advice and
found that "the general opinion was that too much bowdlerizing creates a spineless quality which is not characteristic of these tales"), but
because children deserved to have "the true flavor" of the stories
rather than "lifeless and clumsy" exactitude (*Tales from Grimm* x
and viii).

These quotations come from Wanda Gág's introduction to her volume, where the problems of Grimm translation are discussed—perhaps

for the first time—in relation to the telling of folktales. Like Edgar Taylor she takes her readers into her confidence and discusses what she has done with her sources. The result is fluency and warmth, as we can see by once more returning to the Bremen highway:

> Before long they met a cat. She was sitting by the roadside, with a face as long as a three days' drizzle.
> "Ei, ei, old Whisker-wiper!" said the donkey. "What's wrong with you?"
> "Who can be cheerful when one's life is at stake?" said the cat. (89)

Once again that difficult last sentence is not made to ring perfectly true. Grimms' "Wer kann da lustig sein, wenn's einem an den Kragen geht" appears so simple, yet is so hard to convey naturally into another language (*Kinder- und Hausmärchen: Ausgabe letzter Hand* 1: 161). Few of Wanda Gág's successors have managed to do it, either. What this passage does show, however, is the translator's ear for English storytelling rhythms so rarely discernable among her predecessors. Wanda Gág, with a full awareness of the issues involved, gave priority to the exactness of the sound of the stories rather than to the exactness of a printed equivalent, and in doing so she sanctioned by example a spirit of experimentation from which storytelling and the Grimms alike have benefited. She may have shown, concomitantly, that the scope for variation is endless, and that each generation may have to look for a translation that meets the timbres of its own speech patterns; but like her perceptive predecessor, Edgar Taylor, she shows in every line that she has joined her audience in an "eager relish" for these enduringly "popular stories."

Notes

1. *Kinder- und Hausmärchen: 1837* 23. (Compare the discussion of this passage from "The Frog King" with the treatment in Siegfried Neumann's essay above.—ED.)
2. This collection of "twenty-four choice pieces of Fancy and Fiction" clearly owed much to Tabart's earlier *Popular Stories*. It was, however, newly edited with additional or alternative versions of stories, and it was to

remain in print for over twenty years. It also served as the chief foundation for that important American collection *The Fairy Book,* illustrated by J. A. Adams, and published by Harper Brothers in 1836.

3. Cohen 95. Ruth Michaelis-Jena (185) has already drawn attention to the fact that Edgar Taylor's English title for *Kinder- und Hausmärchen—German Popular Stories*—has a pre-echo in this review by Cohen. On Cohen's influence, see also Bluhm.

4. Thoms makes this remark in a note to his own translation in *The Lays and Legends of Germany* of 1834. This volume includes translations of eleven stories from Grimm, but neither these nor Thoms's retellings of other traditional stories for children (as "Ambrose Merton" in Cundall's "Gammer Gurton" series) show much advance towards an oral mode.

5. I have excluded from consideration here such bibliographically interesting works as the *Household Tales and Traditions* published in London by James Burns in 1845, which included many Grimm stories; the "continuation" of Edgar Taylor's work by his cousin John Edward Taylor in *The Fairy Ring,* illustrated by Richard Doyle (London: Murray, 1846); and the *Home Stories* translated by M. L. Davis and illustrated by G. Thompson (London: Routledge, 1855). Quality and longevity were alike lacking in these versions.

6. See Harris's attack on entrenched prejudice—which he calls "sectionalism"—in his article "Literature in the South" in the *Atlanta Constitution* for 30 November 1879: "We must drop sectionalism and all the outlying prejudices, and along with them must go the selfishness and spite that have misrepresented us at home and abroad. The very spice and flavor of all literature—the very marrow and essence of all literary art—is its localism."

Works Cited

Bluhm, Lothar. "Sir Francis Cohen / Palgrave: Zur frühen Rezeption der Kinder- und Hausmärchen in England." *Brüder Grimm Gedenken* 7 (1987): 224–42.

Cohen, Francis [Sir Francis Palgrave]. Rev. of *Fairy Tales, or the Lilliputian Cabinet, containing Twenty-four choice pieces of Fantasy and Fiction,* by Benjamin Tabart. *Quarterly Review* 21.41 (Jan. 1819): 91–112.

Ellis, John M. *One Fairy Story Too Many: The Brothers Grimm and Their Tales.* Chicago: U of Chicago P, 1983.

Gág, Wanda. *Growing Pains: Diaries and Drawings for the Years 1908–1917.* New York: Coward-McCann, 1940.

————. *Tales from Grimm*. New York: Coward-McCann, 1936.

Grimm, Brothers. *Kinder- und Hausmärchen: Ausgabe letzter Hand mit den Originalanmerkungen der Brüder Grimm*. Ed. Heinz Rölleke. 3 vols. Stuttgart: Reclam, 1980.

————. *Kinder- und Hausmärchen gesammelt durch die Brüder Grimm: Vollständige Ausgabe auf der Grundlage der dritten Auflage (1837)*. Ed. Heinz Rölleke. Frankfurt a.M.: Deutscher Klassiker Verlag, 1985.

————. *Kinder- und Hausmärchen gesammelt durch die Brüder Grimm: Vergrößerter Nachdruck der zweibändigen Erstausgabe von 1812 und 1815*. Ed. Heinz Rölleke and Ulrike Marquardt. 2 vols. and suppl. Göttingen: Vandenhoeck & Ruprecht, 1986.

————. *Kinder- und Hausmärchen: Nach der zweiten vermehrten und verbesserten Auflage von 1819*. Ed. Heinz Rölleke. 2 vols. 1982. Cologne: Diederichs, 1984.

Halliwell-Phillipps, James Orchard. *Popular Rhymes and Nursery Tales: A Sequel to the Nursery Rhymes of England*. London: Smith, 1849.

Harris, Joel Chandler. "Literature in the South." *Atlanta Constitution* 30 Nov. 1879. N. pag.

————. *Nights with Uncle Remus: Myths and Legends of the Old Plantation*. Boston: Osgood, 1883.

————. *Uncle Remus: His Songs and His Sayings. The Folk-lore of the Old Plantation*. 1880. New York: Appleton, 1881.

Hartwig, Otto. "Zur ersten englischen Übersetzung der Kinder- und Hausmärchen der Brüder Grimm: Mit ungedruckten Briefen von Edgar Taylor, J. u. W. Grimm, Walter Scott und G. Benecke." *Centralblatt für Bibliothekswesen* 15 (1898): 1–16.

Hunt, Margaret, trans. *The Complete Grimm's Fairy Tales*. Rev. James Stern. Illus. Josef Scharl. New York: Pantheon, 1944.

————, trans. *Grimm's Household Tales*. 2 vols. London: Bell, 1884. Detroit: Singing Tree Press, 1968.

Jacobs, Joseph. *English Fairy Tales*. London: Nutt, 1890.

Leinstein, Madame. *Unlucky John and His Lump of Silver: A Juvenile Comic Tale*. London: Dean & Munday, 1825.

[Leinstein, Madame?]. *Wishing; or the Fisherman and His Wife: A Juvenile Poem*. London: Dean & Munday, 1825.

Michaelis-Jena, Ruth. "Edgar und John Edward Taylor, die ersten englischen Übersetzer der Kinder- und Hausmärchen." *Brüder Grimm Gedenken* 2 (1975): 183–202.

Paull, Mrs. H. B., trans. *Grimm's Fairy Tales*. Illus. W. J. Weigand. 1868. London: Warne, 1883.

Rölleke, Heinz. Rev. of *One Fairy Story Too Many*, by John Ellis. *Fabula* 25 (1984): 330–32.

Taylor, Edgar. "German Popular and Traditionary Literature." *New Monthly Magazine and Literary Journal* 2 (1821): 146–52, 329–36, 537–44; 4 (1822): 289–96.

Taylor, Edgar, and David Jardine, trans. *German Popular Stories.* Illus. George Cruikshank. Vol. 1. London: Baldwyn, 1823. Vol. 2. London: Robins, 1826. Facs. rpt. London: Frowde, 1904.

Thoms, W. J. *The Lays and Legends of Germany.* London: Cowie, 1834.

The Three Bears and Their Stories. London: Wright, 1841.

Wehnert, Edward H., illus. *Household Stories.* 2 vols. London: Addey, 1853.

The Publishing History of Grimms' Tales: Reception at the Cash Register

Ruth B. Bottigheimer

Summary

BOTH THE GERMAN book-buying public and the books it bought changed in the course of the nineteenth century. Bourgeois taste tending towards the aristocratic dominated the fairy-tale market around 1800 (Gradenwitz). In the course of the nineteenth century, however, book buyers in general came to reject aristocratic styles and instead affirmed consciously bourgeois ones. This resulted in the enormous popularity of Ludwig Bechstein's *Deutsches Märchenbuch*. However, by the turn of the twentieth century taste had further altered, and the folk content, values, and style of the Grimms' *Kinder- und Hausmärchen*, ringing up sales at the cash register, made it the reigning favorite of the fairy-tale world (Schneider; Bottigheimer, "Bechstein's Fairy Tales").

Introduction

"Reception," as this term is used in literary studies, has a history of imprecision. As a critical approach, reception bows inevitably to the simple, arbitrary, and frequently capricious availability of sources: book reviews, private assessments from letters and diaries, scholarly evaluations, and public data like household inventories. With reference to the reception of Grimms' *Fairy Tales* we know that baby Eleanor Marx, Karl's daughter living in London, learned her German from the Grimms' fairy tales (Heilfurth); and we have heard about the negative reception by a little girl who came to Grimm's door with a groschen to begin paying off the skepticism-penalty specified at the end of "The Clever Little Tailor" (No. 114), because Wilhelm reported the incident in a letter to Anna von Arnswaldt (Reifferscheid 189–90). But in general there are precious few childish or parental voices to tell us about how young children or their parents perceived these fairy tales. Literary worthies like Achim von Arnim, Albert Ludwig Grimm, Johann Heinrich Voß, Goethe, Karl Gutzkow, Heinrich Heine, Ferdinand Freiligrath, August Wilhelm and Friedrich Schlegel, Eduard Mörike, Theodor Fontane, and Hugo von Hofmannsthal, on the other hand, were voluble in their praise of the Grimms' tales (Schoof, "150 Jahre").

In the early years of the tales' published life, reactions to them were mixed at best and heartlessly critical at worst. Even Jacob Grimm wrote unfeelingly from Vienna in 1815, taking issue with the book's appearance and content; and Georg Reimer, their publisher, responded to Wilhelm's request for a new edition by calling the 350 copies of volume 2 lying unsold on his Berlin shelves "completely worthless" (letter of 1 October 1818; rpt. in Rölleke, *Kinder- und Hausmärchen: 1819* 2: 550). Eventually the more sympathetic critics carried the day. It is their voices that inform the contemporary imagination, so that the publishing history of the *Kinder- und Hausmärchen* now appears to have been an uninterrupted triumphal progress towards the undeniably remarkable publishing success of the Grimms' fairy tales in the twentieth century (Dégh; Weber-Kellermann; Zipes).

Utterly impossible claims have been inserted into the scholarly literature as fact, for example, that two million copies of the *Kinder- und Hausmärchen* had been published in German by 1857 (*Literatur* 60; Dänhardt). In other cases, one person's memory is mistakenly made to stand for an entire nation's habit, as for instance when Baron von Münchhausen stated that "in an old-fashioned household Grimms' fairy tales occupied a position approximately midway between the cookbook and the hymnal" (qtd. in Schnackenberg 5). The best-informed scholars borrow from the mythicized publishing history of the *Kinder- und Hausmärchen* and refer to its "overwhelming popular success" (Hennig and Lauer 565). The more cautious only claim that Grimm outsold Bechstein between 1850 and 1900, without any further distinctions (Wegehaupt 32). We encounter in this phenomenon the very human tendency to project the experience of the present onto the past, that is, to graft the extraordinarily broad twentieth-century acceptance of the *Kinder- und Hausmärchen* onto its nineteenth-century reception. The actual publishing history of the collection's early years emerges more accurately from the worried letters of Ferdinand Grimm in 1817. They tell a dismal tale of stagnant sales: not a single book sold in Berlin from Christmas to the following August and only a few sales rang up in Leipzig in the same period (Rölleke, *Kinder- und Hausmärchen: 1819* 2: 552).

Despite the disappointing early public response to the *Kinder- und Hausmärchen,* the collection eventually appeared in seven Large and ten Small Editions between 1812 and 1858. The timing of succeeding editions and the pace of their sales allow inferences about patterns of reception at the point of purchase, with the frequency and size of printing taken as a rough measure of the general public's response.[1] Several general assumptions underlie my treatment of the evidence.

Pricing: Cost links buyers' taste and desire for a book and their purchase; pricing is central to selling.

Print runs: Authors generally want more copies of a book printed than does the publisher, and the Grimms were no exception (Schoof, "Jacob Grimm" 494–95).

Publication: Business—not literary, historical, or nationalistic—considerations underlay Georg Reimer's publishing decisions.

Marketing: Reimer published as many copies of a book as he believed he could sell, and when the book sold out, he became interested in reprinting it.

Buyership: The bourgeoisie had more disposable income than lower economic classes.

Sociology of book acquisition: During much of the nineteenth century the bourgeoisie generally preferred, and overwhelmingly bought, fairy tales that reflected their own values (Bottigheimer, "Bechstein's Fairy Tales").

General social ethic: Towards the end of the nineteenth century the folk-oriented values originally espoused by the Romantics finally penetrated both bourgeois and folk culture.

Publishing history: A new folk-oriented value system, together with changing publishing technology, more aggressive marketing decisions, and changes in the nineteenth-century Germany money economy resulted in an increasingly positive reception and an accelerated publishing success for the *Kinder- und Hausmärchen* after the turn of the century. It continues unabated to this day, in capitalist and formerly socialist countries alike.

Wilhelm Grimm's basic editorial principles began to change between the first and second volumes of the first edition, that is, between 1812 and 1815. In terms of provenance, content, and style, the first volume was bourgeois, whereas the second volume of the first edition began to reflect the folk tone and content that the entire collection ultimately embodied (Bottigheimer, "From Gold to Guilt"). Pricing remained similar for volumes 1 and 2 of the first edition, and so the fact that volume 1 sold out in a few years, whereas volume 2 sold less than 550 copies in the four years from 1815 to 1819, strongly suggests that the book-buying public voted decisively with its purse in favor of the "bourgeois" tales and against the "folk" ones.

Printing and Publishing

In the nineteenth century print runs could and did vary enormously. Depending on a book's pricing and consequent profit margin, a firm like Dieterich in Göttingen could cover its costs with as few as four hundred copies, as it did with the first edition of Jacob Grimm's *Deutsche Grammatik* (Schoof, "Jacob Grimm" 493). Scholarly publishing produced smaller profits, however, so that the brothers repeatedly relinquished their honorarium to induce a publisher to accept their manuscripts (Schoof, "Verlegersorgen" 82–84).

Printing practices differed in other ways from twentieth-century norms. For example, flexible paper feeding to printing presses enabled authors in those days to specify different papers for small batch print runs within a total job: vellum for presentation copies for honored friends and patrons, and "Royal" paper for luxury editions, while the bulk of most print runs was produced on ordinary paper, or *Druckpapier*, which was the case with the *Kinder- und Hausmärchen* (Schoof, "Jacob Grimm" 493).

Economically speaking, the early years of the nineteenth century were lean ones, when people bought bread rather than books. Under these circumstances some publishing houses closed down completely for several years, and most publishers were reluctant to risk capital investment in projects with questionable public appeal, like Jacob Grimm's edition of the *Edda,* which sold only one hundred copies. When the Grimms' *Deutsche Sagen* sold poorly, their projected four-volume series was quickly reduced to two.

Thus, when the Grimms' friend Achim von Arnim approached Georg Reimer in 1812 with a proposal to publish their collection of tales, it was in a marketing environment whose general outlook was highly unfavorable. On the other hand, as a commercial genre, *Mährchen* sold well, to judge from the number of titles offered in those years (Heinsius vol. 5). Furthermore, Reimer was an ardent nationalist active both clandestinely and publicly in propagating "the myth of the nation" in the face of the Napoleonic occupation (Johnston). Whether for commercial or ideological reasons, Reimer accepted their manuscript and initiated a turbulent and ultimately stupendously successful publishing venture.

The Publishing and Sales History of the *Kinder- und Hausmärchen*

Five clear phases emerge: (1) during the Grimms' lives, i.e., until 1863, the year of Jacob's death; (2) the thirty-year copyright period until 1893; (3) 1893 until the beginning of World War I; (4) 1914 to 1945; (5) 1945 to the present.

The First Phase: 1812–1863

In December 1812, Georg Reimer's Berlin publishing firm, the Realschulbuchhandlung, began publishing the tales collected by the Grimms, and shortly thereafter Wilhelm received his complimentary copies as specified, eighteen on ordinary paper and two on vellum (Rumpf #3, #4). Reimer did not advertise the book (Federspiel 108), and he omitted the final tale from the first few copies (Schroers; Marquardt); yet the entire print run of approximately nine hundred copies sold out within the next few years at an average rate of three hundred copies per year.[2]

Thus encouraged and with the addition of an entirely new body of material, the Grimms and Reimer undertook a second volume. Priced similarly,[3] printed similarly, and equally unadorned with any form of illustration, volume 2 was a publishing flop. After four years it had sold only 550 copies at an average rate of 137 copies a year (Rölleke, *Kinder- und Hausmärchen: 1819* 2: 549–51).

Despite the failure of volume 2 of the first edition, the Grimms prevailed on Reimer to bring out a second edition in 1819. Friedrich Schleiermacher himself helped proofread it in Berlin during the summer of 1819, and later that year 1,500 copies of the two-volume set were published at 3 Taler 14 Groschen. This book fared no better than volume 2 of the first edition and did not "master the market" either (Rölleke, *Kinder- und Hausmärchen: 1819* 2: 525). Desperate about the book's failure and the total absence of any honorarium, the Grimms turned to a Leipzig publisher, Josef Max, who offered to print and publish a revised edition of the *Kinder- und Hausmärchen*. Reimer created financial obstacles by insisting that Max take the 350 unsold copies of volume 2 off his hands (549–51), which Max was apparently unwilling to do. In fact, in 1834 several hundred copies still languished on Reimer's shelves (556), and the second edition finally sold out only in 1839 at an astonishingly overall low average sales rate of 75 copies per year. It goes without saying that the 1822 volume of notes fared far worse. From a publisher's point of view, the results were disastrous and led to angry correspondence between Reimer and Grimm (Rumpf).

These figures are hardly the stuff of which best-sellers are made. Traditionally volume 2's failure to sell has been attributed partly to the sluggish economy in the years following 1815 (Rölleke, *Kinder- und Hausmärchen: Kleine Ausgabe 1858* 292). The equally low sales of two other 1815 publications, the *Deutsche Sagen* and the *Edda,* support this explanation (Schoof, "Verlegersorgen"). Yet it would be absurd to accept this reason for the period 1819–1837, when the second edition sold at an even slower rate. Nor can the public's abysmal response to volume 2 be attributed to the lack of Grimms' solicitations for favorable notice from their literary friends: over the years they brought their new publications to the attention of an increasingly wide circle of acquaintances and reviewers (Fischer 58; Hübner 38).

The first Small Edition of 1825 is supposed to mark the point at which the Grimms' *Kinder- und Hausmärchen* finally captured the hearts and minds of the German people. Reimer published 1,500 copies of this selection of fifty tales taken equally from volumes 1 and 2 of the Large Edition of 1819. Of these fifty tales, twenty-five had appeared in the (relatively speaking) well-received volume 1 of the first edition. The Small Edition, illustrated by the Grimms' younger brother Ludwig Emil and priced cheaply at 1 Taler, remained available until 1833, selling at an average rate of 187 copies per year. This tops the rates of volume 2 of the first edition (137 copies per year) and of the second Large Edition (87 copies per year), but does not approach the sales of volume 1 of the first edition (300 copies per year). It is even more instructive to compare German sales of the *Kinder- und Hausmärchen* with contemporary sales in England, where the collection's engaging and free translation turned a profit of £15,000 for its publishers, far beyond Reimer's wildest dreams (Emmrich 18).

The mythologized publishing history of the *Kinder- und Hausmärchen* propagated first by German nationalists and later by Marxists begins to crumble in the face of verifiable publishing data, for the troubling and inconvenient fact remains that the most bourgeois of the Grimms' versions of the *Kinder- und Hausmärchen,* volume 1 of the first edition, is precisely the one which sold well in the first decade of the collection's existence, while the editions which successfully incorporated a folk tone sold badly. The inescapable conclusion is that in the years between 1812 and 1837 (and later) the German book-buying public expressed a clear and definite preference for fairy tales in a bourgeois style and with bourgeois values, and rejected those with a folk voice.

Reimer may have been a difficult publisher, but as a good businessman he was willing to republish the *Kinder- und Hausmärchen* when his stocks ran low. Thus he initiated the republication of the Small Edition in 1833 (Rumpf/Grimm Nachlaß 1514, 31/32) and again in 1836, from which we may infer that the 1833 edition sold out in three years. If changes made to "The Virgin Mary's Child" (No. 3) may be taken as a measure of Wilhelm Grimm's editorial intrusion, the tales changed relatively little in those years (Bottigheimer, "Marienkind").

In 1837, Wilhelm Grimm moved the Large Edition to Dieterich in Göttingen, where he and Jacob had lived for seven years. According to Heinz Rölleke, the third Large Edition "brought the long desired success" (*Kinder- und Hausmärchen: 1819* 2: 556); yet without publishing figures indicating the size of the print run in either of the two Small Editions or in the third Large Edition, the dimensions of their success remain conjectural. One may at best assume that the entire print run of the 1837 Large Edition sold out by 1840, when Dieterich republished it. The same remains true of all subsequent editions of the *Kinder- und Hausmärchen* published during the Grimms' lifetimes. Information about publishing figures that would indicate sales rates has not yet been unearthed, but assertions about astronomical sales—for example, two million by 1857—are patently untenable.

A second gauge for the public's taste for the *Kinder- und Hausmärchen* can be developed from a comparison of the publishing histories of the Grimms' and of Bechstein's fairy tales. Between 1845, the year in which Bechstein's *Deutsches Märchenbuch* first appeared, and 1853, Bechstein outsold Grimm from every point of view, whether one counts the number of editions, illustrated versus unillustrated editions, or Large versus Small Editions. In this period Bechstein's *Deutsches Märchenbuch* sold well over sixty thousand copies, perhaps even more than seventy thousand copies in a total of fourteen printings.[4] In contrast, Grimms' *Kinder- und Hausmärchen* appeared in one Large and three Small Editions whose total print run was very unlikely to have been more than a fraction of Bechstein's (Bottigheimer, "Bechstein's Fairy Tales" 82–85). The picture of the *Kinder- und Hausmärchen* as a poor seller during the Grimms' lifetime is further amplified by the appearance of Bechstein's second book of fairy tales in 1856, the *Neues Deutsches Märchenbuch,* which continued as a best-seller in the market served by the Vienna and Pest publishing houses of Hartleben for nearly twenty years after the *Deutsches Märchenbuch* had been relegated to the luxury *Prachtausgabe* market (Bottigheimer, "Bechstein's Fairy Tales" 82–85).

Ruth B. Bottigheimer

The Copyright Period: 1863–1893

After Wilhelm's death, Jacob Grimm and his nephews, Herman and Rudolf Grimm, established a copyright for the *Kinder- und Hausmärchen,* which had important publishing consequences for the period 1863–1893 (Bottigheimer, *Bad Girls and Bold Boys* 7). In 1864, Dieterich published the eighth Large Edition, and six years later the Berlin publishing firm W. Hertz published the ninth Large Edition. Evidently in Herman Grimm's care, the Large Edition continued to be republished by Hertz every year or so until 1893, when the twenty-fifth Large Edition appeared (Kayser). The Small Edition appeared with C. Bertelsmann in Gütersloh and reached its forty-first printing in 1893; it also appeared with F. Duncker in Berlin, which reprinted the 1864 eleventh Small Edition a few times, and with F. Dümmler, which published its thirty-third Small Edition in 1885. Dümmler also reached westward to the United States, where a Chicago branch, the German Book and News Company, brought out a few editions of the *Kinder- und Hausmärchen* for a German-speaking American readership in the 1880s (Heinsius; Kayser; *National Union Catalog*).

Marketing and publishing strategies for the Grimms' fairy tales seem to have been run along very conservative lines. In 1838, the Grimms rejected an overture by Otto Wigand to publish a group of their tales to be selected by Ludwig Bechstein and illustrated by Eugen N. Neureuther (Wegehaupt 25). Bechstein died in 1860 and Jacob Grimm in 1863, with the result that the copyright protection period for Bechstein's two fairy-tale books (1860–1890) covered approximately the same time period as that for the Grimms' *Kinder- und Hausmärchen* (1863–1893). During the thirty years after the Grimms' deaths, their publishers seemed to pursue a conservative marketing strategy. At the same time Bechstein's publishers priced and marketed his tales aggressively, publishing individual tales in profusely illustrated and cheaply priced pamphlet format. The Grimms' publishers adopted this format only eight times between 1871 and 1882 (Kayser). Nonetheless, it was in this period that the Grimms' *Kinder- und Hausmärchen* began to outstrip Bechstein's *Deutsches Märchenbuch.*

It is not sufficient, as in Table 1, simply to compare for this period (1864–1893) the numbers of printings of the Grimms' and Bechstein's fairy-tale collections: forty-nine printings of both Large and Small Editions of the *Kinder- und Hausmärchen* (KHM) and seventy-nine

Table 1. Grimm vs. Bechstein: Publishing Figures 1845–1893
Number of Printings

Period	DMB	NDMB	KHM (large)	KHM (small)	Bechstein	Grimm
1845–53	12	—	2	3	12	5
1854–63	14	1	2	2	15	4
1864–82	12	41	10	19	53	29
1883–93	9	17	9	11	26	20

printings for Bechstein's two collections, the *Deutsches Märchenbuch* (DMB) and the *Neues Deutsches Märchenbuch* (NDMB).[5] These figures give a false idea of how the two authors' books competed against one another, for only Bechstein's *Deutsches Märchenbuch* occupied the same market niche as the Grimms' fairy tales. The *Neues Deutsches Märchenbuch* was published and marketed almost exclusively in the Austro-Hungarian Empire from publishing houses located in Pest and Vienna, cities where the Grimms' tales only began to be published when Gerlach brought out their edition at the beginning of the twentieth century. There are undoubtedly a few exceptions, but by and large Bechstein's two fairy-tale books inhabited two different worlds, the German and the Austro-Hungarian, only one of which overlapped with that in which the Grimms' publishers were active.

When the publishing figures for the *Neues Deutsches Märchenbuch* are omitted from Table 1, it becomes clear that within the German-speaking areas of Europe outside of the Austro-Hungarian Empire the Grimms' tales had already begun to outsell Bechstein's *Deutsches Märchenbuch* during the copyright period, if—and this is a big "if"— we may assume that both collections were printed in runs of approximately the same size. At the present time there is no evidence either for or against this proposition, and advocates of Grimm and Bechstein alike must content themselves with counting the numbers of printings as a rough and probably inaccurate guide to publication and sales success.

Ruth B. Bottigheimer

The Post-Copyright Period to the Beginning of World War I: 1893–1914

This period is characterized by three distinct phenomena: a meteoric rise in the number of publishing houses producing the *Kinder- und Hausmärchen*, the initiation of a public debate about the relative merits of the Grimm and Bechstein collections, and the decisive triumph of the Grimms' tales not only within the German Empire, but within the Austro-Hungarian Empire as well. The numbers of printings cited vary greatly, but all make the same point. Whether there were 250 printings of the *Kinder- und Hausmärchen* between 1912 and 1935 (Schoof, "Verlegersorgen" 85) or 600 printings up to the year 1940 (Federspiel 109), it is clear that the twentieth century is *the* century of the *Kinder- und Hausmärchen*. The Grimms' tales proliferated in school books on both sides of the Atlantic—in the 1880s and 1890s they were used to teach German in the United States—as they already had done in school readers in Germany earlier in the nineteenth century (Schneider 146); and in the next few decades the tales in English and French translation were even used to teach those languages in Germany.

It was above all in newly edited and copyrighted editions and in the production of individual tales or selections from the collection that the *Kinder- und Hausmärchen* continued their steady march towards domination of the market, for example as *Marienkind und andere Märchen, Die Kinder- und Hausmärchen nach ethischen Gesichtspunkten ausgewählt und bearbeitet* by Georg and Lily Gizycki, or *Grimms ausgewählte Märchen in katholischer Bearbeitung*, editions which elicited ridicule from pedagogically oriented critics (Wolgast 92–94).

Whereas Gütersloh and Berlin had for all practical purposes demarcated the two points of publishing and distribution for the Grimm collection up until 1893, the following decades witnessed an outpouring of editions of the tales from additional publishers in Berlin (Besser, A. Weichert, F. Dümmler, and Propyläen) and from points to the south and east: Gütersloh (Bertelsmann), Stuttgart (Deutsche Verlagsanstalt, F. Loewe, G. Weise, and Cotta), Munich (Müller, Braun & Schneider, and O. Beck), Zürich (Conzett & Huber), Vienna (Gerlach), Fürth (G. Lowensohn), Leipzig (F. Simon, E. Kempe, O. Spamer, and Turmverlag), Jena (E. Diederichs), Wesel (W. Düms), and Halle (O. Hendel). Under Herman Grimm's editorship, copyright was renewed with Bertelsmann in Gütersloh for the Small Edition and with W. Hertz in Berlin for

88

the Large Edition. A few of these publishers concurrently carried Bechstein on their lists (for example O. Hendel and F. Loewe), but as a rule different publishers represented the two authors. The *Kinder- und Hausmärchen* swamped both Bechstein's *Deutsches Märchenbuch* and his *Neues Deutsches Märchenbuch* in this period (Fig. 1).[6]

Into this swiftly changing marketing atmosphere panegyric and polemic irrupted and undoubtedly contributed to and hastened the diminution of Bechstein's market share. Leopold Köster's widely used *Geschichte der deutschen Jugendliteratur* apostrophized the Grimms in 1906 (Emmrich 22), and Franz Heyden publicly assaulted Bechstein's *Deutsches Märchenbuch* in a two-part article in the influential *Jugendschriften-Warte* in 1908. Speaking the language of a folk-based nationalism, he castigated Bechstein's tales for their glib humor and non-Germanic style and called for a return to the Grimm collection. Addressed as it was to a schoolteacher readership, the article played an important part in re-forming public perceptions of the *Kinder- und Hausmärchen*.

First anthologized in 1835, the Grimms' *Kinder- und Hausmärchen* continued as an integral part of the Prussian school curriculum in the last third of the nineteenth century in school readers such as Georg Heydner's *Das Lesebuch in der Volksschule* and in guided catechetical discussions.[7] What could be more natural than that the generations that had grown up on the Grimms' tales in school should reflexively choose the *Kinder- und Hausmärchen* for their own children twenty or thirty years later? It would have been a choice made considerably more palatable by changes in the pricing structure of the Grimms' collection. Whereas the Grimms' tales had generally cost at least double that of Bechstein's *Deutsches Märchenbuch* during the copyright period, the opposite became true in the post-copyright years. Faced with a diminished and diminishing market, Bechstein's tales were priced higher as they appeared more frequently in luxury editions in the 1910s and 1920s (Kayser). Thus, both volumes reversed the market positions they had occupied from their inception to the end of the copyright period.

Further impulses towards the Grimms' domination of the fairy-tale market were undoubtedly given by the centenary of the first edition of the *Kinder- und Hausmärchen* celebrated enthusiastically in 1912 by several republications. Diederich's edition inserted the *Kinder- und Hausmärchen* into an increasingly mythologized German past by reprinting the 1857 edition with Friedrich von der Leyen's peculiar

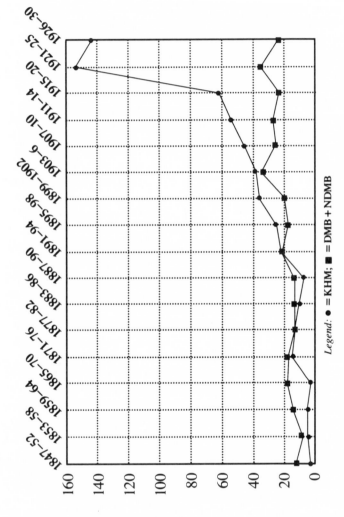

Fig. 1. Grimm (KHM) vs. Bechstein (DMB + NDMB) Number of Printings, 1847–1930.

Legend: ● = KHM; ■ = DMB + NDMB

imprint, that is, his chronological arrangement and indexing according to (his notion of) the date of each tale's genesis.

One is tempted to try to account for the Grimms' tales' triumph between 1893 and 1914 both within Germany and beyond its borders. Nineteenth-century industrialization and urbanization fostered the development of a new proletarian book-buying public in Germany, a development contemporary with the shift in taste from Bechstein to Grimm (Bottigheimer, "Bechstein's Fairy Tales"). The population of the Austro-Hungarian Empire, however, did not experience this social change to the same extent; yet it is certainly possible that Austro-Hungarians' sensitivity toward Prussia's industrial might led them to jettison their traditional favorites, the tales of the *Neues Deutsches Märchenbuch*, as part of their growing awareness of their northern neighbor's dominant and dominating political and economic position in Central Europe.

The Wars: 1914–1945

War fosters nationalism among the masses. Put another way, governments at war have generally fostered nationalism within the population under their control. In the three decades between 1914 and 1945, nationalism, xenophobia, and racism were developed to a fever pitch in Germany. The idea that public rhetoric should be felt at the cash register is easily documented: sales of the Grimms' tales fell off in the United States and in England during the very same period (the 1930s and 1940s) in which they rose in Germany. It is equally worth noting that publication of their tales diminished slightly within Germany during the Weimar period, officially an avowedly internationalist and nonbelligerent era.

It was not that the *Kinder- und Hausmärchen* themselves conspired to produce warlike behavior (Leonard), but that decades of nationalistically steered propaganda had hallowed their "authors" as quintessentially German or Germanic, and therefore as worthy standard-bearers for Germany at war. Wartime editions of the *Kinder- und Hausmärchen* poured off German presses. Two of these editions are especially noteworthy. The first, the complete collection of the Grimms' tales with Otto Ubbelohde's simple illustrations, strongly evoked the Hessian

91

countryside and recalled Early Modern German woodcuts. On cheap paper, it was printed in hundreds of thousands of copies. The same was true of the *Deutsche Märchen* published by the Cigaretten-Bilderdienst. A copy of 1938 indicated that fifty-nine thousand copies had been produced to date; a 1939 edition reached the one hundred thousand mark.

Besides war-spawned nationalism, a second tradition hallowing the Grimms' fairy tales burgeoned alongside the popularization of Jungian and Freudian psychoanalysis, both of which had defined fairy tales apolitically as international and transcendent narratives common to the human condition. Flawed though this argument is (Bottigheimer, "Bettelheims Hexe"), it proved persuasive for thousands of adherents throughout the world and prepared the way for an explosion of editions of Grimms' tales beginning with the end of World War II.

From 1945–1990

The particular attention lavished on the Grimms' tales during the period 1933–1945 had resulted in an equally negative assessment by Americans and English occupation forces between 1945 and 1949. Volumes of the *Kinder- und Hausmärchen* were summarily removed from schools and libraries all over Germany during the military occupation and shipped to libraries outside Germany. A handpress copy of *Muttergottesgläschen,* Grimms' children's legend No. 7, provides an example. Originally printed in a limited edition in 1920, it was acquired by "Krause 9 Apr 45," was confiscated three weeks later on "2 My 45," and was ultimately turned over to the University of Cincinnati Library.[8] This wholesale confiscation has rendered long-range study of the publishing and illustration history of the *Kinder- und Hausmärchen* within Germany far more difficult than would otherwise have been the case.

Despite the efforts of the occupying military forces to strip away from German culture a text that they considered to have exerted a profoundly destructive influence on the German spirit, the Grimms' tales returned immediately to bookstore bookshelves. In 1945 the Stuttgart firm of K. Thienemann published a collection of twenty-nine tales in a press run of twenty-two thousand copies. A curious amalgam of pre- and post-1945 influences, its type was Roman instead of the Gothic favored until 1945; its illustrator, however, was Paul Hey, who had provided the illustrations for the Cigaretten-Bilderdienst's *Deutsche Märchen*, which had been published so widely during the war years; but its content was clearly controlled by postwar social and political requirements. Gone the heathen associations of "Aschenputtel" (No. 21), now black-haired and praying at a typically Bavarian cross on her mother's grave; gone (and unlamented) the dreadful "Jew in the Thornbush" (No. 110).

Some republications of the Grimms' tales were undertaken with the special permission of the occupying forces. One edition of *Hänsel und Gretel*, for example, was licensed on 28 March 1946 by the Information Control Section, Office of Military Government for Greater Hesse. Its witch had a large red clownish nose, breaking with the traditional and politically charged exaggerated hooked nose of so many previously pictured witches. Two years later, licenses were still apparently necessary for publishing the Grimms' tales; and more than once texts assumed the guise of quasi-scholarly editions (Panzer; Keiper), presumably to evade restrictions on their publication.

After the Federal Republic's political independence was formally established with the Constitution of 1949, past anti-Semitic abuses of the *Kinder- und Hausmärchen* conspired to produce genuine disjunctions between title and contents. *Kinder- und Hausmärchen: Vollständige Ausgabe,* published around 1950 by the Reutlingen firm Robert Bardtenschlager, affirmed its completeness by including over two hundred tales, but it resembled Bechstein's collection both visually and in terms of some of its tales and much of its style. Ludwig Richter's illustrations were adopted from the *Deutsches Märchenbuch;* "Puss in Boots" replaced "The Juniper Tree" (No. 47); "Old Hildebrand" (No. 95) and "The Jew in the Thornbush" were happily absent; and dialect tales were translated into High German. The afterword claimed that the edition was based on the 1857 Grimm edition, but it appears rather to be an intentional amalgam of Grimm and Bechstein.

The *Kinder- und Hausmärchen* regained its pre–World War II bestseller status relatively quickly, despite prohibitions, caution, and delicacy of feeling. By 1958 Ensslin and Laiblin had run off 135,000 copies of Grimms' tales, and by 1970 Sändig in Wiesbaden was reproducing a beautiful photo offset reproduction of Elwert's Ubbelohde edition, despite its intimate associations with an unsavory past, that is, with its Nazi-fostered distribution to all German schoolchildren during

93

the war years. Without a frontispiece, the book was presented simply as another artifact, not, as in the nineteenth- and early twentieth-century volumes, as an integral part of a social vision of child-family-magic-nature.

In the German Democratic Republic in the postwar years, the proper place of the Grimms' tales was debated in the context of their exploitation by Fascists versus their value as part of the national heritage. Particularly relevant to this discussion were concerns about reinstating the *Kinder- und Hausmärchen* into the children's literature canon. Sabine Brandt's article, "Rotkäppchen und der Klassenkampf," among others, prepared the way for the tales' official re-canonization. An exhibit in the East Berlin Deutsche Staatsbibliothek entitled The Fairy Tales of the Brothers Grimm—A Vital Inheritance of Our National Culture returned them to unequivocal acceptability, as did the enormous numbers of carefully edited editions of the tales published during postwar governance of the German Democratic Republic by the USSR (Kudrjawzewa 55).

Since the 1970s the *Kinder- und Hausmärchen* have withstood an interval of radical attack from the left wing and have also weathered adoration verging on apotheosis in the Grimm Bicentennial Years, 1985–1986.[9] Neither attack nor adulation has dimmed their publishing appeal, and the *Kinder- und Hausmärchen* continues to flow off the presses at an undiminished pace in many formats: as individual tales, as selections from the corpus, as the complete collection, and as video and audio recordings. They are thoroughly at home in the twentieth century.

Conclusion

The publishing history of the *Kinder- und Hausmärchen* shows it to have had a markedly limited share of the German-language fairy-tale market during much of the nineteenth century, which was dominated for several decades by Ludwig Bechstein's *Deutsches Märchenbuch* within the German Empire and by his *Neues Deutsches Märchenbuch* in the Austro-Hungarian Empire. After the Grimms' deaths their tales appear to have overtaken Bechstein's tales in popularity within the German Empire, while Bechstein's *Neues Deutsches Märchenbuch* continued to hold sway in the Austro-Hungarian Empire. At the expiration of the copyright of the *Kinder- und Hausmärchen* in 1893, marketing, social, political, and economic factors combined, causing the Grimms' fairy tales to displace Bechstein's tales within the German Empire as well as in the Austro-Hungarian Empire. Between the two world wars and afterwards, the dramatic upturn in numbers of printings of the Grimms' tales was sustained. Bolstered by the apolitical arguments of psychoanalysis, sales have continued to soar. Despite their nineteenth-century origins, they have become a quintessentially twentieth-century publishing phenomenon.

Appendix

In preparation for an editorial history of the Grimms' *Kinder- und Hausmärchen,* it has been necessary to locate and verify the seven Large and ten Small Editions of the collection. All lists to date have contained errors with respect to publisher or date (for example, Rölleke, *Kinder- und Hausmärchen: 1819* 2: 555; and Rölleke, *Kinder- und Hausmärchen: 1837* 1164). A reliable and accurate list follows. Asterisked editions are those which Heinz Rölleke has edited and republished, as indicated in the list of Works Cited.

1810*				Ölenberg Manuscript
Large Edition		**Small Edition**		
1812/1815	1st*			Berlin: Realschulbuchhandlung (Reimer)
1819	2nd*			Berlin: G. Reimer
		1825	1st	Berlin: G. Reimer
		1833	2nd	Berlin: G. Reimer
		1836	3rd	Berlin: G. Reimer
1837	3rd*			Göttingen: Dieterich
		1839	4th	Göttingen: Dieterich
1840	4th			Göttingen: Dieterich
		1841?	5th	probably Dieterich
1843	5th			Göttingen: Dieterich
		1844	6th	Berlin: W. Besser
		1847	7th	Berlin: W. Besser

1850	6th			Göttingen: Dieterich
		1850	8th	Berlin: F. Duncker
		1853	9th	Berlin: F. Duncker
1857	7th*			Göttingen: Dieterich
		1858	10th*	Berlin: F. Duncker
		1864	11th	Berlin: J. J. Duncker
1864	8th			Göttingen: Dieterich

It is easy to see a clear pattern in the Grimms' choice of publisher. Their disputes with Reimer led to their removing their *Kinder- und Hausmärchen* business to Göttingen in 1837. When they took up residence in Berlin in 1841, they kept their Large Edition with Dieterich and—given the dislocations inherent in moving—probably published their 1841 Small Edition with Dieterich as well. But beginning with the 1844 Small Edition, they transferred their Small Edition business to W. Besser, transferring it to F. Duncker, business successor to Wilhelm Besser. Jacob Grimm died in 1863, but the publishing tradition continued after his death, with the Small Edition at Duncker, and later at F. Dümmler and C. Bertelsmann. After 1864 the Large Edition passed from Dieterich to Hertz. It would be useful to locate a copy of the fifth Small Edition.

I have not listed the volumes of Grimms' annotations. In the first edition they were integrated into each of the two volumes and appeared after the texts of the tales. They appeared as a separate volume in 1822 and again in 1856. I also have not listed unauthorized (i.e., pirated) editions, which began to appear with the second edition in 1819.

Notes

I would like to thank Dr. Ludwig Denecke, Hannoversch Münden, and Ursula Lange-Lieberknecht, Brüder Grimm-Archiv, Kassel, for their kind assistance in helping me track down several sources.

1. This is not an unproblematic statement. The number of copies printed per edition is known for only the earliest editions. Nonetheless, the number of printings remains the best yardstick available for assessing the public's actual response to the Grimms' collection. See the discussions below.

2. Rißmann 118n26. The figures for the entire print run have been given variously as eight hundred (Rölleke, *Kinder- und Hausmärchen: Ausgabe letzter Hand* 3: 606), nine hundred (Rölleke, *Kinder- und Hausmärchen: 1819* 2: 536), and one thousand (Dielmann).

3. Pricing policy differed from twentieth-century pricing. The primary price represented the body of the book and was higher or lower depending on the quality of the paper chosen. On top of this came the binding. No binding at all, cardboard, "English binding," or English binding with gold stamping represented the kinds of choices each purchaser could make about the *Kinder- und Hausmärchen*—and about other books as well.

4. Bechstein; Bellmann; and Schneider. I am indebted to Lothar Bluhm, Wuppertal, for kindly undertaking to send me a microfiche of the Schneider dissertation. At the time I originally wrote this essay, I had not yet read it, but Schneider's results confirm my conclusions.

5. Table 1 is based on Schneider (125), whose figures are calculated from listings in Kayser and the *Deutsches Bücherverzeichnis.* It is difficult to establish accurate figures in publishing histories. What is significant are the relative totals, which in both cases show Bechstein's fairy tales outselling those of the Grimms during several decades of the nineteenth century. Although these totals may be modified slightly by counts based on different or additional sources, I have confirmed and substantiated the figures and the existence of the editions counted in the documented library holdings published in the *National Union Catalog,* the published catalog of the British Library, the computerized listings of the Research Libraries Network, which access the holdings of major research libraries in the United States, and the computerized listings of the Ohio Classification (OCLC), which accesses the holdings of over three thousand college and university libraries in the United States. American holdings can be held to reflect the numbers of Grimm editions because of the extent to which American occupying forces stripped German libraries of editions of Grimms' tales in the years immediately following World War II.

6. In graphically comparing the numbers of published editions of Bechstein and Grimm, Schneider (131) calculates from 1894 to 1930, while I count from 1847 to 1930. We both, however, set 1930 as the end point. After 1930 the number of Grimm editions spirals upward dizzyingly, and a graph with different proportions entirely would be necessary to accommodate the information. The sources of information for my graph are Kayser and the *Deutsches Bücherverzeichnis.*

7. On the anthologizing of Grimms' tales and their integration into the school curriculum, see Bastian; Jäger 100–102, 108, 118; Gerstl 38–50; Leyen, *Lesebuch; Märchen im Unterricht;* Schmidt; Schneider 146; and Troll. On their use in guided catechetical discussions, see Bastian 70–71.

8. The book is currently in the holdings of the University of Cincinnati (call number Z239.5 G7).

9. For leftist critiques of the Grimms, see Gmelin; Merkel and Richter; Richter; Richter and Vogt; and Zipes. (See the essay by Jack Zipes in this volume on the postwar reception of Grimms' tales in the Federal Republic of Germany and the former German Democratic Republic.—ED.)

Works Cited

Bastian, Ulrike. Die "Kinder- und Hausmärchen" der Brüder Grimm in der literaturpädagogischen Diskussion des 19. und 20. Jahrhunderts. Frankfurt a.M.: Haag & Herchen, 1981.

Bechstein, Ludwig. Foreword. Deutsches Märchenbuch. 1853. Die bibliophilen Taschenbücher 5. Dortmund: Harenberg, 1977.

Bellmann, Werner. "Bechstein, Ludwig." Enzyklopädie des Märchens. Berlin: de Gruyter, 1977–79. 2: 15–19.

Bottigheimer, Ruth B. "Bettelheims Hexe: Die fragwürdige Beziehung zwischen Märchen und Psychoanalyse." Psychotherapie-Psychosomatik-Medizinische Psychologie 39 (1989): 294–99.

———. "From Gold to Guilt: The Forces Which Reshaped Grimms' Tales." The Brothers Grimm and Folktale. Ed. James M. McGlathery. Urbana: U of Illinois P, 1988. 192–204

———. Grimms' Bad Girls and Bold Boys: The Moral and Social Vision of the Tales. New Haven: Yale UP, 1987.

———. "Ludwig Bechstein's Fairy Tales: Nineteenth Century Bestsellers and Bürgerlichkeit." Internationales Archiv für Sozialgeschichte der deutschen Literatur 15.2 (1990): 55–88.

———. "Marienkind (KHM 3): A Computer-Based Study of Editorial Change and Stylistic Development within Grimms' Tales from 1808 to 1864." ARV: Scandinavian Yearbook of Folklore 46 (1990): 7–31.

Brandt, Sabine. "Rotkäppchen und der Klassenkampf." Der Monat 12 (1960): 65–74.

Dänhardt, Reimar. "Grimm-Editionen im Kinderbuchverlag Berlin." Der Gingkobaum 4 (1985): 44–47. Rpt. in Die Brüder Grimm: Erbe und Rezeption: Stockholmer Symposium 1984. Ed. Astrid Stedje. Stockholm: Almqvist & Wiksell, 1985. 51–56.

Dégh, Linda. "Grimm's Household Tales and Its Place in the Household: The Social Relevance of a Controversial Classic." Western Folklore 38.2 (1979): 83–103.

Deutsches Bücherverzeichnis. 22 vols. Leipzig: Börsenverein der Deutschen Buchhändler zu Leipzig, 1916–43.

Dielmann, Karl. "Märchenillustrationen von Ludwig Emil Grimm." *Hanauer Geschichtsblätter* 18 (1962): 281–306.

Emmrich, Christian. "Niemals ohne Beziehung auf das Leben: Zur Märchen-rezeption der Bruder Grimm." *Beiträge zur Kinder- und Jugendliteratur* 83 (1987): 14–33.

Federspiel, Christa. *Vom Volksmärchen zum Kindermärchen.* Vienna: Notring, 1968.

Fischer, Hermann, ed. *Briefwechsel zwischen Jacob Grimm und Friedrich David Graeter aus den Jahren 1810–1813.* Heilbronn: Henninger, 1877.

Gerstl, Quirin. *Der erzieherische Gehalt der Grimmschen Kinder- und Hausmärchen.* Diss. U Munich, 1963. Munich: Uni-Druck, 1963.

Gizycki, Georg and Lily, eds. *Die Kinder- und Hausmärchen nach ethischen Gesichtspunkten ausgewählt und bearbeitet.* Berlin: F. Dümmler, 1894.

Gmelin, Otto. *Böses kommt aus Kinderbüchern: Die verpaßten Möglichkeiten kindlicher Bewußtseinsbildung.* Munich: Kindler, 1972.

Gradenwitz, Peter. "Books and Reading in Germany 200 Years Ago." *Antiquarian Bookman* 7 Sept. 1987: 797–98.

Heilfurth, Gerhard. "Ein Lesefund: Grimms Märchen in der Familie von Karl Marx." *Brüder Grimm Gedenken* 7 (1987): 243–45.

Heinsius, Wilhelm. *Allgemeines Bücher-Lexikon 1799–1892.* 19 vols. Leipzig: Brockhaus, 1812–94. Graz: Akademische Druck- und Verlagsanstalt, 1962–63.

Hennig, Dieter, and Bernhard Lauer, eds. *Die Brüder Grimm: Dokumente ihres Lebens und Wirkens.* Vol. 1 of *200 Jahre Brüder Grimm.* Kassel: Weber & Weidemeyer, 1985.

Heyden, Franz. "Grimm oder Bechstein: Zur Kritik der Bechsteinschen Märchen." *Jugendschriften-Warte* 16.4 (April 1908): 13–15; 16.6 (June 1908): 22–24.

Heydner, Georg. *Das Lesebuch in der Volksschule: Naturgemäße Forderungen.* Nuremberg: Korn, 1891.

Hübner, Rolf. "Unbekannte Briefe der Brüder Grimm an die Weimarer Buchhändler Friedrich Justin und Karl Bertuch." *Forschen und Bilden* 1.2 (1966): 33–40.

Jäger, Georg. *Schule und literarische Kultur: Sozialgeschichte des deutschen Unterrichts an höheren Schulen von der Spätaufklärung bis zum Vormärz.* Stuttgart: Metzler, 1981.

Johnston, Otto W. *The Myth of a Nation: Literature and Politics in Prussia unter der Napoleon.* Columbia, SC: Camden House, 1989.

Kayser, Christian Gottlob. *Vollständiges Bücher-Lexikon 1750–1910.* Leipzig: Tauchnitz, 1834–1911.

Keiper, Wolfgang, ed. *Kinder- und Hausmärchen gesammelt durch die Brüder Grimm: Historische Ausgabe*. Vol. 1. Berlin: Keiper, 1948.

Kudrjawzewa, Lidija. "In der Märchenwelt der Brüder Grimm." *Beiträge zur Kinder- und Jugendliteratur* 83 (1987): 49–55.

Leonard, T. J. "First Steps in Cruelty." *British Zone Review* 1.37 (1947): 10–13.

Leyen, Friedrich von der, ed. *Kinder- und Hausmärchen gesammelt durch die Brüder Grimm*. 2 vols. Jena: Diederichs, 1912.

———. *Lesebuch des deutschen Volksmärchens*. Berlin: Junker & Dünnhaupt, 1934.

Literatur für Kinder und Jugendliche in der DDR. Berlin: Kinderbuchverlag, 1979.

Das Märchen im Unterricht. Spec. issue of *Der Deutschunterricht* 8.6 (1956).

Marienkind und andere Märchen. Illus. Franz Müller-Münster. Berlin: Fischer & Franke, 1901.

Marquardt, Ulrike. "Zur Druckgeschichte der ersten Auflage der Kinder- und Hausmärchen 1812/15: Eine Untersuchung des Grimmschen Handexemplars." *Brüder Grimm Gedenken* 7 (1987): 217–23.

Merkel, Johannes, and Dieter Richter. *Märchen, Phantasie und soziales Lernen*. Berlin: Basis, 1974.

Muttergottesgläschen. Illus. Charlotte Bud. Berlin: Eigenbrödler, [1920].

National Union Catalog: Pre-1956 Imprints. London: Mansell, 1972.

Panzer, Friedrich, ed. *Kinder- und Hausmärchen der Brüder Grimm: Vollständige Ausgabe in der Urfassung*. Wiesbaden: Vollmer, 1947.

Reifferscheid, Alexander, ed. *Freundesbriefe von Wilhelm und Jacob Grimm*. Heilbronn: Henninger, 1878.

Richter, Dieter, ed. *Das politische Kinderbuch: Eine aktuelle historische Dokumentation*. Darmstadt: Luchterhand, 1973.

Richter, Dieter, and Jochen Vogt, eds. *Die heimlichen Erzieher: Kinderbücher und politisches Lernen*. Reinbek bei Hamburg: Rowohlt, 1974.

Rißmann, Jutta. "Zum Briefwechsel der Brüder Grimm mit ihrem Verleger Reimer." *Brüder Grimm Gedenken* 4 (1984): 114–19.

Rölleke, Heinz, ed. *Die älteste Märchensammlung der Brüder Grimm: Synopse der handschriftlichen Urfassung von 1810 und der Erstdrucke von 1812*. Cologny/Geneva: Fondation Martin Bodmer, 1975.

———, ed. *Kinder- und Hausmärchen: Ausgabe letzter Hand mit den Originalanmerkungen der Brüder Grimm*. By the Brothers Grimm. 3 vols. Stuttgart: Reclam, 1980.

———, ed. *Kinder- und Hausmärchen gesammelt durch die Brüder Grimm: Kleine Ausgabe von 1858*. Frankfurt a.M.: Insel, 1985.

———, ed. *Kinder- und Hausmärchen gesammelt durch die Brüder Grimm: Vollständige Ausgabe auf der Grundlage der dritten Auflage (1837)*. Frankfurt a.M.: Deutscher Klassiker Verlag, 1985.

————, ed. *Kinder- und Hausmärchen: Nach der 2. vermehrten und verbesserten Auflage von 1819.* By the Brothers Grimm. 2 vols. Cologne: Diederichs, 1982.

————, and Ulrike Marquardt, eds. *Kinder- und Hausmärchen gesammelt durch die Brüder Grimm: Vergrößerter Nachdruck der zweibändigen Erstausgabe von 1812 und 1815.* 2 vols. and suppl. Göttingen: Vandenhoeck & Ruprecht, 1986.

Rumpf, Marianne. *Volkskundliche Kostproben aus dem "Grimm-Schrank."* Berlin: Staatsbibliothek Preußischer Kulturbesitz Berlin, 1983. N. pag.

Schmidt, Kurt. "Die Texte der Grimmschen Märchen in den Lesebüchern." *Zeitschrift für die Bildung* 11 (1935): 367–87.

Schnackenberg, Ernst, ed. *Brüder Grimm Märchen.* Altona: Meier & Elsner, 1929.

Schneider, Rolf-Rüdiger. "Bechsteins 'Deutches Märchenbuch': Ein Beitrag zur Entstehungs- und Wirkungsgeschichte." Diss. U Wuppertal, 1980.

Schoof, Wilhelm. "150 Jahre 'Kinder- und Hausmärchen': Die Grimmschen Märchen im Urteil der Zeitgenossen." *Wirkendes Wort* 12 (1962): 331–35.

————. "Jacob Grimm als Autor des Dieterichschen Verlages." *Börsenblatt für den deutschen Buchhandel* 11 (5 Aug. 1955): 493–97.

————. "Verlegersorgen der Brüder Grimm." *Börsenblatt für den deutschen Buchhandel* 10 (16 Feb. 1954): 82–85.

Schroers, Paul. "Die erste Ausgabe der Grimmschen Märchen." *Philobiblon* 9 (1965): 263–69.

Troll, Max. *Der Märchenunterricht in der Elementarklasse.* Langensalze: Beyer & Söhne, 1911.

Ubbelohde, Otto, illus. *Kinder- und Hausmärchen: Jubiläumsausgabe.* 3rd ed. 3 vols. Marburg: Elwert, 1922. Wiesbaden: Sändig, 1970.

Weber-Kellermann, Ingeborg. Introduction. *Kinder- und Hausmärchen gesammelt durch die Brüder Grimm.* Frankfurt a.M.: Insel, 1974. 1: 9–18.

Wegehaupt, Heinz. *Mein Vöglein mit dem Ringlein rot.* Berlin: Kinderbuchverlag, 1985.

Wolgast, Heinrich. *Das Elend unserer Jugendliteratur: Ein Beitrag Zur künstlerischen Erziehung der Jugend.* 3rd ed. Leipzig: Teubner, 1905.

Zipes, Jack. *Fairy Tales and the Art of Subversion: The Classical Genre for Children and the Process of Civilization.* New York: Wildman, 1983.

Trivial Pursuit?
Women Deconstructing the
Grimmian Model in the *Kaffeterkreis*

Shawn Jarvis

The *Kaffeterkreis*

IN 1843, the same year the *Kinder- und Hausmärchen* were going into their fifth expanded and improved edition, the order of the *Kaffeterkreis* was called into being. Its members wore pointed brown paper hats with pink veils to hide their blushes when words of praise overwhelmed them or if their forays into a public sphere rendered them meek. The sound of children's rattles signalled displeasure while toy trumpets tooted approval at meetings that President Maiblümchen called to order brandishing a wooden scepter wrapped in ribbons and blossoms. The group met weekly during Berlin's dreary winter months to present the *Kaffeologen's* anonymously submitted art work and literary and musical compositions, and to perform fairy-tale plays to illustrious Berlin audiences. Bettine von Arnim often directed their performances for the Prussian monarch Friedrich Wilhelm IV at the home of Friedrich Karl von Savigny, the Prussian Minister of Justice, with honorary *Kaffeologen* like Eduard Mörike, Hans Christian

Andersen, Emanuel Geibel, even the Prussian crown prince, in atten-
dance. And the original girl-child members were themselves a stately
lot: Gisela, Maximiliane, and Armgart von Arnim; Ottilie von Gräfe;
Marie von Lichtenstein; Marie, Nina, and Hedwig von Olfers; Valeska
von Grabow; Pauline and Anna von Wolzogen; Fernanda von Pappen-
heim; Amalie Herder; and Elisabeth von Königsmarck—the daughters
of Berlin surgeons, zoologists, generals, writers, philosophers, politicians, and saloniéres, and thus children of an intellectual, political,
often monied, aristocracy and developing bourgeoisie. These were
the classes to which generations socialized with the Grimms' primer
might aspire.

The gatherings sounded somewhat less like a hotbed of social and
political discontent or the breeding ground for subversive female voices
and more like a Biedermeier *Kaffeekränzchen* or coffee circle. Bettine
von Arnim's daughters founded the *Kaffeter* with Caroline and Mine
Bardua initially as a riposte to the almost all-male *Maikäferbund*
formed in Bonn in 1840. The men of the *Maikäferbund,* academics
and students, theologians, cultural and art historians, poets, and even a
chemist, met weekly under the directorship of a woman, Johanna
Kinkel—the wife of the theologian and poet Gottfried Kinkel—to sub-
mit and discuss their anonymous literary works before inclusion in
Maikäfer—Eine Zeitschrift für Nicht-Philister, their own privately
printed journal. The club was, one might venture, a Biedermeier
contribution to the literary salon tradition. The *Kaffeter's* founding
members agreed, "We could do that here too!" (Werner 103), and conceived the *Kaffeterkreis* as a virginal order—*Jungfrauenorden*—originally open only to girls and women. The young members of the
Kaffeterkreis (most of them still only adolescents) desired to be on an
equal intellectual footing with male counterparts; they emulated them
by donning male pseudonyms like "Lord Armgart" and "Spatz von
Spatzenheim," and submitted their anonymous works, primarily fairy
tales, to the scrutiny of the *Kaffeologen* before inclusion in the *Kaffeterzeitung,* the protocols of their meetings. The *Kaffeter* thus came as
a direct response to a number of male literary and social activities; and
although males—"only nondangerous ones"—were later admitted as
honorary members, the *Kaffeter* remained a female association (Drewitz 90).

The *Kaffeterkreis* met for the last time on 14 March 1848, in Berlin,
while the city was in the throes of the 1848 Revolution. Attempts to

revive the society failed, and the original members concluded that "The *Kaffeter* was a creature of the pre-Vormärz times" (Werner 188). When the members met again one more time on 26 March 1851, in the Olfers' yellow salon, two of the members had already passed away, and most were spread to the winds, many already married. Some, like Gisela von Arnim and Marie von Olfers, continued their artistic endeavors, but most simply passed into obscurity.

The French and German Salon Traditions

Although the male-dominated *Maikäferbund* was the initial impetus for the daughters of Berlin's intellectual aristocracy, the formation of the *Kaffeter* had strong and obvious predecessors within the female community, both in Germany and, earlier, in France. From the French tradition may have come the *Kaffeter's* interest in fairy tales. Critics trace the genesis of the modern European fairy-tale tradition—the *contes de fées*—to the French salon culture of the late seventeenth century. The early French conversational salon culture poked fun at the rise of classical literature by returning to the archaic and "prelogical" world of the middle ages, of nursemaids, and of children; the major activity in these salons was the spontaneous creation of fairy tales as a "society game for aristocratic ladies" (Baader 226). The ladies of the salons, the *Muses françoises*—among them Madame d'Aulnoy ("Clion" or "l'Eloquente"), Mlle L'Héritier, Mlle Bernard ("Calliope, l'Invincible"), Mlle de la Force ("Thalie, l'Engageante"), and Madame de Murat—produced now-classic literary fairy tales and gained recognition for their efforts. Their work was considered illustrious enough for them to be inducted into the prestigious Accademia dei Ricovrati, a forum for female writers founded in Padua in 1699. And while Charles Perrault, also a guest of Madame d'Aulnoy's salon, has come down in canonical history as the creator of the French fairy tale with his collection *Histoires ou contes du temps passé* (1697), Madame d'Aulnoy actually published the "first" *conte de fées* about the Russian prince Adolphe and the fairy princess Félicité in the novel *Histoire d'Hypolite, comte de Duglas* (1690).[1]

While the female literary production, especially of fairy tales, in the French salons of Madame d'Aulnoy and her contemporaries can be seen as a model for the *Kaffeterkreis,* the German Romantic salon tradition over a century later offered another impetus, one for social and political change. The Romantic salon paved the way for "women's participation in influencing public speech and thereby shaping politics. . . . Through dialogue woman could influence her surroundings and do this by voicing her private and public concerns through a forum which readily synthesized these two spheres" (Waldstein 27). Art and aesthetics were among the many topics discussed: writers and musicians experimented with their work, and aesthetic theories had their origins in discussions of readings and performances. The theories, in turn, became the object of criticism. Women like Rahel Varnhagen and Henriette Herz had dominated the discourse of the German Romantic salon, where they had successfully challenged the "claims to authority . . . by establishing social ties, by creating a sense of rank, order and value in a world in which women prevail" (Rosaldo 36)—a structure that ran contrary to the models in society (and fairy tales).[2]

The young women of the *Kaffeter* synthesized the French and the German salon traditions. They took the French salon's predilection for writing fairy tales while exploiting the blurring of public and private spheres practiced in the German tradition. Like Madame d'Aulnoy and her associates, the girls of the *Kaffeter* combined the characteristics of oral genres with the art of conversation and wrote fairy tales that they presented orally; but, like Varnhagen and Herz and von Arnim, they also created a public—*Öffentlichkeit*—for the ideas they presented by writing and performing fairy-tale plays within the home.[3] Just as the women of the Versailles salons—excluded from the mainstream male discourse—had explored the compensatory nature of fairy tales as a world of wish-fulfillment, and just as the German saloniéres combined public and private spheres, so the girls and women of the *Kaffeter* found in their collaboration the possibility of playing out roles that seemed or were impossible in real life.

Deconstructing the Grimm Model

Although contemporary reports indicate that the *Kaffeterkreis* produced numerous fairy tales and fairy-tale plays, to our knowledge only three texts were published contemporaneously, while a fourth by Gisela von Arnim apparently appeared in a private printing.[4] After the death of the Bardua sisters (the secretaries of the *Kaffeterzeitung*), the protocols were transferred to Maximiliane von Arnim for safekeeping. Johannes Werner, the editor of Maxe's memoirs, planned an edition of the *Kaffeterzeitung,* but the five folio volumes were mysteriously lost between the two world wars, and today only a few manuscripts and transcripts remain scattered in various archives in Germany.

My reading of the few archival remnants of the protocols indicates the tales of the *Kaffeterkreis* broke open the traditional parameters of the *Märchen* as found in Grimms' collection. Grimm model females were passive, silent, industrious, and rewarded with riches and a man to support them, while male models were destined to seek out adventure and take as their reward passive, silent, industrious females. *Kaffeter* fairy tales reversed these roles and presented heroines who found happiness in being educated and single rather than married and brain dead. For example, Gisela von Arnim's "Die garstige kleine Erbse" (The Nasty Little Pea) problematizes the difficulties of being denied speech and subsequent redemption through other modes of communication: (female) peas cast out from the otherwise homogeneous sack and beyond the amalgam of the soup end up happy because they find a new, more satisfying mode of communication in their lives as sweet peas. Other stories, like "Die Rosenwolke" (The Rose Cloud), which I will discuss here at length, are set in a world where only women seem to exist, and tell of girls bent on achieving intellectual growth rather than material gain.

I have chosen "The Rose Cloud" because we can glean from it historical and psychological perspectives on Grimms' *Kinder- und Hausmärchen.* I do not claim it to be representative of all the tales generated in the *Kaffeterkreis* over a five-year span, although it may actually be.[5] It is significant that I presume this story to be from Gisela von Arnim, the heiress to the prestigious Brentano–von Arnim fairy-tale tradition. Born on 30 August 1827 as the third daughter and last of seven children of Bettine Brentano and Achim von Arnim, Gisela—the self-titled "Märchenkind," or fairy-tale child—grew up in a milieu that was strongly influenced by the Arnim-Brentano family tradition of Romanticism and the fairy tale.[6] Her father, Ludwig Achim von Arnim, and her uncle, Clemens Brentano, are counted among the first collectors of folk material with their (albeit somewhat bastardized) "folk" collection *Des Knaben Wunderhorn* (1806–08). Gisela's mother, Bettine, collected and wrote fairy tales, and encouraged the Grimms in their work. Even Gisela's brother Friedmund followed family example and in 1844 published the fairy tales he had collected in Silesia as *Hundert neue Mährchen im Gebirge gesammelt*. In 1857, Gisela married her life-long friend, Herman Grimm, Wilhelm's son.

Gisela's literary oeuvre indicates a firm grounding in the fairy-tale literature of her contemporaries and their predecessors. There are allusions in her works to any number of well-known fairy tales, from Boccaccio's *Decamerone* to Wilhelm Hauff's "Kalif Storch." But she also makes reference to less well-known or even unknown fairy tales written by women. In a series of fairy-tale letters written to her nephew Achim von Arnim, for example, she pays homage to Basile but also draws on the works of Amalie von Helwig (*Sage vom Wolfsbrunnen: Mährchen*, 1814) and Benedikte Naubert ("Die weiße Frau" in *Neue Volksmährchen der Deutschen*, 1789–1793)—works that have been abandoned to obscurity by canonical history.[7]

It is also useful to study the tales from the *Kaffeterkreis* because, chronologically viewed, the girls in the circle were almost all personally acquainted with many of the men who contributed to the fairy-tale canon. The *Kaffeologen* were also familiar with the Grimms' tales and so were one of the first generations to be socialized with the values they expounded.[8] Memoirs and diaries of *Kaffeter* members also indicate a firm grounding in works by Romantic authors: Tieck, Fouqué, Brentano, Hoffmann, Chamisso, Novalis, and Hauff figure prominently in their childhood recollections as visitors to their homes and/or as writers of many favored stories. Hans Christian Andersen, "the fairy-tale man" and honorary member of the group, also had a strong influence. Many of the women, notably Marie von Olfers and Gisela von Arnim, continued to write fairy tales and fairy-tale plays long after the demise of the *Kaffeterkreis*.[9]

What I want to show is how the socialization of girls intimately familiar with the Grimms' model could have caused the need for the forum the *Kaffeter* represented (the *Kaffeter*, by its very existence, rejected the Grimmian model of the silent and passive female), and in turn how the *Kaffeter's* confrontation with and reworking of the fairy tale on numerous levels—as literature, as a pedagogical plan for social relations, as a tool for socialization—yielded new forms of the genre that are yet to be explored and understood.

It is one of the truisms in fairy-tale research that fairy tales generally and the Grimms' stories specifically address how one reaches adulthood, and what happens along the way—that is, the process of maturation or the rights/rites of passage. And while the socialization of the individual takes place along a life-cycle continuum, canonical fairy tales (at least Grimm types) tend to present models for the socialization of individuals at the gateway to adulthood. The Grimms' numerous revisions and reworkings shaped the *Kinder- und Hausmärchen* into the quintessential educational primer—"Erziehungsbuch," as the Grimms themselves described the collection in the second volume of their first edition in 1815 (2: VIII). In this capacity their carefully shaped collection served as a plan for appropriate social and gender relations. The rites and rights of passage in Grimms' tales, as representative research by Ruth Bottigheimer and Maria Tatar has shown, differ depending on gender.[10] Boys are rewarded for transgressing a prohibition, while girls are punished with towery isolations; girls are abjured to silence and passivity, while boys bluster and threaten their way to power. I am interested in showing how women's fairy tales often presented a re-vision of the path. What lessons must a girl learn on the way, who teaches her these lessons (that is, how is she initiated) and where does the initiation lead?

A plot summary of "The Rose Cloud" looks similar to that of any tale with all female characters from the Grimms' collection. Catharine, the protagonist, tends her flock of sheep. One day—distracted by the other activities of childhood—she forgets to herd her favorite lamb, Bichette, home. Catharine sets out at dawn to search for Bichette, finds her at the edge of the pond, scoops her up in her apron, and carries her home. Along the way, she encounters the neighboring shepherd carrying Bichette under his arm. What is really in her apron? A small pink cloud that flies away, singing in a language Catharine does not understand. Shortly thereafter, a terrible storm destroys the apple tree next to her mother's house. Catharine is chided by her mother, Sylvia, for her persistent talk about the rose cloud, and when an interdict against "useless chatter"—that is, female speech—is imposed on her, she becomes a good spinner and reasonable girl ("vernünftig"). On her twelfth birthday, Catharine's mother asks if she would like to visit an impoverished ailing aunt in a distant country. After a long and arduous journey, Sylvia and Catharine reach Aunt Colette's home to discover she is instead the richest farmer and best spinner in her part of the country.

Colette is known as the spinner of clouds. Catharine stays for three months with her mysterious aunt to learn the secret to spinning clouds that will make her rich, happy, and able to secure her impoverished family's future. During the time with her aunt, she encounters the rose cloud again. When Sylvia returns for her three months later, Catharine has unravelled the mysteries of cloud spinning and understands the language of her ethereal companion. She is rewarded with Colette's estate and riches for the rest of her days.

On the surface, parallel to tales of the Grimm genre, "The Rose Cloud" follows the exigencies of the fairy-tale plot. As she reaches puberty, the young protagonist undertakes the journey out. She faces a challenge and must discover a resolution to a conflict. "The question," as Jack Zipes formulates it for Grimms' tales, " . . . is: how can one learn—what must one do to use one's powers rightly in order to be accepted in society or recreate society in keeping with the norms of the *status quo?*" (*Fairy Tales and the Art of Subversion* 57). This also seems to be Catharine's predicament: she must learn to spin. Once she has accomplished this task through hard work and patience, she is rewarded with riches. The re-creation of society Catharine undertakes is not, however, "in keeping with the norms of the *status quo,*" but rather in keeping with a new society women often envision in their tales.

If we trace Catharine's rites of passage in the fourteen chapters of "The Rose Cloud," we see the deconstruction of Grimmian paradigms and the creation of a new prototype. The gender-specific clichés that gloss a female's rite of passage in the Grimms' tales—passivity, obedience, self-sacrifice, hard work, patience, and silence—are all problematized in ways that reject the Grimm world and create a different community. The author of "The Rose Cloud" dis-orders the canonical fairy-tale text. In an exclusively female world, the mother, Sylvia, represents the old social and moral order of the Grimms, Catharine the new prototype, and Aunt Colette the mediating mentor.

In the first three chapters, Catharine is introduced as a character both like and unlike her Grimm counterparts: "Catharine . . . could not yet write or read, but she knew how to converse quite agreeably, and she was a sweet girl—only a bit too curious and fickle" (1). This focus on conversational ability situates the heroine in "The Rose Cloud" firmly in the tradition of her *Kaffeter* and salon sisters, for whom spirited and lambent conversation was the hallmark of success and an important skill for "higher daughters" (Kößler 43). At the same time Catharine is loquacious, she is also a sweet girl—a combination generally unknown in Grimms' stories, where yakking females always presage trouble. Ruth Bottigheimer has found in contrast that "there is a pattern of discourse in Grimms' Tales that discriminates against 'good' girls and produces functionally silent heroines" (*Bad Girls and Bold Boys* 53). Bottigheimer argues that the image and model of the silenced female, as it was reflected in the *Kinder- und Hausmärchen,* was based in sociohistorical conditions for women in the nineteenth century.[11] She suggests that the issue of female voice and voicelessness in the fairy tale can be viewed as deprivation and transformation of power, and that "positively presented, powerful female figures either were deprived of their inherent power [of speech] or else had their power transformed into the godless potency of witchcraft" (76).

In chapter 3, the author problematizes language and speech in a way that anticipates modern feminist critics who view speech as a vehicle to power. As Catharine attempts to understand the rose cloud in a discussion with her mother, Sylvia commands: "Shut up, . . . you know that I can't stand it when people talk nonsense without rhyme or reason" (9). Sylvia imposes the interdict of female silence.[12] The silencing of the female protagonist robs her of a vehicle for expressing what can be understood in words, and it is imposed by the character who represents the Grimm world view. In the Grimm tradition, where so many women were narratively or physically silenced, or had their magic pronouncements reduced to "ungodly" incantations, enforced female silence ensured the passivity that was the hallmark of most Grimm female protagonists.[13]

As Catharine silences her tongue, she is also enjoined to curb her curiosity and inquisitiveness, the equivalent of intellectual activity. Coupled in "The Rose Cloud" with the ban of silence is also a ban on thought as a way to keep heroines "unmündig"—without voice in society. "Curious" and "curiosity" ("neugierig" and "Neugierde") appear in seven of the fourteen chapters in connection with Catharine. The Grimm world in which she still lives abjures curiosity—even the birds in the trees seem to laugh and call, "How curious she is, ugh, how curious!" (10). Female curiosity in the Grimm tradition, just like female loquacity, leads to grave and swift punishment. But as Catharine begins to think for herself, she would still like, despite the birds' scolding, to fly to the clouds. Yet Catharine, while still with her mother, remains of the Grimm ilk: she "remembered that a person was not supposed to talk nonsense and for that reason should not think of silly things. She took up her distaff, spun as well as she could, and tried her hardest to think about nothing, but against her will she kept looking up at the sky" (8). She is obedient, passive, and silent.

It is at this point in the story that the prohibition on speech and thought and the advancement of spinning are conjoined. The prohibition against both speech and thought leaves Catharine with one thing: spinning, a woman's first calling and only destiny. Here spinning remains in the context of ancient tradition for women. In Germany it was, as Ruth Bottigheimer notes, "a task performed by every woman, the task that awaited her when all other household work had been finished."[14] Catharine, too, must spin her measure, although the rose cloud and the inexorable urge to understand the image continue to distract Catharine from her duties in chapter 4. Here we begin to understand the import of the rose cloud, because with Catharine's contemplation of it she neglects her work. Despite her best attempts to continue spinning, she cannot resist glancing to the sky and failing at her task. Father Kempf, an old seafarer passing by, suggests the rose cloud is a "Wetterkorn" and a sign that the need for great labor is ahead: "As soon as one sees this sign at sea, one says: Now there's going to be work, hard work" (11). We get an inkling of what's ahead when the rose cloud transforms itself into an enormous storm cloud and destroys the apple tree in Catharine's mother's garden. It is then that the Grimm equation of female speech with inappropriate behavior is complete: Catharine cannot stop speaking of the cloud, and Sylvia cries to her neighbors, "Oh my God, my little one has gone crazy!" (13). When females speak, insanity is but a step away.

Catharine is called back to the world in which she exists; and because her mother will not tolerate daydreaming and idle chatter (thought and speech are juxtaposed in the text), Catharine, "who was an obedient child" (14), decides to abandon them. Renouncing her daydreaming, she becomes the model of Grimm behavior, learns to love her distaff, and becomes a skilled spinner. But the voyage out, as in all fairy tales, will disrupt the stability Sylvia and the Grimm world have created.

Chapter 5 establishes a break with the model of dangerous female curiosity: as Catharine leaves with her mother to travel to her aunt's, the narrator takes a stand on the positive potential of female curiosity, telling us Catharine was still curious, " but not in any bad way; she just loved to learn'' (15). Female curiosity is necessary for intellectual advancement. This is the critical turning point, as Catharine—who has just turned twelve—has started onto her path to adulthood.

Chapters 6 through 9, the central chapters of the tale, are crucial to the deconstruction of the Grimm model. Aunt Colette, the kindly and wise mediating mentor foreign to most Grimm tales, appears to extol the value of spinning; the distinction between material versus spiritual wealth is addressed (with a choice implicitly made); and the potential for what Jeannine Blackwell describes as ''the psychological continuity and emotional connectedness of characters'' (171) becomes clear.

In chapter 6 we are introduced to Aunt Colette and learn she is a large, pale woman with silver hair and a face ''that was rather pretty'' (19). Following the logic of the Grimm model, Colette's physical beauty reflects her inner virtue. But it is a contradiction in Grimm terms for a woman to be both beautiful and magical. In the Grimm model, beautiful women possess no other powers than their ability to attract a prince, while magical women, most frequently witches, possess not beauty, but rather evil intent. Colette possesses both: beauty and otherworldly powers. She can ''see'' the future in dreams (she is not surprised to see Sylvia and Catharine suddenly at her doorstep, because she dreamt they would come), and she also envisions Catharine's fate. She embraces Catharine, saying: ''That's good, very good! I'm glad this child was born'' (19). Catharine becomes the chosen one, the one to inherit Colette's estate and ''secret.''

It is extremely significant that Colette's first question to Catharine is ''Can you spin, my child?'' (21). Spinning functions in various ways in the Grimms' collection.[15] The author of ''The Rose Cloud'' creates a hybrid: she uses the Grimm type in which spinning functions as a character indicator of female virtue while she also draws on a tradition of women's writing where spinning functions as a path to magicalness. In this hybrid, the positive potential of spinning for a woman—it is the source of Colette's wealth—is revealed.

Spinning, as Bottigheimer and Tatar have amply demonstrated, occupies an extremely ambivalent and ambiguous position in the Grimms' collection. Bottigheimer argues that while Wilhelm Grimm's editorial voice associates spinning with the eventual attainment of riches, ''incontrovertible internal evidence'' within the tales points to the hardship and drudgery of the task. Accordingly, she sums up the role of spinning in Grimms' fairy tales in terms hardly joyous:

[Spinning] identifies subjugated womanhood in "Allerleirauh"; it is an occupation to be escaped in "The Lazy Spinner"; it is also a punishment in "The Water-Nixie," a deforming occupation in "The Three Spinners," "Mother Holle," and "King Thrushbeard"; and at its worst, it is an agent of death or a curse in "Little Briar-Rose." Although many tales declare that spinning mediates wealth in the form of gold, it is primarily associated with poverty in "Tales from the Paddock" and "The Goose-Girl at the Well." Above all, it is the archetypal employment of domesticated, poverty-stricken womanhood in "Eve's Various Children." (*Bad Girls and Bold Boys* 122)

Bottigheimer posits the ambiguity of spinning as a result of Wilhelm's editorial undertaking: while the plots of the tales suggest hard work rewarded, the lexical and narrative levels of the texts betray the hard realities and grueling hardships of women who spun throughout the centuries. Maria Tatar concludes that "the end product of the spinning process may get the heroine a husband, but the process itself is guaranteed to disfigure and deform" (133).

On the other hand, a tradition of spinning unknown in Grimms' tales surfaces in "The Rose Cloud" and harks back to the ancient rites of the spinning of truth. The image of women weaving and spinning, which became increasingly negative in the progression of Grimms' editions, had a strong positive potential. Jeannine Blackwell elucidates this idea in her examination of a tale by Benedikte Naubert, "Der kurze Mantel" (The Short Coat). In this tale—a combination of Arthurian romance and German fairy tale—Frau Rosen explains to Genelas how she lost Frau Holle's protection through careless love and regained it through hard work and kindness. Frau Rosen teaches Genelas to spin and weave the cloth to make a coat which will shrink on the liar and grow to clothe the truth-teller. Blackwell concludes that "wonder women are not born; they are made: the progression from Genelas to Frau Rosen to Frau Holle is merely one of age and experience in weaving the magic cloak of truth. . . . The organizing principle for achieving magic is the search for wisdom and ethics" (167). There are no magic helpers in "The Rose Cloud," no Rumpelstiltskins to spin the finest cloud, no prince as a reward for the woman's labors. Nor does Catharine seek them.

Colette is initiating Catharine into adulthood, and it is significant that she does so by teaching her the magic of spinning clouds. As Karen Rowe points out, the spinning chamber became a central place for the transmission of cultural truths and a staging ground for rites of initiation. *Les sages femmes* (to whose circle Colette certainly belongs) "in its extended meaning . . . comes to signify wise women who transmit culture, whether by presiding over the rites of passage through which young persons pass . . . or by spinning tales that counsel the young through a combination of entertaining story with moral and social instruction" (Rowe 64).

It should be remembered that the tales of the German fairy-tale tradition are often assumed to have travelled through the spinning chamber. Spinning and tale-telling (whereby tale-telling in this context must be construed as a didactic activity, just as the Grimms strove to make their work an educational primer) had been connected since ancient times. In fact, the French, Italian, and English derivatives of *contes de fées,* as Rowe suggests, "compel us to see the origin of 'fairy' as closely related to female acts of birthing, nursing, prophesying, and spinning—as ancient myth makes plain. . . . *Contes de fées* are, therefore, not simply tales told about fairies; implicitly they are tales told by women, descendants of those ancestral Fates, who link once again the craft of spinning with the art of telling fated truths" (63). The fairies and Fates who spun tales of wisdom and cloaks of truth mediated the passage into life.

This, too, is Colette's responsibility in "The Rose Cloud." Her status and ability as the spinner of clouds—"die Wolkenspinnerin"— make her the possessor of both knowledge and material wealth. When Colette shows her work, her "cloud" of extremely fine yarn to Sylvia and Catharine, she is compared to a fairy; but note the connotations: "Catharine let out a cry of wonder, and Sylvia, who imagined her aunt was a fairy or sorceress, went pale with fright" (24). Catharine's receptiveness to Colette's activities and Sylvia's fear of them polarize the Grimm model. When Catharine and Sylvia see the spun cloud, Sylvia experiences fear of the fairy aunt, while Catharine wants the cloud, not because of its monetary value, but because of the skill it represents: " 'Oh, dear Aunt,' cried Catharine, 'if only you would give it to me! It's not because of the money; but I would be so proud to be able to work like you do!' " (25). Grimm heroines seek the secrets to avoiding work—Catharine begs to know the secret to spinning as a metaphor for another truth.

The figures of mother and daughter in "The Rose Cloud" make clear the contrast between the world view of Grimmian tales and the utopian vision of some women's writing. Catharine's prime goal is to achieve a state of knowledge equal to her aunt's, not to aggrandize material goods. While Sylvia is overawed by Colette, "who stood way above her" because of her social status and wealth, Catharine is intimidated by her aunt's wealth of knowledge: "Catharine was also a little taken aback, but not because she was richer or poorer than her aunt, but because she felt how much more educated her aunt was" (20).

In her search for these truths, and in her eventual unravelling of the secrets of Aunt Colette's success and the meaning of the rose cloud, Catharine must reject her mother's interdicts. She is enabled by her aunt, who banishes the specter of the silenced female. Although Sylvia consistently cautions against speaking, Catharine feels such an immediate affinity with her aunt "that she began already on the first day to question her aunt without any inhibitions" (20). When she begins to speak of her encounter with the rose cloud, her mother admonishes her to silence and begs Colette's forgiveness for the "foolish child." Colette, however, gently silences the mother and not the child, saying "but then I won't find out what she wanted to say" (23). Colette listens intently to Catharine's story, offers a moral to the tale (one must mistrust all that is transitory), and finally suggests it would be a shame if she took her secret of spinning clouds to the grave. Now Catharine is faced with a fairy-tale trial, but with a different slant. She must learn her aunt's secret.

In chapter 9, Catharine wishes to remain with her aunt to learn what she believes is the secret behind Colette's ability to spin clouds and Colette's source of wealth. When Sylvia suggests she stay to learn her aunt's secret so that she might become rich and happy, Catharine is relatively unswayed. When Sylvia mentions the next day "that it would be a great injustice to pass up the opportunity to learn something, she wavered" (29). But it is Catharine's ultimate reason for staying with her aunt that signals for me the fundamental break with the Grimm tradition: "Think it over whether you have the right to pass up the opportunity to help *us* all to riches." The typical Grimm plot, as Lutz Röhrich aptly summarizes it, focuses on a clear-cut issue: "With egocentric vigor the fairy tale pushes the fate of relatives, parents, and brothers and sisters aside and concentrates solely on the hero, his self-realization, and his attainment of happiness" (9). What on the surface seems to be an example of Grimmian self-sacrifice, actually becomes part of a bigger picture within women's *Märchen*. Catharine stays so that she may serve another community.[16] She accumulates wealth not for its own sake, but to secure the autonomy of others. This is part of "the psychological continuity and emotional connectedness of characters" that Blackwell has identified.

In chapters 10 and 11, the distinction between Catharine's path to adulthood and that of her Grimmian counterparts becomes apparent. As with the Grimm prototype, her ability to spin becomes the measure of her character. And like the Grimm female, Catharine still connects spinning with enchantment and still waits to uncover the mystery. Catharine believes in the reward system of many Grimm heroines: if she manages to accomplish her task, there will be a reward. So she sets out on a particular day to spin so well that Aunt Colette will have to betray her secret. Willingness and accomplishment equate with reward.

Seeking the fairy-tale solution—magic helpers or magical aids to accomplish the magical cloud—Catharine waits for her aunt to reveal her secret. But instead, Colette simply provides Catharine with flax and a distaff, and allows her, in Rousseauian manner, to spin at her leisure. Whereas Grimm heroines are literally locked away until their quantum is spun, Catharine is set free to spin as she pleases. But "this kind of solitary learning didn't in any way equate with her idea of a great secret, which she had expected suddenly to discover" (31). But the message of "The Rose Cloud" is that the task is not to spin for anyone but herself. Catharine has herself imposed the task, to learn to spin the clouds as her aunt does, and only *she* can fulfill the mission of the text. Colette facilitates the solution by spinning for Catharine, but the solution comes from within the individual, not from without.

Creating one of the most fascinating sequences of the story and the final deconstruction of the Grimm model, the last few chapters deal with the Janus face of the Grimm world. Catharine has grown impatient with her aunt's unwillingness to betray her secret and with her insistence that nothing can replace "willingness and diligence" (38). When she tries to spin, her eyes close and the spindle falls from her fingers. Aunt Colette, suddenly transformed into a fury because Catharine is resting rather than working, demands Catharine follow her to the peak of the mountain. She taunts her niece for dreaming rather than working, drags her through crystal halls across rugs of ermine, and flies with her to the peak of the glacier. She says she will reveal her secret. In a scene vaguely reminiscent of the various household persecutions in Grimms' "King Thrushbeard" (No. 52), Colette tears the distaff from Catharine's hand and replaces it with another, coarser implement, a broom to sweep together the clouds for Colette to hackle. Catharine sweeps, "but neither as well nor as fast as her aunt wished, who kept calling to her: 'Onward, do it faster and better! Keep going! More!' " (42). Colette even insists that Catharine hackle and spin her beloved rose cloud.

In the concluding chapter, we discover this has all been a bad dream, an image from the *Kinder- und Hausmärchen* where girls were forced into menial, impossible domestic tasks that they often could not master alone. It recalls Grimms' tales where, as Maria Tatar points out, "spinning can never be performed with sufficient speed or with the right magical touch to satisfy" (133). In the final paragraphs of the text, the meaning of the rose cloud becomes clear; Aunt Colette, like Catharine, has encountered the image. Her explication of the rose cloud points the way for women to transcend the fairy-tale world in which they, obedient and passive, merely wait for magical solutions. Colette suggests an active approach in which the woman is responsible for the outcome and in which she achieves autonomous control:

> The rose cloud was my whim, a creature of my imagination, my evil destiny. I put it on my good distaff, and the work, the wonderful work, spun such a beautiful thread for the enemy that I couldn't feel the thread at all any more. You'll do as I did. You won't be able to keep the clouds from passing by. But you have collected a reserve of strength. You will grab them, you will hackle them and spin them so well that they will no longer be able to conjure up the storm around and in you. (44–45)

Jeannine Blackwell has found that the mentors in women's fairy tales "are trying to tell us something about mistakes they and the young heroines have made. There is psychological growth and understanding between mortals and wise women" (167). If Blackwell's conclusion is true, "The Rose Cloud" becomes part of a larger picture of the psychological interconnectedness among the characters in women's fairy tales and the tellers and hearers of these tales. Catharine, over time, does indeed learn to spin the finest cloudlike thread and becomes the heiress to Colette's intellectual and material fortune.

One could argue that Aunt Colette's insistence on patience and skill in work as the paths to success and inner happiness is not much of an emancipatory step forward for women. The Grimms, too, rewarded female obedience, self-sacrifice, hard work, and patience in their tales.

117

The distinction between "The Rose Cloud" and Grimms' fairy tales lies, however, in the nature of the reward for such labors. The Grimms' heroines, after suffering their fairy-tale trials, generally have to make do with the princes, whether they wanted them or not. Catharine, the heroine of "The Rose Cloud," does not have material wealth as a goal, nor jewels, nor a man to protect her property rights. Through her wealth, Catharine becomes socially and financially independent, a true fantasy for most women in the nineteenth century. Catharine has achieved riches *and* independence, she has been educated while educating herself, and—most importantly—she has learned to harness inner forces to her advantage because she was allowed to explore and exploit their potential. Her spiritual and financial wealth are the product of forces, goals, and motivations unknown in the Grimms' tales, and not the result of passivity or obedience.

Conclusions

The voices of the *Kaffeter* were silenced for posterity by the 1848 Revolution and by a literary canon that could not or would not understand their message. What was the confrontational impact of the *Kaffeter-Märchen* and *Kaffeterkreis*? They were the products and projections of a community where women had a voice, and where that voice told of opportunities and realms unknown in the Grimms' tradition. The *Kaffeterkreis*—both the forum and the tales it produced—broke the ban of silence imposed on Grimm girls as the virtuous path to adulthood. Female curiosity, the fairy-tale equivalent of intellectual pursuit, was not the death-bringing principle, but rather a prerequisite to meaningful exchange and discovery. Discovery of self requires receptiveness to the other.

The question arises why Gisela von Arnim's and an entire tradition of female-penned fairy tales have been ignored in the critical literature. There are several levels of explanation.

From the early medieval frame narratives about the life and destiny of a woman or a community of women as tellers of tales—as in *The Thousand and One Nights,* Basile's *Pentamerone,* and Boccaccio's *Decamerone*—to "old Marie" of Grimm provenience, women and a real or assumed female oral tradition have played an important, shaping role in the European fairy-tale canon. But the oral and written traditions of women have not fared well. In France, where the modern European canon began, the female tradition of the *contes de fées* came under attack. As early as 1699, when women of Louis XIV's court were already churning out volume after volume of *contes de fées*, the Abbot de Villiers inveighed against the genre, primarily because it was in the main a female product. Interestingly, Charles Perrault, himself a contemporary of these women and a writer of *contes de fées*, rose from the controversy as "the model and corrective for the genre" (Baader 227). Perrault has become, inexplicably for some, the author who has had an undeniable influence on the German fairy-tale tradition (Grätz 22). Given the overwhelming number of women involved in the *contes de fées* tradition who have vanished from the pages of canonical history, one must posit that Perrault's gender indeed influenced the role he has played. Jack Zipes has argued that "the genre as an institution operates to safeguard basic male interests and conventions" (*The Brothers Grimm* 24). However, it is not only the genre per se, but also the canonical principles governing it, the discourse of the discipline itself, which magnifies the male role while diminishing the female contribution (Fox). The Madame d'Aulnoys and Madame de Murats, whose literary product actually constituted the genre of the *contes de fées*, have hardly been received in the critical literature (Baader 237).

In Germany the situation was not much different. The oral tradition of nursemaids and spinners was denigrated by early Enlightenment critics as unworthy of serious attention, although it gained canonical status when it was elevated to the level of the *Buchmärchen*, or "book fairy tale."[17] As a written text, a tale could be and was carefully edited and reworked by the (male) editors according to principles that "safeguard[ed] basic male interests and conventions." To look at the history of German women's fairy-tale collections, or better, the lack thereof, is to suspect that basic male interests and conventions must be missing, since most of these works are unknown to us today and do not constitute the canon.

It is not as if German women did not collect, write, or publish fairy tales. Women wrote *Volksmärchen, Kunstmärchen,* and children's literature in great proportion, long before and long after the Grimms. Benedikte Christiane Naubert, all-too-often forgotten, even ignored, in modern canonical histories, antedated the Grimms by more than two decades with her *Neue Volksmährchen der Deutschen.* More than a

119

decade before the Grimms' first edition appeared, female Romantic writers published texts like Sophie Mereau-Brentano's *Wunderbilder und Träume in eilf Mährchen* (1802), Sophie de la Motte Fouqué's *Drei Mährchen von Serena* (1806), and Amalie von Helwig and Sophie de la Motte Fouqué's *Taschenbuch der Sagen und Legenden* (1812–17). These texts are a testament to the Romantic women's engagement with a form and genre canonical literary history assigns to their brothers, husbands, and lovers. There were also innumerable children's collections like Agnes Franz's 1804 *Kinderlust*, Caroline Stahl's 1818 edition of *Fabeln, Mährchen und Erzählungen für Kinder*, and Amalie Schoppe's voluminous fairy-tale oeuvre made up of works like *Kleine Mährchen-Bibliothek, oder gesammelte Mährchen für die liebe Jugend* (1828) and *Volkssagen, Mährchen und Legenden aus Nord-Deutschland* (1833).

Between 1845 and 1900 women published over two hundred fairy-tale collections in the German-speaking countries. In fact, in the nineteenth century women writers far outnumbered male authors of children's literature—including fairy-tale books. It is thus actually specious to suggest that there has been a "male domination of the genre" (Zipes, *The Brothers Grimm* 24). What there has been is a male domination of the *canonical* genre. Were we to know more about the female fairy-tale tradition preceding and paralleling the Grimm tradition, we might recognize in the female-penned tales of the *Kaffeter* echoes of a now-lost legacy. To suggest, as much of the critical literature does, that the Grimms' *Kinder- und Hausmärchen* was the point of departure for all that ante- and postdated that significant work, is to ignore another tradition that partially influenced and shaped what has come down to us, but which also forms a separate, distinct tradition. What historical records permit us to see is that the Grimms' fairy tales had already become an institution by the 1840s, and positive readership response established the primacy of the *Kinder- und Hausmärchen* by the last third of the nineteenth century.[18]

I suggested earlier that to look at the history of German women's fairy-tale collections is to suspect that basic male interests and conventions must be missing. The Grimm genre—the *Gattung Grimm*—has come to constitute what we in popular culture consider to be true and right about fairy tales. Many critics, from Bruno Bettelheim to Sandra Gilbert and Susan Gubar to Maria Tatar, in various contexts and with various intents, have used this collection to argue that fairy tales represent "internalized" formulas for social—and, by extension, gender—behavior. Linda Dégh has suggested that narratives that depart sharply from traditional folklore patterns, such as *Gattung Grimm* models, are "beyond the scope of folkloristic consideration" (85). This means that texts that reformulate or repostulate the paradigms for human interaction and fulfillment, as elucidated in the Grimms' tales, do not come under the purview of Grimm or fairy-tale scholarship. Women's fairy tales present a different view of reality.

A glance at an introductory comment to a women's collection of fairy tales may clarify what I mean:

> All earthly existence is subject to destruction and transitoriness: the beauty of the body fades; riches and honors change and ebb and flow according to wise, eternal laws; even happiness and emotional well-being, the most beautiful and sweetest jewel of youth, falls prey to time and often is transformed into dour seriousness. It is not this way, however, with the treasurers which you accumulate for your spirit and soul, because no twist of fate, no person can take them from you and they are independent of time and place. But you must protect them, you must always work to increase them, and as you increase them, your inner happiness will increase too, not only in this life, but for all eternity. (Schoppe vi–vii)

Amalie Schoppe (1791–1858), who published innumerable fairy-tale collections and books for children, sums up the focus of so many women's *Märchen*. With these words there is no promise of eternal beauty, no permanent material wealth, no permanent honor, no path to power and domination, as in the Grimms' fairy tales. Here the commandment is to collect spiritual treasures. This leitmotif runs through most collections of fairy tales by women. An independent spirit leads to individual autonomy.

Gisela von Arnim's fairy-tale oeuvre, like that of many other female writers, draws on both oral tradition and the entire corpus of printed fairy tales from both men and women. In the case of male models, we see a reaction to the character configurations and the social statements. In the case of female models, we find a continuation of the leitmotifs that Amalie Schoppe summarized in her foreword. When Gisela von Arnim reacts to the bourgeois fairy tale à la Grimm, she rejects the social structures implicit in it. Her own fairy tales polarize the fairy-tale world of the bourgeois canon and that of the female genre. The texts

121

that became part of the "classical" canon of tales in the nineteenth century were those that affirm the mores of male bourgeois culture, while the less well-received tradition of female fairy-tale authors continues, even today, to offer a new vision for literary and human interaction.

Notes

1. Baader points out that in the final analysis it is not truly important "whether Mlle Bernard's version of *Riquet à la Houppe* or Mlle L'Héritier's *Enchantements* and *L'Adroite princesse* came before the publication of Perrault's *Contes* since the stages of oral transmission cannot be retraced" (228). In any case, the authors travelled in the same circles, knew each other well, and constantly attempted to better each other.
2. Bettine von Arnim—the mother of three *Kaffeologen*—revived the declining salon tradition in the late 1830s and kept it alive until shortly before her death in 1859. See Waldstein for a discussion of Bettine's salon.
3. Titles and characters reveal preoccupation with strong female images. Marie von Olfers's "Ohne Herz" (Without a Heart; loosely based on Wilhelm Hauff's "Das kalte Herz" [The Cold Heart] and performed in 1853) had a cast of all female characters, including Frau Holle, Fürstin Salamandra, Fürstin Luft, Lorely, Undine, and Melusine—some of the potentially strongest female characters in German lore. By writing the plays, the women created new models for social and gender-specific behavior. By performing the plays within the home setting, they taught their children through role-playing that modes of interaction other than those prescribed in Grimms' tales were possible. By performing the plays publicly, the women created a public for the ideas in them.
4. The three contemporaneously published plays were Gisela von Arnim's "Mondkönigstochter" (Moon King's Daughter) and "Aus den Papieren eines Spatzen" (From a Sparrow's Papers), and Armgart von Arnim's "Das Heimelchen: Ein Märchen für die Dämmerstunde" (The Home-Body: A Fairy Tale for Twilight). I am currently preparing a new edition of these and other *Kaffeter* tales for publication (Jarvis, *Märchen aus dem Kaffeterkreis*). Gisela von Arnim's privately printed work was "Das Pfefferkuchenhaus" (The Gingerbread House).
5. I can also not "prove" that it was written by Gisela von Arnim, although there are a number of reasons why I believe it was. The manuscript, written

on the long, white paper used for *Kaffeter*-protocols, is part of Gisela von Arnim's literary estate in the Hessisches Staatsarchiv in Marburg. Although the forty-five–page manuscript is not primarily written in Gisela's hand (it appears to be the work of a copyist), there are numerous marginal notations in Gisela's writing scattered throughout the text. Page references used here correspond to page numbers in the manuscript.

6. The strong, even fateful, influence Romanticism and family tradition had on Gisela affected her later reception as a writer in her own right. Contemporary critics who called her a "born poet" and "poet's child" tempered their comments with the suggestion that she was also "an unschooled or incorrectly schooled, spoiled child of Romanticism" (Seeger 933). For a biography of Gisela von Arnim, see Joeres and the afterword to Jarvis, *Das Leben der Hochgräfin Gritta von Rattenzuhausbeiuns* (205–23).

7. I discuss Gisela's use of both von Helwig and Naubert in the afterword and annotations to Jarvis, *Märchenbriefe an Achim*. For a feminist discussion of Naubert's tale, see Blackwell 166.

8. Maxe von Arnim, for example, recalls watching her cousin Claudine read not just fairy tales, but specifically "Grimms *Märchen*" to her nephew; and Gisela von Arnim critiques her brother Friedmund's own collection of fairy tales by commenting that they were not as lively as the Grimms' because the latter, in contrast to Friedmund, had "decorated theirs here and there with great love and care, and brought forth the best underlying point" (in Gisela's letter of ca. 1844 to Friedmund).

9. The pieces women did publish were judged according to the standards set by the male canon and often criticized by male reviewers for their poor orthography and aberrant narrative styles. See, for example, Gustav Kühne's review, where he discusses Gisela von Arnim's *Märchen* and compares them unfavorably with Eduard Mörike's "Stuttgarter Hutzelmännlein."

10. See my review of Bottigheimer's and Tatar's books, "The Hard Facts about the Bad Girls."

11. For an extremely interesting study of the impact of sociohistorical factors on Wilhelm Grimm's editing principles, see Steinchen.

12. It is interesting to note that Sylvia uses almost the identical language as Hansel when he silences his sister in "Hansel and Gretel," Grimm No. 15. See Bottigheimer, "Silenced Women."

13. On the narrative and physical silencing of women in Grimms' stories, see chapter 7, "Paradigms for Powerlessness," in Bottigheimer, *Bad Girls and Bold Boys* 71–80. Blackwell takes the issue of silenced females beyond plot considerations and suggests that the Grimm silencing of females in their tales has an effect on the auditors of the written text (164–65).

14. Bottigheimer, *Bad Girls and Bold Boys* 112. Spinning and needlework in general continued to be an all-encompassing activity for girls in the

nineteenth century. Witness Sophie Alberg's injunction as late as 1852 regarding such tasks: "Diligence with the needle is a main part of womanly life and must therefore not be taught and endeared to the young girl as the most natural, daily task only when she begins to grow up, . . . but already when she is a child. Knitting really should be the young girl's constant companion" (qtd. in Kößler 4).

15. Bottigheimer identifies four subgroups. In the first, spinning forms the subject of the tale; in the second, spinning is an indicator of the character or characteristics of the female protagonist; in the third, spinning is an action that merely advances the plot; and in the fourth, spinning "symbolizes the female sex and/or onerous tasks per se" (*Bad Girls and Bold Boys* 118).

16. In other tales by Gisela von Arnim, this emphasis on the female community is equally strong. In her fairy-tale novel, *Das Leben der Hochgräfin Gritta von Rattenzuhausbeiuns*, Gritta assents to marriage with the prince in order to secure the safety of her eleven female friends. See my commentary to the first complete edition.

17. In Germany many Enlightenment educators and writers rejected the *Ammenmärchen*—the nursemaid's tale—as "lowly trivial literature" (Ewers 194) and suggested such material, while it may continue to be told by nursemaids, definitely did not need to be seen in published form.

18. Bottigheimer, *Bad Girls and Bold Boys* 14. (Compare also the preceding essay by Bottigheimer in this collection.—ED.)

Works Cited

Arnim, Friedmund von. *Hundert neue Mährchen im Gebirge gesammelt.* Ed. Heinz Rölleke. Cologne: Diederichs, 1986.

Arnim, Gisela von. Letter to Friedmund von Arnim. Ca. 1844. Freies Deutsches Hochstift/Frankfurter Goethemuseum. Hs. 12877.

Baader, Renate. *Dames des lettres: Autorinnen des preziösen, hocharistokratischen und "modernen" Salons (1649–1698): Mlle de Scudéry—Mlle de Montpensier—Mme d'Aulnoy.* Stuttgart: Metzler, 1986.

Bettelheim, Bruno. *The Uses of Enchantment: The Meaning and Importance of Fairy Tales.* New York: Knopf, 1976.

Blackwell, Jeannine. "Fractured Fairy Tales: German Women Authors and the Grimm Tradition." *Germanic Review* 62 (1987): 162–74.

Bottigheimer, Ruth B., ed. *Fairy Tales and Society: Illusion, Allusion, and Paradigm.* Philadelphia: U of Pennsylvania P, 1986.

————. *Grimms' Bad Girls and Bold Boys: The Moral and Social Vision of the Tales.* New Haven: Yale UP, 1987.

————. "Silenced Women in the Grimms' Tales: The 'Fit' between Fairy Tales and Society in Their Historical Context." Bottigheimer, *Fairy Tales and Society* 53–74.

Dégh, Linda. "What Did the Grimm Brothers Give to and Take from the Folk?" McGlathery 66–90.

Drewitz, Ingeborg. *Berliner Salons: Gesellschaft und Literatur zwischen Aufklärung und Industriezeitalter.* Berlin: Haude & Spener, 1979.

Ewers, Hans-Heino. "Märchen." *Kinder- und Jugendliteratur der Romantik: Eine Textsammlung.* Ed. Hans-Heino Ewers. Stuttgart: Reclam, 1984.

Fox, Jennifer. "The Creator Gods: Romantic Nationalism and the Engenderment of Women in Folklore." *Journal of American Folklore* 100 (1987): 563–78.

Gilbert, Sandra, and Susan Gubar. *The Madwoman in the Attic: The Woman Writer and the Nineteenth-Century Literary Imagination.* New Haven: Yale UP, 1979.

Grätz, Manfred. *Das Märchen in der deutschen Aufklärung: Vom Feenmärchen zum Volksmärchen.* Stuttgart: Metzler, 1988.

Grimm, Brothers. *Kinder- und Hausmärchen gesammelt durch die Brüder Grimm: Vergrößerter Nachdruck der zweibändigen Erstausgabe von 1812 und 1815.* Ed. Heinz Rölleke and Ulrike Marquardt. 2 vols. and suppl. Göttingen: Vandenhoeck & Ruprecht, 1986.

Jarvis, Shawn C. "The Hard Facts about the Bad Girls." *The Lion and the Unicorn* 12.2 (1988): 240–43.

————, ed. *Das Leben der Hochgräfin Gritta von Rattenzuhausbeiuns.* By Gisela and Bettine von Arnim. Frankfurt a.M.: Insel, 1986.

————, ed. *Märchenbriefe an Achim.* By Gisela von Arnim. Frankfurt a.M.: Insel; Leipzig: Edition Leipzig, 1991.

————, ed., with Roland Specht Jarvis and Werner Moritz. *Märchen aus dem Kaffeterkreis* [working title]. By Gisela and Armgart von Arnim and Herman Grimm. In preparation.

Joeres, Ruth-Ellen Boetcher. "Gisela von Arnim." *Töchter berühmter Männer: Neun biographische Portraits.* Ed. Luise F. Pusch. Frankfurt a.M.: Insel, 1988. 209–38.

Kößler, Gottfried. *Mädchenkindheit im 19. Jahrhundert.* Gießen: Focus-Verlag, 1979.

Kühne, Gustav. "Die Mährchendichtung von heute: Vier neue Mährchenbücher." *Europa: Chronik der gebildeten Welt* 22 Sept. 1853: 617–20.

McGlathery, James M., ed. *The Brothers Grimm and Folktale.* Urbana: U of Illinois P, 1988.

Röhrich, Lutz. "The Quest of Meaning in Folk Narrative Research." McGlathery 1–15.

Rosaldo, Michelle Zimablist. "Women, Culture, and Society: A Theoretical Overview." *Women, Culture and Society.* Ed. Louise Lampere and Michelle Zimablist Rosaldo. Stanford: Stanford UP, 1974. 17–42.

Rowe, Karen E. "To Spin a Yarn: The Female Voice in Folklore and Fairy Tale." Bottigheimer, *Fairy Tales and Society* 53–74.

Schoppe, Amalie. *Kleine Mährchen-Bibliothek, oder gesammelte Mährchen für die liebe Jugend.* Berlin: Matthisson, 1828.

Seeger, L. Rev. of *Dramatische Werke,* by Gisela von Arnim. *Morgenblatt für gebildete Stände* 52.39 (26 Sept. 1858): 929–33.

Steinchen, Renate. "Märchenerzählerin und Sneewittchen—Zwei Frauenbilder in einer deutschen Märchensammlung: Zur Rekonstruktion der Entstehungsgeschichte Grimmscher Märchenfiguren im Kontext sozial- und kulturhistorischer Entwicklung." *Mythos Frau: Projektionen und Inszenierungen im Patriarchat.* Ed. Barbara Schaeffer-Hegel and Brigitte Wartmann. Berlin: Publica, 1984. 280–308.

Tatar, Maria. *The Hard Facts of the Grimms' Fairy Tales.* Princeton: Princeton UP, 1987.

Waldstein, Edith. *Bettine von Arnim and the Politics of Romantic Conversation.* Columbia, SC: Camden House, 1988.

Werner, Johannes, ed. *Maxe von Arnim: Tochter Bettinas, Gräfin von Oriola 1818–1894.* Leipzig: Koehler und Amelang, 1937.

Zipes, Jack. *The Brothers Grimm: From Enchanted Forests to the Modern World.* New York: Routledge, 1988.

———. *Fairy Tales and the Art of Subversion: The Classical Genre for Children and the Process of Civilization.* New York: Wildman, 1983.

Little Brier Rose:
Young Nietzsche's Sleeping Beauty
Poem as Legend and Swan Song

Richard Perkins

Slumber, oh slumber, so tender and mild,
O wonderfully lovely royal child,
O Little Brier Rose, O Little Brier Rose!

—Nietzsche, 22 September 1862

FRIEDRICH NIETZSCHE passionately despises illusions, especially the ones we are most reluctant to give up, the ones we cling to most desperately. God dies, decomposes, and gradually disappears, moral values dissolve, and truth turns out to be our oldest and most enduring error. Everything is utterly and irrevocably in vain, aimless, senseless, and worthless. Catastrophic nihilism threatens to eclipse modern culture. His philosophy distills its iconoclastic message into radically troubling catchwords: will to power, superman, eternal recurrence. He attempts a transvaluation inverting all traditionally esteemed values and tries to open up a Dionysian play perspective beyond good and evil, beyond truth and falsehood, beyond being and nothingness. But despite all his ranting against our human, all too human, impulse to escape this world and its suffering, against our compulsion to invent other worlds transcending our own earthly experience so as to delude ourselves into thinking our lives possess metaphysically, ethically, or aesthetically determined meanings, he never once suggests dispensing with fairy tales. By playfully making believe in religion and metaphysics, science and art, we eternally resemble children (KSA 2: 493), and children display the innocence, the freedom, and the power we require to live our lives in a world made groundless by God's sudden death.[1]

He grew up among women and clergymen, this philosopher whose hammer was to shatter all our comforting values. He was unusually serious and intensely sensitive to nature. Other children called him the Little Pastor. He wrote melancholy poems. During one summer vacation, it was in 1860, as he wandered along the river Saale near Naumburg, a new realization came over young Fritz, the painfully clear recognition that his education promoted the state rather than culture. Together with his two most intimate comrades, Wilhelm Pinder and Gustav Krug, he resolved to organize an association meant to foster and to direct their creative impulses in art and literature and, as a result, to dedicate their education more formally to culture. He was fifteen years old. So it was that on Wednesday, 25 July, the three boys bought a bottle of red Naumburg wine and in a solemn, festive mood set out to execute their plans at the Schönburg ruins. Reaching the castle, they climbed rickety ladders up to the watchtower battlement, where, ensconced above all inferior concerns, they reviewed their noble aims and ambitions, concluded their vows, toasted their new association, and then, in an ultimate, consummating gesture, hurled the bottle into the deep and christened the union Germania.[2]

Nietzsche contributed some notable pieces to the Germania (HKW 2: 95–99). Among these were a lecture on "Greek History since the Peloponnesian War," an essay dealing with the Ermanaric legend, a symphonic poem entitled "Serbia," a lecture on ethnic origins and culture ("The Childhood of Nations"), a piece on "Napoleon II as President," a Hungarian march, a lecture on Byron's dramatic work, a musical composition called "Pain Is Nature's Keynote," a poem dealing with "Ermanaric's Death," and a lecture on "Fate and History" representing his earliest exercise in speculative philosophy. He was a precocious youngster. "Fate and History" actually anticipates the major themes dominating his mature writings, themes including will to power, superman, and eternal recurrence.[3] On 22 September 1862, he submitted a collection under the unassuming title "Seven Poems" to the Germania as an overdue contribution to its January 1861 meeting.[4] One poem was called "Little Brier Rose" (in German, "Dornröschen"). Its title explicitly recalls the

Grimm fairy tale known as "Dornröschen," which is used loosely as the poem's source.[5]

According to the familiar fairy tale recounted by Marie Hassenpflug and included by Jacob and Wilhelm Grimm in the *Kinder- und Hausmärchen* (No. 50), a childless queen goes bathing and encounters a frog who predicts she is soon to give birth to a daughter. When the baby is born, her royal parents arrange a great feast to celebrate her birth and send out invitations to their guests. Among those they consider honoring with invitations are to be counted thirteen wise women, enchantresses whose generosity to their daughter is to be sought. As it turns out, however, they are short on golden place settings, and so only twelve wise women can be invited. One needs to be dropped. So it goes. As the celebration draws to a close, the twelve wise women show their gratitude by bestowing miraculous attributes on the little princess, just as the Greek gods and goddesses give all their charming virtues to Pandora. The neglected enchantress, however, seething with indignation, suddenly appears to take her revenge. She pronounces a deadly curse. The young princess is one day going to prick her finger with a spindle and die. Luckily, one wise woman has yet to announce her wish, and she manages to ameliorate the wicked spell somewhat by reducing its death sentence to sleep. So the child is destined to sleep a hundred years.

Despite all her father's precautions against the curse, the princess, as a curious adolescent, does prick her finger and does fall into a deep slumber, together with everyone and everything else in the castle. Dense brier hedges spring up, encircling the castle walls, and as time goes on a fascinating tale about a charming young princess sleeping there, Little Brier Rose, circulates around the country. Finally, when a hundred years have come and gone, a brave prince arrives in the district and resolves to venture into the brier thicket where so many princes have already perished. The blossoming hedge magically opens up to let him pass, and he makes his way to the castle tower where the slumbering princess lies. Her beauty inspires him, and he kisses her softly. As she awakens, the castle too revives. In due time, the prince and princess celebrate their wedding and go on to live impossibly happy lives. Marriage is its own consummation. Her parents warn their little girl about sexuality, but she gets the curse anyway. She bleeds. For a seemingly interminable period, while time stands oppressively still, she awaits her darling prince. When he finally comes he will gently

129

penetrate her thorny inhibitions and rescue her. For him she will blossom and open up, and he will awaken her womanly desires.

Nietzsche's sleeping beauty poem radically revises this story. There is a sleeping princess in it, to be sure. But her slumbers are not a lamentable suspension wickedly brought about by a spindle prick or an angry curse. Sleep is her innermost essence. There is also a yearning prince. But although he seeks Little Brier Rose in her enchanted castle, he does not rescue her. She rescues him as he despairs. In almost every significant detail, Nietzsche's narrative inverts its folkloric prototype. The prince becomes the protagonist whose erotic longings are allegorically represented. We encounter an emerging sensuality, to be sure, but it is masculine in nature, and its resolution is treated not socially or psychologically, but metaphysically. Furthermore, the outcome is no comic and societal marriage. It is a tragic and mystical union. Despite its gushy sentiments and its trite romantic images, including glowing sunsets, gloomy longings, swelling waves, breaking hearts, rustling treetops, shimmering moonbeams, resounding horns, soaring swans, tolling bells, singing birds, and so on, its revisionistic innovations make it a poetically engaging composition. Like other juvenile writings, it also anticipates themes basic to Nietzsche's mature thought.

Little Brier Rose
Legend by F. W. Nietzsche

"What charming isle lies sparkling, out in the sunset sea?
The rosy clouds, the golden waters, glittering brilliantly!"
Thus the prince cries out as he stands at the gunwale rail
And gazes so intently at the beckoning cloud-wreathed isle.

The calm waves ripple gently, and gloomy longings pierce
The prince's aching heart and almost move the youth to tears.
"O woods!" he calls in passion, "Green German woods, profound!
Alas, that I might dwell in you, where jubilant horns resound!

"Where oak trees raise their branches into the clouds, upwards,
And there below live countless lovely, merry little birds,
Where brooks spill gently over blossoms and leaves enthralled,
I would dream and suffer forevermore, to behold the sunset gold."

These words the prince speaks sadly, the crew grows more distressed,
Then suddenly three wondrous swans come gliding, swimming past,
Lulling themselves in the sea, as its rippling surface parts.
The prince and his companions sense a saddening fear in their hearts.

The sun sinks deeper still, but the swans soar up to the sky,
From their snowy rustling plumage comes a song, a lullaby.
About Little Brier Rose, so lovely, in a marvellous woodland it tells,
Shimmering moonbeams illumine the sea, its water murmurs and swells.

In the woods, where whispering treetops sound,
Keep an ear to the ground:
There lies a princess in sweet repose,
In warm embrace a spring breeze blows
Blossoms in her golden hair.
Slumber, oh slumber, so tender and mild,
In your marvellous woodland castle there,
O Little Brier Rose, Little Brier Rose!

In the woods, where whispering oak trees sound,
Keep an ear to the ground:
Many a gentle prince comes down,
With sparkling robe, with glittering crown.
Charming golden strings intone:
Slumber, oh slumber, so tender and mild,
You wonderfully lovely royal child,
O Little Brier Rose, Little Brier Rose!

In the woods, where whispering oak trees sound,
Keep an ear to the ground:
The little birds sing many sweet calls,
The treetops murmur like tolling bells,
The spring breeze gently whispers its sound:
Slumber, oh slumber, so tender and mild,
O wonderfully lovely royal child,
O Little Brier Rose, O Little Brier Rose!

Three crowns the swans let drop, diffusing a sunrise glow,
A melancholy sadness swirls the prince in its vertigo.
His blood boils in its veins, his heart nearly breaks in its woe,
The billows rage and he leaps into the gloomy waters below.

The glittering crowns are visible still, the water tenderly foams,
And there upon the murmuring sea the sweet young princess comes,
Her shining, shimmering presence, all bathed in golden light,
She leads the prince to her castle in the woods submerged in night.

As I have presented it here, Nietzsche's ''Little Brier Rose'' is a composite reconstruction based on a sleeping beauty composition written

131

and subsequently rewritten in three successive versions (I, II, and III) between July 1859 and December 1860, while Nietzsche was still in his middle adolescent years (HKW 1: 95–96, 97–98, and 227–28). All these versions carry the title "Little Brier Rose." This integrated composite rendering editorially combines the young author's original, transitional, and final treatments, incorporating them as structural components into a cumulative poem adhering as closely as possible to the basic developmental patterns in its periodic revisions. It converts its diachronic exposition into a synchronic composition.

The composite possesses an outer frame and an inner core. As early as July 1859, Nietzsche briefly mentions two "Little Brier Rose" compositions in notebook entries (HKW 1: 108), presumably acknowledging their distinction. The frame is a narrative ballad comprising seven quatrains rhyming *aabb, ccdd,* and so on. Stanza 6, however, underscores the prince's resolution to drown in the sea with an *eeee* rhyme scheme. Metrically, every stanza begins with three lines possessing six stressed syllables and ends with the last line typically possessing seven. The present translation replaces the six stresses in the second line with seven. The core is a lyric ode including three octets. Each verse opens with a formulaic injunction and closes with an equally formulaic refrain. Rhyme schemes vary slightly between verses, but they approximate an *aabbcdda* pattern. The translation comes fairly close but deviates a bit. In version I, dating to July 1859, Nietzsche generates only the outer frame and numbers its stanzas 1–7. Version II, also dating to July 1859, gives framing stanzas 1–5 but replaces stanzas 6 and 7 with the opening verse in the inner core, apparently presenting it as the song to which line 2 in stanza 5 alludes in passing. With version III, dating to December 1860, the outer framework is completely displaced by its emergent core, now elaborated into three generally repetitive verses bidding the princess to go on sleeping. In this revision "Little Brier Rose" seems also to warrant the title "Swan Song" appearing in Nietzsche's July 1859 notes (KHW 1: 108). No other existing poem bears this title. Throughout these periodic revisions Nietzsche altered punctuation and diction, but there were no other substantive changes. With minor emendations, version III was transcribed, inserted into the "Seven Poems" collection, and submitted to the Germania society in September 1862. Apparently he considered it to be among his best poetic compositions.

The following composite German text follows the transcriptions presented by Hans Joachim Mette in the *Historisch-Kritische Gesamtausgabe*. The opening quatrains preceding the three assimilated octets are given as they appear in version II (HKW 1: 97), the octets reproduce the "Little Brier Rose" revision included in the "Seven Poems" collection (HKW 2: 86), and the closing quatrains following the octets are the last two stanzas in version I (HKW 1: 96). These excerpts have not been amended in any way, so they retain all their flaws.

Dornröschen.
Sage v. FWNietzsche.

Welch' Eiland glänzt so lieblich in der Abendgluth?
Die Wolken erglühen rosig, golden schimmert die Fluth:
Der Königssohn er ruft es, er steht an Schiffes Rand
Und schauet auf das wogenumkränzte Eiland unverwandt.

Sanft kräuseln sich die Wellen; den Königssohn durchdringt
Eine tiefe Wehmuth die ihn fast zu Tränen zwingt
,,O Wald, so ruft er innig, o grüner deutscher Wald
Ach könnt' ich in dir wohnen wo Hörnerjubel in Jauchzen erschallt,

Wo Eichen ihre Wipfel bis in die Wolken heben
Und unter ihnen lustig vielliebe Vöglein leben
Wo mancher sanfte Bach über Blätter und Blüthen rollt!
So träum und leid' ich immer, seh ich der Abendröthe Gold."

Der König sprach es traurig, traurig horchte die Schaar
Da zogen plötzlich vorüber drei Schwäne wunderbar
Die wiegten sich umkräuselt von der hellaufleuchtenden See
Dem König und seinen Genossen ward' es im Herzen bang und weh.

Die Sonne senkte sich nieder, die Schwäne doch schwebten empor
Aus ihrem weißen Gefieder drang ein Gesang hervor
Vom holden Dornenröschen im Waldschloß wundervoll
Dem Mond entquoll viel' Schimmer, die weite Fluth rauschte und schwoll:

Im Walde, wo die Wipfel rauschen,
Wollen wir lauschen:
Da ruht ein holdes Königskind,
Umsäuselt von lauem Frühlingswind
Blüthen fallen aufs gold'ne Haar.
Schlummre, o schlummre weich und lind

133

Im Waldeschlosse wunderbar
O Dornröschen, Dornröschen!

Im Walde, wo die Eichen rauschen,
Wollen wir lauschen:
Da naht manch' zarter Königssohn,
Es blitzet der Purpur, es glänzt die Kron.
Lieblich hallt goldner Saitenklang:
Schlummre, o schlummre weich und lind,
Du wunderschönes Königskind,
O Dornröschen, Dornröschen!

Im Walde, wo die Eichen rauschen,
Wollen wir lauschen:
Die Vöglein singen manch' süßen Schall,
Die Wipfel rauschen wie Glockenhall.
Leise tönet der Frühlingswind:
Schlummre, o schlummre weich und lind
O wunderschönes Königskind,
O Dornröschen, o Dornröschen!

Drei Kronen liesen sie fallen wie Sonnenaufgangsgluth
Dem König wurde so traurig so wehmüthig zu Muth.
Das Herz wollte ihm brechen, ihm wallte des Herzens Blut
Unter ihm erbraußten die Wogen, er sprang in die düstere Fluth

Noch sah man die Krone glänzen, die Wellen rauschten Lind
Da kam auf den Meere das holde Königskind
Ein goldner Schimmer ihre leuchtende Gestalt umfloß
Sie führten den jungen Köning zum nahen Waldesschloß.

The earliest outline suggesting a "Little Brier Rose" project dates to 1856, when Nietzsche was eleven or twelve years old (HKW 1: 363). It sketches out three connected parts. Part 1 was to include childhood memories and an apparition appearing in the forest. Part 2 was to include an episode at sea, a song, and homesickness. These components seem to anticipate most closely the "Little Brier Rose" series he eventually produced. He also took up its basic themes in a juvenile novella fragment entitled "Capri and Helgoland," a story projected in twenty chapters, attempted, and discontinued in July 1859 (HKW 1: 99–106), during the same month he actually began writing and rewriting "Little Brier Rose." The charming isle Nietzsche's prince encounters in the narrative ballad is modelled on Helgoland, a German island in the

North Sea. Part 3 was to include America, a dream, two fairies, and a return. We can only speculate about what role these suggestive elements were meant to play.

The poem's title recalls a German proverb: "Without briers, no roses" (Mieder 67). This bittersweet sentiment, pushed to desperate romantic limits where raging desire necessarily coincides with grieving despair, is arguably Nietzsche's guiding intuition. His gradually developing "Little Brier Rose" composition, artificially reduced by our reconstruction to a single poem within a poem, is essentially an exercise in radical displacement. What he really starts with is the narrative frame and its tragically destructive, mystically redemptive plot progression. A yearning and suffering prince gradually perishes, dying into his own unrelieved longings, as the goldmaking sun hopelessly sets and the restless sea grows ever wilder around him. His very desire to be at one with his own eternally feminine nature drives him to suicide. What Nietzsche finally ends up with, however, is the lyric core and its eternally recurring lullaby. The hero is gone. Only the still and unchanging transcendence he so desperately sought and ultimately attained by dying into its salvation remains. The narrative frame becomes no more than a mere subtext and pretext ineluctably preparing its core text within the suggestive context provided by Grimm and Perrault in their sleeping beauty tales. Consequently, we must literally read into Nietzsche's "Little Brier Rose" as it is presented here. We must spiral inwards, moving from its exterior frame to its interior core, exactly as though we were penetrating to the quiet eye motivating a hurricane. This process is its poetic meaning.

Consider the sleeping beauty slumbering in her enchanted castle. She obviously moves the wandering prince to passion, she apparently moves the warm spring breezes swirling around her in circles expanding outwards to animate the rustling treetops, the tumbling brooks, the soaring swans, and all those shimmering movements quickening her island realm, and she quite conceivably moves the surging waves and the sinking sun, symbolizing a restless mutability surrounding the prince. Yet, as a demiurgically endowed *primum mobile,* she never moves. She is a motionless, sleeping eye centering its hurricane, an axle hub maintaining its rolling wheel in motion, a slumbering beauty binding all oscillating, undulating, pulsing, sweeping movements to inescapable orbits encircling her immobile attraction. Perhaps she embodies Dante's divine love, "l'amor che move il sole e l'altre stelle" (380, canto 33).

She slumbers tenderly and mildly, impassively engendering expanding as well as contracting spirals. Everything is simultaneously loving and dying, winding in and winding out, ascending and descending along the anodic and cathodic pathways Heraclitus asserts to be one and the same. Setting sun and rising moon converge as Nietzsche's narrative reaches its romantic climax. Waxing and waning, the loving, perishing prince disappears under the churning waves, seeking annihilation and transfiguration.

All this is undoubtedly too rampant in its wildly intuitive, associative expression to be easily comprehensible. A more sober presentation is probably in order. There is a ship at sea. From its rail a prince gazes intently at a mysterious isle, wreathed with clouds, gleaming in the sunset. Sadness almost moves him to tears. It lures him irresistibly. He longs to dwell there in its idyllic landscape, dreaming and suffering, taking in the golden sunset. He cries out, giving voice to his passionate longing, and his crew listens in sadness. Meanwhile, the waves are gently rippling. Then three swans suddenly appear and swim past the ship. Fear and sadness once again well up in the prince's heart. The sun sinks lower still, yet the swans take to the air, and as they soar upwards their pure white feathers flutter musically, conjuring up a melancholy song about a sleeping beauty lying peacefully in a castle in the forest on this island gleaming in the sea. The waves are swelling, murmuring inarticulate moans. The swans let their crowns drop into the sea, and the prince's sadness grows in intensity. His heart is about to break. His blood boils in its veins. Now the billowing waves are surging. He leaps into the gloomy waters and drowns. The waves seem to grow calmer, and the ship's crew can still see the glittering crowns. Across the waves, a shining apparition comes, bathed in a golden, shimmering light. It is the slumbering princess, Little Brier Rose, appearing on the foaming sea to guide the desperate prince to her castle.[6] This is the story Nietzsche's swan song displaces, but it is nonetheless where our analysis must begin.

At least twelve major symbolic images are at work in the poem, creating its resonant possibilities. We might take up Cirlot's dictionary, consulting entries pertaining to oceans, ships, princes, islands, forests, swans, crowns, sleeping beauties, and palaces, as well as light, twilight, and water, to come to a fairly reliable reading suggesting a psychic journey into the unconscious in an attempt to realize unity at its mystic center, its innermost certainty, its *sanctum sanctorum* where all

136

tensions, oppositions, and contradictions are resolved in an ultimate conjunction. Our present approach to the poem and its meaning, however, will proceed along more organic lines. It will not focus on symbolic elements as closely as it will on dynamic developments and patterning relationships among these elements. Its basic conclusions may be practically the same as those drawn by interpretive methods relying on symbolic inventory alone, but it will enhance their reliability and specificity by examining the processes animating and motivating the narrative action.

As the legend develops, the sea surrounding the prince's questing ship grows more and more troubled. At the poem's outset the waves are described as gently "rippling," but later on they are represented as "swelling"; and when the prince's passionate suffering finally leads him to plunge to his watery grave, they are described as "raging." As his passion grows in intensity, the sea correspondingly picks up its intensity as well. The verbs Nietzsche uses to indicate this gathering crisis are "kräuseln" (ripple), "schwellen" (swell), and "erbraußen" (rage). The sea, moreover, does not merely mirror the prince's passions sympathetically. It symbolically embodies their urgency. Desires are very rarely simple. The oceanic multiplicity and inconsistency marking his romantic yearnings are reflected in the nouns variously designating their symbolic representation: "Fluth" (waters), "Wellen" (waves), "See" (sea), "Wogen" (billows), and "Meer" (sea). Regarded phenomenologically, passions are similar to the Roman Janus, looking forwards and backwards at the same time, backwards to the aching emptiness inciting us to appetitive desire and forwards to the satisfying object our desire seeks to still its craving. Passions are tinged with a suffering sadness oriented to what they painfully lack as well as with an inspiring happiness oriented to what they pleasurably desire. Satisfaction and dissatisfaction are intermingled. To want something is not only to desire it but also to miss it, to despairingly mourn over its absence and to joyously anticipate its presence at once. The sea is this gloomy, glistening longing, what the mature Nietzsche will come to see as Dionysos or the will to power.[7]

The prince is a sailor. His ship rides the sea's restless, relentless currents, mastering its unruly nature in its own way but still belonging to its contradictory undulations. He stands at its rail gazing longingly at the mysterious isle whose roots are in the watery depths but whose immutability provides a comforting contrast to the sea. As a mythic, mystic topos, this island represents a condition transcending his stormy desires. He turns to it not as to an object among desirable objects promising temporarily to satisfy his eternally recurring cravings but as to a redemptive aim whose attainment will completely drown out his thirst and grant him surcease within its quiet forest sanctuary. He wants to dwell there, surrounded by its lovely birds, its tumbling brooks, its golden sunsets, and comforted by its inner peace and tranquility. He wants to renounce the sea and all its churning needs. His ship is his joyfully and sorrowfully mounted will to transcendence. But it contains a tragic flaw. He urgently *wants* to cease wanting, and as a result he is immediately and inescapably involved once again in a passionate desire which perpetuates its own suffering. Sadness pierces the prince and almost moves him to tears. It overcomes his crew as well. Perhaps these sympathetic companions, mute as they might be, correspond to the reverberating chorus in Attic tragedy.

Then a sign is given. Three wondrous swans glide alongside the ship, elegantly passing it by, and as the sun sinks ever lower in the sky they soar upwards, rustling their chaste plumage to suggest a song. Apparently these emblematic swans are wearing golden crowns, since they later drop them into the raging waters, where they continue to emanate a glow suggesting sunrise. Perhaps these pure white swans are previous princes who have sought the island and attained it in a transfiguring sacrifice. Their crowns certainly attest to their royalty. Their grace and beauty equally attest to their harmonious natures, where all violent emotions are at rest and only poise and balance are in evidence. From their feathers, the prince comes to know a melancholy song telling about a sleeping beauty called Little Brier Rose, a song enjoining her over and over again to go on sleeping. Violent emotions well up within the prince. He obviously wants to sleep with her, to put his tormenting passions to rest. Then the swans drop their crowns into the sea. This is a necessary sign. In order to quiet his desires he must cast his princely strength aside and plunge hopelessly into their churning depths, dissolving his individuated will in their oceanic oneness. Only by submitting to absolute despair can he hope to become as sole and as whole as the swans.

This brings us once again to the sleeping beauty, the guiding princess, Little Brier Rose. We might describe three concentric circles enclosing an axis at their common midpoint. The outermost circle delineates the island, encompassing its immutable precincts against the mutable sea lying open and unlimited beyond its circumscribing, bordering curve. The intermediate circle represents the verdant forest, symbolizing the unconscious and its nurturing, vegetating powers. The prince's longing makes it an idyllic sylvan setting and excludes its darker terrors. The innermost circle is the castle where the princess slumbers, representing the microcosmic core, the occult center whose walls enclose and preserve man's deepest essence. The center point or axis is the sleeping beauty, the psychic animator whose guidance enables her princely counterpart to become whole. This simple geometric paradigm is meant merely to stress the princess's position relative to the domains (castle, forest, and island) within which she quietly reposes. Like Grimms' sleeping beauty, she is encircled, but not by impenetrable brambles. The circles circumscribing her slumber are akin to concentric ripples radiating outwards from an immobile pulsation. They are emanations. Like Grimms' princess, she is also asleep, but no neglected enchantress or spindle is to blame. She *is* sleep, sleep in which polar opposites coincide in harmonious union, expanding and contracting ripples, departing and returning emotions, agonizing and rejoicing suitors, advancing and retreating waves, rising and setting suns. Her name embraces wounding thorns and healing roses in a single mysterious conjunction. She is unity, a superordinate unity that transcends even the distinction between the one and the many. In the end, she *is* the turbulent sea. Like Nietzsche's own eternally feminine Ariadne, she possesses golden hair, and like her too she *is* the very labyrinth she safely guides the hero through.

A passage in Nietzsche's unpublished 1871 fragment on "The Greek Woman" hints at the elementary connection he sees between woman and sleep and gives us a deeper glimpse into Little Brier Rose.

> Woman accordingly signifies to the state what *sleep* does to man. In her nature lies the healing power that replaces what we use up, the salutary rest in which all that is immoderate circumscribes its urges, the eternal sameness with respect to which those given to excess and surplus regulate themselves. Within her dreams the coming generation. Woman is more closely related to nature than man is, and in all basic elements she always remains what she is. (KSA 7: 171)

Nietzsche seems to be anticipating this theme in his "Little Brier Rose" poems when he writes:

> Slumber, oh slumber, so tender and mild,
> O wonderfully lovely royal child,
> O Little Brier Rose, O Little Brier Rose!

It is a refrain repeated with only minor variations three times, monotonously, as though it were a lullaby. Sleep is woman's nature, healing, restricting, unifying sleep in whose native darkness unborn generations come to dream their dreams. Sleep is the feminine principle the prince must regain to restore his fragmentary existence and to restrain his excessive, transgressive passions. She is his storm's calm center, his hurricane's still and gentle eye. There is at least superficially something transparently regressive in this romantic longing. There is, however, an alternative reading that corresponds more closely to Nietzsche's later writings. According to this reading, the protagonist is not seeking absorption and dissolution but rather integration, reunion with his own complementary feminine potentialities. He is seeking a wholeness, a creative power enabling him to express his vitality in dispassionate actions rather than in passionate reactions. This would agree in principle with his ultimate play perspective, especially as it is illustrated in Zarathustra's discourse "On Those Who Are Sublime" (KSA 4: 150–52).[8] The heroic prince moves inexorably towards his ultimate conquest. His sublime will descends into beauty.

One other dynamic element in the story tends to support this tentative reading—the progressing sunset. The sun is already setting as the narrative begins. Evening is coming, a twilight transition that gradually dissolves everything into undifferentiated darkness. The sun's descent parallels the prince's decline. Indeed, the prince takes on solar attributes. He goes down into the sea to rise up again reborn, guided by a princess who comes walking across the water like Aphrodite or Jesus at Galilee. She, in turn, seems to be associated with the moon. As sun and moon alternate by day and night to rule the ocean tides, so male and female energies in oscillating, alternating balance drive the undulating urgencies symbolized by the sea. Since *die Sonne* is a feminine noun in German and *der Mond* is a masculine noun, what emerges is possibly a feminine masculinity and a masculine femininity underscoring the harmonious conjunction to be achieved. Furthermore, the sun's passage is also a swan song. Popular tradition maintains that swans sing most beautifully and sweetly just before they die, and it is in setting, drowning its brilliance in the sea, that the sun glows most beautifully, turning the clouds rosy, giving the waves a glittering, glistening, shimmering radiance, transmuting all there is into precious gold. Going under the waves, the heroic prince redeems his own gloomy despair and goes home to his own sea, home to his own island, home to his own forest, home to his own castle, home to his own sleeping beauty. He becomes who he is. The "Swan Song" version which ultimately displaces this heroic "Legend" lingers on as a reverberating reminder within whose chambers the prince's actions and passions vibrate in reticent silence. In its overt, explicit content, it retains only the haunting, exhilarating strain the prince now sings in voiceless unison with his fellow swans. In it he overcomes his heroic struggles and descends into superheroic beauty.

Assuming this interpretation is essentially correct, we can draw three elementary conclusions concerning Nietzsche's creative response to the Grimms' "Dornröschen." Firstly, he uses the Grimm fairy tale as a prototype on which to base his own transformative reconstruction. His narrative shares very few contact points with its standard predecessor: its title, its sleeping beauty, its yearning prince, its castle, and its encirclement motive. It continues, however, to assume Grimms' tale as its supportive context. Secondly, his wholesale reconstruction involves several basic inversions. The main protagonist is the prince. The princess sleeps owing to her redemptive feminine nature and not because she innocently falls victim to a malevolent curse. She is encircled by generative forces (balmy spring breezes) and not by degenerative obstacles (thorny brier hedges). The sleepwalking princess rescues and saves the prince and leads him to her castle to join her in sleep, not the other way around. Thirdly, Nietzsche consciously turns the existing fairy tale initially into a heroic legend and finally into a swan song. Consequently, the outer narrative frame becomes a subtext invisibly supporting its lyric text. It disappears into its culminating revision.

Considering his extensive involvement in the "Dornröschen" project over a period covering approximately six years, it is surely surprising to discover this: Nietzsche's overt public response to the Grimms is marked by an almost absolute silence. He cites their *Deutsches Wörterbuch* in his 1873 meditation on *David Strauss the Confessor and the Writer* to support arguments calling into question Strauss's alleged accomplishments as a stylist (KSA 1: 236), but beyond this single reference neither Jacob nor Wilhelm Grimm is ever mentioned in his published writings. Explicit references in his unpublished literary remains are also remarkably infrequent.[9] Fourteen direct citations exist. Ten appear in three juvenile philological studies written before Nietzsche was twenty years old: nine in essays dealing with the Ermanaric legend composed in June 1861 and October 1863 (HKW 1: 297 and 2: 293–312), and one in an essay composed in April and May 1864 dealing with Sophocles' *Oedipus Tyrannos* (HKW 2: 382). Four other references appear in mature notebook entries relating to German culture (KSA 7: 691 and 829, 13: 133, and 14: 172–73). From these later notes we can only draw sketchy conclusions regarding his response to the Grimm brothers and their work.

Firstly, he perceives Jacob and Wilhelm Grimm as representing the German Romantic movement and as expressing the desire to revive and to preserve the heroic traditions in which German culture discovers its roots. His allusions are quite obviously primarily to their scholarly researches undertaken in the *Deutsche Sagen* (1816–18), the *Deutsche Heldensage* (1829), and the *Deutsche Mythologie* (1835), and secondarily to their groundbreaking contributions to Germanic philology in the *Deutsches Wörterbuch* and the *Deutsche Grammatik*. Nothing in these scanty citations suggests any direct or indirect concern with the *Kinder- und Hausmärchen*. Allusions to *Märchen* elements, however, do emerge in passages where the Grimms are not mentioned by name. Secondly, he acknowledges their role in establishing contemporary German culture as a necessary one, but he also perceives the influence they continue to exert as a major obstacle to any further development in culture. Cultures restlessly and incessantly overcome themselves, and the conditions once conducive to their emergence during earlier phases in their evolutions invariably become hostile to their changing expressions during later phases. Thirdly, he views their orientations as otherworldly in character, locating meaning in an essentially irretrievable antiquity just as Christian religious impulses locate it in an utterly inaccessible eternity. Since the passages in evidence do not focus on the Grimms' work specifically—their names are variously and indeterminately associated with Goethe, Wagner, and Luther (KSA 7: 691), with Keller, Auerbach, and Heine (KSA 7: 829), with Schlegel, Brentano, and Schopenhauer (KSA 13: 133), and with Schiller, Hoffmann, and Rousseau (KSA 14: 172–73)—only very limited inferences are possible.

Secondary materials, including biographical, exegetical, critical, and bibliographical studies, provide few additional insights. Since Nietzsche says so little about the Grimms, this is not at all surprising. What might strike us as surprising, however, given this almost absolute silence regarding Jacob and Wilhelm Grimm in Nietzsche as well as in Nietzsche studies, are the ways he capitalizes on fairy-tale structures and elements in his writings and speaks about fairy tales themselves. This is particularly surprising since he never once mentions the Grimms in connection with the *Kinder- und Hausmärchen* collection. Nonetheless, we discover distinct and unmistakable allusions to basic elements in various folktales. At two points in *Thus Spoke Zarathustra* (KSA 4: 95–96 and 344) he alludes to the golden ball in "The Frog King" (No. 1).[10] At another point in *Thus Spoke Zarathustra* (KSA 4: 229) as well as in an unpublished fragment sketching a preface to *The Will to Power* (KSA 13: 454) he alludes to the getting-the-creeps theme in "The Boy Who Went Forth to Learn What Fear Was" (No. 4). There is also an obvious allusion to the punishment meted out to the wicked wolves in "The Wolf and the Seven Young Kids" (No. 5) and "Little Red Cap" (No. 26) in *On the Uses and Disadvantages of History for Life* (KSA 1: 272). Nietzsche also employs "The Life Span" (No. 176) as a parodic prototype in elaborately constructing Zarathustra's opening discourse "On the Three Metamorphoses" in *Thus Spoke Zarathustra* (KSA 4: 29–31).[11] "On the Three Metamorphoses" retains the basic syntagmatic and paradigmatic structures patterning "The Life Span" as a framework, but it replaces its ignoble zoomorphic stages with noble ones. The human spirit is still destined to pass through three metamorphoses, taking on sumpter, predator, and jester characteristics in turn, but the degenerating descent accompanying aging, emblematically represented by a donkey, a dog, and a monkey in the Grimm tale and its antecedents, is displaced by Nietzsche's regenerating ascent accompanying overcoming, illustrated by a camel, a lion, and a child. The satiric fable is reconstructed as a parodic parable. It is radically inverted. In particular, the second childhood Nietzsche describes is no longer a pathetic ending marked by infirmity and senility but rather an ecstatic beginning marked by levity and creativity.

Nietzsche occasionally comments on fairy tales in his writings, and in a long passage dating to summer 1873 (KSA 8: 212) appearing among his preliminary work on *Richard Wagner in Bayreuth* he expresses his antipathy toward *Märchen*. In this passage, he contrasts Wagner's creative relationship to a heritage he regards as having been brought to completion in scholarly research with other preservative treatments regarding this archaic heritage and its investigations as something still in progress. Although the contrast represents Wagnerian art as leading a folk song announcing a new beginning in German culture rather than as singing a swan song terminating the Romantic movement, and although Nietzsche here considers Wagner to be a creative genius overcoming Romanticism rather than a culminating spirit submerging with it, as he views him six years later in a preliminary note sketching out aphorism 171 in *Mixed Opinions and Maxims* (KSA 14: 172–73), the contrast is nonetheless significant since it agrees perfectly with Nietzsche's conviction that Romantic yearnings must now be rejected. We can draw at least two important inferences about Nietzsche's attitude toward fairy tales. Firstly, fairy tales are inferior to myths and legends. They represent a degradation, transforming heroic manly stories into old-womanly stories. Tragic myths and heroic legends are replaced by pathetic fairy tales demanding a happy comic ending. He renounces the flabby Romantic, nationalistic, democratic, and optimistic tendencies marking European culture, including those so prominent in fairy tales (compare Zipes) and demands more energetic attitudes. Secondly, fairy tales represent an abortive attempt to return to the naive spirit underpinning German culture. Contemporary Germans, lacking the requisite naive heroism, can never hope successfully to return to their nature, especially through the effeminacy and senility they foolishly exhibit in reworking and preserving fairy tales. It is a childishly silly mistake to attempt to sing the same forgotten song over and over again, and its results are devastating to culture. Genius lies in composing and in conducting a new song through which older remnants and fragments are redeemed and a new spirit is evoked. For these reasons, fairy tales are to be despised.

To suggest that Nietzsche objects to fairy tales because they express Romantic, nationalistic, democratic, and optimistic motives is perhaps a bit too vague. We might justifiably contend that he despises fairy tales for nearly the same reasons he despises Christianity, owing to its slave morality and its mendacity. Slave morality is sharply contrasted with master morality in *On the Genealogy of Morals* (KSA 5: 257–89). According to Nietzsche, master morality reflects a basic *Gut/Schlecht* value structure. Those who are capable and strong designate themselves as "good" and consequently regard those who by comparison are weak and incompetent as "bad." Goodness means excellence, and badness means inadequacy. When we evaluate a writer using the terms *good* or *bad,* we are employing this structure. Slave morality, however, turns master morality upside down and takes revenge on those who are strong and proficient by insisting on a *Gut/Böse* value structure. Here those who are powerfully constituted and effective are designated as "evil" because they are seen to represent a threat, and those who are botched and bungled consequently come to see themselves as "good" because they are harmless and vulnerable. Their very impotence becomes creative. Goodness comes to mean weakness, and potentially dangerous strength is renounced as evil. When we evaluate obedience as "good" and disobedience as "evil," we are adopting this structure. Fairy tales seem to exemplify a slave morality at many points. Many tales are wish-fulfillment fantasies betraying an impoverished spirit longing to compensate its weakness, immaturity, or oppression. Protagonists are generally deficient, mistreated, poor, or otherwise vulnerable diminutives. Power is generally possessed at the outset by malevolent antagonists who are arguably represented as wickedly evil precisely because they are strong, and it is usually seized in the end through trickery, cunning, luck, magic assistance, or wish-fulfilling piety. In short, Paul's promise in 1 Corinthians 1: 26–29 is realized:

> For consider your calling, brethren, that there were not many wise according to the flesh, not many mighty, not many noble: but God has chosen the foolish things of the world to shame the wise, and God has chosen the weak things of the world to shame the things which are strong, and the base things of the world and also the despised, God has chosen, the things that are not, that He might nullify the things that are, that no man should boast before God.

The weaklings thwart their strong counterparts simply because their own wish-fulfilling slave morality demands revenge against anyone who is superior, and in the process they justify their resentment by turning their "oppressors" into witches, wolves, wicked stepmothers, or transparently malevolent monsters similar to Herr Korbes (No. 41) who customarily end up getting just what they deserve. In addition to its underlying slave morality, it is also quite easy to discern a desperate mendacity in this enchanted fairy-tale world engendered by imaginative liars and cheats. They are characteristically so feeble in spirit that the truth—should they ever allow themselves to glimpse it—would destroy them on the spot. Supposing Nietzsche's polemic against fairy tales might be analogous to his polemic against Christianity, this reconstruction approximates a picture we might conceivably sketch. At least it represents a suggestive caricature. Yet much more detailed illustration and documentation would need to be done to shape and to delineate its tentative outlines. Other texts, including aphorism 270 in *Mixed Opinions and Maxims* (KSA 2: 493) and aphorism 46 in *The Gay Science* (KSA 3: 411–12), ameliorate this antagonistic position somewhat by indicating a more tolerant and even enthusiastic attitude towards fairy tales. In these passages, Nietzsche employs the term *Märchen* more generically to designate poetic fictions, heuristic illusions, artistic constructs, and similar systems, even including metaphysics and religion, and not merely to identify fairy tales in the ordinary restricted sense. "We no longer believe fairy tales," he writes in a notebook entry dating to 1867–1870, "but we feel their poetic strength nonetheless" (GW 2: 134).

Notes

1. Nietzsche's mature works are cited from *Sämtliche Werke* in the *Kritische Studienausgabe* (KSA) wherever possible. References to early juvenile writings cite volumes containing *Werke* in the *Historisch-Kritische Gesamtausgabe* (HKW).
2. Elisabeth Förster-Nietzsche provides details concerning this ceremony in *Das Leben Friedrich Nietzsches* 1: 132–33. For an interesting fictionalized account portraying this association and its role in Nietzsche's early cultural development, see his 1870 public lectures *On the Future of Our Educational Institutions* (KSA 1: 652–54).
3. "Fate and History" was written in March 1862 and presented to the Germania at its Easter meeting convened on 16 April 1862. His supplementary essays entitled "Free Will and Fate" and "On Christianity" were prepared and distributed almost immediately. Translations and annotations are provided in Richard Perkins, *Young Nietzsche and Philosophy: Three Juvenile Essays.*
4. Compare Elisabeth Förster-Nietzsche, *The Young Nietzsche* 95.
5. References to the *Kinder- und Hausmärchen* collection are to the seventh edition, published in 1857. Citations indicate tale numbers.
6. In the version I text printed at HKW 1: 95–96, the concluding line in the last stanza begins with the words "Sie führten," meaning "they led." This appears to be a corruption owing to a difficulty in deciphering Nietzsche's

handwriting or perhaps to a minor slip in grammar on Nietzsche's part. There were numerous slips in the manuscript emended in the editor's transcription. Mette documents these corrections in his critical apparatus (HKW 1: 453). In this case, reading "Sie führte," meaning "she led," makes better sense and is almost certainly correct.

7. Sea imagery is also employed to represent a restless will to power in *The Will to Power* 1067 (KSA 11: 610–11). Compare also aphorism 310 comparing "Will and Wave" in *The Gay Science* (KSA 3: 546).

8. This play perspective is examined and its close relationship to Nietzsche's superman is demonstrated in my essay on "The Genius and the Better Player."

9. The most complete indices are Montinari's "Gesamtregister" to the KSA (15: 309), Schlechta's *Nietzsche-Index zu den Werken in drei Bänden* (143), Mette's "Namen-Register" listings in the HKW (1: 470 and 2: 465), and Oehler's "Namen-Register" to the *Gesammelte Werke* (21: 328), subsequently cited as GW.

10. Jung also suggested this attribution during his 13 June 1934 seminar meeting on Nietzsche's *Zarathustra* (1: 107–08).

11. For closer treatments, see my articles on "Metamorphosis in Nietzsche and its Sources in Satiric Fable" and "How the Ape Becomes a Superman."

Works Cited

Cirlot, Juan Eduardo. *A Dictionary of Symbols.* Trans. Jack Sage. New York: Philosophical Library, 1983.

Dante Alighieri. *Paradiso: Text and Commentary.* Trans. Charles S. Singleton. Bollingen Series 80. Princeton: Princeton UP, 1975.

Förster-Nietzsche, Elisabeth. *Das Leben Friedrich Nietzsches.* 2 vols. in 3. Leipzig: Naumann, 1895–1904.

———. *The Young Nietzsche.* Trans. Anthony M. Ludovici. London: Heinemann, 1912.

Grimm, Brothers. *Kinder- und Hausmärchen.* 7th ed. 2 vols. Göttingen: Dieterich, 1857.

Jung, Carl Gustav. *Nietzsche's "Zarathustra".* Ed. James L. Jarrett. 2 vols. Bollingen Series 99. Princeton: Princeton UP, 1988.

Mieder, Wolfgang. *Das Sprichwort in unserer Zeit.* Frauenfeld: Huber, 1975.

Nietzsche, Friedrich. *Gesammelte Werke: Musarionausgabe.* Ed. Richard Oehler, Max Oehler, and Friedrich Chr. Würzbach. 23 vols. Munich: Musarion Verlag, 1920–29.

————. *Sämtliche Werke: Kritische Studienausgabe.* Ed. Giorgio Colli and Mazzino Montinari. 15 vols. Berlin: Walter de Gruyter, 1980.

————. *Werke: Historisch-Kritische Gesamtausgabe.* Ed. Hans Joachim Mette. 5 vols. Munich: Beck, 1933–42.

Perkins, Richard. "The Genius and the Better Player: Superman and the Elements of Play." *International Studies in Philosophy* 15.2 (1983): 13–23.

————. "How the Ape Becomes a Superman: Notes on a Parodic Metamorphosis in Nietzsche." *Nietzsche-Studien* 15 (1986): 180–83.

————. "Metamorphosis in Nietzsche and Its Sources in Satiric Fable." *Comparative Literature Studies* 22.4 (1985): 472–96.

————. *Young Nietzsche and Philosophy: Three Juvenile Essays.* Mt. Pleasant, MI: Enigma Press, 1979.

Schlechta, Karl. *Nietzsche-Index zu den Werken in drei Bänden.* Munich: Carl Hanser Verlag, 1965.

Zipes, Jack. "The Grimms and the German Obsession with Fairy Tales." *Fairy Tales and Society: Illusion, Allusion, and Paradigm.* Ed. Ruth B. Bottigheimer. Philadelphia: U of Pennsylvania P, 1986. 271–85.

Fairy-Tale Allusions in Modern German Aphorisms

Wolfgang Mieder

T HE PAST TWENTY YEARS or so have seen a regular flood of publications that contain serious literary or parodistic rewritings of some of the most popular Grimm fairy tales. Anne Sexton (1928–1974) published her volume of fairy-tale poems so appropriately called *Transformations* in 1971 and thereby followed Sara Henderson Hay's (b. 1906) *Story Hour* (1963), a volume of versified reinterpretations of similar tales.[1] German and American anthologies of such fairy-tale poetry by dozens of authors are ample proof that a literary subgenre of lyrical poetry based on Grimm fairy tales does in fact exist.[2] The same picture exists for prose anthologies, and there are also numerous books containing both lyrical and prose fairy-tale reworkings by many different authors.[3] Traditional fairy tales also play a major role as pictorial motifs in cartoons, comic strips, caricatures, and advertisements. The fact that paperback anthologies of these graphic renderings have been widely sold clearly demonstrates the continuing popularity of Grimms' fairy tales and their juxtaposed modern adaptations.[4]

For such well-known fairy tales as "Little Red Cap" (No. 26) and "The Frog King" (No. 1) we have impressive scholarly books and articles that include vast literary and iconographic examples of adaptations from the nineteenth and twentieth centuries.[5] And yet, despite this wealth of textual and interpretative material, there is one specific type of fairy-tale adaptation that has escaped the attention of scholars. Over the past fifteen years I have collected from the writings of German authors dozens of short aphoristic statements that allude to fairy tales in general or to specific tales and their individual motifs. These allusions can be found not only among the aphorisms of highly intellectual authors but also among the one-liners of modern graffiti. They represent *Schwundstufen* (remnants) of the original fairy tales and form a small subgenre of the aphorism, just as do the so-called *sprichwörtliche Aphorismen* or proverbial aphorisms (Mieder, *Sprichwort, Redensart, Zitat*). Accordingly, I label the texts discussed in the following pages *märchenhafte Aphorismen* (fairy-tale aphorisms).

Let us begin with an aphoristic definition of the fairy tale by Johann Wolfgang von Goethe (1749–1832): "Märchen: das uns unmögliche Begebenheiten unter möglichen oder unmöglichen Bedingungen als möglich darstellt" ("Fairy tale: indicating to us the possibility of impossible occurrences under possible or impossible conditions.")[6] This somewhat paradoxical "maxim," as Goethe called it, might serve as an appropriate leitmotif as we discuss the language, content, and meaning of these texts. The reactions of the various authors to fairy tales in general or to specific motifs appear to reflect this ambiguity between the wishful world of the fairy tale and the reality of everyday life. The dreams, hopes, and fulfillments expressed in fairy tales appear impossible in an imperfect world, but by relating our problems and concerns to the possible solutions in fairy tales, we tend to be able to cope with our sometimes desperate conditions. Gerhart Hauptmann (1862–1946) expressed this thought quite similarly to Goethe's statement in his aphorism "Der Märchenerzähler gewöhnt die Leute an das Ungewöhnliche, und daß dies geschehe, ist von großer Wichtigkeit, denn im Gewöhnlichen erstickt der Mensch" ("The teller of fairy tales gets people used to the unusual, and it is of great importance that this happens because mankind suffocates from the usual"; 1026).

How much the universal nature of fairy tales is also of relevance to people of the modern age was summarized by Elias Canetti (b. 1905) in the mid-1940s: "Ein genaueres Studium der Märchen würde uns darüber belehren, was wir in der Welt noch zu erwarten haben" ("A closer study of fairy tales would teach us what we can still expect from the world"; 61). But we are not to use fairy tales as escapist literature, as Stanislaw Jerzy Lec (1909–1966) warns us: "Glaubt den Märchen nicht. Sie waren wahr" ("Don't believe the fairy tales. They were true"; *Neue unfrisierte Gedanken* 26). Fairy tales, after all, also express cruel aspects of the social reality of the Middle Ages, and once we look at some of the individual scenes of cruelty and fear, fairy tales can in fact reflect the anxieties of the present day as well. Thus Lec claims that "Manche Märchen sind so blutrünstig, daß sie dadurch schon wieder keine mehr sind" ("Some fairy tales are so bloody that they actually cannot be regarded as such"; *Spätlese unfrisierter Gedanken* 129). The same idea is expressed by Josef O'Mayr in his aphorism "Die Schule des Mords und Sadismus beginnt schon mit gewissen Märchen" ("The schooling of murder and sadism begins already with certain fairy tales"; 53). Little wonder that Gabriel Laub (b. 1928) concluded that "Märchen gehören durchaus zur realistischen Literatur. Sie versprechen Glück und Wonne—aber nur im Märchen" ("Fairy tales definitely belong to realistic literature. They promise fortune and joy—but only in the fairy tale"; 27).

Looking at our technological world and its seemingly insurmountable challenges and problems leads aphoristic writers to question the hope for any fairy-tale future for humanity. Either the term "fairy tale" in their aphorisms takes on the secondary meaning of "lie," or the whole concept of a better world "once upon a time" is drastically negated:

"Der Technik kann man nur bescheinigen, daß sie die Zeit beschleunigt; daß sie Zeit spart, ist ein Märchen" ("One can only credit technology with the fact that it speeds up time; that it saves time is a fairy tale [i.e., a lie]"; Sigbert Latzel [b. 1931] 5).
"Die Statistik ist das Märchen der Vernunft" ("Statistics is the fairy tale of rationality"; Martin Kessel [b. 1901] qtd. in Welser 41).
"Auf das 'Es war einmal' des Märchens antworteten die Naturwissenschaften 'Nichts war einmal!'—und daraufhin war auch nichts" ("The natural sciences responded to the 'Once upon a time' of the fairy tale with 'Nothing was once upon a time!'—and as a result there actually was nothing"; Erwin Chargaff [b. 1905] 170).
"Märchen: Es war einmal ein Mensch . . . " ("Fairy tale: Once upon a time there was a man [person] . . . "; Jens Sparschuh 168).

151

The last example, by Jens Sparschuh, formerly of East Germany, creates an ironic pun by juxtaposing the term "fairy tale" with the common introductory formula "Once upon a time." With the nuclear threat and an endangered environment hovering over our heads, it might indeed come to pass that human beings *were* once upon a time.

Such thoughts bring us to textual examples that reflect on recent sociopolitical concerns. The Austrian author Zarko Petan (b. 1929) changed the introductory formula into the future tense to state his view that "Alle sozialistischen Märchen beginnen mit: 'Es wird einmal . . . ' " ("All socialist fairy tales begin with: 'Once upon a time there will be . . . ' "; *Mit leerem Kopf* 11). Six years later Birtha Gahlsdorf, a reader of the tabloid German newspaper *Bild,* submitted for publication the following *Spruch* or saying, which contains a similar ironic twist regarding the socioeconomic differences between capitalism and socialism: " 'Es war einmal,' so beginnen die Märchen im Westen. 'Es wird einmal,' so fangen sie im Osten an" (" 'Once upon a time there was,' so begin the fairy tales in the West. 'Once upon a time there will be,' so they start in the East").[7] With the same hope for improvements in the standard of living in what was once East Germany, Wolfgang Mocker penned the aphorism "Moderne Märchen beginnen mit: 'Es wird einmal . . . ' " ("Modern fairy tales begin with: 'Once upon a time there will be . . . ' "; 171). In all of these examples playing on the conventional introductory formula, "fairy tale" stands for a better future.

Aphorists with sociopolitical concerns also exploit the traditional closing formula of the fairy tale: "Und wenn sie nicht gestorben sind, dann leben sie noch heute" ("And if they haven't died, then they are still alive today"; i.e., they lived happily ever after). For those people who are sick of waiting and hearing yet another promise from their leaders, the following poster parody might be an appropriate cynical remark: "Und wenn sie nicht gestorben sind dann warten sie noch heute" ("And if they haven't died, then they are still waiting today"; Neumann 321). The traditional fairy-tale closing was also used by the Swiss satirist Albert Ehrismann (b. 1908) in a short text that reflects on the dangers of war as we move towards the end of the twentieth century:

Kinder

Und wenn sie nicht gestorben sind,
so leben sie noch heute:
in den Träumen von Vätern und Müttern, die hoffen,
daß ihre Enkel und Urenkel einst in Frieden würden wohnen können.

Children

And if they haven't died,
they are still alive today:
in the dreams of fathers and mothers, who hope
that their grandchildren and great-grandchildren might be
able to live in peace one day. (14)

Such pessimism is commonplace in these modern fairy-tale aphorisms. Politicians are seen as liars by Werner Sprenger (b. 1923), who believes that they are paying only lip service to whatever cause happens to be in vogue at any given time: "Die meisten Politiker sind nichts als berufsmäßige Hochstapler, die mit würdevollen Gesichtern die Märchen erzählen, die gerade am beliebtesten sind" ("Most politicians are nothing but occupational swindlers who with dignified faces tell those fairy tales which happen to be the most popular"; 29). Very aggressive against the "haves" of our society is Nikolaus Cybinski's (b. 1936) cynical aphorism "Märchen sind die Digestive der Satten, mit deren Hilfe sie versuchen, ihre alten Utopien restlos zu verdauen" ("Fairy tales are the digestive medicine of those who are full and who try to completely digest their old utopias with their help"; 44). And finally there is the telling aphorism by Rudolf Rolfs (b. 1920), which once again shows that fairy tales do represent basic human needs, desires, and laws: " 'Lieben Sie Märchen?' Ja, ich lese gern im Grundgesetz" (" 'Do you love fairy tales?' Yes, I love to read in the basic law book"; 36).

These basic laws or truths are also expressed in those aphorisms that allude to particular fairy tales and their motifs. Alluding to "The Frog King," the East German author Peter Tille (b. 1938) reminds us that "Wer dem Kind den Froschkönig vorliest, muß am Ende seine eignen Versprechen halten" ("He who reads the Frog King to the child must in the end keep his own promises"; 84). The old didacticism of the traditional fairy-tale message is maintained here, and Tille points out that the idea of keeping promises clearly affects children and adults alike. Nikolaus Cybinski, on the other hand, warns us that fairy-tale transformations cannot necessarily be transposed into the reality of our everyday lives, especially not when these tales deal with the final perfect outcome of human relationships: "Unsere neuerliche Sehnsucht nach Märchen ist gefährlich. Haben wir vergessen, daß aus dem Frosch nicht jedesmal ein schöner Prinz wird?" ("Our newest longing for fairy tales is dangerous. Have we forgotten that the frog does not turn into a beautiful prince every time?"; 29). This type of unromantic reflection also resulted in the reduction of this particular fairy tale to the new American proverb "You have to kiss a lot of frogs before you meet a prince" and its variant "Before you meet the handsome prince you have to kiss a lot of toads." Examples of these texts can be found on T-shirts, greeting cards, book marks, puzzles, posters, and so on; and in the meantime this proverb based on a fairy tale has even gained currency in Germany as a loan translation (Mieder, "Sprichwörtliche Schwundstufen"). The many collections of graffiti often include examples of this aphoristic, or better proverbial, parody of the first Grimm fairy tale. In fact, texts like "Man muß viele Frösche küssen, bevor man einen Prinzen findet" ("You have to kiss many frogs before you find a prince"; Maaß 137) and "Bevor du deinen Prinzen findest, mußt du eine Menge häßliche Frösche küssen" ("Before you find your prince you have to kiss a lot of ugly frogs"; Franz 73) have become proverbial in the German language as well. Finally, there are also two anonymous graffiti texts from the youth culture which allude to the sexual content of this fairy tale: "Mädchen, küßt eure Märchenprinzen, damit ihr seht, was ihr für Frösche habt" ("Girls, kiss your fairy-tale princes so that you see what kind of frogs you have"; Rauchberger and Harten 33) and "Lieber eine Nacht mit einem Prinzen als ein ganzes Leben mit einem Frosch" ("Better one night with a prince than a whole life with a frog"; Thomsen, *Wer im Bett lacht* 30). The colloquial usage of the word "Frosch" (frog) implies the meaning of "weak or scary", and so these texts are telling female views on modern sexual politics.

Reducing fairy tales to proverbial aphorisms is actually nothing new. Already in the nineteenth century the German humorist Wilhelm Busch (1832–1908) rephrased a central scene from "Hansel and Gretel" (No. 15) in the form of a wellerism filled with black humor: " 'Das wird ein warmer Tag!' sagte die Hexe, da sollte sie verbrannt werden" (" 'This will be a warm day!' said the witch when she was about to be burnt").[8]

154

The Swiss satirist Fritz Herdi, on the other hand, took the proverb "Was Hänschen nicht lernt, lernt Hans nimmermehr" ("What little Jack doesn't learn, Jack will never learn") and formulated the parodistic *Antisprichwort* or antiproverb with obvious sexual undertones: "Was Hänschen nicht lernt, wird Gretchen ihm später schon beibringen" ("What little Jack doesn't learn, Gretchen [Jill] will surely teach him later"; 2). Finally Heinz Müller-Dietz (b. 1931) has created the wonderful pun "Manche Gretel wird gehänselt" ("Many a Gretel is teased by Hansel"; 32) based on the name "Hänsel" and the verb "hänseln," which means "to tease." Although this is only wordplay, it very concisely negates the perfect relationship of Hansel and Gretel in the fairy tale. Reality is, to be sure, not as saccharine as the fairy-tale siblings would have us believe.

Moving on to a few examples based on the fairy tale "Brier Rose" (No. 50), we can see clearly how the content of these aphoristic remnants quickly moves from the sublime to the ridiculous. Franz Fühmann (1922–1984), the East German poet who became known for his fairy-tale poetry, uses "Brier Rose" in the following insightful aphorism to comment on the maturation process and the problem of appropriate timing: "Es ist die alte Geschichte von Dornröschen. Hunderte Ritter mußten elend im Gestrüpp krepieren, und vor dem einen, dem letzten dann öffnete sich das Tor, und er bekam die Königstochter, und das war kein Unrecht" ("It is the old story of Brier Rose: Hundreds of knights had to croak miserably, but in front of the last one the gate finally opened itself and he got the king's daughter, and that was no injustice").[9] According to Zarko Petan, however, mature modern women are much more awake and ready for the sexual encounter: "Dornröschen von heute sind wach und warten auf den Prinzen, der mit ihnen schlafen geht" ("Brier Roses of today are awake and wait for the prince who will go to bed with them"; *Vor uns die Sintflut*). Should these Sleeping Beauties by chance oversleep, modern technology will awaken them just in time, as the satirical aphoristic writer Helmut Arntzen (b. 1931) points out: "Eine stille Straße am Sommermittag. Das Auto biegt lärmend um die Ecke. Dornröschen erwacht, ehe der Prinz es küßt" ("A quiet street at noontime in the summer. A car turns noisily around the corner. Brier Rose awakens before the prince kisses her"; 17). The next two very similar rhyming couplets from the oral and written sayings of the German youth culture are mere wordplay, but they indicate how fairy-tale literacy plays a role in the humorous

155

communication of young people: "Auch Dornröschen / trug ein Höschen" ("Brier Rose, too, wore panties"); Glismann, *Ich denke*) and "Auch Dornröschen / trug kein Höschen" ("Brier Rose, too, wore no panties"; Thomsen, *Pissen ist Macht*).

The last text enters once again the sexual sphere, and it should come as no surprise to find numerous sexually oriented aphorisms based on "Snow White" (No. 53). In *Wer im Bett lacht, lacht am besten*—a collection of erotic one-liners, puns, graffiti, jokes, and aphorisms edited by Bernd Thomsen in 1986—we find three such texts: "Du hast den Körper von Schneewittchen—keinen Arsch und keine Tittchen" ("You have the body of Snow White—no ass and not even little tits"; 15);[10] "Lieber einmal mit Schneewittchen als siebenmal mit den Zwergen" ("Better once with Snow White than seven times with the dwarfs"; 37); and " 'Natürlich habe ich stets von sieben Zentimetern geträumt,' klagt Schneewittchen, 'aber doch nicht von einem nach dem anderen' " (" 'Of course I've always dreamed of seven centimeters,' complains Snow White, 'but definitely not one centimeter after another' "; 148).[11] Sexual promiscuity and the lust of the seven dwarfs led to the aphoristic question "Wußten Sie schon, daß Schneewittchen an keinem Tag in der Woche zur Ruhe kam?" ("Did you know that Snow White had no rest on any day of the week?"; Gernhardt, Bernstein, and Waechter 43). The anal preoccupation of some Germans is reflected in the altered verse "Spieglein, Spieglein auf dem Klo, / wer hat in unserem Büro / von allen Damen den schönsten Po?" ("Mirror, mirror, in the bathroom, who of all the ladies in our office has the nicest fanny?"; Thomsen, *Neue Büro-Sprüche*). After all this, it is not surprising that Bernd Thomsen was also in a position to collect the graffiti verse "Spieglein, Spieglein an der Wand— / wer ist die größte Sau im Land?" ("Mirror, mirror, on the wall, who is the biggest pig [in the sense of being obscene or dirty] of them all?"; *Wer im Bett lacht* 19).

The situation is not any different with parodies of the famous verse from "Rumpelstiltskin" (No. 55): "Ach, wie gut ist, daß niemand weiß, / daß ich Rumpelstilzchen heiß" ("Oh, how good it is that nobody knows that I am called Rumpelstiltskin"). The scatological rhyme "Ach wie gut, daß niemand weiß, / daß ich unabhängig scheiß" ("Oh, how good that nobody knows that I shit independently") has become quite popular among students and the youth scene in Germany.[12] This preoccupation with scatology is also evident in the more political statement "Ach wie gut, daß niemand weiß, / daß ich auf den Kanzler scheiß" ("Oh, how good that nobody knows that I shit on the federal chancellor" [i.e., that he can kiss my ass]).[13]

Crude sex, on the other hand, is expressed in yet another variation of this couplet, in which the person called "Rumpelheinzchen" might be interpreted as a trashy or no-good smallish male named Heinz who has had sexual intercourse with the female speaker of the altered fairy-tale formula: "Ach wie gut, daß niemand weiß, / daß mich Rumpelheinzchen stieß" ("Oh, how good that nobody knows that no good Heinz screwed me"; Biscioni 81). Luckily Gerhard Uhlenbruck (b. 1929), a prolific aphoristic writer and medical doctor from Cologne, rescues us from such base reinterpretations of fairy-tale verses by Germany's youth. His definitorial aphorisms "Rumpelstilzchen: Das personifizierte Prinzip der Neidvermeidung" ("Rumpelstiltskin: The personified principle of envy prevention"; *Frust-Rationen* 60) and "Auch die Anonymität hat einen Namen: Rumpelstilzchen" ("Anonymity also has a name: Rumpelstiltskin"; . . . *einFach gesimpelt* 48) deal once again with the basic human problems of honesty and identity that underlie the message of this fairy tale.

The most prolific "producer" of fairy-tale aphorisms is without doubt Werner Mitsch (b. 1936) from Stuttgart. He has published about a dozen books of aphorisms in which he often rephrases such folkloric genres as proverbs, proverbial expressions, legends, folk songs, and above all fairy tales.[14] I have found about fifty fairy-tale aphorisms in his works, ranging once again from general remarks concerning fairy tales in the modern age to reactions to motifs of the better-known fairy tales. Many of his texts are rather mundane, if not banal, while others are significant sociopolitical reflections on modern society, which is anything but a fairy tale. Some of the texts are based on proverbial structures, others contain marvellous wordplays, and there are also examples that are simply poignant prose sentences that shock the reader into critical thought by juxtaposing the aphoristic statement with the actual message of the traditional fairy tale. What follows is a list of twenty-two such aphorisms to show their range of possibilities both in style and content. While Werner Mitsch has interspersed these texts randomly throughout his books, I have ordered them according to the tales to which they allude, whether directly or indirectly. First come those aphorisms that comment on fairy tales in general:

"Die Gebrüder Grimm erweckten unsere Märchen aus ihrem Dornröschenschlaf" ("The Brothers Grimm awakened our fairy tales from their

Brier Rose sleep''; *Pferde* 11).
"In den meisten Märchen siegt das Gute. Deshalb heißen Märchen Märchen" ("Good wins in most fairy tales. That's why fairy tales are called fairy tales"; 12).
"Märchen heißen Märchen, weil man in Märchen nur insgesamt drei Prüfungen bestehen muß" ("Fairy tales are called fairy tales because you only have to pass a total of three tests in fairy tales"; 33).
"Deutsche Märchen haben kein Happy-End. In deutschen Märchen siegen Könige und Prinzen" ("German fairy tales have no happy-end. In German fairy tales kings and princes win"; 34).
In alten Märchen steckt oft mehr Wahrheit als in neuen Regierungserklärungen" ("There is often more truth contained in old fairy tales than in new governmental platforms"; *Hunde* 31).
"Sie bekam ihren Prinzen und der Prinz seine Gebärmaschine" ("She got her prince and the prince got his birth machine"; 32).
"Für Märchen ist die Welt zu hektisch geworden. Oder zu gut?" ("The world has become too hectic for fairy tales. Or too good?"; 58).
"In der guten alten Zeit, als die Märchen noch keine Elektronik im Leibe hatten" ("In the good old days when fairy tales didn't yet have any electronics in their body" [i.e., when there were no recordings and films of fairy tales]; *Das Schwarze* 55).

As can be seen from these texts, Mitsch is well aware that the Brothers Grimm and the various editions of their fairy-tale collection were instrumental in revitalizing the interest in fairy tales by people of all walks of life and age groups in Germany and elsewhere. He also feels that the fairy-tale world with its always-resolved trials and tribulations is quite different from social reality with its deceptive governments, dictators, materialism, technology, and male chauvinism. Little wonder that Mitsch asks in the last two aphorisms whether fairy tales have perhaps lost their effectiveness when nobody has time to tell tales any longer and when their oral or even written transmission has been reduced to recordings and films.

And yet, Mitsch obviously believes rightfully that Grimms' tales must still be in sufficient currency among the people, for otherwise his aphorisms based on motifs from specific tales would really make no sense at all. In each of the examples listed below, Mitsch clearly assumes that his readers have attained the level of cultural literacy that enables them to think of the actual fairy tale while reading the aphorisms that allude to them.[15] It is, after all, this interplay of tradition and innovation that brings about the meaningful communication between Mitsch and his readers.

These examples have been arranged by fairy tales according to the order in which they appear in the Grimm collection. Unfortunately many of Mitsch's aphorisms depend on fascinating wordplays that would be lost in translation. Therefore, I have included only those texts that suit themselves to at least some degree of meaningful translation:

"Rapunzel" (No. 12):

"Er war herablassend wie Rapunzel in punkto Haare" ("He was as condescending ['herablassen' = to let down, to lower] as Rapunzel in regard to hair"; *"Grund- & Boden-Sätze"* 21).

"Es war einmal eine Jungfrau, die wohnte in einem Turm und ging eines Tages zur Dauerwelle. Sehr zum Leidwesen der Gebrüder Grimm" ("There once was a young woman who lived in a tower and who one day got a permanent. Much to the dismay of the Brothers Grimm"; *Neue Hin- und Wider Sprüche* 77).

"Hansel and Gretel" (No. 15):

"Hänsel und Gretel verirrten sich im Wolf. Dort spielte Schneewittchen mit Rumpelstilzchen Golf" ("Hansel and Gretel got lost in the wolf. There Snow White played golf with Rumpelstiltskin"; *Bienen* 118).

"Gretel ist eine Hexe. Man sollte sie deshalb aber nicht hänseln" ("Gretel is a witch. But you shouldn't tease ['hänseln' is, of course, a wordplay on "Hänsel'] her because of this"; *Neue Hin- und Wider Sprüche* 93).

"The Brave Little Tailor" (No. 20):

"Ein guter Liebhaber schafft's fünfmal. Das tapfere Schneiderlein aber schaffte es siebenmal auf einmal" ("A good lover can do it five times. The brave little tailor, however, was able to do it seven times at once"; *Hunde* 96).

"Cinderella" (No. 21):

"Feminismus. Lieber Blut im Schuh, als einen Prinzen am Hals" ("Feminism. Better blood in the shoe than a prince around your neck"; *Das Schwarze* 88).

"Little Red Cap" (No. 26):

"Als die Großmutter ihre Märchen erzählte, sahen die Kinder vor lauter Rotkäppchen den Wald nicht mehr" ("When the grandmother told her fairy tales the children couldn't see the forest for all the Little Red Caps any longer"; *Bienen* 21).

159

"Aller guten Dinge sind drei, sagte der Wolf und nahm den Jäger als Nachspeise" ("All good things come in threes, said the wolf and took the huntsman as his dessert"; *Das Schwarze* 112).

"Wäre der Wolf im Rotkäppchen-Märchen nicht zahnlos gewesen, so hätte die Geschichte eine völlig andere Wendung genommen" ("If the wolf in the fairy tale of Little Red Cap had not been toothless the story would have taken a completely different turn"; *"Grund- & Boden-Sätze"* 93).

"Snow White" (No. 53):

"Die sieben Zwerge konnten dem Schneewittchen zwar den Kaffee reichen, nicht aber dem Prinzen das Wasser" ("To be sure, the seven dwarfs could serve Snow White coffee but could not serve the prince water" [i.e., they could not hold a candle to the prince]; *Das Schwarze* 16).

"Sieben Hügel machen noch keinen Berg und sieben Zwerge noch keinen Prinzen" ("Seven hills don't make a mountain and seven dwarfs don't make a prince"; 18).

"Durch glückliche Fügung bekam Schneewittchen einen Prinzen, der sich eines Tages zum Schneekönig mauserte" ("Through a lucky coincidence Snow White got a prince who one day changed into a Snow King"; 63).

"Rumpelstiltskin" (No. 55):

"Heute back ich, morgen brau ich, übermorgen mach ich der Schwägerin ein Kind. Wie gut ist's, daß es niemand weiß, daß ich wie mein Bruder heiß!" ("Today I'll bake, tomorrow I'll brew, and the next day I get my sister-in-law pregnant. How good it is that nobody knows that my name is the same as my brother's"; *Hunde* 93).

"Was nützt es dem Menschen, wenn er Stroh zu Gold spinnen kann und trotzdem ein Leben lang ein Rumpelstilzchen bleibt?" ("What good does it do a person if he/she can spin straw into gold and still remains his/her whole life long a Rumpelstiltskin?"; *Spinnen* 79).

This last aphorism in the form of a question can serve well to introduce some concluding remarks. The traditional fairy tales represent utopian steps towards a better life in which love, faith, and hope rule supreme. Those fairy-tale characters who do not achieve this state of bliss go to their doom, and they populate the so-called *Antimärchen* or anti-fairy tale that reveals the other side of the coin (Jolles 242). The many fairy-tale aphorisms assembled and discussed here for the first time clearly belong to the anti-fairy tale category, for they show primarily that modern existence is not at all like a perfect fairy tale.

Power, crime, violence, selfishness, greed, materialism, sex, and hedonism abound and prevent people from becoming responsible, fair, and compassionate individuals. Instead, many of us play the role of Rumpelstiltskin throughout our lives, never quite attaining our full potential as social beings. We hide behind a makeshift facade of deception like the emperor in Hans Christian Andersen's (1805–1875) popular tale "The Emperor's New Clothes," which the American poet Idries Shah (b. 1924) reduced to the telling aphorism "It is not always a question of the Emperor having no clothes on. Sometimes it is, 'Is that an Emperor at all?' "[16] The questions of identity, character, and truthfulness are all addressed in the old fairy tales, and when modern aphoristic and graffiti writers present us with laconic antipodes based on them, they express a deep moral commitment to bringing about a change towards a more fairy-tale-like existence. To every humorous, ironic, or satirical fairy-tale aphorism belongs a seriously positive fairy tale that might just show us a way out of the dilemma of modern existence. Let's be ever mindful of Elias Canetti's superbly formulated fairy-tale aphorism that was already quoted above: "A closer study of fairy tales would teach us what we can still expect from the world." Perhaps fairy-tale aphorisms might be helpful along these lines, as might the modern poems and prose adaptations that have been studied in much more detail (Bausinger). All these responses, reactions and revisions bear witness to the importance of fairy tales as part of cultural literacy in a world that is becoming increasingly heterogeneous. Drawing at least in part on the universal knowledge about humankind expressed in fairy tales, we might just be able to continue our search towards a utopian world.

Notes

1. Wherever possible I have supplied dates for the authors mentioned. Some of them are quite unknown and birthdates could not be obtained.
2. See Mieder, *Mädchen, pfeif auf den Prinzen!* and *Disenchantments.*
3. Prose anthologies include Claus and Kutschera; Fetscher; Konrad; and Mieder, *Grimmige Märchen.* Anthologies containing both lyric and prose adaptations include Frank; Gelberg; Jung; Kaiser and Pilz; Lauer and Mieder; Mieder, *Grimms Märchen—modern;* Rumold; and Scheibner.

4. See Horn's studies "Grimmsche Märchen" and "Märchenmotive"; and the following anthologies: Langer; and Ritz, *Bilder vom Rotkäppchen.*
5. See Dundes, *Little Red Riding Hood;* Mieder, "Modern Anglo-American Variants of 'The Frog Prince,' " "Survival Forms of 'Little Red Riding Hood,' " and *Tradition and Innovation;* Ritz, *Die Geschichte vom Rotkäppchen;* Röhrich, *Gebärde, Metapher, Parodie* and *Wage es, den Frosch zu küssen!;* and Zipes.
6. Goethe 498. Translations are all my own, but I thank my wife Barbara Mieder as well as my colleague and friend David Scrase for their helpful suggestions.
7. *Bild* 19 October 1985: 2. I owe this reference to my father, Horst Mieder.
8. Busch 67. For other wellerisms based on fairy tales see Mieder, "Sprichwörtliche Schwundstufen" 263–65.
9. Fühmann 164. See also Maurer; and Mieder, *Mädchen, pfeif auf den Prinzen!.*
10. See also the rhymed couplet "S' wär' nicht das Schneewittchen, / hätt' es nicht kühle Tittchen!" ("It wouldn't be Snow White if she didn't have cool tits") printed on the leaf for 6–12 March 1978 of a humorous toilet calendar *Locus vivendi 1978: Sentenzen fürs Klo* (Munich: Heyne, 1978).
11. This text might well be a German translation of the earlier English version that appeared in *Playboy* March 1982: 132: " 'Gee, guys,' said Snow White, 'I've always dreamed of getting seven inches—but not an inch at a time.' " On the transformation of fairy tales into jokes, see Jones.
12. Glismann, *Edel sei der Mensch.* This text is also cited by the folklorist Rainer Wehse (325) as an example of a fairy-tale parody. My research now shows that there is a whole subgenre of such short parodies.
13. Moriz. For more on the issue of scatological preoccupation, see Dundes, *Life Is Like a Chicken Coop Ladder.*
14. On Mitsch's proverbial expressions, see Mieder, " 'Wahrheiten.' "
15. On the concept and crisis of cultural literacy, especially in the United States, see Hirsch; and Hirsch, Kett, and Trefil.
16. Shah 145. I have also collected many German aphorisms dealing with this particular Andersen tale. It should also be pointed out that numerous aphorisms exist relating to *The Thousand and One Nights* and in particular to the magic words "open sesame," which are spoken to open the door of the robbers' den in the story of Ali Baba.

Works Cited

Arntzen, Helmut. *Kurzer Prozeß: Aphorismen und Fabeln.* Munich: Nymphenburger Verlagsbuchhandlung, 1966.

Bausinger, Hermann. "Möglichkeiten des Märchens in der Gegenwart." *Märchen, Mythos, Dichtung: Festschrift zum 90. Geburtstag Friedrich von der Leyens.* Ed. Hugo Kuhn and Kurt Schier. Munich: Beck, 1963. 15–30.

Biscioni, Renato. " . . . *außer Rolf, der klebt am Golf"": Kindersprüche—rotsfrech.* Munich: Goldmann, 1987.

Busch, Wilhelm. *Wilhelm Busch Gesamtausgabe.* Ed. Otto Nöldeke. Munich: Braun & Schneider, 1943.

Canetti, Elias. *Aufzeichnungen 1942–1948.* Munich: Hanser, 1965.

Chargaff, Erwin. *Bemerkungen.* Stuttgart: Klett-Cotta, 1981.

Claus, Uta, and Rolf Kutschera. *Total tote Hose: 12 bockstarke Märchen.* Frankfurt: Eichborn, 1984.

Cybinski, Nikolaus. *Die Unfreiheit hassen wir nun. Wann fangen wir an, die Freiheit zu lieben? Aphorismen.* Freiburg: Isele, 1987.

Dundes, Alan. *Life Is Like a Chicken Coop Ladder: A Portrait of German Culture through Folklore.* New York: Columbia UP, 1984.

———, ed. *Little Red Riding Hood: A Casebook.* Madison: U of Wisconsin P, 1989.

Ehrismann, Albert. "Gegen Ende des 2. Jahrtausends." *Nebelspalter* 26 (28 June 1983): 14.

Fetscher, Iring. *Wer hat Dornröschen wachgeküßt? Das Märchen-Verwirrbuch.* Frankfurt: Fischer, 1974.

Frank, Karlhans, ed. *Märchen.* Munich: Goethe-Institut, 1985.

Franz, Angelika, ed. *Das endgültige Buch der Sprüche & Graffiti.* Munich: Heyne, 1987.

Fühmann, Franz. *Zweiundzwanzig Tage oder Die Hälfte des Lebens.* Rostock: Hinstorff, 1973.

Gelberg, Hans-Joachim, ed. *Neues vom Rumpelstilzchen und andere Haus-Märchen von 43 Autoren.* Weinheim: Beltz, 1976.

Gernhardt, Robert, F. W. Bernstein, and F. K. Waechter, eds. *Welt im Spiegel, 1964–1976.* Frankfurt: Zweitausendeins, 1979.

Glismann, Claudia, ed. *Edel sei der Mensch, Zwieback und gut: Szene-Sprüche.* Munich: Heyne, 1984. N. pag.

———, ed. *Ich denke, also spinn ich: Schüler-Sprüche.* Munich: Heyne, 1984. N. pag.

Goethe, Johann Wolfgang von. *Goethes Werke.* Ed. Erich Trunz. Vol. 12. Hamburg: Wegner, 1953.

Hauptmann, Gerhart. *Sämtliche Werke.* Ed. Hans-Egon Hass. Vol. 6. Frankfurt: Propyläen, 1963.

Hay, Sara Henderson. *Story Hour.* Fayetteville: U of Arkansas P, 1963.

Herdi, Fritz. "Sprüch und Witz." *Nebelspalter* 30 (27 July 1982): 2.

Hirsch, E. D. *Cultural Literacy: What Every American Needs to Know.* Boston: Houghton Mifflin, 1987.

————, Joseph F. Kett, and James Trefil. *The Dictionary of Cultural Literacy.* Boston: Houghton Mifflin, 1988.

Horn, Katalin. "Grimmsche Märchen als Quellen für Metaphern und Vergleiche in der Sprache der Werbung, des Journalismus und der Literatur." *Muttersprache* 91 (1981): 106–15.

————. "Märchenmotive und gezeichneter Witz: Einige Möglichkeiten der Adaptation." *Österreichische Zeitschrift für Volkskunde* 86 (1983): 209–37.

Jolles, André. *Einfache Formen.* 3rd ed. Tübingen: Niemeyer, 1965.

Jones, Steven Swann. "Joking Transformations of Popular Fairy Tales: A Comparative Analysis of Five Jokes and Their Fairy Tale Sources." *Western Folklore* 44 (1985): 97–114.

Jung, Jochen, ed. *Bilderbogengeschichten: Märchen, Sagen, Abenteuer: Neu erzählt von Autoren unserer Zeit.* Munich: Deutscher Taschenbuch Verlag, 1976.

Kaiser, Erich, and Georg Pilz, eds. *Erzähl mir doch (k)ein Märchen.* Frankfurt: Diesterweg, 1981.

Konrad, Johann Friedrich. *Hexen-Memoiren: Märchen, entwirrt und neu erzählt.* Frankfurt: Eichborn, 1981.

Langer, Heinz. *Grimmige Märchen: Cartoons.* Munich: Deutscher Taschenbuch Verlag, 1984.

Latzel, Sigbert. *Stichhaltiges: Aphorismen.* St. Michael: Bläschke, 1983.

Laub, Gabriel. *Verärgerte Logik: Aphorismen.* Munich: Hanser, 1969.

Lauer, Rosemarie, and Wolfgang Mieder, eds. *Kein Hänsel ohne Gretel: Da lachen selbst die Grimms im Grab.* Frankfurt: Eichborn, 1988.

Lec, Stanislaw Jerzy. *Neue unfrisierte Gedanken.* Ed. Karl Dedecius. Munich: Hanser, 1964.

————. *Spätlese unfrisierter Gedanken.* Ed. Karl Dedecius. Munich: Hanser, 1976.

Maaß, Winfried, ed. *Worte der Woche: Die stärksten Sprüche bekannter Zeitgenossen.* Hamburg: Stern-Buch, 1988.

Maurer, Georg. "Näher der Wurzel der Dinge: Das Märchenmotiv bei Franz Fühmann." *Neue deutsche Literatur* 12 (1964): 111–27.

Mieder, Wolfgang, ed. *Disenchantments: An Anthology of Modern Fairy Tale Poetry.* Hanover, NH: UP of New England, 1985.

————, ed. *Grimmige Märchen: Prosatexte von Ilse Aichinger bis Martin Walser.* Frankfurt: R. G. Fischer, 1986.

————, ed. *Grimms Märchen—modern: Prosa, Gedichte, Karikaturen.* Stuttgart: Reclam, 1979.

————, ed. *Mädchen, pfeif auf den Prinzen! Märchengedichte von Günter Grass bis Sarah Kirsch.* Cologne: Diederichs, 1983.

————. "Modern Anglo-American Variants of 'The Frog Prince' " (AT 440). *New York Folklore* 6 (1980): 111–35.

———. *Sprichwort, Redensart, Zitat: Tradierte Formelsprache in der Moderne.* Bern: Lang, 1985.

———. "Sprichwörtliche Schwundstufen des Märchens: Zum 200. Geburtstag der Brüder Grimm." *Proverbium: Yearbook of International Proverb Scholarship* 3 (1986): 257–71.

———. "Survival Forms of 'Little Red Riding Hood' in Modern Society." *International Folklore Review* 2 (1982): 23–40.

———. *Tradition and Innovation in Folk Literature.* Hanover, NH: UP of New England, 1987.

———. " 'Wahrheiten: Phantasmen aus Logik und Alltag.' Zu den sprichwörtlichen Aphorismen von Werner Mitsch." *Muttersprache* 98 (1988): 121–32.

Mitsch, Werner. *Bienen, die nur wohnen, heißen Drohnen. Sprüche. Nichts als Sprüche.* Stuttgart: Letsch, 1982.

———. *"Grund- & Boden-Sätze." Sprüche. Nichts als Sprüche.* Stuttgart: Letsch, 1984.

———. *Hunde, die schielen, beißen daneben. Sprüche. Nichts als Sprüche.* Stuttgart: Letsch, 1981.

———. *Neue Hin- und Wider Sprüche.* Rosenheim: Förg, 1988.

———. *Pferde, die arbeiten, nennt man Esel. Sprüche. Nichts als Sprüche.* Stuttgart: Letsch, 1980.

———. *Das Schwarze unterm Fingernagel. Sprüche. Nichts als Sprüche.* Stuttgart: Letsch, 1983.

———. *Spinnen, die nicht spinnen, spinnen. Sprüche. Nichts als Sprüche.* Stuttgart: Letsch, 1978.

Mocker, Wolfgang. "Euphorismen." *Neue deutsche Literatur* 30 (1982): 171.

Moriz, Eduard, ed. *Lieber intim als in petto: Sponti-Sprüche No. 5.* Frankfurt: Eichborn, 1984. N. pag.

Müller-Dietz, Heinz. *Recht sprechen & rechtsprechen: Neue Aphorismen und Glossen.* Heidelberg: Müller, 1987.

Neumann, Renate. *Das wilde Schreiben: Graffiti, Sprüche und Zeichen am Rand der Straßen.* Essen: Verlag Die Blaue Eule, 1986.

O'Mayr, Josef Meier. *Wo lassen Sie denken: Weisheiten und Naseweisheiten.* Pfaffenhofen: Ludwig, 1983.

Petan, Zarko. *Mit leerem Kopf nickt es sich leichter: Satirische Aphorismen.* Graz: Styria, 1979.

———. *Vor uns die Sintflut: Aphorismen.* Graz: Styria, 1983. N. pag.

Rauchberger, Karl Heinz, and Ulf Harten, eds. *"Club-Sprüche": Eingesandt von Hörern der NDR-Jugendsendung "Der Club".* Hamburg: Verlag Hanseatische Edition, 1983.

Ritz, Hans, ed. *Bilder vom Rotkäppchen: Das Märchen in 100 Illustrationen, Karikaturen und Cartoons.* Munich: Heyne, 1986.

————. *Die Geschichte vom Rotkäppchen: Ursprünge, Analysen, Parodien eines Märchens.* Göttingen: Muriverlag, 1981.

Röhrich, Lutz. *Gebärde, Metapher, Parodie: Studien zur Sprache und Volksdichtung.* Düsseldorf: Schwann, 1967.

————. *Wage es, den Frosch zu küssen! Das Grimmsche Märchen Nummer Eins in seinen Wandlungen.* Cologne: Diederichs, 1987.

Rolfs, Rudolf. *Fragen Sie August Pi! Ein Circus d'esprit mit 1444 Widersprüchen.* Frankfurt: Die Schmiere, 1980.

Rumold, Barbara, ed. *Schneewittchen total: Bilder und Geschichten.* Frankfurt: Eichborn, 1987.

Scheibner, Hans, ed. *Das ist ja wie im Märchen: Satiren aus dem Volk.* Göttingen: Steidl, 1985.

Sexton, Anne. *Transformations.* Boston: Houghton Mifflin, 1971.

Shah, Idries. *Reflections.* Baltimore: Penguin, 1968.

Sparschuh, Jens. "Aphorismen." *Neue deutsche Literatur* 31 (1983): 168.

Sprenger, Werner. *Ordensunreife Gedanken I: Eindeutige Sätze gegen höchst zweideutige Zustände.* Freiburg: Nie/nie/sagen-Verlag, 1978.

Thomsen, Bernd, ed. *Neue Büro-Sprüche: Lieber die dunkelste Kneipe als den hellsten Arbeitsplatz.* Munich: Heyne, 1986. N. pag.

————, ed. *Pissen ist Macht: Neue Klo-Sprüche.* Munich: Heyne, 1986. N. pag.

————, ed. *Wer im Bett lacht, lacht am besten: Horizontale Graffiti, Witze, Bilder und Sprüche.* Munich: Heyne, 1986.

Tille, Peter. *Sommersprossen: 666 aphoristische Gesichtspunkte.* Halle: Mitteldeutscher Verlag, 1983.

Uhlenbruck, Gerhard. . . . *einFach gesimpelt: Aphorismen.* Aachen: Stippak, 1979.

————. *Frust-Rationen: Aphorismen.* Aachen: Stippak, 1980.

Wehse, Rainer. "Parodie—eine neue Einfache Form?" *Jahrbuch für Volksliedforschung* 27–28 (1982–1983): 316–34.

Welser, Klaus von, ed. *Deutsche Aphorismen.* Munich: Piper, 1988.

Zipes, Jack. *The Trials and Tribulations of Little Red Riding Hood: Versions of the Tale in Sociocultural Context.* London: Heinemann, 1982.

The Struggle for
the Grimms' Throne:
The Legacy of the Grimms' Tales
in the FRG and GDR since 1945

Jack Zipes

N O SOONER DID World War II come to a close than explanations were urgently sought to explain why the Germans had committed atrocious acts. Given the importance that fairy tales played in the German socialization process, particularly the Grimms' tales, is was not by chance that the occupation forces, led by the British, banned the publication of fairy tales in 1945 (Bastian 186). According to the military authorities, the brutality in the fairy tales was partially responsible for generating attitudes that led to the acceptance of the Nazis and their monstrous crimes. Moreover, the tales allegedly gave children a false impression of the world that made them susceptible to lies and irrationalism.

The decision by the occupation forces led the Germans themselves to debate the value of fairy tales,[1] and it should be noted that the Grimms' tales were practically synonymous with the general use of the term *Märchen*. That is, the Grimms' collection, especially during the Nazi regime, had become identical with a German national tradition and character, as if all the Grimms' tales were "purely" German and belonged to the German cultural tradition. Therefore, unless a distinction was made in the discussions about fairy tales and folktales after 1945, it was always understood that one meant the Grimms' tales. They ruled the realm of this genre, and thus they were also held partially responsible for what had happened during the German Reich.

Although the ban against publishing fairy tales was lifted by 1946, the discussion about their brutality and connection to Nazism continued into the early 1950s. There were two general arguments in this debate: (1) the Grimms' tales had conditioned German children to accept brutal acts and prepared them for a savage regime; (2) the tales had nothing to do with the barbarism of the Nazis; rather, the cruelty of the Nazis had to be understood in light of traditional German authoritarianism and socioeconomic factors. The controversy over the Grimms' tales was never resolved, largely because the viewpoints expressed could not be documented and because very little research had been done about the effects of fairy tales on children and adults. However, the debate about the Grimms' tales set the tone for their reception in both Germanys, and two distinctive Grimm traditions emerged in the Federal Republic of Germany (FRG) and the German Democratic Republic (GDR).

In fact, the overall reception of the Grimms' tales in the postwar period is a complex one, and there are numerous factors that must be taken into consideration: (1) the customary attitude of the German people towards the Grimms' tales as part of their cultural legacy; (2) the policies of publishers and the government; (3) the use of the Grimms' tales at home and in schools, libraries, and the mass media; (4) the influence of scholarly and critical works on the Grimms by academics, psychologists, and folklorists; (5) the differences in the reception of the Grimms' tales by children and adults, as well as gender differences; and (6) the references to the Grimms' tales in advertisements, commercials, and cartoons. In this essay, my focus will be limited to the ways creative writers in the FRG and GDR have responded to the Grimms' tales in short prose narratives and have sought to dethrone the Grimms as the ideological rulers of fairy tales. That is, I am concerned most with the *critical and productive* attitudes that German writers bring to their revisions of the Grimms' tales and how their attitudes are articulated in the reformulations of the Grimms' tales. Interestingly, the experiments with the Grimms' tales are not simply to be considered innovative attempts by contemporary writers to come to terms with the legacy of the Brothers Grimm; they must also be regarded as endeavors to explore, challenge, and define the cultural determinants and parameters of West and East Germany. In this regard, though there are clear differences between the revised Grimms' tales for children and those for adults, I shall not deal at length with them since these differences are often blurred and since I am more generally concerned with how the production of new "Grimm-like" tales goes against or with the grain of the Grimms' tradition.

West Germany

Once the Federal Republic was established in 1949, there was an apparent need to make compromises with the Nazi past and create propitious conditions to reclaim the German classics in the name of democratic humanism. Historians and other academics have often referred to the period of the 1950s as one of nonideology, when Germans were afraid of ideological extremes and preferred a middle if not neutral path in politics. *Nonideology* is a deceptive term. In fact, the prevalent ideological position at this point was anticommunist and procapitalist with many Germans fearful of conflict and another war. Nonideological, therefore, meant a rejection of Nazism, an avoidance of radical politics of any kind, an acceptance of a capitalist welfare state, and partiality for the conservative middle stream that promised economic security above everything else. Given the conservative if not patriarchal nature of the Grimms' tales, they were clearly suited for this period. Consequently, the Grimms' *Kinder- und Hausmärchen* was published and circulated again in the thousands, both as a collection and individually in single volumes.

Despite the short ban on fairy tales and the debate about their effect, the reception of the Grimms' tales never really experienced a rupture within the German socialization process. If there was a major change during the 1950s in West Germany, it was the elimination of the explicit racist interpretations and the more violent episodes of the tales in editions intended for children. Otherwise, the Grimms' tales quickly made their way back into the school curriculums, libraries, theaters, radio, and even television. A major fairy-tale society called *Die Gesellschaft zur Pflege des Märchengutes* (The Society for the Preservation of the Fairy-Tale Treasure)[2] was founded in 1955 to perpetuate the fairy-tale tradition, and this group had strong folk if not *völkisch* tendencies. Indeed, the climate for the reception of the Grimms' tales in the 1950s had not changed radically from that of the 1940s: the Grimms' tales were considered "purely" German and healthy for the soul of both young and old. The only thing missing was the explicit Nazi ideological framework that had previously set the conditions for the reception of the Grimms' tales.

If one were to talk about schools of thought that influenced the reception from 1949 to approximately the mid-1960s, there were basically four that were all in agreement about the positive nature of the tales: the psychological, the anthroposophical, the structural, and the moralistic. Though their approaches to the tales were and are different, each one of these currents stressed the healing and educational nature of fairy tales. In the case of the psychological movement, the Jungian school that had triumphed over Freudian psychology during the 1930s and 1940s remained dominant, whereby archetypical/mythic identification and the harmony of the anima and animus were the overriding foci of interpretations. Readers, so it was and is claimed even today, can learn to become whole if not wholesome through the absorption of fairy tales. Closely related to Jungian ideology, the anthroposophical mode of thinking, influenced by Rudolf Steiner and developed in practice at the Waldorf schools, stressed that fairy tales can help us regain touch with the innocence of childhood and the oneness with nature. The structural approaches to fairy tales were elaborated in different ways, but they were all geared towards the appreciation of the aesthetic composition of the tales as marvellous artifacts. Content and history were disregarded in favor of the morphological study of the tales, which were purported to be universal statements about the ontological nature of humankind. Here the moralistic approach complemented the structural insofar as it placed more emphasis on contents. The tales were often treated as transmissions of morals and ethics that contributed to the building of character. Through the emulation of a particular protagonist, one could learn to develop Christian charity, the proper work habits, patience, and so on.

From 1946 to 1966 there were hardly any major revisions of the Grimms' tales. It was as if they were sacrosanct and part of the healing process necessary for the rebuilding of a humanist German culture. There were indeed new collections of folk and fairy tales by other authors, but they were neither explicit nor implicit commentaries on the

Grimms' tales, though there may have been some influence by the Grimms' stories. More important was the prevailing desire to cure and reconstruct the German nation. Indicative of this attitude was the short preface that Ernst Wiechert wrote for the publication of his two volumes of *Märchen* in 1946:

> This book was begun during the last winter of the war when hate and fire scorched the earth and our hearts. It was written for all of the poor children of all of the poor people and for my own heart so that I would not lose my faith in truth and justice. For the world as it is depicted in the fairy tale is not the world of miracles and magicians but that of the great and final justice about which the children and people of all times have dreamed. (2: 7)

The more notable collections along the lines of Wiechert's compassionate and stimulating fairy tales published during the immediate postwar period up to 1965 were: Otto Flake, *Kinderland* (1946); Ina Seidel, *Das wunderbare Geißleinbuch* (1949); Hans Watzlik, *Girliz und Mixel* (1949); Hanns Arens, ed., *Märchen deutscher Dichter der Gegenwart* (1951); and Paul Alverdes, *Vom Schlaraffenland* (1965). Most of these works were not directly related to the Grimms' tales, but the general reconciliatory attitude towards the fairy tale determined the overall reception of the Grimms' tales during this period. The fairy tales were intended to help bring about a redemption from the past both for children and adults. In those instances where the Grimms' tales were used as the basis for "new" tales, the references were also redemptive. Two good examples are Seidel's *Das wunderbare Geißleinbuch* and Arens's *Märchen deutscher Dichter der Gegenwart*.

Though published first in 1925, Seidel's *Geißleinbuch* was reissued in 1949 and reprinted until 1962, and its popular reception reveals how strong the nostalgia for the Grimms' tales and the atavistic mythic tradition remained among Germans. The plot and setting of the book recall a longing for an idyllic, Teutonic lifestyle. Young Peter lives with his mother and father on the edge of a forest because his father is a forester. Each night his mother tells him a story, and one evening she tells him the tale about "The Wolf and the Seven Kids." During the narration, Peter asks many questions, and when it is over, his mother has him say his prayers and wishes him sweet dreams about the seven kids. From this point on, Peter has several dreams about visiting the mother goat and her seven kids, and each dream is an adventure that includes characters from the Grimms' tales: Red Riding Hood, her grandmother, the hunter, the Bremen Town Musicians, Hansel and Gretel, and the seven dwarfs. Towards the end of the book, he attends a wedding of a prince and princess and experiences a storm during which the father goat scares him because the goat, related to the Germanic goat who pulls Thor's coach during storms, jumps all over the place. Peter is comforted by the mother goat, who in the end turns into his own mother holding him on her lap and whispering that it was only a dream.

Seidel's narrative can be considered a maternal discourse: the tone and style are predicated on nurturing the imagination of the protagonist/young reader and especially on comforting the hero. All the gruesome elements in the Grimms' tales are modified and defused so that the fairy-tale characters appear to be part of one happy family. In fact, the restoration of the family and German tradition through the fairy tale is the major theme of the book, and its atavistic quality made it useful for the healing of the wounds of the postwar period, but it did not point to utopian alternatives for a better future.

Jens Tismar has argued that most of the fairy tales printed or written in the immediate postwar period were mainly concerned with reestablishing continuity with German tradition in an unhistorical and uncritical way (133–39). In particular, he criticizes Arens's *Märchen deutscher Dichter der Gegenwart* for its retrogressive tendencies and claims that the title is misleading since most of the forty-one tales were written before 1945, and many of the authors had contributed to the *völkisch* cause during the Nazi period, including Arens himself.

> Evidently the keyword "contemporary German poets" was to include that period from the end of the 19th century to the postwar years as a continuity not to be questioned and not to be more exactly determined than it was. In other words, since the Nazi period could not be undone, this fairy-tale book provided the consolation that the poets, insofar as they might have stood above their times, made something beautiful that will have permanence and last over the years and beyond catastrophes. For none of the contributions to the volume sheds clear light on the respective historical situation. (Tismar 133)

As Tismar points out, there are only two tales that had immediate relevance for the postwar situation in Germany, and interestingly they are tales with a direct reference to the Grimms' "The Sweet Porridge":

Flake's *Das Milchbrünnchen* and Luise Rinser's *Das Märchen vom Mäusetöpfchen*. Flake's tale originally appeared in 1931 and draws an apparent analogy with the Great Depression of that time. A water spring wishes to provide milk for all those who visit it, and the Christ child grants the spring its wish. However, the people abuse the abundant supply of milk, and the owner of the land makes a business out of it. The Christ child returns to the spring and empowers it to provide milk only for helpless animals and for those children who tell it a fairy tale in return for the milk. Rinser's tale, written after World War II, involves a poor cleaning woman and her daughter Hanni, who finds a dirty pot among some rubbish. The pot is magical and steals food and supplies from a grocer to help the poor family. The grocer tries to catch and get rid of the pot, but he is put to shame when he learns how poverty-stricken Hanni and her mother are. From that point on, the pot is no longer necessary, for the grocer decides to provide food and provisions for Hanni and her mother at no cost.

The emphasis in both these tales is on Christian charity, compassion for the downtrodden, and survival. Throughout the 1950s these themes reappeared in the analysis of the Grimms' tales, which were regarded as cultural treasures, and in new literary fairy tales, whether or not they relied on motifs and topoi from the Grimms' collection. By the late 1960s, however, the cultural climate and economic conditions in West Germany had changed, and there was little talk about reverence for German tradition, philanthropy, and healing the wounds of the past. If anything, the key slogans of this period had more to do with anti-authoritarianism, rebellion, revamping German tradition, and alternative cultural choices for the future.

In fact, there was a radical break in the reception of the Grimms' fairy tales, and several factors must be considered if one is to grasp the plethora of anti-Grimm fairy tales that have been produced since the 1970s.[3]

1. The student movement revolted against all the traditional institutions of culture and education and sought radical models from the Weimar period on which to base their own collective experiments to bring about greater democracy, if not socialism, in West Germany. In particular, the work of such progressive psychologists as Siegfried Bernfeld, Otto Kranitz, Otto Rühle, Alfred Adler, and Wilhelm Reich was rediscovered, their ideas were implemented in schools and collective daycare centers, and students began demanding and writing children's

books that corresponded to the antiauthoritarian ideology that prevailed from 1968 to 1972.

2. Radical fairy-tale proponents and writers from the Weimar period such as Edwin Hoernle, Hermynia Zur Mühlen, and Walter Benjamin were rediscovered, and their ideas stimulated contemporary writers to experiment with the traditional fairy tales. Pirated editions of Zur Mühlen's tales and Benjamin's theories were published by radical collectives and had a strong influence on writers and publishers.

3. In keeping with the student movement, left-wing publishing houses were established to promote a progressive children's literature: Basis Verlag, Oberbaum, and Das rote Kinderbuch in Berlin and Weissmann Verlag in Munich. Major publishers such as Rowohlt, Insel, Campe, and Beltz developed new series of experimental children's books. Radical journals of education, such as *betrifft:erziehung* and *päd. extra,* were founded, and children's literature became a topic discussed in leading journals throughout West Germany. In general the entire publishing industry adjusted its attitude towards publishing books for children. While traditional editions of the Grimms' tales kept appearing, there were pressing social issues ranging from war, racism, and sexism to economic exploitation and domestic problems that found expression in experimental fairy tales and in a more "realistic" literature that avoided speaking to young people in a condescending manner.

4. During the 1970s a new generation of young teachers entered the school system and initiated reforms that led to a greater demand for innovative children's literature that was antisexist, nonracist, and antimilitaristic. These teachers supported cultural experimentation in all the media including children's theater, films, and television.

5. The desire to produce new radical fairy tales came from students and adults, who apparently felt that the Grimms' tales that had been so much a part of their early socialization needed to be re-formed. In fact, the alternative fairy-tale realms imaginatively projected by adults are often utopian and dystopian options that provoke readers to reconsider the ideological message of the Grimms' tales as well as the prevailing ideology in their immediate surroundings.

While radical experimentation with fairy tales became widespread after 1968, there were a few significant transitional works published during the early 1960s. Even then there were writers who were dissatisfied with the reception of the Grimms' tales and who desired to embark on a new more adventurous path with the Grimms' tales in mind.

Strikingly, two of the first endeavors to break with the Grimms' tradition were revisions of "Hansel and Gretel": Hans Traxler's *Die Wahrheit über Hänsel und Gretel* (The Truth about Hansel and Gretel, 1963) and Paul Maar's "Die Geschichte vom bösen Hänsel, der bösen Gretel und der Hexe" (The Story about Evil Hansel, Evil Gretel and the Witch, 1968).[4] If any tale from the Grimms' collection had represented the perfect ideological picture of familial reconciliation for Germans after 1945, then it was certainly this tale that was often performed on stage during Christmas in Engelbert Humperdinck's operatic version. Nothing could be more holy than "Hansel and Gretel" for Germans, and this is exactly why Traxler and Maar created their antiauthoritarian tales. Traxler's book is a sober, tongue-in-check scholarly study that purports to demonstrate through photos and sketches of ruins, relics, manuscripts, and other documents that Hansel and Gretel were actually bakers, who stole the recipe for the Nürnberger Lebkuchen from an old woman who lived alone in a forest. Indeed, claims Traxler, who bases his evidence on the work of the researcher Georg Ossegg, Hansel and Gretel killed the old woman to obtain her recipe and became rich and famous because of the old woman's Lebkuchen.

Traxler's book, which has a format similar to a scholarly study, parodies the work of folklorists and traditional academics while at the same time debunking the idyllic biedermeier reception of the tale by transforming it into a tale of murder. Traxler indicates that there is something dark, dangerous, and evil concealed beneath the superficial happy end of the Grimm tale.[5] Like Traxler, Maar reveals in his collection of tales, *Der tätowierte Hund*, intended for young readers, that the poor witch was indeed murdered by Hansel and Gretel despite the fact that she was kind and wanted to help them. His short tale provokes readers to reconsider the truth about the tale and witches, for he asserts that the witch had lost her powers and had retired to the forest to build the most beautiful "*Hexenhaus*" in the world. Hansel and Gretel have no respect for her work or her age. Their only concern is to fill their stomachs and steal her jewels—obviously a reference to the pursuit of material well-being of Germans in the 1950s.

Both Traxler and Maar do not want simply to question the "truth" of the Grimms' "Hänsel und Gretel." They want to compel readers to consider possible alternatives to the Grimms' tales and to change the manner in which they receive fairy tales. The truth of the tale is not so much in the contents of the tale itself but in the authoritative and

175

authoritarian rules that govern the way tales are disseminated, interpreted, and accepted.

The key factor at the beginning of the movement to revise the manner in which Germans, young and old, receive the Grimms' tales was insubordination. The innovative writers of fairy tales did not want to follow the Grimms' tradition blithely and to subordinate themselves to ideas, rules, laws, and customs that had become suspect. Most typical of the new breed of writer/publisher was Hans-Joachim Gelberg, who played a major role in bringing about a new more emancipatory children's literature in West Germany. Soon after joining the Beltz Verlag, he edited a series of Jahrbücher der Kinderliteratur (Yearbooks of Children's Literature) and promoted the publication of highly experimental fairy tales that departed greatly in style and tone from the Grimms' tale. In section 2 of his first yearbook, *Geh und spiel mit dem Riesen* (1971), he published twenty different fairy tales in prose, verse, and cartoon, four of which (by Richard Bletschacher, Janosch, Lisa Loviscach, and Iring Fetscher) are direct parodies of Grimms' tales. Gelberg argued in his "Afterword for Adults" that

> the child's need for entertainment is not limited to traditional forms. There are many possibilities to create tension, and a good deal in children's literature begins new and entirely different every year. Poems, plays, reports, letters, pictures, photos—even the slick advertisements that resound in our ears every day can be fused to new contents if we learn to regard the entertainment of children, their encounter with language and form, not just in a one-dimensional traditional way. And it is in this way that even the good old fairy tale will take on a new aspect. (Gelberg, *Erstes Jahrbuch* 341)

As an example of what direction he thought the "new" fairy tale should take, he quoted the East German writer Franz Fühmann's poem "Lob des Ungehorsams" (In Praise of Disobedience, 1966), which is important to record in full here:

> They were seven young kids
> allowed to look into everything
> with the exception of the clock case,
> for that could ruin the clock,
> so their mother had said.
>
> They were seven good young kids,
> who wanted to look into everything

176

with the exception of the clock case,
for that could ruin the clock,
so their mother had said.

There was a disobedient kid
who wanted to look into everything
even into the clock case,
and so it ruined the clock,
just as his mother had said.

Then came the big bad wolf.

There were six good young kids,
who hid themselves when the wolf came,
under the table, under the bed, under the chair,
none in the clock case.
They were all eaten by the wolf.

There was one naughty young kid,
who jumped into the clock case,
for it knew that it was empty.
The wolf did not find it there,
and so it remained alive.

In this case the mother goat was quite glad.
(Gelberg, *Erstes Jahrbuch* 341)[6]

In keeping with the spirit of disobedience, Gelberg published Janosch's "Der Däumling" (Thumbling), which is a terse narrative about a son, who leaves home forever because he can never please his father, no matter what he accomplishes. To a certain extent, all the major "revisionist" writers of the Grimms' fairy tales since 1970 break with their fathers via the Brothers Grimm. That is, their rupture with the Grimms or challenge to the Grimms can be viewed as a critique of the older generation in Germany and a desire to project the possibilities for other modes of living and thinking. Chief among the rebellious fairy-tale writers is Janosch, whose remarkable book *Janosch erzählt Grimm's Märchen* (1972) signalled that the time for toppling the Grimms from their throne had come. As Gelberg, his publisher in this common affair, remarked in his afterword to this edition:

> The fairy tales of the Brothers Grimm originated in a time long since past and have been passed on by word of mouth. They present social structures that we have overcome or reject. It's said there that whoever is

177

poor must be humble and obedient—only this way can it happen that the poor man from the common people is rewarded, that the rich prince marries the miller's daughter. . . . In many variations and ideas that are often shrewd and continually new, Janosch blurs the schemes of the Grimms' fairy tales and parodies them without forcing anything. There are not many writers who could come to terms with these rigid fairy tales—Janosch senses with a reliable instinct where and how the tone of the folk can become captured in language. And yet his (fifty) fairy tales retain something of the timeless "truth" of fairy tales. (Janosch 250, 252)

Janosch holds nothing and no one sacred. His tales debunk the good, clean bourgeois values of the Grimms and reveal how inappropriate they are in the contemporary *Leistungsgesellschaft*, a society where achievement and money are the standards by which we measure ourselves. In his version of "Hans mein Igel" (Hans My Hedgehog), for example, Hans is gladly sent packing by his father because of his strange looks and habits. However, as soon as Hans becomes a famous rock and roll star, he is welcomed back by his father and the entire village. In "Doktor Allwissend" (Doctor Know-It-All) a farmer transforms himself into a rich doctor with the help of his wife, who has leaned that charlatanism is the basis of the medical knowledge that most doctors disperse. In "Vom tapferen Schneider" (About the Brave Tailor) a tailor is constantly rewarded for killing a king's enemies from afar with weapons that the king places at his disposal. Finally, when the tailor has weapons enough to destroy entire lands, he uses all his courage to connect them, after which he pushes a button and blows up the entire world. In "König Drosselbart" (King Thrushbeard) the daughter of a rich man defies her father, who wants her to marry a wealthy man with a chin like a thrushbeard. She runs away, joins up with a young hippie, and tramps about Europe until life becomes too hard for her. Then she returns home only to discover that the young hippie is the son of the man with the thrushbeard, and she consents to marry him since he has returned to the fold as well.

Janosch's tales deal with generation conflicts, hypocrisy, war, greed, the false dreams of the petty bourgeoisie, and sexism. His drawings and language are terse, sober, and unpretentious. It is as if he were the child from Andersen's "The Emperor's New Clothes," seeking to denude the Grimms' tales and the artificiality of contemporary German society.

Indeed, one could summarize the general attitude of the best fairy-tale writers from 1970 to reunification as one that seeks to denude the Grimms while exposing all that is false in West German society. But perhaps the expression used by Erich Kaiser is more apropos in describing the attitude of most of the writers who have revised the Grimms' tales. He uses the term *ent-Grimm-te Märchen,* or de-Grimmed fairy tales (448), to describe those tales created by authors who have reacted to an overdose of Grimms' tales and want to get rid of a bad habit by cleansing the tales of negative and useless elements. For him, "the common denominator of the de-Grimmed fairy tales, which are incidentally very different from one another, is therefore the rejuvenation of the basic components that can be utilized by the respective authors for pedagogical, sociopolitical critical, parodistic, or free poetical purposes" (449–50).

While "de-Grimmed" can be a useful term for many of the revised Grimms' tales, it suggests depletion or cleansing, and this process does not actually take place. I prefer the political term *Umfunktionierung,* or reutilization, because it suggests that German authors have taken the Grimms' tales and turned their function around so that the motifs and themes of the tales work against the old anachronistic ones through new, more rigorous forms and formulations. A "reutilized" Grimm tale breaks down the closure of the original to open up new perspectives not only on the original version but on contemporary social conditions and aesthetics. Since there are so many techniques that West German authors have used to reutilize the Grimms' tales, it is not easy to categorize them (nor should one necessarily do this). However, certain categories can be helpful in describing the types of experimentation conducted with the Grimms' tales since 1970. In all, I find six basic types: (1) social satire; (2) utopian; (3) pedagogical; (4) feminist; (5) comic parody; and (6) spiritual. In considering some examples of these types, I must emphasize again that I am using these categories primarily for descriptive purposes since they enable us to understand the critical and productive attitudes of the authors. Of course, the attitudes are often complex, and many of the tales can be considered under two or three headings. For example, a feminist tale may not only be a tale written against sexism and in behalf of women, but it may also be utopian and satirical. In essence, a tale may contain different voices (often depending on the reader) and carry on several dialogues all at the same time. Yet, at the bottom of *all* the reutilized Grimms' tales is a dialogue with the famous Brothers and their legacy.

Social Satire Fairy Tales

The satirical fairy tales generally have a twofold purpose of debunking the style and ideology of the Grimms' tales and of mocking the prevailing ideology of contemporary West Germany. Unlike the utopian revisions of the Grimms' tales, no alternatives to the existing social conditions are indicated. As we have seen in the works of Traxler, Maar, and Janosch, most authors of satirical tales demonstrate the destructive, hypocritical, and pathetic aspects of the Grimms' tales and West German society without leaving the reader with much hope for a better future. The general aim of the social satires is provocative and subversive: the reader is to reflect critically about the status quo of the Grimms' tales as classics and their relationship to contemporary social conditions, and is challenged *not* to accept the accepted. Some examples:

Max von der Grün's "Rotkäppchen" (Little Red Cap, 1972), published in Jochen Jung's anthology *Bilderbogengeschichten,*[7] transforms the Grimms' tale into a biting satire about conformism in West Germany. Whereas Grimms' tale implicitly warns youngsters and sets a lesson of obedience, von der Grün speaks out against conformity by showing how it can lead to fascistic behavior. His little girl, who receives a red cap with a silver star on it as a present, is made an outcast and ultimately attacked by a band of schoolchildren because she is different. Such stigmatization recalls Nazi behavior, for only after the girl and her family are beaten into submission, so to say, are they reintegrated into the German community.

Iring Fetscher's *Wer hat Dornröschen wachgeküßt?* (1972) contains thirteen sardonic versions of Grimms' tales that also mock different critical approaches to the tales such as the philological, psychoanalytical, and historical materialist methods. In "Cinderella's Awakening," Fetscher depicts how the poor exploited maiden does not wait for a fairy godmother to help her. Instead, she organizes all the maids in her town to demand better wages and working conditions. When she founds a union and has success, the prince hears about her, and upon meeting her, proposes. However, she does not want to betray her movement and tells the prince that if he really loves her, he will convince his father, the king, to abolish the feudal conditions in his land and to recognize the union. The king reacts violently and has Cinderella arrested. After she serves her term, she emigrates to America where there are no princes and kings, and the prince is said to have committed suicide.

In Peter Paul Zahl's "Die Rückkehr der Meisterdiebe" (The Return of the Master Thieves), published in the anthology *Deutsche Märchen* (1981), edited by Günter Kämpf und Vilma Link,[8] two brothers, after many years of separation, return home one after the other to their poor parents, who live in the Kreuzberg section of Berlin. Since the first one is a common thief, his parents turn him in to the police, and he is imprisoned. The second one is a rich real estate speculator, and he takes care of his parents by sending them to an old-age home. Then he buys their decrepit building and has it torn down to make way for a profitable parking lot. Zahl ends his story by commenting, "if he hasn't died yet, he's still, since we live in times in which mere wishing does not help, living today in a splendid villa in the south side of the city" (148).

The acrimonious tone of Zahl's and also Janosch's tales and the sarcastic critique of the false values resulting from the so-called economic miracle in West Germany can also be found in Margaret Kassajep's amusing book, *"Deutsche Hausmärchen" frisch getrimmt* ("German Household Tales" Freshly Trimmed, 1980). Her twenty-eight radical tales were originally published in the newspaper *Die Süddeutsche* and focused on the savage and brutal quality of life in West Germany. For instance, in "Rotkäppchen mit Sturzhelm" (Little Red Cap with Crash Helmet), the granddaughter and her friend Wolfi kill grandmother in an old-age home because they want her money. Then the two lovers take off for Copenhagen on Wolfi's Suzuki, feeling no remorse about their crime. In "König Drosselbarts Ende" (King Thrushbeard's End), a ruthless entrepeneur drives another businessman into bankruptcy because the businessman's daughter had mocked him during a tennis match and had called him King Thrushbeard. Now poor, the businessman's daughter is driven to study and work hard at menial jobs until she is finally employed by Thrushbeard. Then she puts to use everything she has learned to drive Thrushbeard into bankruptcy and opens her own large banking account in Switzerland.

Utopian Fairy Tales

Whereas the satirical fairy tale often has a skeptical or cynical viewpoint about social change, the plot of the utopian fairy tale most often maps out the possibility for alternative lifestyles. Implicit is a major critique of the Grimms' tales that are primarily concerned with individual happiness and power: utopian fairy tales depict change through collective action and equal participation in the benefits of such work. The humor in these tales tends to be more burlesque than satirical, and the central theme is the overcoming of oppression.

The early children's books of Basis Verlag published at the beginning of the 1970s all tend to have a utopian message. For example, *Zwei Korken für Schlienz* (Two Corks for Schlienz) is a highly innovative revision of the Grimms' "How Six Made Their Way in the World." Using photographs of real people acting out fictitious roles in contemporary Berlin as illustrations, the story focuses on housing problems and exploitation by landlords. Four young people (all in their twenties) decide to live together: Schlienz, who can smell extraordinarily well; Minzl, who can hear long distances; Gorch, who can run faster than cars; and Atta, who is tremendously strong. They rent an apartment, and the landlord tries to cheat them. However, they are too smart for him, ultimately organizing the other tenants in the entire building to fight an arbitrary hike in the rent. Although they use their extraordinary talents to the collective's advantage, they have difficulties because the tenants come from different classes (teacher, bank clerk, metal worker, insurance inspector and railroad worker) and have different interests. So the landlord is able to play upon the divisiveness in the coalition and, with the help of the police, defeat the tenants' strike. Schlienz, Minzl, Gorch and Atta are arrested. Nevertheless, while in prison, they reconsider their strategy and make plans so that they can be successful the next time they try to organize the tenants. Although the four heroes (two men and two women) do not succeed, the plot indicates that they are not dejected and hope to learn from their mistakes. Here the emphasis is not so much on gaining a victory but on creating a sense of need for collective action.

However, in Friedrich Karl Waechter's *Tischlein deck dich und Knüppel aus dem Sack* (Table Be Covered and Stick Out of the Sack, 1972), there is a victory of the collective, and it is sweet. Waechter's tale takes place in a small town named Breitenrode a long time ago. (From the illustrations by Waechter himself the time can be estimated to be the early twentieth century.) Fat Jacob Bock, who owns a large lumber mill and most of the town, exploits his workers to the utmost. When a young carpenter named Philip invents a magic table that provides all the food one can eat upon command and a powerful stick that jumps out of a sack to hit people, Bock appropriates these inventions since they were done on company time. However, Philip, his fellow workers, and an elf named Xram (Marx spelled backwards) band together and expose Bock's duplicity. Eventually, they drive him out of town and share the fruits of their labor with one another. The reading of this tale (along with the visuals) becomes a learning process about socialization and work in capitalist society. The workers experience how the products of collective labor are expropriated by Bock, and with the help of Xram (i.e., the insights of Marx) they learn to take control of the products of their own labor and share them equally among themselves.

The utopian fairy tales are generally based on wish fulfillments, yearnings for a better life. In Irmela Brender's "Das Rumpelstilzchen hat mir immer leid getan" (I Always Felt Sorry for Rumpelstiltskin, 1976), the author suggests that Rumpelstiltskin must have been a gifted, but very lonely, man. If only the miller's daughter had asked him to join her, the king, and their child, he probably would have accepted, and they *all* would have lived happily ever after. "But the way it is now in the fairy tale, there's no justice" (200).

Pedagogical Fairy Tales

Though their positive outlook towards social change parallels the utopian narratives, the pedagogical fairy tales are more concerned with eliminating violence, sexism, racism, and other elements that the authors consider harmful for children. Therefore, the major revisions of the Grimms' tales delete elements antithetical to the authors' conception of responsible socialization. The focus is on depicting the possibilities for harmony and a "healthy" development. There is very little humor in these tales, and any innovation is often compromised by a didactic message or a contrived closure.

Among the more prominent writers of the pedagogical movement in the early 1970s was Otto F. Gmelin. His critical study, *Böses kommt aus Kinderbüchern* (1972), argued that "books for children must be oriented functionally in regard to the total social strategy. They must be dialectical insofar as they must first cancel out the perpetual nonsynchronicites and contradictions according to the programmatic sense of an antipatriarchal action put into practice" (112). To present examples of his theories, Gmelin published with Doris Lerche *Märchen für tapfere Mädchen* (1978), in which he changed "Little Red Cap" so it ended with the wolf transformed into a young boy with black eyebrows and blond hair, who remains with Little Red Cap and her grandmother. In addition, his Hansel and Gretel go into the woods voluntarily to help their poor parents. Once lost, they encounter an old woman who had been banished to the forest by the villagers because she was no longer productive. Although she does not want to kill and eat the children, she does want to exploit them and make them work for her. After a while they manage to escape, not by killing her but by using some magical instruments; and they return to both their parents, who are glad to see them. As we can see, Gmelin diminishes the anxiety children might feel in reading this tale by making the children much more active in determining their fate. Gone is the nasty stepmother, the expulsion of the children, the cannibalistic witch, the helpless Gretel, the killing of the witch, the return home with jewels just to the father.

Like Gmelin, Burckhard and Gisela Garbe have retold the Grimms' tales from a more progressive viewpoint. Their book, *Der ungestiefelte Kater* (1985), contains thirty-two revised Grimms' tales, in which Burckhard Garbe as writer sought to retain such values as ''honesty, friendliness, helpfulness, gratitude, industriousness, and courage from the original Grimms' tales. To be sure,'' Garbe explains, ''I eliminated such authoritarian 'virtues' that serve the state as humility, obsequiousness, fatalism, inaction on the part of the individual as a result of submission to God, fate, or men, the acceptance of social injustice on the basis of axiomatic faith in God's justice, the nonquestioning of the 'necessity' of war, one-dimensional fixing of roles for women and men to the disadvantage of women'' (225–26).

Garbe's version of ''Hansel and Gretel'' reveals a pedagogical viewpoint different from Gmelin's. The mother beats the children and makes them work hard. However, when she proposes to the father that they abandon Hansel and Gretel in the woods, he refuses and joins forces with the children. Together they desert the mother in the woods, and she makes her way to a wise woman, who punishes her by making her work as hard as she made her children toil. Meanwhile Hansel and Gretel live peacefully and happily with their father even though they never become rich. In general Garbe favors simple role reversals in his tales so that ''King Thrushbeard'' becomes ''Princess Thrushbeard,'' in which the theme of the taming of the shrew is changed into the taming of the male chauvinist.

Feminist Fairy Tales

Obviously the feminist revisions of the Grimms' tales are related to the pedagogical fairy tales since they basically want to teach nonsexist behavior or to impart notions that contradict the stereotypical images of male-female relations found in the Grimms' tales. However, the focus is not so much on the pedagogical aspect. Feminist fairy tales tend to be confrontational and provocative, and often there is no strict feminist line that they follow.[9]

Typical of those tales that expose the Grimms' patriarchal attitudes and confront male exploitation is Rosemarie Kunzler's "Rumpelstilzchen" (1976), in which the miller's daughter refuses to give Rumpelstiltskin her child or to marry the king.[10] Of course Rumpelstiltskin becomes enraged and stamps his foot so deep into the ground that the door of the chamber flies open, which allows the miller's daughter to flee into the wide world. The rejection of manipulation by men is also apparent in Annette Laun's "Rapunzel" (1985), in which the prince seduces Rapunzel with sweet promises and then abandons her.[11] Later Rapunzel cuts off her hair and goes to live in a city where she gives birth to twins. One day she passes the castle of the prince, who has meanwhile become the king, and she enters a tower where she hears sad tones from the queen. Rapunzel calls her and tells her to cut off her black hair and make a ladder out of it. The queen joins Rapunzel, and together they live on.

This notion of female solidarity is perhaps best exemplified in Christa Reinig's tale, "Kluge Else, Katy und Gänsemagd als Bremerstadtmusikanten" (Clever Else, Katy, and the Goose Girl as the Bremen Town Musicians, 1976) based on three of Grimms' tales.[12] Clever Else becomes tired of being mocked by her father and fiancé. So she leaves home and recruits Katy, whose husband has locked her out of her house, and the goose girl, who has left her husband, to go with her to Bremen and start a rock band. On their way through the forest they scare a group of soldiers, who think the women are the Russians. The men abandon the house they were using as headquarters, and the women set up home together.

While most feminists have radically altered the Grimms' tales like Reinig, there are some like Svende Merian, who, in her book *Der Mann aus Zucker* (The Man Made of Sugar, 1985), has made slight variations to alter the passive roles and sexist ideology of the Grimms' tales. There are also more scholarly studies like *Scheewittchen hat viele*

Schwestern (Snow White Has Many Sisters, 1988) by Ines Köhler-Zülch and Christine Shojaei Kawan, who demonstrate the wide variety of tales with women as the major protagonists. Finally, unusual feminist fairy tales with motifs from the Grimms' tales can be found in various anthologies and journals such as the special issue of *Schreiben* entitled *Blut im Schuh: Märchen* (Blood in the Shoe: Fairy Tales, 1984).[13]

Comic Parody Fairy Tales

Though related to the socially satirical tales, the fairy tale as comic parody tends to mock the conventions of the Grimms' fairy tales without necessarily providing a socially relevant message. Nothing is sacred in the parody, and often both the Grimms' tradition and contemporary mores are mocked at the same time. Typical of Grimm parodies are three recent works: Uta Claus and Rolf Kutschera, *Total tote Hose* (1984); Heinz Langer, *Grimmige Märchen* (1984); and Chris Schrauff, *Der Wolf und seine Steine* (1986). All three books have highly amusing illustrations that reinforce the comic nature of the fairy-tale revisions. Claus has taken twelve well-known tales and rewritten them in the slang and hip language of contemporary German youth. For example, her version of "Snow White" starts like this: "The whole story all started because Whitey's filthy rich dad couldn't keep going without some broad. So he brought a horny old lady back to their place. She was an unbelievable mess, and the only thing buzzing in her bean was makeup and clothes. And whenever she saw another woman that looked more tremendous than she did, she became mad as a hatter. Well, Whitey looked amazingly hot, and that's why the old bag wanted to bump her off" (39). Claus follows the basic plotline of the Grimms' tale, but her witty slang undermines the romantic aspect of the classical version, and totally debunks all the characters and virtues of "Snow White" (Fig. 2).

Langer's technique is completely different from Claus's use of slang. He parodies thirty-eight of Grimms' tales with full-page illustrations facing brief passages from the classical versions. The illustrations are generally totally different from the texts, and the disparity between text and image creates the parody. For instance, in one illustration of "Snow White" (26–27) he depicts two dwarfs standing by the side of the road and trying to hitch a ride. Next to them is the glass coffin with Snow White, who has the core of an apple jutting from her mouth. Down the road one can see a hearse heading toward the dwarfs (Fig. 3).

Fig. 2. Uta Claus and Rolf Kutschera, *Total tote Hose* (Frankfurt a.M.: Eichborn Verlag, 1984). Illustration © Eichborn Verlag.

Langer's illustration of "Cinderella" (56–57) shows the prince, who has tripped over roller skates, flying through the air in the entrance of a disco. Throughout the book the anachronistic language and ideas of the Grimms' text are contrasted with cartoons that mix modern settings and characters with traditional fairy-tale motifs.

Finally Schrauff, whose terse narratives are illustrated by Karl Volkmann, mocks various aspects of the Grimms' tales by jolting the reader with unexpected combinations of motifs. For instance, one of his versions reads: "Once upon a time there was a prince, who found a sleeping Snow White. And since she lay there so beautiful and peaceful, he slit her throat, took her apple, and ate it himself." There is a touch of cynicism in all his tales since there is never a happy ending. One prince who looks for Snow White finds her coffin empty and himself turned into one of the common dwarfs. A frog, tired of being thrown against walls by princesses who want to see if he is a prince, decides to throw a princess against a wall, but she dies from the collision. Like Claus

187

Fig. 3. Heinz Langer, *Grimmige Märchen* (München: Hugendubel, 1984). Illustration © Heinz Langer.

and Langer, Schrauff focuses on implied meanings of the old tales for contemporary audiences. Most of all, their parodies achieve their effects by causing their readers to laugh at irreconcilable contradictions between the Grimms' mode of writing and thinking and contemporary social conditions.

Spiritual Fairy Tales

The so-called spiritual tales are either religious or moralistic in nature and tend to employ the Grimms' tales in a therapeutic and didactic way so that the reader may be uplifted. Generally speaking, the Grimms' version is not so much revised as it is reinterpreted to reveal its benefits for the individual reader's edification. Leading the way in promoting the spiritual effect of the fairy tales is the Kreuz publishing house with its series Weisheit im Märchen (Wisdom in the Fairy Tale), edited by Theodor Seifert. All the editions have basically the same format: the classical version of the particular Grimms' tale is reprinted, and then there are several explicatory chapters about the essential nature of the tale and how it leads to wholesome living.[14] In Seifert's own edition of "Snow White," interpreted as a demonstration of how one can win back a happy life that seems to have been lost, he begins by advising: "Let the fairy tale calmly have an effect on you. Try to capture the feelings that it stimulates. Let yourself be enchanted by its own power and vision. Let yourself be surprised by your own reactions. . . . Fairy tales are counselors and anticipatory images of the most different situations and difficulties of life. That is why we can use them with trust to orient ourselves because there is no personal intention of a particular author behind them" (8–9). Seifert then examines passages from "Snow White" and advises his readers on how they too might deepen their spiritual lives and see alternatives to a life that appears deadened.

While Seifert's tips for better living tend to be obvious and his tone condescending, J. F. Konrad's revisions of nine Grimms' tales in *Hexen-Memoiren* (1981) are modern and amusing. For instance, "The Frog King" is entitled "Der Lustfrosch" (The Lecherous Frog) and is told in the first person from the frog's perspective. All he can think of is seducing the princess, but as he realizes how much revulsion he causes and how much he makes the princess suffer, he decides not to persecute her anymore. To his surprise, his decision makes him feel humane, and the princess is then free herself to treat him with compassion. In Konrad's notes for the use of his tales at home and in the school, he comments: "The revision has been conceived with a view toward adolescents and is intended to help in connection with other media and texts to free sex and eros from egotism, exploitation, and boasting, and also from inhibition, besmirching and smut and to enable them to form a partnership that lives from consideration and fulfillment" (125).

East Germany

The postwar debate about the harmful effects of the Grimms' tales was always tied in the German Democratic Republic to questions about the cultural heritage. That is, once the communists solidified their power in 1949, all literature that was considered bourgeois was to be evaluated and appropriated in a dialectical sense to further the nation's progress toward genuine socialism and eventually communism (Steinitz). The Grimms' tales were rather easy to appropriate since they were considered part of the oral folk tradition and thus depicted how people from the lower classes overcame oppression and fought to improve their lot. Two early scholary works of the 1950s by Gerhard Kahlo and Waltraud Woeller elaborated this position to show the folktale's connection to the historical reality of the peasants' experiences. In other words, it was argued that the Grimms' tales and other German folktales contained positive elements of the class struggle and were part of a grand European tradition that corresponded to the internationalist aspect of communism. Moreover, the tales were considered helpful in developing the moral character of young people. As Anneliese Kocialek stated in her work on the importance of the folktale in elementary education:

> The moral and aesthetic education of pupils through folktales in the primary levels of the schools in the German Democratic Republic are inseparably fused with one another. The special attributes of the artistic fairy-tale forms make the children more receptive to the moral content and simultaneously provide aesthetic pleasure. The tales of our own people are superbly suited to maintain in our children a love for their homeland, and the tales of other peoples waken in them a respect for their cultural achievements. (183)

Since specific criteria for the moral and political development of the people in the GDR were stringently set by the state and party leadership, the Grimms' tales came under close scrutiny and, beginning in 1952, the early editions of the Grimms' tales all underwent revision so that they conformed to the value system of the state: racist and religious elements were eliminated; violence and brutality were diminished; moral statements were added. It was not until 1955 that the first unabridged complete edition of the Grimms' tales was published, but even after that event the censorship and/or revision of the Grimms' tales continued. The result was a dehistorization of the Grimms' tales due to an endeavor to transform them into genuine folktales that could be used for the moral and political elevation of the people. From 1952 to 1975 there were forty-eight different editions of the Grimms' tales published in the GDR (Bennung 292; Bastian 225) with very little criticism of the possible regressive elements in the tales and with changes based on a one-dimensional view of what a folktale is or should be. The Grimms' tales were considered sacrosanct: perfect for the moral upbringing of children; perfect for making adults aware of the class struggle.

Given the high status of the Grimms' tales, GDR writers were not encouraged to tamper with them, and certainly not to mock them. The only major writer who rewrote them in a critical manner before 1970 was Franz Fühmann, who published compelling verse renditions of the Grimms' tales in *Die Richtung der Märchen* (1962) that generally addressed the theme of the Nazi past and problems of authoritarianism. For instance his poem, "In Frau Trudes Haus" (In Mother Trudy's House), begins this way:

> When the child entered Mother Trudy's house,
> it saw a black man standing on the stairs,
> his head was a dead skull,
> claws were on his fingers.

> My child, what you're looking at, said Mother Trudy,
> what've you been imagining,
> it was only the good charcoal burner,
> who's brought me wood to burn.

In contrast to the Grimms' "Mother Trudy," in which a disobedient child is approvingly burned as a log, Fühmann's poem recalls images of Nazi Germany, and the child is murdered because it sees everything only too clearly.

191

Fühmann's 1962 poems were indeed an exception in East Germany,[15] and it was only after a change in the government leadership from Walther Ulbricht to Erich Honecker in 1971 that writers were encouraged to write more imaginative, if not fantastic, literature (Castein, *Es wird einmal* 198). This does not mean that there were no fairy tales whatsoever produced before 1971. In fact there was a fair amount produced that departed from the Grimms' tales in interesting ways. For instance, Friedrich Wolf published some interesting tales for children following World War II, and such writers as Lilo Hardel, Fred Rodrian, Werner Heiduczek, Benno Pludra, and Stefan Heym experimented with the genre (Bennung 296–305). Yet, like the fairy tales published in West Germany during this period, these tales tended to create a sense of harmony and to stress the importance of moral behavior commensurate with the expectations of the state. However, they reflected little about the hard realities of life in the GDR during the 1950s and 1960s. Ironically, it was only with the thaw of socialist realism that writers dared to address social contradictions and produce highly innovative fairy tales that broke with the Grimms' tradition in a critical way. The important factors that led to the endeavors to rewrite the Grimms' tales were: (1) the influence of West German writers whose work was known in the GDR; (2) a more positive reception of German Romanticism; (3) the great overall familiarity of the writers and their public with the Grimms' tales, which could be used thus more effectively as shared symbolical vehicles to criticize the state; (4) greater cultural freedom that allowed writers to address social problems in a more obvious manner (Castein, ''Arbeiten'').

Since the production of reutilized Grimms' tales was much more limited in the GDR than in the FRG, and only achieved significance during the last 15 years, I want to focus largely on tales included in three important anthologies—*Die Rettung des Saragossameeres*, 1976; *Die Verbesserung des Menschen*, 1982; *Es wird einmal*, 1988—to consider tales representative of some of the best work done in East Germany. Most of these tales were first published in individual volumes by their authors, and they, too, can be loosely categorized according to their satirical, parodistic, feminist, and pedagogical aspects, although there are no religious or spiritual narratives. The common thread running throughout most of them is political and, although there was no antiauthoritarian movement at the end of the 1960s in the German

Democratic Republic, insubordination also plays a role in the Grimms' tales that have been *umfunktioniert.*

In his essay "Metamorphose des Märchens," Joachim Walther, one of the editors of *Die Rettung des Saragossameeres,* associates the endeavor to write new literary fairy tales in the GDR with the radical antibourgeois and utopian tales of early German Romanticism, not with the Grimms' "folk" tales. In fact, he argues that "the form of the folktale that has been handed down to us cannot become the model for the new contents" (132). Walther maintains that the changed conditions of production and the social needs of the people in the GDR must serve as the basis for new, utopian fairy tales, if the literary fairy tale is to overcome a transitional phase in which it mixes elements from different genres and assume an important social function.

In his own anthology there are several examples in which authors attempt to use the Grimms' tales as models that can be revised with new contents to address social problems in the GDR, yet they are anything but utopian. Klaus Rahn's "Frau Holle" (Mother Holle) recalls an episode in which a young Polish woman named Irina is raped by a German farmer during World War II. Irina burns down the farm and herself, muttering "Mother Holle" before she dies. Her story lives on in former East Germany, and the narrator stimulates German readers through surrealistic imagery to return to the land where it happened and to associate it with contemporary attitudes toward the Poles today. Waltraud Jähnichen's version of "Brier Rose" is less serious than Rahn's tale and pokes fun at the state ceremonies in the GDR. A top chef is missing on the day of an important celebration, and nobody else knows the recipe for the pastry. The kitchen boy is sent to the state library to try to discover it but cannot get the book he needs. So he finally looks into a thick fairy-tale book and wakes the chef who was about to give the kitchen-boy a slap in the face. Now the chef gets mad again and is about to slap the kitchen boy from Berlin, but the minister president's young wife pricks her finger with a thorn in her eye. Everyone falls asleep, and the next day the top chef returns and is puzzled to find everyone in a coma with the fairy-tale book turned to the tale of "Brier Rose." More complex and more sardonic than Jähnichen's parody is Martin Stade's "Der Traum vom Hühnchen und vom Hähnchen nach Grimm" (The Dream of the Little Hen and the Little Rooster according to Grimm), in which Stade interweaves passages from the Grimms' tale

193

with a first-person recollection of a futuristic dream. The reader is compelled to reconcile the fatalism of the old Grimms' tale about "The Death of the Hen" with the narrator's recollection of a sterile automated future.

Interestingly the three tales by Rahn, Jähnichen, and Stade are all satirical and open-ended. The revised Grimms' tales reflect more about the difficulties of resolving contradictions in the GDR society than indicating utopian alternatives and tendencies. This is also true of Günter Kunert's fairy tales in *Die geheime Bibliothek* (1973), which preceded the publication of *Die Rettung des Saragossameeres* by three years. In particular his "Brier Rose" is a brief recapitulation of the tale in which he seeks to undermine the idyllic happy ending and belief in a rosy future by showing the reality as it must have been for the prince, who supposedly makes his way through the thorny hedges after one hundred years have passed: "He enters the castle, runs up the stairs, enters the chamber where the sleeping woman is resting, her toothless mouth half-opened, slobbering, sunken lids, her hairless skull rippled on the temples by blue wormlike veins, spotted, dirty, a snoring hag. Oh blessed are all, who, dreaming of Brier Rose, died in the hedge and in the belief that behind the hedge a time would prevail in which time would finally stop once and for all and be definite" (Castein, *Es wird einmal* 8). Obviously, Kunert is casting doubt on the future of the GDR as did other writers of fairy tales in the early 1970s after having been prevented from developing fairy tales and other genres of fantasy literature. The questioning spirit of all the revised Grimms' tales during the 1970s is skeptical because the writers were still dubious abut whether the thaw would bring about a new flood of suppression of cultural freedoms.

A good example of the skeptical nature of the satirical fairy tales based on a Grimms' tale is Arnim Stolper's "Der Wolf, nicht totzukriegen" (The Wolf That Can't Be Killed, 1979). The focus is on a German professor who tries to dissuade Little Red Riding Hood from believing in such fantastic stories as fairy tales. He is a man of reason, who represents the cultural authorities of the GDR. When he sees Little Red Riding Hood returning from her grandmother's house, he refuses to believe what happened to her. And even when he is eaten by a wolf, he tries to repress the reality of fantasy. However, after several years in the wolf's stomach, he discovers his own subjectivity, is transformed

194

into a young man in his best years, and goes home with Little Red Riding Hood and her fairy-tale book.

Another parody of a Grimms' tale critiquing higher authorities in the GDR is Karl Hermann Roehricht's "Von einem, der auszog, die Höflichkeit zu lernen" (About a Young Man, Who Went Out to Learn about Politeness, 1980). Here a young simpleton leaves his hometown with the advice from an old woman to say only one sentence to the people he meets: "From the bottom of my heart I am sorry." However, this sentence and two others that he thinks up cause him to have difficulties with kings who incarcerate him. Finally, fed up with kings, he returns to his hometown with the sentence "I have complete understanding for everything." Eventually, even though he remains simple-minded, people turn to him for advice in his old age, and he becomes a professor who teaches the art of politeness.

Like Roehricht's parody, Lothar Kusche's "Froschkönig" (Frog King, 1979) mocks audience expectations concerning fairy tales while presenting a critique of contemporary society. Here a young woman loses an earring in a fountain, and the frog visits her in her apartment, where she flings him against a wall because he becomes too irksome. When he is transformed into the Prince Alwin von und zu Schaumburg-lippe auf Knödelstein von Hessen-Nassau with an upper-class nasal manner of speaking, she compels him to leave because she does not want to have anything to do with princes. Kusche concludes that the tale explains that most people are repelled by frogs because they fear that a frog could be transformed unexpectedly into an old German prince.

Aside from the socially critical fairy tales that debunk the authorities and any form of class hegemony, there have been various parodies that are basically intended to mock the old versions of the Grimms and to provide amusement for readers. For instance Stefan Heym's "Wie es mit Rotkäppchen weiterging" (The Further Adventures of Little Red Cap, 1979) pokes fun at Little Red Riding Hood's desire for more fame after she has told her neighbors and villagers about her encounter with the wolf.[16] She becomes bored at home and neglects Felix, the boy next door. Therefore she hopes that she will meet another wolf and become famous again on another visit to Granny. However, neither her grandmother nor the son of the big bad wolf agrees to repeat the previous adventure, and she returns home where Felix invites her to play the game of Little Red Riding Hood and the Wolf, in which she will be gobbled up out of love. What is ironical sexual innuendo in Heym's narrative becomes the explicit meaning of all the short illustrated parodies in Thomas Schleusing's *Es war einmal . . .* (Once Upon a Time, 1979). Similar to the technique employed by the West German caricaturist Heinz Langer, Schleusing takes a short passage from the traditional Grimms' tale and then juxtaposes it with an erotic illustration that brings out some of the underlying sexual meanings of the tale. In his "Der Froschkönig" (The Frog King) he quotes the part where the frog says he is tired and wants to sleep with her, and then shows the princess in a revealing nightie with the frog between her legs. As she looks down at him, she remarks, "Oh, don't be a frog!" (41). Even more explicit in its sexual if not sexist connotation is his version of Rapunzel based on the passage where the prince calls her to let her hair down. There she is pictured smiling from a window in her tower as a group of princes have formed a line to take their turn having their pleasure with her.

Although most of the reutilized fairy tales in the GDR are comic in tone, there are some that are deadly serious and do away with magic and fantasy. For instance, Horst Matthies's collection of tales *Der goldene Fisch* (The Golden Fish, 1980) has the subtitle *Not a Fairy-Tale Book (Kein Märchenbuch),* and indeed his revisions of such tales as "The Wolf and the Seven Young Kids," "Brier Rose," "Lucky Hans," and "The Devil with the Three Golden Hairs" have more to do with stark realism than with symbolic literature. Moreover, Matthies concentrates specifically on the problems that women have encountered since the foundation of the GDR in 1949, and he exposes the romantic myths underlying the Grimms' fairy tales. In "The Wolf and the Seven Kids," Matthies focuses on a young woman who, in a span of eighteen years, has seven girls with different fathers. Most of the times she is treated shabbily by men, and she also has shabby jobs since she has never been able to educate herself or qualify for high-skilled work. She constantly tells her daughters to beware of men taking advantage of them, and when she goes on her vacation one summer, she returns to find that a repairman is sleeping in her apartment because of major repairs he must make on the gasline in the building. After an initial distrust on the mother's part, she soon learns to accept him and gets married. On the steps of the city hall, she then says to her daughters: "What's rumbling and pumbling around in my stomach . . . ?" (35). This delightful ending can be contrasted to Matthies's version of "Brier

Rose," in which a young woman loses her mother in an air attack a day or so before World War II ends. An orphan, she takes a job as an archivist in a small town and spends the rest of her life afraid to make contact with men, yet waiting for a man to save her. Life passes her by, and she remains a lonely anxious person whose deep desires will never be fulfilled.

What is one to conclude from all the experiments with the Grimms' fairy tales in East and West Germany? Have the Grimms been toppled from their throne? Will it ever be possible to surpass the Grimms' fairy tales, which are second only to the Bible as a best-seller in all parts of Germany? If we begin with a comparison of the "productive" reception of the Grimms' tales in the FRG and GDR, we can note that there have been distinctly different historical phases, and yet writers in both countries have arrived at the same goal.

In West Germany up to 1968, the Grimms' tales were treated as gems of the German cultural tradition that were therapeutic and could help heal the wounds of World War II. The antiauthoritarian movement and student revolts brought about a radical change in the attitude towards the Grimms' tales so that those major writers who have reutilized them seek to expose their regressive ideological aspects and deceptive idyllic messages. The experimentation with the Grimms' fairy tales is based on *insubordination* or a healthy skepticism towards blind acceptance of the so-called humanistic German cultural tradition. In this respect, the Grimms' tales are touchstones in a literary discourse within the public sphere. They serve as symbolical reference points for critical writers who reutilize them to have a dialogue about sex, politics, social conditions, religion, and so on.

From 1949 to 1971 in the GDR, there was a similar "religious" attitude towards the Grimms' tales, with one major difference. Whereas the overriding ideological reception in West Germany was connected to traditional religious and bourgeois values and served a social function of healing and reinforcing a mood of existentialism, mystery, and miracle, the reception in the GDR was linked to a rationalization and legitimization of the so-called socialist policies of the state. The ethics and morals of the tales were shaped to promote class struggle, and the social function of the tales was to promote an understanding of how one must strive to overcome exploitation. Since the Grimms' tales were

197

considered part of the GDR's cultural heritage, it was taboo to criticize them until 1971. Since then, East German writers have purposely used the Grimms' tales in much the same way as West German writers with one important exception. There are no endeavors to continue or reconstruct an anthroposophical, Jungian, or Christian discourse through the Grimms' tales. The reutilization of the Grimms' tales was part of a vigorous dialogue pertaining to state policies and social conditions in the GDR, and it is in this sense that writers in East and West Germany have come together, for their tales are socially symbolical gestures that want to open up questions abut the German past and point to ways to change the institutions of their respective public spheres.

For the most part the reutilized Grimms' tales in East and West Germany are *not* utopian, whereas it is easy to point to the utopian aspects of the original Grimms' tales—tales written during a revolutionary period when the bourgeoisie was on the rise and establishing the norms of its civilizing process. To the extent that this civilizing process remains firm (even though it has been qualitatively different in both the GDR and FRG), it will be difficult to topple the Grimms from their fairy-tale throne. Nevertheless, it can be clearly seen that the "realm" of fairy-tale production changed immensely in both countries after 1970,[17] and experimentation in literary fairy tales and fantasy transcended the Grimms. In this regard, one must extend the study of the reception of the Grimms' tales to see how they have been fully transformed or by-passed in other contemporary fairy tales. Moreover, since the two Germanys became united in the fall of 1990, there will undoubtedly be numerous fairy tales addressing the problems of nationalism and reunification. As Germany enters a new historical phase, there are bound to be "new German" fairy tales about the legacy of the Grimms, the direction that the united Germany will take, and the hopes and wishes of the German people, who have longed to overcome the dark past of Nazism. But that is another story with an ending that has yet to be written. . . .

Notes

1. See Boettger; Gong and Privat; Langfeldt; Lenartz; and Petzet.
2. In 1981 the society changed its name to the *Europäische Märchengesellschaft* (European Fairy Tale Society) and indicated that it was becoming

more open to sociological, philological, and historical approaches to the folk- and fairy-tale tradition.

3. For more detailed treatments of this period, see Dankert; Hengst; and Zipes, "Down with Heidi."

4. For other revisions of "Hansel and Gretel," see Mieder, *Grimms Märchen—modern* 9–34; and Mieder, *Grimmige Märchen* 91–112. Among the German authors who have created their own versions of the Grimms' tale are Wolfram Siebeck, Günter Bruno Fuchs, Michael Ende, Karin Struck, Josef Wittmann, Julius Nef, and Josef Reding.

5. One of the most gifted political satirists in the Federal Republic, Traxler often works together with Robert J. Gernhardt, F. W. Bernstein, and Friedrich K. Waechter. In fact, some interesting political fairy tales can be found in Bernstein, Gernhardt, and Waechter, *Die Drei*, which contains some of their best work of the last twenty years.

6. Published first in Fühmann, *Die Richtung der Märchen*.

7. Jung commissioned twenty-eight leading contemporary authors to choose an old broadside from the nineteenth century and to write their own tale based on the images of the broadside. Among those authors who chose a Grimm tale are Ilse Aichinger, Jürgen Becker, Nicolas Born, Peter O. Chotejewitz, Jörg Drews, Fabius von Gugel, Peter Härtling, Herbert Heckmann, Katrine von Hutten, Marie Luise Kaschnitz, Karl Krolow, Barbara König, Hermann Lenz, Friederike Mayröcker, and Jung himself. Most of the tales fall under the category of social satire.

8. The format of this book is somewhat similar to that of Jochen Jung's anthology. The editors took fairy-tale collages (based on Grimms' tales) by the artist Heinrich Dreidoppel, sent them to seventy German writers, and asked them to react to the images by writing new fairy tales "in which actual experiences would be connected to historical ones and German traumas would perhaps be given new expression" (151). The authors who participated in this experiment are Peter Härtling, Karin Struck, Jochen Link, Robert Jarowoy, Hans-Jürgen Linke, Bernd Bohmeier, Vilma Link, Jens Hagen, Rolf Haubl, Bernd Hackländer, Norbert Relenberg, Walter Höllerer, Karl Riha, Hans-Dieter Eberhard, Eckhard Henscheid, Gertrude von Wasmuth, Jochen Gerz, Urs Jaeggi, Fritz Teufel, and Peter Paul Zahl.

9. Other feminist tales and anthologies of significance that I shall not be able to deal with here are Ursula Eggli, *Fortschritt in Grimmsland* and *Querflöte*. Many feminist fairy tales can be found in collections that are mixed, such as Gmelin's and Garbe's books as well as Gelberg's anthologies.

10. This tale was published in Gelberg's anthology *Neues vom Rumpelstilzchen*.

11. This tale is in Brigitte Heidebrecht's anthology *Dornröschen nimmt die Heckenschere* 50–52.

199

12. This tale is in Gelberg's anthology *Neues vom Rumpelstilzchen* 63–69.

13. See also Beese, *Von Nixen und Brunnenfrauen;* Schmölders, *Die wilde Frau;* and Moog, *Die Wasserfrau.*

14. Among the titles published by the Kreuz Verlag in Seifert's series are Angela Waiblinger, *Rumpelstilzchen: Gold statt Liebe* (1983); Theodor Seifert, *Schneewittchen: Das fast verlorene Leben* (1983); Hildegunde Wöller, *Aschenputtel: Energie der Liebe* (1984); Lutz Müller, *Das tapfere Schneiderlein: List als Lebenskunst* (1985); Hans Dieckmann, *Der blaue Vogel: Der charmante Held und seine Heldin* (1985); Hans Jellouschek, *Der Froschkönig: Geschichte einer Beziehung* (1985); Helmut Hark, *Gevatter Tod: Auseinandersetzung mit der Sterblichkeit* (1985); Marie-Louise von Franz, *Die Katze: Entwicklung des Weiblichen* (1986); Ursula Eschenbach, *Hänsel und Gretel: Der Sohn im mütterlichen Dunkel* (1986). See my critical discussion of the Kreuz series in Zipes, *The Brothers Grimm* 117–19.

15. Another exception was Günter de Bruyn, who, in *Maskareden,* parodied the words of Fühmann, Erwin Strittmatter, and Johannes Bobrowski using Grimms' tales.

16. For an entirely different version of "Little Red Cap" that pokes fun at male chauvinism, see Hans Joachim Schädlich's "Kriminalmärchen" in *Versuchte Nähe.*

17. See the works by Irmtraud Morgner in the GDR and Michael Ende in the FRG.

References

Primary Literature

The following compilation of fairy tales and adaptations of the Grimms' tales is more extensive than the tales cited in the text because I wanted to provide the reader with additional references that might be useful for further research in the field.

Arens, Hanns, ed. *Märchen deutscher Dichter der Gegenwart.* Esslingen: Bechtle, 1951.

Beese, Henriette, ed. *Von Nixen und Brunnenfrauen.* Berlin: Ullstein, 1972.

Bernstein, F. W., Robert Gernhardt, and F. K. Waechter. *Die Drei.* Frankfurt a.M.: Zweitausendundeins, 1981.

Blut im Schuh: Märchen. Spec. Issue of *Schreiben.* Bremen: Zeichen + Spuren, 1984.

Borchers, Elisabeth, ed. *Märchen deutscher Dichter.* Frankfurt a.M.: Insel, 1972.

Brenda, Irmela. "Das Rumpelstilzchen hat mir immer leid getan." *Neues vom Rumpelstilzchen und andere Haus-Märchen von 43 Autoren.* Ed. Hans-Joachim Gelberg. Weinheim: Beltz & Gelberg, 1976. 198–200.

Brezan, Jurij. *Der Mäuseturm.* Berlin: Verlag Neues Leben, 1970.

Bruyn, Günter de. *Maskeraden.* Halle: Mitteldeutscher Verlag, 1966.

Castein, Hanne, ed. *Es wird einmal: Märchen für morgen.* Frankfurt a.M.: Suhrkamp, 1988.

Chotjewitz, Peter O. *Kinder, Kinder! Ein Märchen aus sieben Märchen.* Hannover: Fackelträger, 1973.

Claus, Uta, and Rolf Kutschera. *Total tote Hose: 12 bockstarke Märchen.* Frankfurt a.M.: Eichborn, 1984.

Eggli, Ursula. *Fortschritt in Grimmsland: Ein Märchen für Mädchen und Frauen.* Bern: RIURS, 1983.

Ende, Michael. *Momo.* Stuttgart: Klett, 1973.

———. *Unendliche Geschichte.* Stuttgart, Klett, 1979.

Fetscher, Iring. *Der Nulltarif der Wichtelmänner: Märchen- und andere Verwirrspiele.* Hamburg: Claassen, 1982.

———. *Wer hat Dornröschen wachgeküßt? Das Märchen-Verwirrbuch.* Hamburg: Claassen, 1972.

Fuchs, Günter Bruno. "Behauptung." *Deutsche Unsinnspoesie.* Ed. Klaus Peter Dencker. Stuttgart: Reclam, 1978. 295.

Fühmann, Franz. *Märchen auf Bestellung.* Rostock: Hinstorff, 1982.

———. *Die Richtung der Märchen.* Berlin: Aufbau, 1962.

Garbe, Burckhard, and Gisela Garbe. *Der ungestiefelte Kater: Grimms Märchen umerzählt.* Göttingen: sage & schreibe, 1985.

Gelberg, Hans-Joachim. *Erstes Jahrbuch der Kinderliteratur 1: Geh und spiel mit dem Riesen.* Weinheim: Beltz & Gelberg, 1971.

———. *Zweites Jahrbuch der Kinderliteratur 2: Am Montag fängt die Woche an.* Weinheim: Beltz & Gelberg, 1973.

———. *Drittes Jahrbuch der Kinderliteratur 3: Menschengeschichten.* Weinheim: Beltz & Gelberg, 1975.

———. *Viertes Jahrbuch der Kinderliteratur 4: Der fliegende Robert.* Weinheim: Beltz & Gelberg, 1977.

———. *Neues vom Rumpelstilzchen und andere Haus-Märchen von 43 Autoren.* Weinheim: Beltz & Gelberg. 1976.

Goes, Albrecht. "Sterntaler." *Gedichte.* Frankfurt a.M.: Fischer, 1958. 116.

Günzel, Manfred. *Deutsche Märchen.* Frankfurt a.M.: Metopen-Verlag, 1968.

Hägele, Rainer. *Ich dachte, es wäre der Froschkönig.* Stuttgart: Spectrum, 1984.

Hammer, Klaus, ed. *Der Holzwurm und der König: Märchenhaftes und Wundersames für Erwachsene.* Halle: Mitteldeutscher Verlag, 1985.

Hardel, Lilo. *Otto und der Zauberer Faulebaul.* Berlin: Kinderbuchverlag, 1956.

Heidebrecht, Brigitte, ed. *Dornröschen nimmt die Heckenschere: Märchenhaftes von 30 Autorinnen.* Bonn: verlag kleine schritte, 1985.

Heidtmann, Horst, ed. *Die Verbesserung des Menschen: Märchen von Franz Fühmann, Peter Hacks, Irmtraud Morgner, Anna Seghers und vielen anderen Autoren aus der DDR.* Darmstadt: Luchterhand, 1982.

Heiduczek, Werner. *Jana und der kleine Stern.* Berlin: Kinderbuchverlag, 1968.

Helmecke, Monika. *Klopfzeichen.* Berlin: Verlag Neues Leben, 1979.

Heym, Stefan. *Cymbelinchen.* Munich: Bertelsmann, 1975.

————. *Der kleine König, der ein Kind kriegen mußte und andere neue Märchen für kluge Kinder.* Munich: Goldmann, 1977.

Holtz-Baumert, Gerhard. *Sieben und dreimal sieben Geschichten.* Berlin: Kinderbuchverlag, 1979.

Janosch. *Janosch erzählt Grimm's Märchen.* Weinheim: Beltz & Gelberg, 1972.

Jentzsch, Bernd. *Ratsch und ade!* Rostock: Hinstorff, 1975.

Jung, Jochen, ed. *Bilderbogengeschichten: Märchen, Sagen, Abenteuer.* Munich: Moos, 1974.

Kahn, Lisa. *Wer mehr liebt.* Berlin: Stoedtner, 1984.

Kämpf, Günter, and Vilma Link, eds. *Deutsche Märchen.* Gießen: Anabas, 1981.

Kaschnitz, Marie Luise. "Bräutigam Froschkönig." *Überallnie: Ausgewählte Gedichte 1928–1965.* Munich: dtv, 1969. 150.

Kassajep, Margaret. *"Deutsche Hausmärchen" frisch getrimmt.* Dachau: Baedeker & Lang, 1980.

Kirsch, Rainer. *Auszog das Fürchten zu lernen.* Reinbek: Rowohlt, 1978.

Knauth, Joachim. *Vier Theatermärchen und ein Essay.* Berlin: Henschel, 1981.

Köhler-Zülch, Ines, and Christine Shojaei Kawan. *Schneewittchen hat viele Schwestern.* Gütersloh: Gütersloher Verlagshaus, 1988.

Konrad, Johann Friedrich. *Hexen-Memoiren: Märchen, entwirrt und neu erzählt.* Frankfurt a.M.: Eichborn, 1981.

Körner, Heinz, ed. *Die Farben der Wirklichkeit: Ein Märchenbuch.* Fellbach: Körner, 1983.

Kraus, Barbara, ed. *Gestohlene Märchen.*Munich: Trikont, 1979.

Kriegel, Volker. *Der Rock 'n' König.* Aarau: Saurländer, 1982.

Kunert, Günter. *Die geheime Bibliothek.* Berlin: Aufbau, 1973.

Kunze, Reiner. *Der Löwe Leopold: Fast Märchen, fast Geschichten.* Frankfurt a.M.: Fischer, 1974.

Kusche, Lothar. *Lothar Kusche's Drucksachen.* Berlin: Eulenspiegel, 1979.

Langer, Heinz. *Grimmige Märchen.* Munich: Hugendubel, 1984.

Lerche, Doris, and Otto F. Gmelin. *Märchen für tapfere Mädchen.* Gießen: edition schlot, 1978.

Maar, Paul. *Der tätowierte Hund.* Hamburg: Oetinger, 1968.

Matthies, Horst. *Der goldene Fisch: Kein Märchenbuch.* Halle: Mitteldeutscher Verlag, 1980.

Merian, Svende. *Der Mann aus Zucker: Mein Märchenbuch.* Darmstadt: Luchterhand, 1985.

Merkel, Johannes. *Zwei Korken für Schlienz.* Berlin: Basis, 1972.

Mieder, Wolfgang, ed. *Grimmige Märchen: Prosatexte von Ilse Aichinger bis Martin Walser.* Frankfurt a.M.: R. G. Fischer, 1986.

————, ed. *Grimms Märchen—modern: Prosa, Gedichte, Karikaturen.* Stuttgart: Reclam, 1979.

Mitru, Alexander. *Die verwöhnte Prinzessin.* Berlin: Kinderbuchverlag, 1983.

Moderne Märchen. Versuche: Saarländische Zeitschrift für Literatur & Graphik 12 (1978).

Moog, Hanna, ed. *Die Wasserfrau: Von geheimen Kräften, Sehnsüchten und Ungeheuern mit Namen Hans.* Cologne: Diederichs, 1987.

Morgner, Irmtraud. *Leben und Abenteuer der Trobodora Beatriz.* Berlin: Aufbau, 1974.

Mucke, Dieter. *Die Sorgen des Teufels.* Berlin: Eulenspiegel, 1979.

Nieboj-Preuss, Grete. *Rübezahl einmal ganz anders und weitere ergötzliche Märchen.* Karlsruhe: Moninger, 1952.

Péhan, Wolfgang. *Grimm 2000.* Vienna: Intercity, 1977.

Pludra, Benno. *Vom Bären, der nicht mehr schlafen konnte.* Berlin: Kinderbuchverlag, 1967.

Pribil, Willy. "Schneewittchen—frei nach Sigmund Freud." *Scherz beiseite.* Ed. G. H. Herzog and Ehrhardt Heinhold. Munich: Scherz, 1966. 489–90.

Querflöte: Märchen & fantastische Erzählungen. Vienna: Wiener Frauenverlag, 1984.

Rodrian, Fed. *Der Märchenschimmel.* Berlin: Kinderbuchverlag, 1959.

————. *Das Wolkenschaf.* Berlin: Kinderbuchverlag, 1958.

Roehricht, Karl Hermann. *Die unzufriedenen Wörter und andere Märchen.* Berlin: Rütten und Loening, 1980.

Rühmkorf, Peter. *Der Hüter des Misthaufens: Aufgeklärte Märchen.* Reinbek: Rowohlt, 1983.

Sangerberg, Georg. *Gänsehaut: Geschichten für sensible Leser.* Frankfurt a.M.: Bärmeier und Nikel, 1964.

Schädlich, Hans Joachim. *Versuchte Nähe.* Reinbek: Rowohlt, 1977.

Schlesier, Clara Maria. *Die Osterquelle.* Berlin: Pinguin, 1947.

Schleusing, Thomas. *Es war einmal . . . Märchen für Erwachsene.* Berlin: Eulenspiegel, 1979.

Schmölders, Claudia, ed. *Die wilde Frau: Mythische Geschichten zum Staunen, Fürchten und Begehren.* Cologne: Diederichs, 1983.

Schnitzler, Sonja, and Manfred Wolter, eds. *Die Tarnkappe.* Berlin: Eulenspiegel, 1978.

Schrauff, Chris. *Der Wolf und seine Steine.* Hannover: SOAK, 1986. N. pag.

Schrauff, Christoffer. *Der arbeitslose Prinz.* Berlin: Basis, 1982.

Schubert, Helga. *Blickwinkel.* Berlin: Aufbau, 1984.

Seidel, Ina. *Das wunderbare Geißleinbuch: Neue Geschichten für Kinder, die die alten Märchen gut kennen.*Reutlingen: Ensslin & Laiblin, 1949.

Seidemann, Maria. *Der Tag, an dem Sir Henry starb.* Berlin: Eulenspiegel, 1980.

Seifert, Theodor. *Schneewittchen: Das fast verlorene Leben.* Stuttgart: Kreuz, 1983.

Siebeck, Wolfram. "Sommermärchen vom Wirte wundermild." *Scherz beiseite.* Ed. G. H. Herzog and Ehrhardt Heinhold. Munich: Scherz, 1966. 543–45.

Spielnagel, Johann Christoph. *Zauberflöte und Honigtopf: Erotische Märchen.* Munich: Scherz, 1979.

Stachowa, Angela. *Geschichten für Maja.* Halle: Mitteldeutscher Verlag, 1978.

Stamer, Barbara, ed. *Dornröschen und der Rosenbey: Motivgleiche Märchen.* Frankfurt a.M.: Fischer, 1985.

Stepan, Bohumil. *Knusperhäuschen: Ein Bilderbuch zum Anschauen und Theaterspielen, un-autoritär und ent-Grimm-t.* Ravensburg: Maier, 1973.

Stephan, Martin, *Der verliebte Drache.* Berlin: Eulenspiegel, 1978.

Stolper, Arnim. *Die Karriere des Seiltänzers.* Rostock: Hinstorff, 1979.

Strauß, Ludwig. *Die Brautfahrt nach Schweigenland.* Olten: Walter, 1982.

Traxler, Hans. *Die Wahrheit über Hänsel und Gretel: Die Dokumentation des Märchens der Gebrüder Grimm.* Frankfurt a.M.: Bärmeier und Nikel, 1963.

Waechter, Friedrich Karl. *Die Bauern im Brunnen.* Zürich: Diogenes, 1978.

———. *Tischlein deck dich und Knüppel aus dem Sack.* Reinbek: Rowohlt, 1972.

Walther, Joachim, and Manfred Wolter, eds. *Die Rettung des Saragossameeres: Märchen.* Berlin: Buchverlag der Moren, 1976.

Wiechert, Ernst. *Märchen.* 2 vols. Munich: Desch, 1946.

Wolf, Friedrich. *Märchen für große und kleine Kinder.* Berlin: Aufbau, 1947.

Critical Works Cited

Bastian, Ulrike. *Die "Kinder- und Hausmärchen" der Brüder Grimm in der literaturpädagogischen Diskussion des 19. und 20. Jahrhunderts.* Frankfurt a.M.: Haag & Herchen, 1981.

Bennung, Isa. "Das deutsche Märchen als Kinderliteratur: Eine Untersuchung von den Anfängen bis zur Entwicklung in der DDR." Diss. Martin-Luther-U, Halle, 1975.

Boettger, Gerhard. "Das Gute und Böse im Märchen." *Lehrerrundbrief* 3 (1948): 290–91.

Castein, Hanne. "Arbeiten mit der Romantik heute: Zur Romantikrezeption der DDR, unter Berücksichtigung des Märchens." *Deutsche Romantik und das 20. Jahrhundert.* Ed. Hanne Castein and Alexander Stillmark. Stuttgart: Akademischer Verlag, 1986. 5–23.

Dankert, Birgit. "Die antiautoritäre Kinder- und Jungendliteratur." *Jungendliteratur in einer veränderten Welt.* Ed. Karl Ernst Maier. Bad Heilbrunn: Klinkhardt, 1972. 68–84.

Gmelin, Otto F. *Böses kommt aus Kinderbüchern: Die verpaßten Möglichkeiten kindlicher Bewußtseinsbildung.* Munich: Kindler, 1972.

Gong, Walter, and Karl Privat. "Vorschule der Grausamkeit? Eine Diskussion um die Märchen der Brüder Grimm." *Der Tagesspiegel* 7 Feb. 1947. N. pag.

Hengst, Heinz. "Emanzipatorische Belletristik für Kinder! Probleme politischer Sozialisation in linken Kinderbüchern." *Die heimlichen Erzieher: Kinderbücher und politisches Lernen.* Ed. Dieter Richer and Jochen Vogt. Reinbek: Rowohlt, 1974. 91–100.

Kahlo, Gerhard. *Die Wahrheit unserer Märchen.* Halle: Niemeyer, 1954.

Kaiser, Erich. "Ent-Grimm-te Märchen?" *Westermanns Pädagogische Beiträge* 8 (1975): 448–59.

Kocialek, Anneliese. "Die Bedeutung der Volksmärchen für Unterricht und Erziehung in der Unterstufe der deutschen demokratischen Schule." Diss. Humboldt-U, Berlin, 1951.

Langfeldt, Johannes. "Märchen und Pädagogik." *Pädagogische Rundschau* 2 (1948): 521–25.

Lenartz, Werner. "Von der erzieherischen Kraft des Märchens." *Pädagogische Rundschau* 2 (1948): 330–36.

Petzet, Wolfgang. "Verteidigung des Märchens gegen seine Verleumder." *Prisma* 1 (1947): 3, 11.

Steinitz, Wolfgang. "Das deutsche Volksmärchen: Ein wichtiger Teil nationalen Kulturerbes." *Neues Deutschland* 17 Nov. 1951.

Tismar, Jens. *Das deutsche Kunstmärchen des zwanzigsten Jahrhunderts.* Stuttgart: Metzler, 1981.

Walther, Joachim. "Metamorphose des Märchens." *Arbeiten mit der Romantik heute.* Ed. Heide Hess and Peter Liebers. Akademie der Künste der DDR, Arbeitsheft 26. Berlin: Henschel, 1978. 130–32.

Woeller, Waltraud. "Der soziale Gehalt und die soziale Funktion der deutschen Volksmärchen." Habilitations-Schrift der Humboldt-Universität zu Berlin, 1955. Rpt. in *Wissenschaftliche Zeitschrift der Humboldt-Universität zu Berlin.* Gesellschafts- und sprachwissenschaftliche Reihe 10 (1961): 395–459; 11 (1962): 281–307.

Zipes, Jack. *The Brothers Grimm: From Enchanted Forests to the Modern World.* New York: Routledge, 1988.

————. "Down with Heidi, Down with Struwwelpeter, Three Cheers for the Revolution: Towards a New Socialist Children's Literature in West Germany." *Children's Literature* 5 (1976): 162–79.

Wilhelm Grimm/Maurice Sendak: *Dear Mili* and the Literary Culture of Childhood

Maria Tatar

> Now children! I have only one piece of serious,
> important advice to give you all, so attend to me!—
> Never crack nuts with your teeth!
>
> —Catherine Sinclair, *Holiday House*

WHEN HENRY SHARPE HORSELY published *The Affectionate Parent's Gift, and the Good Child's Reward* in 1828, he felt that the "sincerity of intention" behind his efforts separated this collection of poems and essays for children from the vast quantities of frivolous reading matter for children:

> It is an acknowledged fact, and much to be lamented, that the greater part of the Books published for the use of children, are either ridiculous in themselves, unfit to instruct or inform, or are of an improper tendency, calculated only to mislead the susceptible and tender minds of youth; and, consequently, ought to be rejected by the parents and guardians of children with as much indignation, as a proffered poisonous ingredient for mixture or infusion into the food of their children. (119)

Horsely never names any of the "objectionable and contaminating" volumes against which he rails, but we can infer, after a reading of his own poems, that he is probably referring to stories without any apparent didactic thrust. His own plots, however, do not seem to deviate materially from the reward-and-punishment model that dominated the

207

market for children's literature at the time of his writing. "I have endeavored to pourtray vice in its heinous character, and its evil tendencies," he writes, "to picture the milder virtues of the mind, as being alone worthy of cultivation" (119). Predictably, he has also "endeavored to enforce obedience, and inculcate sincerity and truth" (120).

Horsely's book is breathtaking in its sweep. There are the usual meditations on idleness:

> An idle girl, or idle boy,
> Is hated as a pest;
> Like dirty pigs, they always love
> In slothfulness to rest. (127)

But Horsely also includes a poem about the death of a mother, in which the woman's dying words are recorded:

> "Soon your mother will be lifeless,
> For you I'd wish but to be spar'd;
> Ah, why this wish, I n'er shall have it,
> Never see my children rear'd." (126)

Fathers are also mortal, and so we are treated to "The Death of a Father" with a well-pointed moral:

> Children, prize a tender father,
> Best protectors of the young;
> Never let your conduct grieve them,
> Never vex them with your tongue. (121)

There are also poems about visits to Newgate "just for example's sake," trips to the blind asylum where "all hands are busy in their rooms," a stop at the lunatic asylum to see "the throngs of those who don't possess their reason," meetings with orphans who are "clad in rags and patches," and an encounter with a crippled girl who affords "gen'rous Mary" the chance to make a show of her compassion.

Horsely makes a point of exposing children to the hard facts of everyday life in a fashion characteristic of nineteenth-century writers. Beggars, blind men, and thieves have one sole purpose in life, which is to teach lessons or to remind children to be grateful for what they have. The admitted aim of *The Affectionate Parent's Gift, and the Good Child's Reward* (the title's unintentional irony speaks volumes) is to awaken "sentiments of gratitude, obedience, and humanity" in chil-

dren. If Horsely and his contemporaries erred in the direction of showing children too many of the harsh realities of everyday life (for all the
wrong reasons and in all the wrong ways), there were those who moved
to the opposite end of the spectrum and presented idealized and senti-
mentalized versions of reality. Here we have books like *The History of
Little Goody Two-Shoes,* or stories like "The Schoolgirl," that feature
a heroine "playful, and innocent as the dove" (Upton 3).

For Maurice Sendak, Goody Two-Shoes and her literary cousins are
the real villains in the history of children's literature. Even today many
writers of children's books embrace "the great nineteenth-century fantasy that paints childhood as an eternally innocent paradise" and create
hopelessly dull stories that have one purpose alone—"they don't
frighten adults" (*Caldecott & Co.* 153). False sentimentality, with its
denial of the emotional complexities of childhood, evades the very issues that children's books ought to represent and enact. What Sendak
aims to do, in his books for children, is to "reconstruct and defuse
dreadful moments of childhood" (210). In *Outside Over There,* for example, Sendak claims to have created a narrative whose subtext was his
own childhood anxiety about the Lindbergh case ("In it, I am the Lindbergh baby, and my sister saves me"—*Caldecott & Co.* 210) and his
sister's resentment about being stuck all the time with baby Maurice.
Writing the book helped Sendak in a wonderfully economical way to
master his childhood fears about being kidnapped, to discharge the
guilt in his relationship with his sister, and to make peace with a mother
who had transferred responsibility for her son to her daughter in all too
light a fashion. Sendak sees children's literature as a therapeutic form
of play in which author, character, and reader participate to purge themselves of childhood anger, resentment, fear, frustration, and confusion.
Max, Kenny, Martin, and Rosie, like his other fictional creations, "all
have the same need to master the uncontrollable and frightening aspects
of their lives, and they all turn to fantasy to accomplish this" (152).

The rhetoric of mastery that permeates Sendak's writings about children's books dovetails neatly with the model of reading as therapy developed by Bruno Bettelheim in his *Uses of Enchantment.* Bettelheim
too deplores the fallacy of innocence that informs children's literature.
With the best of intentions, adults expose children "only to the sunny
side of things," drawing attention away from what troubles the child
most, "nameless anxieties" and "chaotic, angry, and even violent fantasies" (7). That fairy tales "give body to . . . anxieties" is precisely

209

what makes them so beneficial for adults and children alike. As the tales enact anxieties and fears, they also "relieve" them (hence the "uses of enchantment"), often "without this ever coming to conscious awareness" (15).

That representation leads to resolution stands as the cornerstone of Sendak's philosophy of children's literature just as it informs Bettelheim's model of psychological growth through identification and abreaction. Sendak insistently celebrates fantasy as an empowering mode, enabling children to tame "ungovernable" and "dangerous" emotions by providing a healthy catharsis: "Through fantasy, Max [the hero of *Where the Wild Things Are*] discharges his anger against his mother, and returns to the real world sleepy, hungry, and at peace with himself" (*Caldecott & Co.* 151).[1] Children's literature becomes a miniature Aristotelian tragedy that secures a child's identification with its protagonists and promotes a cathartic effect. Is it any wonder that Sendak used the very term *catharsis* to describe the powerful feelings that overcame him once he had finished *Where the Wild Things Are?* "When I write and draw I'm experiencing what the child in the book is going through. I was as relieved to get back from Max's journey as he was. . . . It's only after the act of writing the book that, as an adult, I can see what has happened and talk about fantasy as catharsis, about Max acting out his anger as he fights to grow" (Hentoff 344).

Sendak's observations raise a number of questions, among them one that an early commentator on children's literature framed by asking "Do children need horror in stories? If so, how much and how soon?" (Pickard 1). Sendak would probably not ask about the proper dose and its timing but about the disease that the medicine is meant to cure. Take the case of Carlo Collodi's *Pinocchio*, a story that, in Sendak's own words, does not suffer from "whimsicality or sentimentality" yet is nonetheless "a cruel and frightening tale" built on a "sickening" premise (*Caldecott & Co.* 112–13). Collodi creates a world in which children are inherently lazy, disobedient, and dishonest—the same world we encounter in most nineteenth-century cautionary tales and reward-and-punishment tales. At every bend in the road evil forces, incarnated in the ethos of "Playland" (which was to become Walt Disney's "Pleasure Island"), stand ready to seduce the child and to turn him into the little beast that he really is. That the text is punctuated with stern lectures about the importance of hard work, obedience, and truth (always just after Pinocchio has realized the error of his ways and just before he slips once again into a "naughty" mode) makes it a dreary story, designed more to satisfy adults than children. "From now on I shall lead a different life, and become an obedient boy. I have learnt the lesson that disobedient children never prosper, and never gain anything" (67), the backsliding boy declares to himself in a pathetic speech delivered without a great deal of conviction.

Collodi's tale, with its emphasis on the importance of suppressing the desire to play and have fun in order to find salvation through hard work, conforms almost to the letter with our understanding of the ethical world of nineteenth-century children's literature. Yet despite its endless harping on the evils of "Playland," the book's focus is on adventure—on a sequence of breathtakingly exciting brushes with death framed by scenes at home—and this, even more than Walt Disney, has given the book its staying power. The structure of the adventures is not so different from the one Sendak himself uses in *Outside Over There, Where the Wild Things Are,* and *In the Night Kitchen.* But where Collodi uses moral glosses to set things right lest the reader perceive the book as a mere celebration of adventure, Sendak never spells out a single lesson. As one might expect from a man who sees himself above all as an illustrator and interpreter of children's books, Sendak sends powerful messages through the images and between the lines of the book. Take the case, once again, of Max. Fantasy has for him a real instrumental value. Once he has discharged his anger against his mother through fantasy, he is "at peace with himself," as Sendak tells us, and returns to his bedroom, where a "still hot" supper that includes a generous slice of layer cake awaits him. What Sendak does not tell us, but what is crucially important, is that Max must also be at peace with his mother and therefore less likely to be defiant or disobedient, those same traits that were the nineteenth-century's cardinal sins of childhood.

Both Sendak and Bettelheim argue for the instrumentalization of fantasy (whether in adventure books or in fairy tales) even as they deplore children's literature that takes an explicitly didactic turn. Stories can convey lessons and purify children of "ungovernable" (Sendak's term is telling in view of his need for mastery) emotions, but they must never put those lessons into words. Twentieth-century children's literature has witnessed a gradual fading of the (adult) judgmental narrative voice that was so strident a presence in books such as *Pinocchio* but

211

also in the great nineteenth-century collections of fairy tales. Jacqueline Rose has observed that there was a time when children's books were "*only* justified by the presence of the adult, who laid out for that other adult presumed to be buying the book exactly what he or she was doing" (59). A book without a lesson was hardly worth the paper on which it was printed.

Bettelheim takes essentially the same line on fairy tales that Sendak adopts for his books by placing an equal sign between didacticism and repression while making the case for the vanishing adult: "Explaining to a child why a fairy tale is so captivating to him destroys . . . the story's enchantment. . . . With the forfeiture of this power to enchant goes also a loss of the story's potential for helping the child struggle on his own, and master all by himself the problem which has made the story meaningful to him in the first place" (18).

Bettelheim's diction is telling. Even as he concedes the power of a text to manipulate its reader—a story is "captivating" and has the "power to enchant"—he claims autonomy for the child reader, who struggles "on his own" to "master" a story "all by himself." Let us bracket for the moment whether it is really a good thing for a child to struggle "on his own" in order to ask whether the child really does struggle "on his own" with the problem that makes the story so attractive. Early on in *The Uses of Enchantment,* Bettelheim celebrates fairy tales as vehicles of "a moral education which *subtly,* and *by implication* only, conveys to him the advantages of moral behavior, not through abstract ethical concepts but through that which seems tangibly right and therefore meaningful to him" (5; my emphasis). Bettelheim's fairy tales do not seem able to escape what Roger Duvoisin ascribes to most literature written by adults for children: "that little sneaking desire to teach and to moralize, to pass on to children what we think of our world" (358). Bettelheim endows children with a power over the text that they do not in reality possess. The fact that fairy tales guide feelings and control responses gives the lie to the notion that children work their way from dependence to autonomy through literature.

With their insistence on a noninterventionist policy on the part of adults who read to their children, Sendak and Bettelheim privilege the text, extending its power, while affecting that children control the text as they work their way from powerlessness to autonomy. This privileging of the text is particularly wrongheaded, however, when it comes to fairy tales. Forgetting that fairy tales originally circulated as oral stories that showed extraordinary resilience even as they were reshaped by tellers from different cultures, Bettelheim writes: "The true meaning and impact of a fairy tale can be appreciated, its enchantment can be experienced, only from the story in its original form" (19). Once again, Bettelheim transfers authority and power to a stable, ideal text that in reality is nothing more than one of many artificial constructs created by adults. When it comes to folktales (of which fairy tales are a subcategory), there is no "original text," only an infinite number of variants, each anchored in a specific time and place. For this reason, the reading of fairy tales is precisely the activity that invites adult intervention, for the "original version" that has been captured between the pages of a book has the "power to enchant," but perhaps in a way that may not be appropriate for the time and place in which it is being retold. Do we really want to tell our children about Mother Trudy (No. 43), the woman in the Grimms' *Nursery and Household Tales* who turns disobedient children into logs and warms herself as they burn? How will girls react to the heroine of Perrault's "Bluebeard," who prostrates herself before her husband "asking his pardon with tears, and with all the signs of a true repentance for her disobedience" (83)? Can we expect them to realize how odd it is for a woman whose husband is a mass murderer to reproach herself for opening the door that contains the evidence for his crimes? Are we really that keen to recite to our children the catalog of horrors ("slimy toads," "fat snakes," and "great fat waddling spiders") that plague the proud Inger in Andersen's "The Girl Who Trod on the Loaf"? Nowhere is selectivity more vital than when an adult decides to use fairy tales for bedtime reading. Much as Bettelheim sees himself as the advocate of children in his effort to sanctify children's literature by purging it of the evils of adult interpretation (an impossible task since children's literature is produced by adults), his efforts misfire when it comes to fairy tales.[2] Fairy tales may appear to be a form of literature uncontaminated by adult didacticism, but they remain the creation of adults.

The ideal of a text that is as innocent and as unreflecting as the child to whom it is read has haunted the children's literature industry ever since its inception. For this reason, fairy tales, which seem to represent both the childhood of fiction and the fiction of childhood, occupy a privileged position in the hierarchy of children's literature. But the notion of childlike innocence and naturalness implies that the adult world is tainted with corruption and artificiality. Is it any wonder that writers and critics of children's literature seem eager to keep the adult out of the picture and out of the story? Yet to declare that adults should stay out of children's literature is utterly unrealistic—adults write the books, publish them, review them, buy them, and read them.[3] To argue that adults should not interfere in the reading process is as misguided as arguing that adults should not intrude on children's lives. Letting children be wholly on their own as the readers of a story can, in some situations, count as a not-so-benign form of neglect that leaves them without a compass to guide them as they enter, pass through, and exit a world of fiction.

Sendak's child characters are experts in the art of fending for themselves in the world of fantasy just as Bettelheim's child readers do not need a road map to chart a path through enchanted woods. To achieve autonomy (the ultimate goal in the process of mastery), the child must move into an autonomous mode, giving up helpers and guides on the royal road to independence and integration. This male developmental model defines the self through separation and mastery, in contrast with Carol Gilligan's female model of affiliation and dependence and in contrast with the actual facts of many of the fairy tales analyzed by Bettelheim. Heroes and heroines alike must sever ties to their family, but through the helpers and donors they encounter en route to a second home, they enter an intricate web of relationships that envelops and protects them. The fairy-tale world is a world in which compassion counts—the good deeds of hero and heroine single them out from trios of siblings and mark them as the beneficiaries of helpers and donors. No matter how trivial a favor may seem, it is repaid in generous terms. The boy who spares the life of an ant and the girl who shares her crust of bread end by ruling over a kingdom. But rather than acting autonomously, fairy-tale heroes again and again depend on help from sources of the most improbable kind in order to reach the goal of reaffiliation symbolized by marriage and monarchy.

Bettelheim's views on the "lessons" of "Cinderella" reveal how he typically divides fairy-tale life into two phases, each marked by a clear sense of separation from community—being "on one's own," as Bettelheim habitually puts it: " 'Cinderella' guides the child from his greatest disappointments—oedipal disillusionment, castration anxiety, low opinion of himself because of the imagined low opinion of others— toward developing his autonomy, becoming industrious [note how the work ethic inadvertently slips in], and gaining a positive identity of his own" (276). The very sense of isolation and lack of affiliation experienced by the heroine at the tale's beginning is repeated in a conclusion that "elevates" the heroine to a condition of supposed autonomy. Even so sensitive a critic of Bettelheim as Jack Zipes, who faults the child psychologist for attempting to construct "static literary models to be internalized for therapeutic consumption," comes down in the end (though for different reasons) on the side of "greater individual autonomy" (*Breaking the Magic Spell* 177) for fairy-tale recipients. Readers and protagonists alike must all march relentlessly down the royal road that leads to autonomy.

Given Sendak's penchant for telling tales in which children retreat into a world of fantasy to master unruly feelings on their own and his distaste for tales that send explicit messages, it is surprising to find him drawn so strongly to the Grimms' *Nursery and Household Tales,* and in particular to the "recently discovered" Grimm tale "Dear Mili." To be sure, Sendak has had a long love affair with the *Nursery and Household Tales,* beginning with his illustrations of 1973 for *The Juniper Tree and Other Tales from Grimm,* translated by Lore Segal.[4] That he and Lore Segal, who collaborated in selecting twenty-seven tales from the collection, chose to call the anthology *The Juniper Tree* is telling in that it suggests a desire to resurrect and rehabilitate precisely those tales that our culture has turned away from, in large part because of their open display of family conflicts, domestic violence, and illicit sexual desire. Virtually no other collection of this size, with the exception of the Grimms' own *Kleine Ausgabe* (the abridged Small Edition of fifty tales), includes "Thousandfurs" (No. 65), a story in which a king wants to marry his own daughter, and "Mother Trudy," a tale that we have already mentioned for the alarmingly cruel way in which it punishes the curiosity of its protagonist.

Sendak's literary preferences and his choice of authors to illustrate suggest that it may not then be so strange that he chose to collaborate with the translator Ralph Manheim to produce the spectacular publishing success *Dear Mili.* That story does not, by any stretch of the imagination, paint childhood as an "eternally innocent paradise"—its heroine is exposed to perils that exceed a child's worst fears, and the story ends with the death of mother and child. But *Dear Mili* also has a didactic overlay deeper and denser than almost any text in the

Grimms' *Nursery and Household Tales.* Before we look more closely at the logic of Sendak's three-year labor of love in producing the illustrations for *Dear Mili,* we need to take a closer look at the origins of the Grimms' text and to examine its status as a "lost" text.

On 28 September 1983, a front-page headline in the *New York Times* announced: "A Fairy Tale by Grimm Comes to Light" (McDowell). "After more than 150 years," it dramatically declared, "Hansel and Gretel, Snow White, Rumpelstiltskin and Cinderella will be joined by another Grimm fairy-tale character." This new character did not come cheap. But the "substantial five-figure price" ($26,000 according to later newspaper reports) paid by Farrar, Straus & Giroux for the tale carried with it a certificate of authenticity. The Schiller Company, a firm specializing in rare children's books, guaranteed in writing that the manuscript had never been published previously and promised to refund the purchase price "if this is ever found not to be the case." As John M. Ellis has noted, it was "very strange" that this unique manuscript had been available since 1974 but had found no buyers. "The first and only addition to a collection that is one of the major documents of Western culture, the first and only fairy tale manuscript in Wilhelm Grimm's hand since 1810 . . . and no one is interested?" he writes in mock astonishment (88). Ellis concluded that the tale recorded in the pricey manuscript could not possibly stand out from the masses of published and unpublished folkloric material not included by the Grimms in the 210 numbered texts of their *Nursery and Household Tales.*

While the article in the *New York Times* conceded that there were "brief elements in the story of an earlier Grimm tale, 'Saint Joseph in the Woods,' " it avoided pursuing the point by veering off, in midsentence, to a non sequitur warning readers that the new tale, like other stories by the Grimms, "does not admit to easy interpretation or analysis." In fact, *Dear Mili* contains much more than "brief elements" from another tale—it comes very close to being a conflation of two texts from the ten "Legends for Children" that form the coda to the *Nursery and Household Tales.*

Before taking a closer look at the two texts that were merged to form the basis for *Dear Mili,* let us pause to examine the matter and the manner of the narrative itself. *Dear Mili* is not a complicated narrative. It tells of a young girl whose mother sends her into the woods to save her from the turmoil of war. There the pious, obedient girl meets Saint Joseph and stays with him for what she believes to be three days but what

216

turns out to be thirty years. Saint Joseph instructs the girl to return home with a rosebud, telling her not to be afraid, for she will return to him once the rose is in full bloom. Reunited with her aged mother, the girl spends the evening with her, then goes to bed "calmly and cheerfully." In the morning, neighbors find the woman and her daughter dead: "They had fallen happily asleep, and between them lay Saint Joseph's rose in full bloom."

Just what is it about this tale that led Maurice Sendak to describe it as "wonderful, beautiful and touching?" When you "make an excavation," he added, "you don't expect to find Pompeii" (McDowell). But here was, for him, the Pompeii of fairy-tale digs. Not surprisingly, what Sendak generally likes about the Grimms is that they tell rather than show or comment: "[The Grimms] did not punctuate everything with morals or messages; that's why they are so good" (McDowell).[5] This remark seems more than odd in the context of *Dear Mili,* a text that may not state one clear message but that forcefully guides the reader through the story by constantly passing judgment on the heroine's behavior and commenting on the events that befall her.

Dear Mili begins in the epistolary mode with a letter, penned by the author. In it, the storyteller builds a bridge between himself and "dear Mili." Though he has never set eyes on Mili, his heart goes out to her and reaches her to tell the story set forth in his letter. The prefatory remarks draw attention to a topic close to Wilhelm Grimm's heart: the rift between man and nature. They contrast the ease with which flowers floating in separate brooks can drift towards each other when the streams converge with the difficulty humans encounter in their efforts to meet. "Great mountains and rivers, forests and meadows, cities and villages lie in between . . . and humans cannot fly." Nature is thus privileged in its ease of communication, with no natural or artificial barriers blocking communion between its component parts. Though the narrator claims to have sent his heart out to Mili and that this heart "speaks" even as Mili "listens," it is in fact the written word—that most artificial of signifiers—that bridges the gap between him and Mili. The narrator's insistence on turning the word into the agent that overcomes the barriers separating man from nature reminds us of the degree to which the Grimms and others unwittingly divested language of its artificiality and invested it with natural qualities when it was placed in the service of telling stories, in particular children's stories. The preface thus enunciates the naiveté of the text and declares it to

217

be an unreflected and direct narrative lacking the stylized self-consciousness of "literary" works, which are products of culture rather than of nature. We are led to believe that the voice of nature, speaking in a register at once timeless and universal, addresses us rather than the voice of a narrator like Wilhelm Grimm, who is anchored in a specific time and place.

Dear Mili begins on a less than cheerful note. We are introduced to a widow who lives at the edge of a village and who lives with her one surviving daughter: "Her children had died, all but one daughter, whom she loved dearly." The girl is a model of good behavior: "She was a dear, good little girl, who was always obedient and said her prayers before going to bed and in the morning when she got up." The effect of all this goodness becomes immediately apparent to the reader, who learns in the very next sentence that "everything she did went well." "When she planted something in her little garden patch, a clump of violets or a sprig of rosemary, it took root so well that you could see it growing"—a truly amazing consequence of being dear, good, and obedient. More importantly, we learn that the heroine must have a guardian angel, for "when danger threatened the little girl, she was always saved." After the girl meets up with Saint Joseph, she is more tractable and agreeable than ever, if that is at all possible. Not only does she share her Sunday cake with him and cook his food, she also volunteers to sleep on the floor ("A little straw on the floor will be soft enough for me") and happily follows his instructions to take charge of gathering food in the forest ("It was because he didn't want her to be idle that he had sent her out to work"). To be sure, the girl does get a chance to play (with her guardian angel) after the two have dug the roots that are to constitute dinner, but she has to work surprisingly hard in view of the fact that she has died and gone to heaven.

Sendak is right on one count when it comes to *Dear Mili*. "You have to be careful about reading things into the Grimms' stories," he warns (McDowell). For *Dear Mili* this is especially the case, in part because the tale sends mixed signals to the reader, and, as a result, produces a message that is almost hopelessly scrambled. The heroine, we recall, is a "dear, good little girl" blessed with good fortune. But all her prayers and good behavior seem to backfire, for not only does war break out around her, but her mother decides to send her into the woods for "three days" to protect her from "wicked men." While the girl is in the woods, it begins to dawn on the reader that she has met her death there and gone to heaven. When the heroine returns home, we learn that "her mother had thought wild beasts had torn her to pieces years ago." In fact, it is highly probable that the girl perished in exactly that way in the forest, then entered the domestic paradise ruled by Saint Joseph. Observe what happens on the girl's first night away from home while she is contemplating the stars: "One by one the stars came out, and looking up at them the child said: 'How bright are the nails on the great door of heaven! What a joy it will be when God opens it!' Then suddenly a star seemed to have fallen to the ground. As the child came nearer, the light grew bigger and bigger until at length she came to a little house and saw that the light was shining from the window." Can there be any doubt that the girl has entered a celestial abode?

Why, then, is it that the mother favored sending her daughter on her own into the woods, where the chances for survival must have been slim, over keeping her at home, where the risks were obviously not as grave? The question becomes an urgent one, not because children's literature must adhere to an iron logic of naturalistic motivation, but because most children who read the story in its new incarnation and realize that the heroine dies while the mother survives will be puzzled by the mother's decision to send her daughter away and will not be satisfied with the mother's misplaced faith in Providence ("God in His mercy will show you the way," she tells her daughter at the edge of the woods).

The significance of the mother's decision nonetheless pales by comparison with the weightiness of the final image and final page in the book. With outstretched arms and eyes that seem blinded by age, the mother greets her daughter, who marches homeward, rosebud in hand, against the background of a brilliant sunset. Here is the full version of the tale's "happy end" in its verbal form: "All evening they sat happily together. Then they went to bed calmly and cheerfully, and next morning the neighbors found them dead. They had fallen happily asleep, and between them lay Saint Joseph's rose in full bloom." The blossoming of the rose presumably offers the promise of eternal life, for Saint Joseph had handed the rose to the heroine with the reassurance of a return when the flower came to full bloom. This orientation to otherworldly salvation is very much in keeping with the story's overlay of religious piety. The heroine not only spends a great deal of her time praying, but also appeals to God whenever she is in need ("Oh, dear God, help your child to go on") and is confident that he will provide for her ("God is feeding his sheep with roses, why would He forget me?").[6]

In one sense, *Dear Mili* delivers a consistent message, for it can be read as a Christian parable in which eternal life stands as the reward for a life of piety and goodness. But at the same time, as a story that draws on fairy-tale conventions and as a text selected by Maurice Sendak for illustration, it arouses specific expectations, at least on the part of adult readers. Returning to Saint Joseph may be some people's idea of a reward, but it does not correspond to what most fairy-tale heroines acquire once they make their way out of the woods. What of the earthly rewards usually stored up for the protagonists and the eternal punishments reserved for the villains? It is hard to believe that children can find in death an ending more satisfying than wealth and a return home to *live* happily ever after. And why is it that Maurice Sendak, who usually gives us adventure stories that end with the hero's return to reality (to the here and now) and reconciliation with mother, suddenly chooses to spend three years on a text that promises the reward of eternal salvation? Even leaving Maurice Sendak out of the picture, looking at the text alone, it remains difficult to square the otherworldly orientation of this particular story with the secularity of children's literature today. There are good reasons why we do not start out stories with descriptions of widows who have lost all their children but one or end them with images of mother and daughter lying down and dying. This is not to say that children should be shielded from descriptions of material hardships and death, only that they are not necessarily better off when entertained with stories that reflect or take as their point of departure the social and cultural realities of an age other than their own.

Let us, at long last, look at the textual traces of the tale's origins. When Wilhelm Grimm wrote to Mili in 1816, he had not yet published the ten children's legends appended to the *Nursery and Household Tales*. These ten legends appeared for the first time in the second edition of the tales published in 1819. "Saint Joseph in the Forest," the first of the ten stories, is, as the Grimms themselves noted in their annotations to the tale, a variant of "The Three Little Men in the Woods" (No. 13). Both stories are shaped by the reward-and-punishment pattern characteristic of stories about kind and unkind girls. But "Saint Joseph in the Forest" deviates slightly from the norm by plotting the fortunes of three girls—the oldest is "mischievous and wicked," the second is "much better," while the third is "a pious and kind child."[7] More importantly, the benevolent figure that all three girls meet is very different from the gnomes and witches who usually take up residence in the woods to test or to take in fairy-tale heroines. But the Saint Joseph in this particular tale rewards the "pious and kind child" in typical fairy-tale fashion. After demonstrating her willingness to work and to sacrifice her own comfort to ease the lot of others, the young girl retires for the evening. She awakens to find her virtues rewarded:

> She got up and searched for [Saint Joseph], but he was nowhere to be found. Finally, she noticed a bag with money behind the door, and it was so heavy that she could barely carry it. A note on the bag said that the money was for the girl who slept there that night. So the girl took the bag and hurried straight home with it to her mother. She gave all the money to her mother as a present, and the woman was totally satisfied with her daughter. (634–35)

The youngest child, whom the mother once "could not stand," has now found favor in her mother's eyes. Saint Joseph gives the girl exactly the reward she needs in order to live happily ever after. But just as he rewards virtue, so he punishes vice. The oldest daughter also makes the journey to Saint Joseph, who quickly determines that she is a selfish opportunist and punishes her by attaching a second nose to her face. The girl, mortified by the disfiguring effect, pleads with Saint Joseph to relent and remove the nose, which he does. But when the wicked girl returns home, her mother takes her back to the woods to find the bag of money to which she feels entitled. Here is how Saint Joseph punishes evil: "Along the way . . . they were attacked by so many lizards and snakes that they could not protect themselves. The wicked girl was finally stung to death, and the mother was stung all over her feet for not having raised her daughter in a proper way" (636).

This narrative combines exemplary story with cautionary tale to produce the classic reward-and-punishment pattern. The child-victim turns the table on her oppressor, just as the child-transgressor is punished. This is very different from *Dear Mili,* which shows us the good child as victim coming to an unhappy end. In this sense *Dear Mili* stands as an anomaly in the world of the Grimms' fairy tales, for it shows us a heroine who, for all her goodness, hard work, and obedience, comes to a bad end. Of course, there are many who would argue that the heroine's death is more reward than punishment. Indeed, this must have been precisely what Wilhelm Grimm meant to demonstrate.

In the second text that influenced Wilhelm Grimm's letter to Mili, we have a classic example of the consolatory tale, a story designed to provide comfort to those whose parents or children had suffered an untimely death. "The Rose," the third of the "Legends for Children," tells of a poor woman with two children. The younger of the two must go into the woods every day to fetch wood. There the child is protected and aided by its guardian angel who, one day, brings a rosebud for the child. The mother puts the rosebud in water: "One morning her son did not get out of bed. So she went to his bed and found him dead, but he lay there looking very content. And the rose reached full bloom that very same morning."[8] This tale may have served a useful, indeed therapeutic, function in another age, when the death of small children was an occurrence of distressing frequency, but it seems less than appropriate as a bedtime story for children in certain cultures of our own age.

What Wilhelm Grimm did in drafting his letter to Mili amounts to a clumsy attempt to cross two different types of tales. "The Rose," a consolatory tale probably designed to comfort parents grieving for a child, was grafted onto "Saint Joseph in the Forest," a reward-and-punishment tale oriented very much, despite the figure in the title, to this world and to its rewards. The result is an impossible hybrid form, one that tries to reward a good child with something that most children can consider only as a punishment.

Dear Mili is, of course, not unprecedented in its status as a children's book that celebrates the death of a child. But we do have to go far back in time to find something comparable. James Janeway's *A Token for Children* (1671), which inspired Cotton Mather's *A Token, for the Children of New-England* (1700) and countless other books, praises early death as a path to salvation and gives us the short lives and protracted deaths of numerous saintly children. Judging by the number of editions printed, these books were immensely popular with adults. There is some evidence that children did read them, if only to please their parents. When the eight-year-old Sarah Camme died in Westmoreland in 1682, her parents, Thomas and Anne Camme, took it upon themselves to write a brief biography of the child. In it, they described Sarah's favorite books. While alive, she "delighted much in reading the holy Scripture; . . . she took great Delight to read the Testimony of Friends to the Appearance of God's Power in Young Children, whether in their Health, or on their Dying Beds; and had got several printed Books that had relation thereto" (Sloane 52). Sarah may have been as delighted as her parents allege, yet it is important to bear in mind that we have nothing more than the testimony of her parents—both of whom happened to be Quaker preachers—to substantiate her love of scripture and biographical narratives.

Janeway, as F. J. Harvey Darton has charitably pointed out, had the best of intentions when he published his stories (58). From Janeway's point of view, it was a sacred duty to salvage the souls of those who are "not too little to go to Hell" (qtd. in Darton 56). The exemplary tales in *A Token for Children* were also designed to provide comfort to children faced with the tragedy of a sibling's death or confronted with their own mortality when visited by some dread disease. At age two and a half, Maurice Sendak himself had just this kind of brush with death—in the form of a thirteen-week bout with measles followed by double pneumonia—that left him frail for most of his childhood and also marked him psychologically. "I remember being terrified of death as a child," Sendak observed. "I think a lot of children are, but I was scared because I heard talk of it all around me. There was always the possibility I might have died of the measles or its aftermath. Certainly my parents were afraid I wouldn't survive" (Lanes 16).

Sendak's childhood preoccupation with death is further reflected in the vivid recollection of a story told by his father. Of the many "beautiful" and "imaginative" stories Maurice Sendak heard as a child, this one remained fixed in memory. The tale begins with a child taking a walk with his parents. Here is how Sendak retells the rest of the story: "Somehow he becomes separated from [his parents] and snow begins to fall. The child shivers in the cold and huddles under a tree, sobbing in terror. Then, an enormous, angelic figure hovers over him and says, as he draws the boy up, 'I am Abraham, your father.' His fear is gone, the child looks up and also sees Sarah. When his mother and father find him, he is dead" (Lanes 12). Sendak's admitted "obsession" with his own childhood, his need to replay it and hence to defuse some of the powerful emotions associated with it, determines to a great extent not only the plots of the tales he tells but also the kinds of stories he chooses to illustrate. The mystery of his fascination with *Dear Mili* partially unravels with a look at his own childhood and its texts.

The agenda of children's literature has always been fixed by adults. From its inception, with ABC primers that proclaimed "In Adam's Fall, we sinned all," children's literature moved in the theological/redemptive mode only to shift gradually, with the introduction of discipline through instruction, into the didactic/moralistic mode. The nineteenth century, which witnessed the great flowering of children's literature, placed, with some notable Victorian exceptions, an unprecedented premium on sending messages through children's literature even as it nervously sought to preserve the notion of childhood as a wide-eyed, innocent, uncontaminated stage of life. Consider, for example, the Grimms' preface to their *Nursery and Household Tales,* where the brothers write about the purity that makes children appear "so marvellous and blessed" (1: 16) and then proceed to tell stories about stubborn, obstinate, strong-willed children who are put to death.

The nineteenth-century celebration of childish innocence and the creation of a special literary preserve characterized by naturalness and naiveté were shadowed by a didactic mode anchored in the culture of surveillance so convincingly mapped by Michel Foucault in *Discipline and Punish.* We need look no further than the popular child-rearing manuals of the time, with their medieval restraining devices and projects for discipline, to recognize the extent to which manipulation feeds on idealization. For many parents, however, control could be exercised more effectively through visual means than through either words or material forms of restraint. Children's books first became implicated in a culture of surveillance by propagating the threat of an all-seeing and vengeful God. In *The Child's Instructor,* a young girl vows to herself: "I will always behave well, even when I find myself in the greatest solitude; recollecting that, wherever I am, the eye of my Creator is upon me; and to HIM I must look for that blessing which is the reward of a virtuous life" (34). The notorious Fairchild children of Mrs. Sherwood's nineteenth-century children's classic learn to recite a prayer addressed to a "great and dreadful God! who seest every thing and knowest everything; from whom I cannot hide even one thought of my heart; whose eye can go down into the deepest and darkest place!" (Sherwood 2: 107). But they are also kept under the strict supervision of their parents. Mr. and Mrs. Fairchild never seem to take their eyes off their children—when their daughter Lucy boasts that she and her siblings have been exceptionally well behaved and not punished for a long time, Mrs. Fairchild responds by quoting scripture about the evils of boasting and adds: "If you have not done any very naughty thing lately, it is not because there is any goodness or wisdom in you, but because your papa and I have been always with you, carefully watching and guiding you from morning till night" (2: 68). This watchful parental-eye was forever trained on the child, seeking to control it with punishments, gazes, words, pictures, and whatever else could be added to the arsenal of parental weapons.

Our own culture has moved into yet another mode of telling children's stories, one that might best be described as empathetic/cathartic, resting as it does on a therapeutic model. Any adult who has read stories to children knows how readily they slide into the role of the tale's main character, usurping all the pains and privileges attending the role of primary actor. The ease with which children identify with storybook characters encouraged Bettelheim and Sendak to endorse children's stories that enact the pains of childhood and help children face and work through their deepest anxieties. But even Bettelheim concedes that "we cannot know at what age a particular fairy tale will be most important to a particular child" and that therefore "we cannot ourselves decide which of the many tales he should be told at any given time or why" (17). Through a process of trial and error, the adult can eventually determine which stories have special meaning for a child and promote identification and abreaction. Adults, in short, do need to intervene, even if for Bettelheim only in a rather haphazard process of selection. Sendak, by contrast, delegates even responsibility for selection to the child. To a mother who insisted, despite her daughter's protests, on reading *Where the Wild Things Are* with her because it was a "Caldecott book," Sendak wrote: "If a kid doesn't like a book, *throw it away*. Children don't give a damn about awards. Why should they? We should let children choose their own books. What they don't like *they will toss aside*" (Lanes 106; my emphasis). This is all well and good, but Sendak seems unwittingly to acknowledge adult control even as he repudiates it. Forgetting that the adult has the real power to throw a book away (the girl in question evidently had to suffer through at least ten readings of *Where the Wild Things Are* before her mother wrote to its author for advice), Sendak mistakenly claims that the child can elect to toss a book aside.

It may seem churlish to mount a critique of those who wish to restore to children what seems rightfully theirs and who have done much to steer us away from the self-righteous and often cruel didactic tale of an earlier age. Both Bettelheim and Sendak have directed our attention to the desires and needs of the child, but it is important to recognize that those desires and needs remain an eternal mystery to adults, who have the real power when it comes to determining what is to constitute children's literature. Adults produce the texts passed on to children, and, as Sendak himself acknowledges, it is *their* childhood anxieties and fears that are reconstructed and mastered through the writing of the texts, though there is also a chance that the adult gets it right and captures the feelings and experiences of the child. "It may be that in projecting how I felt as a child onto the children I draw I'm being terribly biased and inaccurate," Sendak admits. "But all I have to go on is what I know—not only about my childhood then but about the child I was as he exists now" (Hentoff 329). Children's literature is now still really as much for adults as it is for children. "There was a time in history," Sendak has observed, "when books like *Alice in Wonderland* and the fairy tales of George MacDonald were read by everybody. They were not designated as being 'for children.' The Grimm tales are about the pure essence of life—incest, murder, insane mothers, love, sex—what have you" (Lanes 206). Jacob Grimm himself stated that the *Nursery and Household Tales* were not recorded for children, but he was delighted to find that they numbered among those who became avid readers of the book (Steig 269).

This simple fact of children's literature as a product of adult reconstructions of childhood realities does much to unravel one of the mysteries of fairy tales. Why is it that tales originally written by adults for adults so insistently take the child's point of view and are so obsessed with such childhood matters as sibling rivalry and fear of abandonment? The answer is Sendak's answer to why he writes children's stories: to "reconstruct" childhood anxieties and to "defuse" their explosive power. The real question does not turn on the false dichotomy between adult authors/adult recipients and child protagonists/childhood themes, but on the issue of why we have turned the Grimms' tales and other such folkloristic monuments into literature that is targeted almost exclusively for children. Sendak's description of the genesis of his books reminds us that the line separating children's literature from "adult literature" is really somewhat more fluid than we imagine it to be. Adults make all the decisions about children's literature, and there is no reason why they should not also be active recipients of the tales. As we have seen, decisions about what makes a good storybook shift from one era to another. Our current preferences may seem vastly superior to Janeway's luridly sanctimonious descriptions of dying children, or Dr. Heinrich Hoffmann's unforgettable images of thumbsuckers getting their thumbs sheared off and disobedient children going up in flames, but they are ultimately our adult preferences about what we want to see in books and what is "for their own good."

Notes

1. Jennifer R. Waller finds that *Where the Wild Things Are* and *In the Night Kitchen* are "not therapeutic in intent." For her, Sendak's books "simply attempt to reflect and evoke the child's imaginative experience" (135).
2. On children's literature as a creation of adults (hence its impossibility), see especially Jacqueline Rose, *The Case of Peter Pan or The Impossibility of Children's Fiction.*
3. This point, obvious as it may seem, cannot be emphasized enough. John Rowe Townsend stresses it, as does Penelope Mortimer.
4. For expert commentary, from the German point of view, on the illustrations, see Heinz Rölleke's essay on Sendak, "Tales from Grimm."
5. P. L. Travers appreciates this same lack of a didactic turn when she writes that the Grimms "spread out the story just as it was" (21).
6. On Christian elements in the Grimms' *Nursery and Household Tales,* see Heinz Rölleke, "Das Bild Gottes," and Ruth B. Bottigheimer 143–55.
7. English translations of the text refer to Jack Zipes's translation, *The Complete Fairy Tales of the Brothers Grimm.* Here 634.
8. The original does not specify the child's gender (638).

Works Cited

Andersen, Hans Christian. *Eighty Fairy Tales.* Trans. R. P. Keigwin. New York: Pantheon, 1976.

Bettelheim, Bruno. *The Uses of Enchantment: The Meaning and Importance of Fairy Tales.* New York: Random House-Vintage Books, 1976.

Bottigheimer, Ruth B. *Grimms' Bad Girls and Bold Boys: The Moral and Social Vision of the Tales.* New Haven: Yale UP, 1987.

The Child's Instructor; intended as a first book, for children. By a fellow of the Royal Society. London: Thorp and Burch, 1828.

Collodi, Carlo. *The Adventures of Pinocchio.* Trans. E. Harden. New York: Knopf, 1988.

Darton, F. J. Harvey. *Children's Books in England: Five Centuries of Social Life*. Cambridge: Cambridge UP, 1932.

Duvoisin, Roger. "Children's Book Illustration: The Pleasures and Problems." Egoff, *Only Connect* 357–74.

Egoff, Sheila, et al., eds. *Only Connect: Readings in Children's Literature*. Toronto: Oxford UP, 1969.

Ellis, John M. "What Really Is the Value of the 'New' Grimm Discovery?" *German Quarterly* 58 (1985): 87–90.

Foucault, Michel. *Discipline and Punish: The Birth of the Prison*. Trans. Alan Sheridan. New York: Random House-Vintage Books, 1977.

Gilligan, Carol. *In a Different Voice: Psychological Theory and Women's Development*. Cambridge: Harvard UP, 1982.

Grimm, Brothers. *Kinder- und Hausmärchen: Ausgabe letzter Hand mit den Originalanmerkungen der Brüder Grimm*. Ed. Heinz Rölleke. 3 vols. Stuttgart: Reclam, 1980.

———. *The Juniper Tree and Other Tales from Grimm*. Trans. Lore Segal, with four tales trans. Randall Jarrell. Illus. Maurice Sendak. New York: Farrar, Straus & Giroux, 1973.

Grimm, Wilhelm. *Dear Mili*. Trans. Ralph Manheim. Illus. Maurice Sendak. New York: Farrar, Straus & Giroux, 1988.

Hentoff, Nat. "Among the Wild Things." Egoff, *Only Connect* 323–46.

The History of Little Goody Two-Shoes; Otherwise called, Mrs. Margery Two-Shoes. London: John Newbery, 1765.

Horsely, Henry Sharpe. *The Affectionate Parent's Gift, and the Good Child's Reward. Flowers of Delight*. Ed. Leonard de Vries. London: Dennis Dobson, 1965. 119–29.

Janeway, James. *A Token for Children; Being an Account of the Conversion, Holy and Exemplary Lives, and Joyful Deaths, of Several Young Children*. 1671. London: Francis Westley, 1825.

Lanes, Selma G. *The Art of Maurice Sendak*. New York: Harry N. Abrams, 1980.

McDowell, Edwin. "A Fairy Tale by Grimm Comes to Light." *New York Times* 28 Sept. 1983.

Mortimer, Penelope. "Thoughts Concerning Children's Books." Egoff, *Only Connect* 97–105.

Perrault's Complete Fairy Tales. Trans. A. E. Johnson et al. New York: Dodd, Mead, 1961.

Pickard, P. M. *I Could a Tale Unfold: Violence, Horror and Sensationalism in Stories for Children*. London: Tavistock, 1961.

Rölleke, Heinz. "Das Bild Gottes in den Märchen der Brüder Grimm." *"Wo das Wünschen noch geholfen hat": Gesammelte Aufsätze zu den "Kinder- und Hausmärchen" der Brüder Grimm*. Bonn: Bouvier, 1985. 207–19.

———. "Tales from Grimm—Pictures by Maurice Sendak: Entdeckungen und Vermutungen." *Brüder Grimm Gedenken* 2 (1975): 242–45.

Rose, Jacqueline. *The Case of Peter Pan or The Impossibility of Children's Fiction.* London: MacMillan, 1984.

Sendak, Maurice. *Caldecott & Co.* New York: Farrar, Straus and Giroux, Michael di Capua Books, 1988.

———. *In the Night Kitchen.* New York: Harper & Row, 1970.

———. *Outside Over There.* New York: Harper & Row, 1981.

———. *Where the Wild Things Are.* New York: Harper & Row, 1963.

Sherwood, Mary Martha. *History of the Fairchild Family.* Vol. 2 of *The Works of Mrs. Sherwood.* New York: Harper & Brothers, 1864.

Sloane, William. *Children's Books in England and America in the Seventeenth Century.* New York: King's Crown Press, 1955.

Steig, Reinhold, ed. *Achim von Arnim und Jacob und Wilhelm Grimm.* Stuttgart: Cotta, 1904.

Townsend, John Rowe. "Didacticism in Modern Dress." Egoff, *Only Connect* 33–40.

Travers, P. L. "On Not Writing for Children." *Children's Literature* 4 (1975): 15–22.

Upton, William. "The School Girl: A Poem." London: William Darton, 1820.

Waller, Jennifer R. "Maurice Sendak and the Blakean Vision of Childhood." *Children's Literature* 6 (1977): 130–40.

Zipes, Jack. *Breaking the Magic Spell: Radical Theories of Folk & Fairy Tales.* Austin: U of Texas P, 1979.

———, trans. *The Complete Fairy Tales of the Brothers Grimm.* New York: Bantam, 1987.

Response and Responsibility in Reading Grimms' Fairy Tales

Donald Haase

T HE ENGRAVER RESPONSIBLE for the title page of the nineteenth-century American edition of Grimms' tales translated by Edgar Taylor evidently was given the original German text to work from. And he evidently had some trouble deciphering the German typeface he encountered. Little did he know it was the *Kinder- und Hausmärchen* he had before him and not—as we read on the American title page—the *Rinder und Hans Märchen* (Alderson n2). Fortunately, the error did no lasting damage, and the Grimms' *Children's and Household Tales* did not become known to Americans as the *Cattle and Hans Tales.* But the error is worth noting, not simply for its humor but also for what it suggests about responsibility in reading Grimms' fairy tales. The engraver responsible was in one sense not responsible enough. Without the necessary information, experience, and context, he understandably took the Fraktur *K* for an *R,* and the *u* for an *n.* Irresponsible? Well, yes, in that this constitutes an inappropriate response to the foreign lettering. But certainly he had no reason to assume the letters were any others than those he perceived them to be.

In fact, he made sense of an otherwise unintelligible language in the best way he could—by responding to the individual letters as shapes resembling those he knew. Responding to the text, he distorted it in one sense; yet in another sense he gave what might have seemed to him a distorted text shape and meaning.

Our engraver is not so different from Katy in Grimms' tale of "Freddy and Katy" (No. 59). Unable to make sense of her husband's idiomatic and metaphoric language except on a literal level, she carries out his instructions in ways that seem bizarre and irresponsible to him but appear perfectly sensible and logical to her. If we were to level charges of irresponsibility at the engraver—or the reader—who responds to a text without the requisite context, then we might expect a reply echoing Katy's: "I didn't know that. You should have told me" (*Complete Fairy Tales* 226).

This is precisely what contemporary Grimm scholars have undertaken to do: to tell the uninformed what it is they need to know in order to respond responsibly to the *Kinder- und Hausmärchen*. Weary of psychotherapists, spiritualists, astrologers, and other assorted interpreters reading Grimms' tales with the same blind spot as our nineteenth-century engraver, informed Grimm scholars have begun a process of reeducation by defining what a responsible reading is and what a reader needs to know to arrive at one. Here I want to review this critical reception of the Grimms' tales and explore the implications for reading, understanding, and responding to them.

Heinz Rölleke has led the way in laying out the ground rules for an informed understanding of the *Kinder- und Hausmärchen*. His meticulous philological-historical studies and text-editions have illuminated the genesis, development, and nature of the Grimms' collection; and he has persuasively argued that a responsible interpretation of any single tale must be based on a thorough philological and text-historical analysis.[1] His point is lucidly made in a discussion of "Brier Rose" (No. 50) in his 1985 introduction to the Grimms' tales:

> One would hope that philological-literary and folkloric research would offer in the future a more solid foundation for fairy-tale interpretation, which is running wild everywhere. The make up of texts and appropriate textual understanding should become indispensable prerequisites for every fairy-tale interpretation; otherwise the way is open for sheer caprice. Only when the textual history of Grimms' tale of "Brier Rose" [for example] has been illuminated as much as possible, when the historical and

cultural, as well as the generic prerequisites are generally recognized, can a sound interpretation be generated by any of the variously emphasized positions of those disciplines that have in the meantime turned their attention to the fairy tale—whether the text is analyzed from theological, mythological, psychoanalytic, anthroposophic, pedagogical, or literary perspectives. (*Die Märchen* 97)

Rölleke has no sympathy for interpretations that have not considered a specific tale's textual ancestry. While he allows that fairy tales are "rich enough . . . to permit" private and undisciplined readings, he insists that "serious" scholary commentary must take into account facts surrounding the origin and development of the texts (*Die wahren Märchen* 315). Not only the Grimms' editorial revisions must be taken into account, including those in both the seven Large Editions and the ten Small Editions of the *Kinder- und Hausmärchen,* but also the identity of their informants and/or the written sources, insofar as these can be established. Such "filters"[2] have all shaped the content, style, and meaning of the text in some way, so that any more or less definitive statements about the text's significance must be based on an accurate recognition and understanding of these. For example, Rölleke has repeatedly corrected Helmut Brackert's claim to see sociohistorical significance in "Hansel and Gretel" (No. 15), particularly in the tale's introductory reference to "a great famine." This "große Teuerung," Rölleke cautions, could not be taken as evidence that the tale reflects "social conditions and problems of earliest times" if readers like Brackert knew that the motif was first inserted into the story by Wilhelm Grimm in 1843, when he borrowed it from a version of the tale published by August Stöber in 1842.[3]

But the actual extent and implications of Rölleke's well-founded scholarly position on responsibility become most evident in his contention that before we can make any interpretive claims about the nature and significance of the *Kinder- und Hausmärchen* as a whole, we need "some 240 individual studies" of the tales the Grimms published in, deleted from, or used to compile and annotate their collection throughout its publishing history:

> For each text, one would need to describe its history before the Grimms; to uncover the form in which the Grimms became familiar with the tale, through hearing or reading it; and to document and interpret the changes

made, whether as a result of a misunderstanding, for reasons of stylistic improvement, motivation, embellishment, or abridgement, or above all as the result of manifold contamination. And this must be done not only for the first edition of 1812–15, but for all seventeen editions of the collection, . . . taking into account, of course, the manuscript material in the form of inscribed notations and textual changes. ("New Results" 101–2)

Only after putting all these pieces of an enormous jigsaw puzzle together can we begin to understand and interpret the Grimms' stories and their collection responsibly. Until then, Rölleke warns, "all wholesale judgments . . . must remain unprovable" (102). In fact, from this perspective, responsible—let alone definitive—interpretation appears to be indefinitely deferred. Given the likely impossibility of fully reconstructing the complete heritage of every Grimm text and pre-text, as well as the fact that "one does not find, either, in direct testimony or statements by the Grimm brothers or their contributors, so much as a hint that would render permissible such deductive conclusions," we might well ask whether responsible interpretation and understanding are possible at all under the circumstances Rölleke describes.

Rölleke's formidable view of the reader's responsibility is clearly informed by his philological orientation and expertise. The American folklorist Alan Dundes, on the other hand, offers an equally demanding prescription for responsible fairy-tale interpretation that reflects his specific folkloric interests and expertise. Dundes has emphasized the inadequacy both of folkloristic investigations that collect variants of a tale type without interpretive effort and literary interpretations that fail to consider a tale's "full panoply of oral texts" (41). Literary critics who privilege a specific text—and it is normally the Grimm version of a tale—too quickly deduce its meaning and make interpretive or cultural generalizations on the basis of this single variant alone. Only when the full stock of variants is considered and understood as manifestations of a single *tale type* can a reader responsibly propose an interpretation and draw broader conclusions.

Like Rölleke, Dundes insists on a textual reconstruction undertaken by viewing the tale in a context of multiple texts. But unlike Rölleke, Dundes, as a folklorist, seeks not to reconstruct the textual history of a tale philologically and to use earlier texts to understand a specific Grimm tale or even the collection as a whole; rather, he uses variants—

which may be philologically unrelated—to reconstruct a generally representative and hypothetical text that implicitly becomes the object of interpretation.

Dundes's position raises significant questions about the ontology of the interpreted fairy-tale text that go beyond the scope of my arguments here. More pertinent is the notion that responsible readings of Grimms' tales involve more than the reader and the specific Grimm texts, and even more than their immediate contexts. In fact, Dundes's responsible interpretation emerges from multiple readings of multiple texts and is, in the final analysis, a reading of a hypothetical composite text that transcends the actual, individual texts considered. "There is no one single text in folklore," writes Dundes, "there are only texts" (16). In this interpretive scenario, responsibility is not dictated by the reader's response to a text, but by his or her attention to a full (but necessarily incomplete) complement of international variants.

From a sociohistorical perspective, Jack Zipes articulates yet another view of the fairy tale that places specific demands on the reader to adopt a multidimensional view of any text. Eschewing a one-dimensional view, Zipes emphasizes the multiple layers of sociohistorical references and values that inform Grimms' tales—strata of significance that reflect the perspectives of the various tellers who have helped give any specific tale its current shape (*The Brothers Grimm* 43–61, 135–46). These are basically the filters of which Rölleke writes. But Zipes goes a step beyond Rölleke and speculates not only about the Grimms' contributions to a tale, about the traces of their informants and sources, but also about the unspecified yet inevitably present tellers of the tale from even further back in history and the chain of storytellers. In any given Grimm text we might find the voice of the Grimms' informant, the voice of either Jacob or Wilhelm himself, the voice of the tale's "submerged creator," and the voices of the "intervening tale tellers who pass on the narrative from author to listeners and future tellers" (50). So Zipes is more likely to attribute certain motifs in "Cinderella" (No. 21) to storytellers from a past and unspecified matriarchal society than is Rölleke, whose philological orientation is not conducive to such speculation, and who would thus focus only on what he knows about the identifiable sources and informants (137–38; Rölleke, "Die Frau").

Furthermore, because fairy tales consist of multiple layers of often contradictory values, Zipes recommends that readers begin "exploring historical paths'' in the tales (*The Brothers Grimm* 43–61). In other words, the reader's responsibility is to tease apart the layers of socio-historical evidence in the tales so as to understand better each story's historical development and reception, and to understand our own responses to the meanings and values discovered in the tales (46). This procedure becomes crucial if we are to comprehend the often contradictory values that fairy tales seem to contain and the contradictory reception they receive. And it is crucial if we are to grasp both the hazardous and liberating potential of fairy tales as agents of socialization (27).

All these positions usefully clarify the problem of critical responsibility in fairy-tale interpretation. The parade of filters, variants, and voices makes one thing evident: the Grimm fairy tale is not necessarily an integrated symbolic gesture with an inherent, immutable, and clearly defined meaning. I contest Maria Tatar's assertion that "the symbolic codes woven into fairy tales are relatively easy to decipher" (92). Rather, I would make two arguments: (1) fairy tales consist of chaotic symbolic codes that have become highly ambiguous and invite quite diverse responses; and (2) these responses will reflect a recipient's experience, perspective, or predisposition.

Despite the various methodological stipulations that seek to reconstruct a tale's "actual" meaning and to control the outcome of fairy-tale interpretation, there is a growing consensus that the significance of a fairy-tale text frequently remains elusive. Gerhard Haas's remarks are representative of this consensus:

> What fairy tales originally and actually meant can hardly ever be determined with any certainty. . . . The European folktales that have been fixed in literary form were, over centuries, composed of so many narrative layers, different perspectives, experiences, and forms of sensibility that it is just inconceivable that these texts could have preserved a unified—as is generally presumed—statement about the nature of human beings. Any other assumption is pure wishful thinking.[4]

There is compelling evidence for the ambiguous nature of fairy tales and the limitations of responsible fairy-tale interpretation. In the first place, the longevity of the fairy tale—its reception by diverse societies in diverse contexts—attests to its broad interpretive potential and its apparent flexibility (Dégh 76–77). Grimms' tales have served the needs of the Nazis, Freudian psychoanalysts, theologians, feminists, and the Waldorf schools—to name just a few of the diverse groups who have utilized them—and this wide applicability implies that instability in the tales' symbolic associations and core values accounts for their stability in the world-wide canon.

Similarly, the diversity of critical fairy-tale interpretations encourages sober consideration of the genre's remarkable potential for meaning. With similar ideological premises, some feminists berate Grimms' "Cinderella" and tales of its type for the heroine's passivity and dependency, while others praise the story for its positive depiction of female independence.[5] In the case of "Little Red Riding Hood" (No. 26), Erich Fromm interprets the tale as the product of men-hating women, while Jack Zipes, discussing the *Trials and Tribulations of Little Red Riding Hood,* sees the story as a projection of misogynous males. For Bruno Bettelheim the tale focuses on adolescence and genital obsessions (166–83), while for Alan Dundes it revolves around orality and infantile fantasies (43).

How is it that so many reasonable people reach so many diverse and often contradictory conclusions about the same texts? One answer, of course, is that many readers have been operating irresponsibly—like the engraver of the "Cattle and Hans Tales." Bruno Bettelheim, for example, can make universal psychotherapeutic claims for Grimms' tales because he is almost thoroughly uninformed. He ignores diverse variants of the tales; he falsely assumes that the stories accurately reflect ancient oral narratives; and he neglects the sociohistorical setting in which they were revised and edited. Beyond such scholarly irresponsibility, however, the motley history of fairy-tale interpretation finds an explanation in the scholarly rediscovery of the complex editorial history surrounding Grimms' tales. Over the last fifteen years, Grimm scholarship has been dominated by Heinz Rölleke's philological investigation of Grimms' informants and variants, and by the search for multiple historical voices speaking simultaneously in the tales. These complementary research projects, which identify diverse narrators and layers of sociohistorical reality, have exposed the palimpsest-like nature of Grimms' texts and undercut the idea of one-dimensional meaning.

The feminist critic Karen Rowe, for example, uses the bifocal vision of a fairy tale's significance to explain how contradictory interpretations are equally legitimate. Noting the coexistence of repressive, misogynistic elements and an overall message of rebirth, coming of age, or liberation, she discerns two voices in the classical fairy tales: a patriarchal voice speaking to and for a male-dominated society, and a sub-merged female voice speaking a code of liberation. As she puts it, a fairy tale is "speaking at one level to a total culture, but at another to a sisterhood of readers who will understand the hidden language, the secret revelations of the tale" (15). Rowe's notion of a hidden language speaking to a sisterhood of readers suggests not only the double potential in responding to fairy tales, but also the potential problems in undertaking a responsible reading of fairy tales, in particular the difficulty for male readers who may be deaf to the sister's voice.[6] In this case we could ask whether responses and responsibility to fairy tales differ by gender.

Wolfgang Mieder puts a more general twist on this double potential of the fairy tale and the reader's response when he comments on the role of the reader's perspective in contemporary fairy-tale reception: "The moment one ceases to look at a fairy tale as a symbolic expression of the idea and belief that everything will work out in the end, the cathartic nature of the tale vanishes. Rather than enjoying the final happy state of the fairy tale heroes and heroines at the very end of the fairy tale, modern adults tend to concentrate on the specific problems of the fairy tales, since they reflect today's social reality in a striking fashion" (6). In other words, focusing macroscopically on the utopian plot of fairy tales gives us one view of its significance, while attending microscopically to the details of specific characters and motifs—such as the passivity of classic heroines—gives us a quite different understanding and evokes a different response. So the reader's focus or perspective determines his or her understanding of a tale.

But why should the reader's own perspective override that of the tale itself? Ostensibly a product of "low" or popular culture, the fairy tale, with its simple structures and language, might be thought more singly denotative and resistant to such caprice and ambiguity. Richly connotative structures and discourse, after all, are traditionally characteristic of "high" or literary culture. The Grimm fairy tale, however, is—despite its apparent simplicity—an institutionalized literary genre. And while its language is apparently simple, it is one-dimensional and denotative only in terms of the fictional and generically determined world it represents. The absence of an identifiable narrator (indeed the presence of multiple, incomplete, and conflicting narrative voices) gives little direction as the reader fills out the details of the story. In this way, the reader—like the storyteller who retells a fairy tale—is invited into

237

the re-creative process and made responsible for concretizing the characterizations, settings, motivations, and valuations that the text itself has not specified. So, the reader's understanding of the text and response to it are potentially wide open, making the structures and language of the fairy tale richly multivalent and dependent on the reader's own projections. Whether those projections reflect an institutionalized understanding of the fairy tale or an idiosyncratic response depends on the experience of the reader and the circumstances of reception.

In dealing with the Grimms' tales we have ambiguous texts that belong to both the classical canon and the popular canon. Because of their surface simplicity, Grimms' tales are not only fully accessible to but also produced and marketed for a "lay" audience outside the interpretive institutions. Accordingly, the recipients of fairy tales are overwhelmingly not scholars. Instead, the fairy-tale audience comprises a wide spectrum of readers and auditors, but in particular children. And there is "a necessary difference" between these recipients and the "licensed practitioners" of institutional interpretation (Kermode 73). Lacking a sense of critical responsibility, these recipients possess a response-ability—an ability to respond that will not wait for and could not use the 240 dissertations that scholars need to understand Grimms' collection definitively.

The responses of popular fairy-tale recipients occur not only in ignorance of scholarly data and in reaction to ambiguous texts; they also occur to some extent outside the constraints imposed by a public context. While traditional storytelling was a public event that to some degree controlled the individual response, the printing of texts has increasingly privatized fairy-tale reception (Schenda 85), which increases individual control over the text. Kay Stone has argued that "told stories have more possibilities for openness than do those in printed and filmed media," but she ultimately acknowledges the freedom of the individual recipient to respond outside the interpretive limits imposed by each medium ("Three Transformations" 54). Moreover, because some traditional folkloric symbols have lost their original significance for new generations or foreign cultures, they are now "empty" and are no longer interpreted by readers but used to conform to the individual's own frame of reference. The fairy-tale recipient, in the words of Hermann Bausinger, is limited by an individual "horizon of symbolic understanding" ("Aschenputtel" 147–50). Irresponsible readings may ensue, but they nonetheless reflect the actual conditions of most fairy-tale reception.

Try as we will, and should, to stress responsible historical readings, to publicize the facts of Grimms' fairy tales and the complexities of fairy-tale interpretation, we cannot ignore the recipients and their irresponsible responses. By attending to their responses, we can learn a great deal about how fairy tales generate meaning and function in contemporary society. As an illustration, allow me a personal and admittedly anecdotal example. Once, when reading "Rumpelstiltskin" (No. 55) to my six-year-old daughter for what I believe was the first time, I casually experimented to gauge whether she had already developed a sense of common fairy-tale vocabulary, motifs, and style. While reading (from Zipes's translation *The Complete Fairy Tales of the Brothers Grimm*), I would pause at certain points and ask her to guess the next word. Generally, the results were predictable. For example, "Once upon a ——there was a miller who was poor, but he had a beautiful ——" elicited correctly from her the words "time" and "daughter" (209). The most interesting responses, however, were the following concerning the trials of the miller's daughter. In the first trial, the king locks the maiden in a room with the straw and commands, "Now get to work! If you don't spin this straw into gold by morning, then you must ——." "Die" was my daughter's correct response. The second trial also involves the threat of death. In the third trial, there is a shift. Here the king offers not a threat but a reward. When the king states, "You must spin all this into gold tonight. If you succeed, you shall become my ——," my daughter hesitated and came forth not with the actual word "wife" (211), but instead with a word revealing her own interpretation of the events: "slave."

This response illuminates the story's "meaning"—its potential for reception. While opposing critical camps may argue whether the tale is misogynistic or not, whether it depicts a woman's oppression by men or her ultimate achievement of autonomy and power over men, this naive response cuts to the core of the issue and vividly displays not only the tale's potential significance, but also precisely how fairy tales appear to function in the socialization process. The child's choice of the word "slave" for the text's own use of "wife" reveals the tale's ability literally to define social roles. The response effectively exposes the tale's equation of domestic exploitation—that is, slavery—with the concept

239

of marriage. It is thus not only a legitimate response that can be confirmed by more scholarly analysis, but it is also and more importantly a response that illuminates the meaningful operation of fairy tales in a contemporary social context. It opens a window on the generation of meaning in fairy tales and on the significance of fairy-tale language in a communicative context. In other words, the study of response productively shifts the emphasis from *what* fairy tales mean or meant historically to the question of *how* fairy tales mean in a given context.

For all the debate and controversy over the meaning of Grimms' tales in society, there have been in fact few studies of a practical or experimental nature that attempt to determine how fairy tales are actually received in diverse contexts. The focus of research on Grimm reception has been for the most part on more or less conventional literary-historical questions of influence, adaptation, and what used to be called in comparative literary scholarship "fortune studies." While such studies do elucidate important forms of public response, other equally significant manifestations of private response are only beginning to receive attention. The problem, of course, is in part one of accessibility. While the documentation and analysis of editions, translations, adaptations, and other published responses to Grimms' tales are relatively easy to undertake, the reliable documentation of individual subjective responses is much more difficult. As a consequence, most of the scholarship on the reception of Grimms' tales by children, for example, does not actually examine children's responses. Instead, like Bruno Bettelheim's influential work, it interprets tales abstractly according to a specific theory of reception. Unlike Jack Zipes, who also proposes a theory of fairy-tale reception, few in the debate over the Grimms have actually recognized that the reader's response to a fairy tale is "difficult to interpret, since the reception of an individual tale varies according to the background and experience of the reader" (*Fairy Tales and the Art of Subversion* 174).

The relatively few studies that have attempted to understand individual responses to Grimms' tales have approached the problem with varying perspectives and diverse methods. While psychologists such as Anne-Marie Tausch have experimentally studied responses to Grimms' tales in order to gauge their emotional and ethical effects on children, Rudolf Messner has interviewed children more informally to try to understand what makes fairy tales appropriate or inappropriate at different times. Pedagogues, on the other hand, have been concerned with what children's responses to fairy tales can tell us about the effects of reading in a didactic context. Michael Sahr's experiments with children's responses to Grimms' "Old Sultan" (No. 48), for example, were devised to determine the long- and short-term effects of hearing a fairy tale on children's attitudes and to discern the pedagogical implications of various media adaptations ("Zur experimentellen Erschließung"; "Zur Wirkung"). Similarly concerned with the process of reading and the effects of media on understanding, Helge Weinrebe has studied children's responses to investigate how verbal texts and illustrations influence personal responses to fairy tales.

While these studies reach general conclusions about the operation of specific texts and the effects of their content or form, others have asked how particular groups of recipients respond to Grimms' stories. Jessica Schmitz and Renate Meyer zur Capellen have collaborated to study the responses of kindergartners from five different German schools, including the children of foreign workers and affluent German families. Schmitz's transcripts of discussions with the children about "The Wolf and the Seven Young Kids" (No. 5) have been analyzed from a psychoanalytic perspective by Meyer zur Capellen against the socioeconomic background of each group. Focusing on another class of readers entirely—sick children—Gisela Haas has examined the fairy-tale drawings of hospitalized children and concluded that their diverse responses are shaped by the unique problems and desires of the individual.

The few studies that intentionally set out to examine the responses of children as individuals have been done by parents using their own children as subjects, much like early studies of childhood language acquisition conducted by linguists. That can be both an advantage and disadvantage depending on the methods employed. Ben Rubenstein's study of his daughter's responses to "Cinderella" is not so much a study of a child's response as it is his own Freudian reading of the tale and of his daughter's relationship to himself. Eugen Mahler's informal reports on conversations with his two children about Andersen's "The Ugly Duckling" and Grimm Nos. 4 and 6 are openly characterized as the "observations and thoughts of a father." Unfortunately, his observations remain ultimately inconclusive and do not give us a useful model for eliciting responses. Nina Mikkelsen, on the other hand, attempts a somewhat more methodical study of her daughter's responses to versions of "Snow White" (No. 53) during her third and fourth

241

years. Especially interested in how preliterate children "read" and create meaning, Mikkelsen provides an illuminating analysis of her daughter's changing responses to the different Snow White texts over time.

Despite the diverse perspectives, experimental rigor, and methods of these studies, some conclusions indicate how the study of response illuminates significant issues in fairy-tale scholarship. Three examples are particularly revealing. The first involves two psychological experiments that have tested Bettelheim's assertion that fairy tales have therapeutic effects on children. While psychological testing of children by William C. Crain et al. appears to support Bettelheim's contention that children find fairy tales meaningful and thought-provoking, there is only speculation about how this might be the case. When Patricia Guérin Thomas studied the responses of kindergarten and third-grade pupils to "Brother and Sister" (No. 11) and "The Queen Bee" (No. 62), she found that their responses do depend on the children's developmentally determined inner conflicts and cognitive understanding of moral themes. Neither study, however, found evidence in the children's responses that would confirm Bettelheim's thesis that fairy tales actually help children resolve psychological conflicts.

The study of response has also shed light on the question of sexism in Grimms' tales. Like Bettelheim's assertions about the therapeutic role of fairy tales, discussions of sexism and its effect on readers rarely rely on the responses of real people. Instead, pronouncements about the influence of fairy tales on perceptions of gender roles normally revolve around a critic's own interpretation and the theoretical effects of fairy tales on recipients. Recognizing that scholars often presume to speak for readers, Kay Stone has undertaken to restore the reader's voice and to "describe actual rather than theoretical connections between fairy tales and their readers" ("Misuses of Enchantment" 126). She has done this by conducting formal interviews about the Cinderella story and analyzing "the reactions of readers of various ages and backgrounds, both male and female" (130). Stone's study of readers' reactions to "Cinderella" leads to two important conclusions. First, because the story elicits diverse responses among readers, she concludes that there is no single truth about the meaning and impact of fairy tales, especially when it comes to the question of sexism. Second, despite the diversity of responses, Stone identifies patterns that indicate women read and respond to tales differently from men. Women in particular may continue to perceive the female models found in fairy tales as problematic, and may interpret and reinterpret them as they struggle with their own identity. So by turning to the reactions of actual readers, Stone cuts through the unresolved theoretical speculation and delivers concrete insights into the tale's actual reception. In doing so she clarifies the issue of sexist content in fairy tales, the genre's impact on readers' perceptions of gender, and the role of gender itself in reading the tales.

A final example of how the study of readers' reactions can illuminate larger issues is provided by Kristin Wardetzky. Like Stone, Wardetzky advocates an empirical investigation to bring credibility to the abstract theoretical debates about the effects of fairy tales on children. Whereas Stone used interviews with North American subjects of diverse ages, Wardetzky (as part of a larger study) asked 1,577 children between eight and ten years of age in former East Germany to invent fairy tales stimulated by given story openers. Wardetzky's discovery that the children's tales differ in significant ways from the Grimms' leads her to reject the conventional wisdom that Grimms' stories exert a paradigmatic influence on children's understanding of fairy tales. In fact, Wardetzky's study suggests that far from being controlled by traditional fairy tales and preoccupied through them with social or moral issues, children may adapt tales to serve their own imaginative needs for heroic status (172). Like the experimental studies of psychologists testing Bettelheim's therapeutic theories and like Stone's investigation of sexism in fairy tales, Wardetzky's empirical study of children's fairy tales represents a serious challenge to conventional theories about the psychosocial function of Grimms' tales.

Despite my focus on subjective responses to Grimms' fairy tales, it should be clear that I am not arguing that we abandon responsible readings of the kind prescribed in the first part of this essay. Nor am I proposing that we discontinue reeducating readers about the facts of Grimms' fairy tales and the implications of these facts for an understanding of the texts. After all, analyses informed by the important data resulting from the work of Heinz Rölleke, for example, demystify the genre and correct the pseudoscholarly interpretations that make unjustifiable historical claims or implications. But I am suggesting that private readings of fairy tales can be equally illuminating, even if the responses are irresponsible from a scholarly point of view. Both the private and public reception of fairy tales demand our attention because they tell us something about the living meaning of fairy tales and their role in society. As the history of fairy-tale interpretation and fairy-tale exploitation has shown, the recipient and context of reception are as much a determinant of meaning as the text itself. So I am arguing as well that there is as much danger in institutionalizing response as there is in institutionalizing the genre.

If, as Christa Bürger has claimed, the emancipatory potential of the fairy tale resides not in its content but in its reception (103), then institutionalizing interpretation betrays the genre's liberating function. When the Grimms appropriated the folktale in the nineteenth century for scientific purposes, they institutionalized the genre and gave scholars considerable authority over it. Scholars, along with editors and publishers, not only determined which tales would be privileged in print, which variants would be standardized and canonized, and what shape the published text would ultimately take; they also legitimized the text's interpretation. The chilling extent of that authority is evident when Bruno Jöckel, in a 1939 study written in fascist Germany, refers to "official fairy-tale research" (5), an expression that finds its ironic echo in 1980 when Hermann Bausinger knowingly refers to "Verwalter des Märchenerbes," or "custodians of the fairy-tale inheritance" ("Anmerkungen" 45). To insist too strongly on the scholar's custodial role denies the individual reader's power over fairy tales (Haase). The role of the scholar is not to be a ventriloquist for the reader. The scholar's burden of responsibility lies in reconstructing the meaning of a fairy tale not only by attending to the voices that speak through it, but also by acknowledging the diverse voices that speak in response to it.

"The Golden Key"—the last of Grimms' two hundred tales—is conventionally interpreted as a parable about the inexhaustible meaning of fairy tales.[7] For me, however, the story goes even further and tells us that significance lies in reception. The Grimms—perhaps denying or camouflaging their own appropriation of the stories they edited—want us to believe that it is not scholars who hold the key to fairy tales, but a solitary child who accidentally finds one in the snow. The focus of the story is not on what the child finds, but on his process of discovery. Finding a key, he posits the existence of a lock. Finding a locked casket, he searches for a keyhole. Finding a keyhole, he inserts the key and begins turning it. The discovery of what lies in the casket, however, remains under his—not our—control, for "we must wait until he unlocks the casket and completely lifts the cover. That's when we'll learn what wonderful things he found" (*Complete Fairy Tales* 631). The "things" themselves remain undefined and indeterminate, not simply because fairy tales have an endless potential for meaning, but because they are the child's discovery, not ours. We cannot dictate what the child—or any other reader—will find; we must wait for him (or her) to show us what can be found. And so it is in recognizing the recipient's control over the text's meaning that we also recognize the central place of reader response in studying Grimms' fairy tales.

Notes

1. Rölleke's important essays are collected in *"Nebeninschriften"* and *"Wo das Wünschen noch geholfen hat."*
2. Rölleke, *Die Märchen* 84. See also Dollerup, Reventlow, and Hansen.
3. Rölleke chides Brackert in "August Stöbers Einfluß" 86; "Die Stellung" 128; "New Results" 108; and "Homo oeconomicus" 37–38.
4. Gerhard Haas 15. See also Bausinger, "Aschenputtel"; Holbek; Lange 84–85; Röhrich; Simonsen; Wolfersdorf 9. While all these writers question whether the ultimate, original, or inherent significance of the fairy tale can be discerned, they do so with varying degrees of skepticism and from different points of view. Folklorist Holbek, for example, does not doubt "that tales do possess inherent cores of meaning," but he admits the possibility that these meanings "may . . . forever remain elusive" (27).
5. See, for example, Bernikow; Kavablum; Kolbenschlag 61–99; Lieberman 192–94; Lüthi 61; and Yolen. See also Vera Dika on Ericka Beckman's feminist revision of the Cinderella tale in her 1986 film.
6. See Jeannine Blackwell's description of the subversive female narrative voice speaking to daughters in fairy tales as told by nineteenth-century German women. The double voice of women narrators, albeit in a different cultural context, is also taken up by Bar-Itzhak and Shenhar in *Jewish Moroccan Folk Narratives from Israel.*
7. See Rölleke's commentary in Grimm, *Kinder- und Hausmärchen: 1837* 1265; and *Kinder- und Hausmärchen: Ausgabe letzter Hand* 3: 516.

Works Cited

Alderson, Brian. *Grimm Tales in English.* British Library exhibition notes. London: British Library, 1985. N. pag.

Bar-Itzhak, Haya, and Aliza Shenhar, eds. and trans. *Jewish Moroccan Folk Narratives from Israel*. Detroit: Wayne State UP, 1993.

Bausinger, Hermann. "Anmerkungen zu Schneewittchen." Brackert, *Und wenn sie nicht gestorben sind* 39–70.

———. "Aschenputtel: Zum Problem der Märchensymbolik." *Zeitschrift für Volkskunde* 52 (1955): 144–55.

Bernikow, Louise. "Cinderella: Saturday Afternoon at the Movies." *Among Women*. New York: Harmony Books, 1980. 17–38, 271–72.

Bettelheim, Bruno. *The Uses of Enchantment: The Meaning and Importance of Fairy Tales*. New York: Knopf, 1976.

Blackwell, Jeannine. "Fractured Fairy Tales: German Women Authors and the Grimm Tradition." *Germanic Review* 62 (1987): 162–74.

Bottigheimer, Ruth B., ed. *Fairy Tales and Society: Illusion, Allusion, and Paradigm*. Philadelphia: U of Pennsylvania P, 1986.

Brackert, Helmut. "Hänsel und Gretel oder Möglichkeiten und Grenzen literaturwissenschaftlicher Märchen-Interpretation." Brackert, *Und wenn sie nicht gestorben sind* 9–38.

———, ed. *Und wenn sie nicht gestorben sind . . . : Perspektiven auf das Märchen*. Frankfurt a.M.: Suhrkamp, 1980.

Bürger, Christa. "Zur ideologischen Betrachtung von Sagen und Märchen." *Phantasie und Realität in der Kinderliteratur*. Ed. Karl E. Maier. Bad Heilbrunn: Klinkhardt, 1976, 102–7.

Crain, William C., et al. "The Impact of Hearing a Fairy Tale on Children's Immediate Behavior." *Journal of Genetic Psychology* 143 (1983): 9–17.

Dégh, Linda. "What Did the Grimm Brothers Give to and Take from the Folk?" McGlathery 66–90.

Dika, Vera. "A Feminist Fairy Tale." *Art in America* 75 (April 1987): 31–33.

Dollerup, Cay, Iven Reventlow, and Carsten Rosenberg Hansen. "A Case Study of Editorial Filters in Folktales: A Discussion of the *Allerleirauh* Tales in Grimm." *Fabula* 27 (1986): 12–30.

Dundes, Alan. "Interpreting Little Red Riding Hood Psychoanalytically." McGlathery 16–51.

Fromm, Erich. *The Forgotten Language: An Introduction to the Understanding of Dreams, Fairy Tales and Myths*. New York: Rinehart, 1951. 235–41.

Garlichs, Ariane, ed. *Kinder leben mit Märchen*. Kassel: Röth, 1988.

Grimm, Brothers. *The Complete Fairy Tales of the Brothers Grimm*. Trans. Jack Zipes. New York: Bantam, 1987.

———. *Kinder- und Hausmärchen: Ausgabe letzter Hand mit den Originalanmerkungen der Brüder Grimm*. Ed. Heinz Rölleke. 3 vols. Stuttgart: Reclam, 1980.

———. *Kinder- und Hausmärchen gesammelt durch die Brüder Grimm: Vollständige Ausgabe auf der Grundlage der dritten Auflage (1837)*. Ed. Heinz Rölleke. Frankfurt a.M.: Deutscher Klassiker Verlag, 1985.

Haas, Gerhard. "Die 'Logik' der Märchen: Überlegungen zur zeitgenössischen Märcheninterpretation und Märchendidaktik." *Märchen in Erziehung und Unterricht.* Ed. Ottilie Dinges, Monika Born, and Jürgen Janning. Kassel: Röth, 1986.

Haas, Gisela. "Kranke Kinder malen Märchen." Garlichs 36–54.

Haase, Donald. "Yours, Mine, or Ours? Perrault, the Brothers Grimm, and the Ownership of Fairy Tales." *Once upon a Folktale: Capturing the Folklore Process with Children.* Ed. Gloria Blatt. New York: Teachers College Press, 1993. 63–77.

Holbek, Bengt. "The Many Abodes of Fata Morgana or the Quest for Meaning in Fairy Tales." *Journal of Folklore Research* 22 (1985): 19–28.

Jöckel, Bruno. *Der Weg zum Märchen.* Berlin-Steglitz: Dion, 1939.

Kavablum, Lea. *Cinderella: Radical Feminist, Alchemist.* N.p.: privately printed, 1973.

Kermode, Frank. "Institutional Control of Interpretation." *Salmagundi* 43 (1979): 72–86.

Kolbenschlag, Madonna. *Kiss Sleeping Beauty Good-Bye: Breaking the Spell of Feminine Myths and Models.* 1979. New York: Bantam, 1981.

Lange, Günter. "Grimms' Märchen aus der Sicht eines Religionspädagogen." *Hanau 1985–1986: 200 Jahre Brüder Grimm.* Ed. Stadt Hanau/Hauptamt. Hanau: Stadt Hanau, 1986. 73–90.

Lieberman, Marcia. " 'Some Day My Prince Will Come': Female Acculturation through the Fairy Tale." *College English* 34 (1972): 383–95. Rpt. in *Don't Bet on the Prince: Contemporary Feminist Fairy Tales in North America and England.* Ed. Jack Zipes. New York: Methuen, 1986. 185–200.

Lüthi, Max. *Once upon a Time: On the Nature of Fairy Tales.* Trans. Lee Chadeayne and Paul Gottwald. Bloomington: Indiana UP, 1976.

Mahler, Eugen. "Gespräche über Märchen: Beobachtungen und Gedanken eines Vaters." Garlichs 55–70, 110–11.

McGlathery, James M., ed. *The Brothers Grimm and Folktale.* Urbana: U of Illinois P, 1988.

Messner, Rudolf. "Kinder und Märchen—was sie verbindet und was sie trennt." Garlichs 106–9.

Meyer zur Capellen, Renate. "Kinder hören ein Märchen, fürchten sich und wehren sich." Brackert, *Und wenn sie nicht gestorben sind* 210–22.

Mieder, Wolfgang. "Grimm Variations: From Fairy Tales to Modern Anti-Fairy Tales." *Tradition and Innovation in Folk Literature.* Hanover: UP of New England, 1987. 1–44.

Mikkelsen, Nina. "Sendak, *Snow White,* and the Child as Literary Critic." *Language Arts* 62 (1985): 362–73.

Röhrich, Lutz. "The Quest of Meaning in Folk Narrative Research." McGlathery 1–15.

247

Rölleke, Heinz. "August Stöbers Einfluß auf die *Kinder- und Hausmärchen* der Brüder Grimm." *Fabula* 24 (1983): 11–20. Rpt. in Rölleke, *"Wo das Wünschen noch geholfen hat"* 75–87.

———. "Die Frau in den Märchen der Brüder Grimm." *Die Frau im Märchen*. Ed. Sigrid Früh and Rainer Wehse. Kassel: Röth, 1985. 72–88.

———. "Der Homo oeconomicus im Märchen." *Der literarische Homo oeconomicus: Vom Märchenhelden zum Manager: Beiträge zum Ökonomieverständnis in der Literatur*. Ed. Werner Wunderlich. Bern: Haupt, 1989. 23–40.

———. *Die Märchen der Brüder Grimm: Eine Einführung*. Munich: Artemis, 1985.

———. *"Nebeninschriften": Brüder Grimm–Arnim und Brentano–Droste-Hülshoff: Literarhistorische Studien*. Bonn: Bouvier, 1980.

———. "New Results of Research on *Grimms' Fairy Tales*." McGlathery 101–11. (Trans. of "Neue Ergebnisse zu den 'Kinder- und Hausmärchen' der Brüder Grimm." *Jacob und Wilhelm Grimm: Vorträge und Ansprachen*. Göttingen: Vandenhoeck & Ruprecht, 1986. 39–48.)

———. "Die Stellung des Dornröschenmärchens zum Mythos und zur Heldensage." *Antiker Mythos in unseren Märchen*. Ed. Wolfdietrich Siegmund. Kassel: Röth, 1984. 125–37, 197–98.

———, ed. *Die wahren Märchen der Brüder Grimm*. Frankfurt a.M.: Fischer, 1989.

———. *"Wo das Wünschen noch geholfen hat": Gesammelte Aufsätze zu den 'Kinder- und Hausmärchen' der Brüder Grimm*. Bonn: Bouvier, 1985.

Rowe, Karen. "To Spin a Yarn: The Female Voice in Folklore and Fairy Tale." Bottigheimer 53–74.

Rubenstein, Ben. "The Meaning of the Cinderella Story in the Development of a Little Girl." *American Imago* 12 (1955): 197–205. Rpt. in *Cinderella: A Casebook*. Ed. Alan Dundes. 1982. New York: Wildman: 1983. 219–28.

Sahr, Michael. "Zur experimentellen Erschließung von Lesewirkungen: Eine empirische Studie zum Märchen 'Der alte Sultan.'" *Zeitschrift für Pädagogik* 26 (1980): 365–81.

———. "Zur Wirkung von Märchen: Eine medienvergleichende Betrachtung zum Grimmschen Märchen: Der alte Sultan." *Das gute Jugendbuch* 27 (1977): 67–75. Rpt. in *Kinderliteratur und Rezeption: Beiträge der Kinderliteraturforschung zur literaturwissenschaftlichen Pragmatik*. Ed. Bettina Hurrelmann. Baltmannsweiler: Schneider, 1980. 351–65.

Schenda, Rudolf. "Telling Tales—Spreading Tales: Changes in the Communicative Form of a Popular Genre." Bottigheimer 74–94.

Schmitz, Jessica. "Erfahrungen beim Erzählen eines Märchens im Kindergarten am Beispiel *Der Wolf und die sieben jungen Geißlein*." Brackert, *Und wenn sie nicht gestorben sind* 193–210.

Simonsen, Michèle. "Do Fairy Tales Make Sense?" *Journal of Folklore Research* 22 (1985): 29–36.

Stone, Kay F. "The Misuses of Enchantment: Controversies on the Significance of Fairy Tales." *Women's Folklore, Women's Culture.* Ed. Rosan A. Jordan and Susan J. Kalcik. Philadelphia: U of Philadelphia P, 1985. 125–45. (Rev. and trans. of "Mißbrauchte Verzauberung: Aschenputtel als Weiblichkeitsideal in Nordamerika." *Über Märchen für Kinder von heute: Essays zu ihrem Wandel und ihrer Funktion.* Ed. Klaus Doderer. Weinheim: Beltz, 1983. 78–93.)

———. "Three Transformations of Snow White." McGlathery 52–65.

Tatar, Maria. *The Hard Facts of the Grimms' Fairy Tales.* Princeton: Princeton UP, 1987.

Tausch, Anne-Marie. "Einige Auswirkungen von Märcheninhalten." *Psychologische Rundschau* 18 (1967): 104–16.

Thomas, Patricia Guérin. "Children's Responses to Fairy Tales: A Developmental Perspective." Diss. Adelphi U, 1983.

Wardetzky, Kristin. "The Structure and Interpretation of Fairy Tales Composed by Children." *Journal of American Folklore* 103 (1990): 157–76.

Weinrebe, Helge M. A. *Märchen, Bilder, Wirkungen: Zur Wirkung und Rezeptionsgeschichte von illustrierten Märchen der Brüder Grimm nach 1945.* Frankfurt a.M.: Lang, 1987.

Wolfersdorf, Peter. *Märchen und Sage in Forschung, Schule und Jugendpflege.* Braunschweig: Waisenhaus, 1958.

Yolen, Jane. "America's Cinderella." *Children's Literature in Education* 8 (1977): 21–29.

Zipes, Jack. *The Brothers Grimm: From Enchanted Forests to the Modern World.* New York: Routledge, 1988

———. *Fairy Tales and the Art of Subversion: The Classical Genre for Children and the Process of Civilization.* New York: Wildman, 1983.

———. *The Trials and Tribulations of Little Red Riding Hood: Versions of the Tale in Sociocultural Context.* South Hadley, MA: Bergin & Garvey, 1983. 1–65.

Once Upon a Time Today: Grimm Tales for Contemporary Performers

Kay F. Stone

IN THE PAST fifteen years I have been an observer of and then a
participant in the so-called storytelling revival that has sprung up
with apparent spontaneity in both Europe and North America. As
an observing folklorist I have become fascinated with the folktale as a
part of an oral literature created thousands of years before writing was
dimly conceived of as another way for human beings to speak to one
another. Most folklorists examine folktales in the natural environment
of an orally creative community, often one in which writing is still absent or at least weak as an artistic expression. My folkloristic interest,
however, has been drawn to urban professional tellers with no experience of any fully oral community.

I have found that many urban storytellers I have heard in performance and in conversation have developed an understanding of the creative dynamics of oral composition. They do not merely repeat tales,
they re-create them at each performance. It is possible for a narrative
scholar to examine the correlations between texture, context, and text.
Folk narrative research has sought to discover such correlations in tra-

ditional oral communities where individual tellers are often too immersed in their art to answer the endless questions academics are capable of asking. Articulate urban performers are equally absorbed in their art, but since they have had to learn it consciously rather than absorb it as part of an entire culture, they retain a self-consciousness that can respond to detailed academic queries. Not surprisingly, storytellers love to talk.

As a folklorist I have been able to question a number of urban tellers about their understanding of the oral process in which they are involved. Most particularly I have wanted to find out the fate of the powerful *Märchen,* which has risen out of the long enchantment of "neverneverland" for many urban tellers. The folklorist in me asks how this sophisticated metaphoric genre manifests itself on the lips of those who know it only from childhood books—notably from the many translations of a handful of Grimm tales.

My view as a full participant in the storytelling revival—that is, my view as a performer—is bound to be different. It is of direct personal interest to me that the *Märchen* seems to have returned to a full existence with adult audiences who respond positively to the transformational and cathartic powers of this sort of narrative. Sweep away all the nostalgic trifles written today about quaint old peasants whiling away the hours before a comfortable fire—which is the sentimental view of traditional narration held by too many modern performers—and you will still find many tellers who understand that old stories do retain an ancient and uncompromising power.

The two streams of this essay flow along in their own channels and occasionally intersect. The first stream is my folkloric search for the place of traditional folktales in modern repertoires, and I use the Grimm collection as a model since it is still central to North American childhood reading. The other stream, which insists on continually flooding its banks here, is my storyteller's quest for the elusive muses of narrative artistry. How in the world can we *tell* stories, particularly old and seemingly outdated ones, that carry the same expressive weight as good written stories, especially in an age where written literature is supreme? Let me begin with the Grimm tales, because, as I have said, these are still the archetype and the stereotype of the folktale for many North American readers and listeners.

When I was conducting my dissertation research in the early 1970s, one woman reported that she assumed that the Grimm tales she read in

English were English folktales. Her German-born mother had told her German stories in German (Rita Romsa-Ross, in Stone, "Romantic Heroines" 314). I was surprised to find this was true of most of the adults and children I interviewed at that time. They did not think of the Grimm tales as Germanic, but rather as "world" folktales that belonged to everyone.

Despite the continuing popularity of this collection and its perceived position as a world treasury, I have heard very few Grimm tales told by the professional storytellers I have listened to. Since the tales had been so central to the dozens of people I had questioned in the 1970s, I wondered if these tellers were deliberately avoiding them, or if the Grimm collection had lost its hold on North American readers. In order to find out, I selected a number of professional urban performers across North America, all but one of whom I had heard in actual performance at storytelling festivals in New England, Tennessee, and California, as well as at smaller and more informal sessions.

I sent out a questionnaire to twenty-five tellers and received seventeen responses.[1] The questions I asked were meant not only to discover the place of the Grimm tales in their repertoires, but also to uncover the storytellers' understanding of the complexities of oral composition. I chose tellers who favored traditional stories and who treated them as serious literature rather than as something to parody. One teller said specifically: "I prefer not to 'fracture' fairy tales to make them more palatable to contemporary values" (Lynn Rubright, letter of 5 January 1988). This is important to note, since some contemporary performers do "fracture" such tales, performing well-known tales ("Cinderella," "The Frog Prince," and "Hansel and Gretel" are favorite choices) as satires or parodies that proceed more from stereotypes of "fairy tales" or "happily ever after stories" than from any profound understanding of the *Märchen* genre.

The seventeen urban tellers who responded (often in depth) to my queries revealed that although the Grimm collection was certainly familiar to them, most chose to draw from less familiar material. Yet the few Grimm tales they included in their repertoires were carefully chosen for specific reasons and for particular listeners.

In order to allow these tellers to speak their own words as much as possible within the limits of this brief essay, I will structure my first section in three parts, arranged according to the three basic questions I asked. The first of these was: "What part (if any) have the Grimm tales played in your tellings, both past and present?'' Most responded that as children they had read the Grimms avidly and later found them to be important models for oral narration. For example, Barbara Reed from Connecticut says: ''I consider these tales at the heart of (folk) fairy tales, and folktales at the heart of storytelling. Some I have told so long I don't remember when or where I first met them'' (Barbara Reed, 2 January 1988). Another professional performer, Lynn Rubright of St. Louis, describes her early experience in strikingly similar words when she recalls not only the tales themselves but the human context in which these were told:

> Grimm tales played an enormous role in developing my love of story as a child. My grandmother used to tell me Red Riding Hood, Jack in the Beanstalk [*not* Grimm] and Hansel and Gretel while I was nestled next to her warm body under the featherbed in the back bedroom during nap time when I was about four years old. It wasn't until years later that I recalled the warm and loving environment in which I was introduced to the Grimms' tales. (Lynn Rubright, 5 January 1988)

Elizabeth Ellis is a southern teller with knowledge of traditional Appalachian tales as well as childhood familiarity with the Grimm collection. She identified several Kentucky tales as being local variants of recognizable Grimm tales: ''I tell some Grimm-based fairytales. I grew up hearing Appalachian Mountain versions of some of those stories. I still tell some of them. I've messed with some of them, but others I tell pretty much the way I heard them'' (Elizabeth Ellis, undated 1988).

Another woman, Ruthilde Kronberg of German descent, found the Grimm tales even more central in her childhood: ''As a child in Nazi Germany I used to get in trouble because I didn't do my homework. I read fairy tales instead. I think they saved my sanity because they taught me that the evil which was taking place around me would burn itself out. Which it did'' (Ruthilde Kronberg, undated 1987).

Not all contemporary tellers retained the Grimms as part of their active repertoire, however. Washington State storyteller Cathryn Wellner comments:

> Though I do not tell tales from the Grimms, they have influenced me enormously. To call them favorite childhood tales is to ignore the fact that they were very nearly *the only folktales* I heard then. They taught me the pattern which still provides the frame on which I hang a tale: introduction, problem, development, denouement, conclusion. From them I

learned that good triumphs over evil, that the weak can outwit the strong, that industriousness leads to success, that loyalty and honor are among the highest virtues. (Cathryn Wellner, 7 January 1988)

It was interesting to me that the storytellers I questioned in 1987 gave the Grimm tales the same central place that they had had for the children and adults I had questioned fifteen years earlier as part of my dissertation research. The stories had not lost their popularity, as I speculated at the beginning of this essay. Quite the opposite. Respondents from both groups (1970s and 1980s) were able to name specific tales and give accurate plot summaries.

Interestingly, those who were now storytellers listed a greater variety of tale titles (even when they were no longer telling Grimm tales) in response to my second question: "Can you describe any specific Grimm tales you've favoured either now or in the past, and can you describe why these appealed to both you and to audiences?" Some mentioned only a few, others offered many titles. I quote Elizabeth Ellis in full because her response is both concise and detailed:

The June Apple Tree (The Juniper tree) I tell a lot. I love telling it because it helps people focus on those things in our culture that devour the lives of our children. Three Golden Shirts and Finger Ring (Seven Ravens) I enjoy telling, I guess because I have felt mute most of my life with my family. Don't Fall in My Beans (The Lad Who Went Forth to Learn What Fear Is) is a perfect opening story—a scary/funny ghost tale. One of the most used tales in my repertoire. Beauty and Her Aunts (The Three Spinners) never fails to get a laugh. Useful with adult audiences. Everyone appreciates a good scam. Jack and the Devil's Grandmother (Devil with Three Golden Hairs) I used to tell, but not so much now. I really enjoy riddling stories and seriously plotted tales. Mr. Fox (The Robber Bridegroom) I tell a lot. I like its haunted quality. I also enjoy the spunky heroine.[2]

Barbara Reed names a dozen Grimm tales as part of her regular repertoire, commenting that she includes "all the old favorites, in B. Reed versions suited to the occasion."[3] She is one of the few tellers who incorporated "old favorites" instead of seeking out the lesser-known tales.

The desire to find less commonly known tales was so strong that even a teller who favors the Grimms says, "I stay away from the ones popularized in this country such as 'Little Red Riding Hood,' 'Hansel and Gretel,' 'Cinderella,' 'Sleeping Beauty,' etc.'' (Renate Schneider, 1988). Similarly Marvyne Jenoff, a Toronto writer and occasional storyteller, avoids certain stories precisely because they are well known. She says that the overpopularization of some stories "spurred me quite energetically in pursuit of unusual materials" (Marvyne Jenoff, December 1987). A Winnipeg teacher and teller agrees that the Grimm collection is only one of many to select from: "There are so many stories to draw from that often I choose something else—eg. Nanabush, Anansi, Jack Tales" (Mary-Louise Quanbury, November 1988). Cathryn Wellner is even more specific in her rejection of the more popularized Grimm tales: "Another of the problems in using Grimms' tales is that their adaptations and commercial uses have set up certain expectations for them. Children hearing 'Hansel and Gretel' or 'Rumpelstiltskin' have pre-formed images that skew the way in which they listen to the tales. I prefer to tell stories that do not set off an automatic reaction."

Of the seventeen performers who responded to my questionnaire, only five identify Grimm tales as having a significant part in their usual repertoires. Only two of these, both German-born, build their repertoires around the Grimms. Ruthilde Kronberg writes that "over the years I have told about 50 Grimm tales." She says that she includes both well-known and obscure tales. Renate Schneider indicates that twenty of the fifty tales she tells regularly are less commonly known stories from the Grimms, and many of the others are German tales from other sources: "Grimm tales play, of course, a big part in my repertory since I grew up with them and for me they represent and express the German countryside, where these particular versions were shaped. I tell only certain ones which to me give the special flavor of German philosophy and mood and myth." For the two German-born narrators (Schneider and Kronberg) the Grimm tales are not just a collection of world tales but an intimate part of their cultural identity. As already noted, others regarded the texts in a more universal light.

Though she tells far fewer Grimm tales than Kronberg and Schneider, Elizabeth Ellis was as committed as they in expressing her reasons for regarding these tales as central: "I include the Grimm tales because they are rich and opulent sources of meaning. I can tell them over and over without tiring of them because there is always something there I never noticed before, always something powerfully parallel to my own life. I figure that must also be true of my listeners.'' Barbara Reed named fewer than a dozen Grimm tales that she tells regularly, but still felt that these were central to her as a storyteller (as noted earlier):

> I look back at the Random House/Pantheon edition [of Grimm tales], but I feel quite free and entitled to do my own versions of The Fishermen and His Wife, The Frog Prince, Snow White—fun to undo Disney—Cinderella when requested, Sleeping Beauty when I find a class of children so tired I want to put them to sleep. The Wolf and Seven Kids, Rumpelstiltskin, Rapunzel, Hansel and Gretel.

Maryland storyteller Susan Gordon wrote that she often did not know why a particular story appealed to her but had learned that when a story (particularly from the Grimm narratives) caught her attention, it usually had something deeply personal to offer her and would therefore have the potential of touching others as well. In speaking of two of her Grimm narratives, ''The Juniper Tree'' and ''The Handless Maiden,'' she says:

> The stories seem to be touching needs and areas of growth which I would not have named myself. [When I choose a story] my desire is to tell them a story that is, in some way, their story, which will provide them the opportunity to reflect on their own lives. In each of these instances the storytelling becomes very mutual, with the listeners not only helping you tell the story by their presence, but recreating the story and deepening it for both listeners and teller. (Susan Gordon, December 1987–January 1988)

Even though Gordon includes only the four tales (''The Handless Maiden,'' ''The Juniper Tree,'' ''The Boy Who Set Out to Study Fear,'' and ''The Golden Goose'') in her repertoire of ''50 to 60,'' she insists that these are as important to her as any of her other narratives: ''All of these stories make a whole for me, none is more important than the other.'' Like other storytellers, she notes the absence in her repertoire of the more popular titles, which she identifies as ''the typical female stories, Snow White, Cinderella, Sleeping Beauty, etc.''

When I compiled a full list of the stories named by these tellers I found a surprising variety of titles mentioned. I also noticed that while three of the more popular tales do still appear at the head of the list, their positions were far less prominent than they were with those I interviewed in the 1970s. These titles are presented in the order in which

I took them from tellers' responses. Frequency of response is in parentheses, followed by Grimm (KHM) and Aarne-Thompson (AT) index numbers.

Tales (# responses)	Grimm No.	Aarne-Thompson No.
Cinderella (5)	KHM 21	AT 510A
Snow White (3)	KHM 53	AT 709
Hansel and Gretel (3)	KHM 15	AT 327A
Rapunzel (3)	KHM 12	AT 310
Rumpelstiltskin (3)	KHM 55	AT 500
King Thrushbeard (3)	KHM 52	AT 900
The Goose Girl (3)	KHM 89	AT 533
The Wedding of Mrs. Fox (3)	KHM 38	AT 65
The White Snake (3)	KHM 17	AT 673
The Juniper Tree (3)	KHM 47	AT 720
The Frog King (2)	KHM 1	AT 440
The Seven Ravens (2)	KHM 25	AT 451
Snow White and Rose Red (2)	KHM 161	AT 426
The Robber Bridegroom (2)	KHM 40	AT 955
The Three Spinners (2)	KHM 14	AT 501
The Gifts of the Little Folk (2)	KHM 182	AT 503
Maid Maleen (2)	KHM 198	AT 870
The Poor Man and the Rich Man (2)	KHM 87	AT 750A
The Boy Who Went Forth . . . (2)	KHM 4	AT 326
Mother Holle (1)	KHM 24	AT 480
Brother and Sister (1)	KHM 11	AT 450
Jorinda and Joringel (1)	KHM 69	AT 405
The Three Little Gnomes in the Forest (1)	KHM 13	AT 403B
The Three Feathers (1)	KHM 63	AT 402
The Water of Life (1)	KHM 97	AT 551
The Star Coins (1)	KHM 153	AT 779
The Singing Bone (1)	KHM 28	AT 780
The Twelve Brothers (1)	KHM 9	AT 451
The Two Brothers (1)	KHM 60	AT 567A
The Marvelous Minstrel (1)	KHM 8	AT 151
The Turnip (1)	KHM 146	AT 1960D

The Old Man and His Grandson (1)	KHM 78	AT 930B
The Devil with the Three Golden Hairs (1)	KHM 29	AT 930
The Golden Goose (1)	KHM 64	AT 571
The Maiden without Hands (1)	KHM 31	AT 706
The Bremen Town Musicians (1)	KHM 27	AT 130
The Three Sons of Fortune (1)	KHM 70	AT 1650
The Queen Bee (1)	KHM 62	AT 554
The Three Green Twigs (1)	Children's Legend 6	AT 756A
Spindle, Shuttle, and Needle (1)	KHM 188	AT 585
The Fishermen and His Wife (1)	KHM 19	AT 555
Brier Rose (1)	KHM 50	AT 410
The Wolf and the Seven Young Kids (1)	KHM 5	AT 123
The Tailor in Heaven (1)	KHM 35	AT 800
Mother Trudy (1)	KHM 43	AT 334

As this list reveals, even "Cinderella" has only five tellers, and the other favored tales only two each. "Brier Rose" (or "Sleeping Beauty") was named by a single teller, and "Little Red Cap" does not appear at all except as a tale that is avoided because of its popularity (both Jenoff and Renate Schneider mention it negatively). Of the forty-six titles mentioned, forty are in the category of "romantic" or "magic" tales. Only four are animal tales (AT 65, 123, 130, 151) and two are humorous anecdotes (AT 1650 and 1960D). Interestingly the latter are named by male tellers. These titles reflect the exaggerated position that romantic "fairy tale" texts hold in most popular English translations that feature only thirty to sixty of the full Grimm collection.

Seven tellers maintained that the Grimm tales were not a regular part of their performing repertoire, six of these explaining that they preferred lesser-known sources. Only one, Elizabeth Nash of Winnipeg, rejected the Grimms completely on the basis of their violence, although she did recall a few childhood favorites:

I don't remember ever telling a Grimm story. That was not the result of a conscious decision. The brutality of some of the stories shakes me even now: the community that drove spikes into a barrel, forced an old lady into it and rolled it down the hill; the gang that heated iron shoes red hot, jammed them on an erring woman's feet and made her dance until she dies. *This* child was distressed to tears by them on more than one occasion, and possibly that's why *this* adult has not told Grimm stories. (Elizabeth Nash, 10 December 1987)

Interestingly, she lists "Hansel and Gretel" and "Rumpelstiltskin" as former favorites, though both have violent resolutions. She also remarks that as a result of completing the questionnaire she decided she might try to tell "King Thrushbeard," a current favorite.[4]

John Harrell is another teller/author who has told very few Grimm tales. He names only "The Bremen Town Musicians" and "The Three Gifts of Fortune" (i.e., "The Three Sons of Fortune"). In explaining why he tells these two, he reveals his own understanding about the inherent power of old oral stories: "Bremen Town Musicians was a favorite tale of my wife's and when I would tell it to her, it always made her laugh heartily. It was good therapy. I [also] liked Three Gifts of Fortune because, like Bremen, it is so easy to tell" (John Harrell, 1988). It is true that the Grimms have been justifiably recognized as editors of (rather than as scientific collectors of) authentic orally generated stories. Many of their reworked texts manage to express the not-so-simple simplicity Harrell mentions.

It is almost two centuries since the "Grimm Tales" were gathered together, without a developed scholarly approach to authentic collecting, in another place and in another time, and then translated into other languages and spread to other times and places. And still they have the potential to become vibrantly relevant to non-German people like most of the tellers I have introduced thus far. In response to my third and last question—"Why do you either include *or* exclude Grimm tales in your repertoire now?"—all of these narrators were able to give a clear idea of their reasons for telling tales orally, Grimm and otherwise. For example, Susan Gordon comments on her storytelling as a human expression that goes beyond theatrical diversion:

When I entertain, it is my intent to just tell the story absolutely alive and let it do and be whatever it is supposed to be—funny, mysterious, scary, etc. That same thing holds true in any setting, but in therapeutic, educational and religious settings, the story is chosen with care to the occasion, with some knowledge of the people I'm telling it to. In those settings, often I have developed some ways to help us reflect on the story, think about it, and feel it more deeply, as well as providing a way for people to respond creatively.

Gordon seems to have developed a thorough understanding of this aspect of verbal artistry from her own experiences, despite her lack of contact with any specific oral tradition.

Several expressed this developed sense of narration as an emergent exchange between narrators and listeners brought together in storytelling events (see Bauman). John Harrell, for instance, highlights the difference between narrating and reading: "I prefer to tell tales rather than to read them because the communication is direct between me and the other person(s). With reading, the story is in the book. With telling, the story is part of me and I'm giving that part of me to you" (Harrell, 1988). Toronto performer Marylyn Peringer also underlines the direct power of spoken rather than read or recited words: "I don't ever write out a text that I am learning. Writing freezes it, and then it freezes me. I just talk to myself when I'm alone—out loud, of course, getting through the story part by part until it sounds right" (Marylyn Peringer, 10 January 1988). For Jane Yolen, who both writes and tells stories, finding one's own "voice" is important: "I keep defining and then redefining what stories mean to me and how I can transmit that feeling (and those stories) in the best possible manner to others. When I listen to others tell, I realize that as good as they are, they are not me. I have to take the story again into my own mouth" (Jane Yolen, 7 February 1987).

Each of the seventeen tellers had their own firm idea of what the oral process meant to them as recreated through their own words. California artist Ruth Stotter, for example, asserted that she found her personal connections while preparing and telling a story, and often was able to give her listeners a chance to discover and reveal their own: "At present I tell just a few stories from the Grimms—those that fascinate me by their symbolic interpretations and my psychological reverberations— giving me a chance to step back and ponder life. I often tell Grimm tales to adult audiences and we usually have a discussion afterward" (Ruth Stotter, 1987).

Many of the seventeen considered their storytelling role as potentially transformational for the listeners as well as for the story. The words of Cathryn Wellner are most appropriate:

> Though I avoid moralistic and didactic stories like some dread disease and squirm when I am forced to sit through one, I nevertheless perceive the storyteller's role as that of moral and spiritual bellwether in a secular society. The first task of the story is to entertain, for only entertaining stories will be heeded. But once the attention is focused we must ask ourselves, "To what end?" I want my stories to be affirmations of hope, of belief in humanity's basic goodness.

At first glance these words seem to echo the sentiments expressed by Jack Zipes in the introduction to his translation of the Grimm tales, when he says:

> Today we have inherited [the Grimm brothers'] concerns and contradictions, and their tales still read like innovative strategies for survival. Most of all they provide hope that there is more to life than mastering the art of survival. Their "once upon a time" keeps alive our utopian longing for a better world that can be created out of our dreams and actions. (Zipes xxxi)

Indeed, these tellers would agree that the Grimm tales have offered them, as children if not still as adults, "innovative strategies for survival." But because story*telling* is most effectively done in the ethnographic present, the survival strategies are not utopian, not dreams of the future. These old stories still have the potential power they have always had to identify and address the most basic human concerns and contradictions as they manifest themselves today.

A more concrete example will bring this immediate aspect of told stories more clearly into focus. I use "The Juniper Tree," which was commented on by four of my respondents. This is one of the very few Grimm tales in which a victimized protagonist, in this case the boy murdered and cooked by his mother, avenges himself directly rather than having the villain punished obliquely. Here the boy returns to life as a bird and rewards his loving sister and father by dropping down gifts, but punishes his mother by dropping a millstone on her. He then regains his human shape.

Each of the four storytellers expressed their own immediate reasons for finding this particular tale so compelling. Marylyn Peringer was moved by the simplicity of the story as told by a French performer: "I heard Bruno LaSalle tell it simply, movingly, and [he] sang the song of the bird as composed by one of the musicians in his storytelling troupe." Marvyne Jenoff comments on the current popularity of the story with adult and mixed-age Toronto audiences as a result of two particularly influential tellers (Joan Bodger, who is a therapist, and Alice Kane): "Both seem to feel that children need the violence in folktales to help them understand and articulate their own lives, which include at least the *awareness* of violence" (Jenoff, 2 March 1989). Elizabeth Ellis says that she herself tells the story often in its Appalachian variant ("The June Apple Tree"). In fact she lists it first among the stories she identified as "Grimm" tales. As I quoted earlier, she says: "I love telling it because it helps people focus on those things in our culture that devour the lives of our children." Ellis's telling is close to the variant told by Kentucky narrator Uncle Blessing, who told it to Marie Campbell in the 1930s.

Susan Gordon also tells this tale frequently, and she is considerably more expansive on her reasons for so doing:

> Juniper Tree is a story which I told initially at a conference on the existence of evil. I had never told it before, but had developed the song for it. I planned to tell other stories, but the types of evil people were discussing—rape, batterings, sexual abuse, etc.—just seemed to call for that story. I talked to the fellow who hired me to tell, and he remembers the story as being as frightening as Stephen King is frightening, but offering hope.

Gordon stresses that in telling it she follows the Grimm tale "with great beauty and faithfulness" while at the same time developing its immediate relevance, first by working through the characters and motivating forces for herself as she prepares the tale, and then through discussions with the audience.

> The trick of this story for me was allowing each character to stand out on their own. One of the best responses this story has received is when I told it to a long-term spiritual direction group I was leading and then had the listeners each take a character from the story and relive the story from that point of view, asking themselves what culpability each character had in the boy's death. It was an extraordinary process, in which each person was able to address how they had contributed to the child's death and we began to see the step-mother as not just evil, but as incredibly isolated.

With Gordon and the other narrators "Juniper Tree" returns fully to life, ever emerging anew for each teller and for each audience. I too have experienced this emergent aspect while developing the Grimm tale "Frau Trude," also called "Mother Trudy." In this odd little tale a girl who is too curious encounters a witch who rewards her curiosity by turning her into a block of wood and throwing her on the fire. Interestingly, the story does not actually state that the girl is destroyed, which gives the tale a sense of incomplete resolution that leaves room for further creativity. I began playing with the idea of fire as an element of transformation, which brought the girl back to life in the form of a fiery bird. Through a succession of elemental transformations by Frau Trude the girl passes through the four elements of fire (as wood), air (as bird), water (as fish), and earth (as hare). After this she is challenged to free herself by telling one story that has never been heard before, and she goes out into the world to learn all the stories she can. When she returns a year and a day later to tell her stories, she finds that Frau Trude has heard them all. Lacking any other, she begins in desperation to tell the story of her own adventures, and thus discovers that this is the unknown story that frees her.[5]

In June 1988 I was telling this story for an audience in Windsor, Ontario. I had just completed the girl's desperate words of her own story, "Once there was a girl who was too curious," and the audience began to applaud before I could reach the concluding lines, "and so she went free." I stopped in surprise, then realized that they had spontaneously discovered a more natural ending to my story, one that makes the tale circular by beginning and ending with the same words. This became my usual resolution from that time on.

Later that same year I told the story to a small audience gathered at the home of a friend in Quebec City, where I was visiting. Her daughter wondered why the girl had to go through all of the transformations. These seemed unnecessarily complex and puzzling to her. I recognized her instinctive recognition of the story's natural simplicity, and reduced the transformations to fire/wood and air/bird, having her cross over water and earth to complete the cycle in her own shape.

Finally, in the spring of 1989 my story was retold to me (and the rest of the adult audience) by an eleven-year-old boy who had heard it once from his mother. They both insisted that they told it exactly as I had, but in his variant the girl remained in the same shape of the bird until she had successfully told her story. It was immediately obvious to me that this was a more genuine and organic form for her, since she is more clearly in Frau Trude's power until her story is finally told.

Each of these transformations clarified the story by intuitively simplifying and rationalizing it. This delicate and vibrant balance between traditional stability and individual innovation is the very core of the creative process in oral composition. The narration of story is a perpetually emergent form of artistic expression; in the context of storytelling the texture of the story emerges as narrator and audience interact. Cathryn Wellner describes this exchange eloquently:

> The real work and the real joy come when I tell the partially formed story to an audience for the first time. I used to nearly work a story to death before testing it on an audience. Now I lay the framework and then begin telling it. There are a few things with which I am comfortable at that point: I know the story line, the nature of the characters, essential details, places in which I want to use a chant or a song, and something of the culture. The audience teaches me what the story is about, and each audience teaches me something slightly different. Through their reactions, I see where the story takes wings and where it is earthbound. Eventually, after many tellings, the story takes a shape which I tend to return to each time. It will always be fluid and unrepeatable. Sometimes an especially attuned audience will give me a moment of such clarity that I am stunned. The story becomes fresh and new.

The immediacy of the storytelling experience as described by Wellner and others quoted here emphasizes the fact that for them storytelling is not primarily a theatrical event confined by the convention of the fourth wall. Instead they address themselves candidly to the audience, and in some cases (particularly in more informal contexts) the audience responds with equal directness.

We have seen that the Grimm tales have lost their primacy in terms of quantity; most of the tellers do not feature many of the Grimm texts in their repertoire. However, the variety of titles mentioned is much greater than those recalled by the children and adults I interviewed in the early 1970s. Also, several tellers identified the Grimm collection as having provided a valuable model for an oral repertoire even when they no longer told Grimm tales.

But why do urban performers bother with any traditional tales at all? In considering this question I have kept in mind the works of two narrative scholars, Max Lüthi and Linda Dégh, who in their own separate ways have devoted careful attention to the *Märchen* as a profound human expression.

While Dégh focuses on tales and tellers as they live in actual performance, Max Lüthi takes a more traditional literary view and examines tales in depth as artistic expressions that transcend tellers and times. In fact, Lüthi becomes so deeply involved in describing traditional literature—notably the *Märchen*—that he himself becomes a storyteller who ponders the fate of traditional narratives that have served humankind for centuries. In a concluding chapter of *The European Folktale,* Lüthi—invoking Hermann Hesse—asks what new form of expression might equal the *Märchen* in offering a "new language of symbols," a modern expression that might "offer a playful overview of human existence": "In this future 'glass bead game,' science and art, fragmentary perception and comprehensive vision, and actuality and potentiality would come together as a unity, and the ancient contrast between folktale and legend would cease to exist" (Lüthi 106). His inspiration comes from Hermann Hesse's last novel, *The Glass Bead Game,* in which the fictional narrator describes the twentieth century as a time of "gigantic consumption of empty whimsies" (20), an age in which people have "struggled through a deluge of isolated cultural facts and fragments of knowledge robbed of all meaning" (23). In response, a few creative thinkers have formulated a complex and meaningful form of play called The Glass Bead Game, "a new alphabet, a new language of symbols through which they [the players] could formulate and exchange their new intellectual experience" (36).

In this interpretation of Hesse's inspired words Lüthi, a formalist, seems to assume that any "new language of symbols" would be expressed in a new literary form that would supersede old oral forms. I find Lüthi's optimism refreshing in his hope for a "new folktale" that will join poets and scientists in creative collaboration, but I think he has failed to give the told story its due as a continuing artistic expression.

Folklorist Dégh has always been interested in examining the endlessly creative methods that traditional narrators employ in weaving together tellers and tales and listeners. She has studied a glass bead game as it actually lives in our own world. And she has listened carefully and remembered thoughtfully. In a recent article on "The Snakeprince"

(AT 425) she observes that the telling of any tale takes place in the ethnographic present, and that each tale has the possibility "of making the world of fantasy palpable by connecting it with the world of everyday reality" (Dégh 48). The urban tellers I questioned seem on the whole to be doing exactly this—performing in an ethnographic present, using old fantasies to speak to current realities without sacrificing the integrity of any traditional narratives they use. Dégh also emphasizes the deeply personal connection between tale and teller in words that are applicable to contemporary performance: "The told story also mirrors the narrator's specific conceptualization of the world and its affairs: his cultural and personal meanings. . . . The storyteller is never neutral but emotionally involved when creating the personality of the cast" (48). It is clear from the words of the tellers themselves that they are as personally involved in their stories as are good traditional narrators. But they are not self-indulgently so. Their interest is in breaking through the boundaries of the individual self, as well as breaking through the borders of the conventional fourth wall of the theater. For them the told tale is the personal vehicle for this breakthrough and reconnection.

I often hear from my students that storytelling is a dead art, that the fairy tale in particular is frivolous and irrelevant. Not so. With many contemporary narrators these old stories take on new relevance, whether told fully, as with "The Juniper Tree" or "Frau Trude," or told more indirectly, as in the personal narratives of tellers like Wellner. Contemporary urban narration offers an impassioned challenge now, in this ethnographic present, and not in some utopian future. Wellner observes, for example:

> There is a carelessness that runs through the industrialized western world. . . . If our only stories are those we read in the newspaper or watch on television or film, we can hardly be blamed for a sense of hopelessness. We need other stories, stories which celebrate life in all its complexity, stories that prod us to look at the world in fresh ways, stories that pose hard questions.

Wellner is one of many contemporary tellers for whom childhood contact with old oral tales, filtered through the printed medium, leads to an understanding of a creative process paralleling traditional oral composition. For such tellers the old *Märchen* (and other types of tales) have offered direct and indirect models for a personal, face-to-face artistic exchange that has the potential for simultaneously transforming tellers, tales, and listeners. In the immediate context of storytelling events, old stories take on newly textured contours. The echoes of Grimm tales can still be heard in this new "glass bead game."[6]

Notes

1. Actually two separate questionnaires were sent to the twenty-five selected tellers in the fall of 1987. The first was a fairly complex form with several questions; but when I received only a handful of replies, I sent the second, with only three questions, to those who had not yet responded. Over the next few months I received a dozen more replies, and these form the central portion of this essay. The seventeen who responded are: Elizabeth Nash, Mary-Louise Quanbury, Joyce Birch, Gerri Serrette (all from Winnipeg); Elizabeth Ellis (Texas); Susan Gordon (Maryland); Jane Yolen (Massachusetts); John Harrell and Ruth Stotter (California); Marvyne Jenoff and Marylyn Peringer (Toronto); Renate and Robert Schneider, and Barbara Reed (Connecticut); Lynn Rubright and Ruthilde Kronberg (Missouri); and Cathryn Wellner (state of Washington).
2. Several of the titles she mentions are from Marie Campbell's collection of Kentucky folktales, *Tales from the Cloud Walking Country.*
3. She lists "The Fisherman and His Wife," "The Frog Prince," "Snow White," "Cinderella," "Sleeping Beauty," "The Wolf and the Seven Young Kids," "Rumpelstiltskin," "Rapunzel," "Hansel and Gretel," "The Goose Girl," and "The White Snake."
4. And in fact she did try it at a small and informal Winnipeg storytelling group, Stone Soup Stories, in the winter of 1988. Her story was well received.
5. I have made a thorough description of the story of this story in my essay "Burning Brightly."
6. I am deeply grateful to each of those who contributed to the creation of this essay. In particular I appreciate the responses of John Harrell, Marvyne Jenoff, Cathryn Wellner, and Susan Gordon.

Works Cited

Bauman, Richard. *Verbal Art as Performance.* Prospect Heights, IL: Waveland Press, 1977.

Campbell, Marie. *Tales from the Cloud Walking Country.* 1958. Westport, CN: Greenwood Press, 1976.

Dégh, Linda. "How Storytellers Interpret the Snakeprince Tale." *The Telling of Stories: Approaches to a Traditional Craft. A Symposium.* Ed. Morten Nøjgaard et al. Odense: Odense UP, 1990. 47–62.

Hesse, Hermann. *The Glass Bead Game.* Trans. Richard and Clara Winston. New York: Holt, Rinehart and Winston, 1969.

Lüthi, Max. *The European Folktale: Form and Nature.* Trans. John D. Niles. Philadelphia: ISHI, 1982.

Stone, Kay F. "Burning Brightly." *Feminist Messages: Coding in Women's Folk Culture.* Ed. Joan N. Radner. Urbana: U of Illinois P, 1993. 289–305.

———. "Romantic Heroines in Anglo-American Folk and Popular Literature." Diss. Indiana U, 1975.

Zipes, Jack, trans. *The Complete Fairy Tales of the Brothers Grimm.* New York: Bantam, 1987.

Personal Reflections on the Scholarly Reception of Grimms' Tales in France

Jacques Barchilon

THIS ESSAY IS not a systematic attempt to gauge the French reception of Grimms' *Kinder- und Hausmärchen* in their original language or in translations. It is instead a focused effort to present the Grimms and their tales as "received" by a somewhat typical cultivated representative of French culture. This is, in other words, a description of my own reception of Grimms' fairy tales. Moreover, since my private response has been shaped in part by the published work of a few perceptive French scholars, I will address selected works of French Grimm scholarship to illuminate not only these critical responses to Grimms' stories but also their effects on my personal understanding of the *Kinder- und Hausmärchen*.

My own *early* personal response to Grimms' tales was the result of a superficial French cultural bias that favored Perrault's tales over the Grimms'. I could not read and understand the tales fluently in the original, so I had to rely on French and English translations. My approach was prejudiced from the start: I assumed that Charles Perrault's *Contes* of 1697 obviously "came first," bringing to the world the classic texts of some of the most famous fairy tales of our Western culture, and that the Brothers Grimm just followed in their French predecessor's footsteps. I did have to admit, however reluctantly, that the famous German brothers did collect far more tales than Perrault's mere dozen stories. Their "record" or total of 210 tales seemed impressive. When, in due course, I came to know Perrault's tales very well, I also had to become better acquainted with the Grimms' stories, if only for the purpose of comparison. So my research led me to Harry Velten's well-documented article concerning "The Influence of Charles Perrault's *Contes de ma Mère l'Oie* on German Folklore."

This article, which reprints part of a thesis on the same subject, reproduces side by side corresponding passages from Perrault's *Contes* and from the Grimms' collection. This juxtaposition shows the unmistakable influence of Perrault's 1697 texts on specific Grimm tales, from the pervasive resemblance between tales such as "La barbe bleue" and Grimms' "Bluebeard," which was omitted after the first edition precisely because of its sole dependence on Perrault's text, to the similarities of stories such as "Les fées" and "The Three Little Gnomes in the Forest" (No. 13). These French "facts" bearing witness to the dependence of certain Grimm tales on models in Perrault's *Contes* are now well known to Grimm scholars, just as they became known to the Grimms themselves after collecting and publishing the very first edition.

Much data of this kind had been duly recorded in the indispensable *Anmerkungen zu den Kinder- und Hausmärchen der Brüder Grimm* (1913–32) as edited by Johannes Bolte and Georg Polívka. Perusing the *Anmerkungen* during this phase of my research, the naive graduate student I was at the time discovered something both obvious and necessary: there were even earlier versions or analogues of not only the Grimms' but also Perrault's stories. So I was compelled to go back further and further, and to examine Renaissance and Medieval texts in French, Catalan, and Italian.

In one way my response to Perrault's tales and the *Kinder- und Hausmärchen* is similar to that of the Brothers Grimm. They believed their tales were mostly of German origin, only to discover (or to be shown by fellow scholars) that their texts belonged to a vast fund of cosmopolitan popular and literary tradition. Although this is obvious to us now, it was not so immediately obvious to the Grimms. And of course it could not be otherwise.

No French reader of the Grimms' collection will ever come to a true appreciation of these masterpieces of German and world literature until he or she goes beyond that first stage of cultural chauvinism and looks for something else in the Grimms' stories than a simple echo of Perrault. Even that echo can be suggestive and lend itself to interesting comparisons that prove the Grimms to be more than mere imitators of Perrault. As for the stories that do not evoke Perrault, they are many, some quite a feast for the mind. My favorites since my graduate student days are the stories of animal transformations: "The Twelve Brothers" (No. 9), "The Seven Ravens" (No. 25), "The Six Swans" (No. 49), and "The Lilting, Leaping Lark" (No. 88). My immediate response is that they seem at once familiar and somewhat new, especially "The Lilting, Leaping Lark," whose title in French sounds just as musical, "L'alouette sauteuse et dansante." This "déjà vu, déjà entendu" response comes from the irrepressible resonance of previous acquaintance with French versions. Grimm No. 88 is, after all, a variant of "Beauty and the Beast," which Mme Leprince de Beaumont immortalized in her version of 1756. Now—corollary to my response—I have to ask myself two questions. Do I like this Grimm No. 88 more than the "original" French? Secondly, did this Grimm version influence Jean Cocteau's conception of the beast in his famous film, *La Belle et la Bête* (1946)?

The answer to the first question is both yes and no. I am seduced by the wonderfully smooth narrative, the quickly articulated sequence of events, and I like the mysterious, almost mystical atmosphere of the story. It is a German-Romantic story, but I miss my French *Bête*. Should I forget such silly nationalistic distinctions and love the story for itself? Sometimes I really do. The lion as a beast is a charming surprise. In fact, a lion as a beast that Beauty will eventually disenchant is certainly less repulsive than the indescribably fearful and dangerous beast of Mme Leprince de Beaumont's version. In any case the Grimms' lion may have inspired the almost attractive leonine monster of Jean Cocteau, so aptly played by Jean Marais; it may also have inspired Angela Carter's witty remake, "The Courtship of Mr. Lyon" (1979). I tend to believe, however, that the imagination of both artists simply created the lion as an apt symbol, without any influence from the Grimm version. The artist's imagination can very well create a lion the "equal" of anything found in the folktale.

But let us turn to the tale of "The Twelve Brothers," a story that did not elicit from me a déjà vu reaction and thus brought me to the next stage of my response. The transformation of the twelve brothers into twelve ravens after the inadvertent cutting of the flowers by the devoted younger sister had for me a certain seductive eeriness. Poetic as this feature of the tale may be, its beginning had (still has?) something disturbing: a father ready to sacrifice his twelve sons, just for being sons, in favor of the newborn sister. And topping this cruelty with gory realism were the twelve coffins filled with wood shavings and the mortuary pillows. This was a terrifying account, which I could not understand, like a riddle waiting for a solution.

The stages of my response to Grimms' fairy tales could thus be summarized as follows: prejudice, then overcoming of prejudice, fascinated interest, and a certain puzzlement about some of my favorite tales. My experience with the collection is in no way similar to that of millions of young Germans who grew up with the Grimms' tales and who have "internalized" their texts as one internalizes religious or cultural notions. I came to the Grimms' tales as an adult. I was thus "condemned" to search for their meaning and import through works of criticism. At this stage, I discovered Ernest Tonnelat's monumental two-part thesis, *Les Frères Grimm* and *Les contes des Frères Grimm* (1912). Much of what I found in the work of that eminent Germanist is now familiar to contemporary scholars, thanks to the availability of works in English by Jack Zipes, Ruth B. Bottigheimer, Maria Tatar, and others. But from 1950 to 1955, there was not much more than Tonnelat's volumes available in the French language. And even today, these two volumes are still useful and are still liberally quoted. My youthful idealism was deflated when Tonnelat burst my illusion that the Grimm Brothers, if not Perrault, had been the founders of folklore because they had faithfully transcribed folktales from the mouths of German peasants. In fact, as Tonnelat showed me, Grimms' tales were a work of synthesis of various sources, and very few of them were "popular." The tales were not faithful transcriptions but literary retellings, "not the exact word for word renditions, but the minuscule notation of all the traditional details in a form closest to that used by members of the popular classes when they tell a tale, that is to say a language very simple in its syntax, abounding in images and in comparisons, concrete and expressive, but mixed with proverbs, maxims, interjections, onomatopoeias" (Tonnelat, *Les contes* 72). In other words, the Grimm Brothers began to look more and more like Perrault.

The following statement sums it all up: "The Brothers Grimm believed they had only recovered the original popular language: in reality they had purified and refined it. They were, when all was said and done, the creators of a literary form" (*Les Frères Grimm* 207). So it was through the work of a French scholar that I was taught to appreciate the Grimms' fairy tales for what they are, works of literature, like the tales of Perrault, which I had always admired for their literary charm.

While Tonnelat placed Grimms' stories in a literary context for me, another interesting French scholar, Marthe Robert, returns to a mythic notion of the Grimms as bards of the German people. (I believe, in fact, that the Grimms are the creators of a voice for the German soul, rather than its listeners; but since I am not a Germanist, I would not dare engage myself in that polemical direction.) Acknowledged as the best recent translator of the *Kinder- und Hausmärchen,* Robert has articulated her opinions and critical views in the introduction to her translation, *Contes de Grimm* (1959), and in her critical volume, *Roman des origines et origines du roman* (1972). There is no doubt that for her the Grimms' stories are "superior" to the French fairy tale in general. She praises the Brothers Grimm for having respected oral tradition and having preserved or restored the folktale's initiatory function. Fairy tales describe passages from childhood to adolescence, then to adulthood. All this happens while the child or young man is lost in a forest, only to be rescued by a wise supernatural being (*Contes* 13). The French folk and fairy tale, Robert claims, has lost something the Grimms have recaptured: "While the French tradition weakens the initiatory character of the tale in order to promote a weakly disguised eroticism and ethical values most often of a conformist nature, the German tale, evidently less 'civilized,' preserves all its vigor" (*Contes* 13).

One might disagree with this statement that the French tradition is weaker in its "initiatory character," but Marthe Robert is entitled to adopt a more relativistic attitude and feel that each national tradition normally leans towards its own limits and "ideal" expression, one tradition not necessarily being superior or inferior, or closer to the ideal model than another. It is in their individual and national diversity that folk and fairy tales produce their best fruits. And I admire equally the folktale and fairy tale when they are beautifully expressed. Since the passage above seems like a veiled attack on Perrault, I quote Max

Lüthi, who speaks for me when he writes that "We would not care to do without the elegance and the incisiveness of Perrault" (34).

Marthe Robert's reading of Grimms' tales is most insightful when she notices that the German tales do not rely on fairies as the French do: "One would look in vain in most of the tales of this collection for the fairy with the glistening dress who, a star on her forehead and displaying a wand, appears in the nick of time to straighten out the love affairs of young people" (*Contes* 13). The observation is quite correct, for the old women who obstruct or favor the protagonists of the Grimms' tales are not called "fairies," but "wise women" in the original German text. Robert's translation reflects this observation when she states that she has retained this expression, which in French becomes "sage-femme," or "midwife." She explains that she has "kept this expression in our text precisely because of its double meaning and because of the possibilities for interpretation that it suggests" (*Contes* 14). This translator-editor of Grimms' tales rightly insists on double meaning and interpretation—on the part of listeners.

So, we are reminded once again that there is no response that is not—most often—interpretation. Is it a sin? Is it an inveterate critical temptation? It seems, in any case, that interpretation is the soul of folk-tale and fairy-tale appreciation.

An interesting example of this is the work of Antoine Faivre, *Les contes de Grimm, mythe et initiation* (1979). Faivre's book constitutes a vast and complex survey of Grimms' fairy tales seen through various approaches—Proppian, Lévi-Straussian, and ultimately Jungian or "Durandian" (after Gilbert Durand, an influential scholar at Grenoble University). In Faivre's survey, however, the words and ideas of Mircea Eliade seem to stand out:

> One could almost say that the tale repeats, on another plane and with other means, the exemplary initiatic scenario. The tale repeats and prolongs the "initiation" at the imaginary level. If it constitutes an amusement or an evasion, it is so only for modern man's mind; in the deeper psyche, the initiatory scenarios do keep their seriousness and continue to transmit their messages, and to operate mutations. (Eliade 243–44)

The question is: What is this initiation? According to Eliade, it is simply learning that life is an unending series of trials, of "deaths" and "resurrections," or "whatever other terms used in our modern language to translate these originally religious experiences" might be

274

(244). To illustrate how Grimms' tales provide this initiation to life, Antoine Faivre—using schematics borrowed from Simone Vierne's *Rite, roman, initiation* (1973)—analyzes "The Devil with the Three Golden Hairs" (No. 29). To be sure, this tale apparently conforms to the following sequence: Preparation-Initiatory Death = Rites of Entry and Trip to another World (Hell), and finally, Rebirth. One might say that this is wonderful, that the tales are all clear. But, one might ask, are they all the more enjoyable? And what if one does not ask, or rather, does not feel like asking? Interpreters will say that what the common mortal or child might ask, or not ask, is irrelevant. The meaning of the tale is forever there and will continue to elicit interpretation-responses from those whose purpose in life is to read meaning into all forms of expression. Perhaps Lévi-Strauss says it best, provided we accept his notion that there is no difference between myth and fairy tales: "Myth . . . [is] the mode of discourse where the value of the formula *traduttore, tradittore* tends to become practically untrue" because "the myth's value as myth persists in spite of its worst translation" (232).

The trouble with this dogmatism is that it most satisfies those who formulate it and those who choose to espouse its tenets. This is not a reproach, but a simple observation. But this observation is why I was intrigued by the approach of Pierre Péju, who refused a priori to interpret Grimms' tales: "I would like to write in favor of fairy tales a book deliberately refusing to interpret them no matter what and so reduce them to some dry and silent models . . . without wishing at all costs to deduce their components . . . to that silly question: 'What does it mean?' . . . Could one, with these tales, write a book of pleasure?" (14–15). In order to justify his noninterpretive approach, Péju chose to "debunk" Bruno Bettelheim's famous exegesis, *The Uses of Enchantment* (1976), whose title is betrayed by the French translation *Psychanalyse des contes de fées*. Here, for instance, is Péju's account of Bettelheim's reading of "Sleeping Beauty": "The story of Sleeping Beauty [according to Bettelheim] enables children to understand that a certain traumatic event—such as bleeding at the beginning of puberty, and later at the occasion of the first sexual intercourse—has very happy effects" (77). Our French critic responds to Bettelheim's interpretation with these two statements: "One can only feel a certain disappointment," and "Well, might as well go back to sleep." Now, if one should ask, "But, how *does* this Frenchman see Grimms' tales?" we might get an answer like this: There are stages of desire other than the obvious

275

Oedipus complex and the Freudian family romance in the stories. These stages of desire are often something that Jacob and Wilhelm had noticed fairly early in their research and collecting: a certain "communion with nature," in the sense that these stories elicit, in the child's or adult's unconscious, images and desire to become animal or vegetal, rock or stone, or frog or rat, "which have nothing to do with this or that moment of the libido . . . nothing to do with a phantasm of pervasive power" (89). These feelings and images correspond to another world that haunts our imagination, like fragments of a puzzle that we cannot always join together. This seems to be the final lesson of Péju's courageous and perceptive study: fragments to enjoy, without too much worry.

And here it must be stated that Pierre Péju is much more a novelist and storyteller than a critic, for he has written many stories in which there is an element of unresolved mystery that is always slightly fantastic, but never macabre. His stories belong to the tradition of the *Wundermärchen,* like a modern reflection of Grimms' tales in the French language. I recommend his story "Le poisson-chat" (The Fish Cat), in which a child is at times a cat, a fish, or both, going through the three stages without herself understanding her successive transformations. But Péju carefully resists explaining. Must we wait forever, just as we wait in No. 200 for the golden key to open the iron casket containing wonderful things?

And yet, our need for a key is so strong that we cannot refrain from constantly searching until we find the one that fits for us, like the shoe that finally fits Cinderella's foot. I myself have finally discovered a key in Bellemin-Noël's *Les contes et leurs fantasmes.* I might hypocritically write that I "regret to say" that this key is a psychoanalytic one, and a Freudian one at that, albeit with a very strong French accent. The book is structured like a menu, literally, as if we were reading the description of a gourmet meal. The foreword is entitled "Apéritif," the introduction is called "Hors-d'oeuvre," and the first chapter, an analysis of "The Twelve Brothers," is wittily entitled "Ortolans en brochette," to refer to the twelve brothers' unfortunate avatars. The next chapter, an analysis of "The Seven Ravens," is just as appropriately entitled "Terrine de volaille," since the ravens do not fare so well either, and so on.

Earlier in this essay I noted one story's mixture of "cruelty with gory realism," represented by "the twelve coffins filled with wood shavings and the mortuary pillows." "This," I wrote, "is a somewhat terrifying account, which I could not understand, like a riddle waiting for a solution." This describes my feeling of "malaise" toward No. 9, "The Twelve Brothers." With opportune coincidence, I found in Bellemin-Noël's first chapter an answer I could understand. Our French critic writes that the cruel king who orders the death of his twelve sons if his next offspring happens to be a girl is a very familiar figure at the phantasmatic level, almost the anthropological level postulated by Frazer and Freud: "How can we fail to recognize there the jealous patriarch of the *primitive band* of which Freud made so much? Or Laius attempting to oppose the oracle's threats by disposing of Oedipus?" (34). Here Bellemin-Noël is doing for the psychoanalysis of fairy tales exactly what Propp tried to do in terms of their structure. Propp stated that all tales have—more or less—the same structure. Bellemin-Noël is stating that all fairy tales are retellings of what Freud called the "family romance." Under another phrasing even Jacob and Wilhelm Grimm had noticed, and many others as well, that most fairy tales involve what we now call the "nuclear family." For this French critic, the father in this tale is the "same" father as Laius in Greek tragedy or Abraham in the Bible. In a striking short circuit of phrasing we are reminded that in terms of reader or auditor response, our unconscious is the current that carries meaning to our "phantasmatic mind" as we savor a fairy tale:

> When the tale presents the vision of a father savagely determined to destroy his sons, it suggests that this is the exact negative of the son's wish with respect to the father. The listener-reader perceives, recognizes this reciprocal structure, recognizes the self in it, in double terms of victim and sacrificer. *It's Abraham whose throat is sliced by Oedipus, because Laius has raised the knife over Isaac: each ideology emphasizes the myths which suit its culture, but the Unconscious knows all of them, deciphers all of them as complementary, reversible.* (35; emphasis mine)

Before Bellemin-Noël and I myself are condemned as overly reductive Freudians, let us listen a little longer. Why, at the beginning of this tale, does the king entrust his wife with the dreadful knowledge that her twelve sons will be killed? Why do the youngest son and the mother conspire to save the condemned sons? We are in the phantasmatic realm of the unconscious. We *know* that no worthy mother will ever accept the killing of her sons. The beginning of this tale is a disguised dialogue

277

between father and mother. It is as if the mother were taking revenge on the father, letting go of her anger (37), saying in substance: You are sacrificing everything (everyone) for "your" daughter, but I am protecting "my" sons. Which is also a way of saying: "My father was just as good as your mother" (37).

Why does this improbable king ask his own wife to guard the room with the twelve coffins? Why does he give her the key to the room? These questions were to remain riddles for me until Bellemin-Noël decoded them. He proposes to equate "room" for "his wife-woman's belly." This interpretation might seem "too much," but who has a better answer? Bellemin-Noël tells us that if we refuse the Freudian identification of rooms with the female body, we can at least accept the metaphorical connection between the twelve coffins and the one woman, of all women, who is entrusted as their guardian, which is an impossibility in normal terms. (What parents are ready to kill their children?) In other words, and again at the phantasmatic level, it is as if the king were telling his wife: "All right, let us not kill our sons, put them back in your belly . . . give them another chance to be reborn." This last interpretation is not quite Bellemin-Noël's, but mine. It so happens that the twelve sons are metamorphosed into ravens, but only after the sister has found them and served as their "mother" by living with them and forming a sort of happy "incestuous" relation with the youngest son, the Benjamin of the family.

There are many suggestive and convincing rapprochements in these phantasms, even if they are accepted with humor as mere heuristic phantasms. It would be tempting to reject them if Bellemin-Noël did not know the German language. But he knows it very well and documents his exegesis with an informed sense of the linguistic texture of Grimms' collection. For instance, he reminds us that in German there is alliteration in the reference to the younger sister, who wears the very symbol of her femininity, a jewel, on her forehead: "einen Stern auf der Stirne." As he observes: "It is the superior middle part of the face that is emphasized instead of the lower part of the body, the center of thought replaces that of the sensual drives. . . . In sum, the little girl's sex becomes a metaphor from that star on her forehead" (57).

The linguistic authority supporting Bellemin-Noël's psychoanalytic exegesis is evident elsewhere, too. We are informed that the German word *Vogel* (bird—the brothers are transformed into birds) commonly refers to the penis, just as in French *zizi* recalls the sound of *zoizeau* (birds) in childish language to refer to the penis. So, when the brothers are transformed into twelve ravens, they are reduced to their simplest virile expression and are to disappear, or hide, until their wholeness can be reasserted in the realm of adulthood. The other example is perhaps the most suggestive of all. At the tale's end there is one bad mother, the queen mother. Bellemin-Noël takes to task Marthe Robert, who was neither inspired nor accurate, when she identified this wicked queen as a mere "stepmother." The expression will not do. There is another expression, perfectly appropriate in the German language, an expression without equivalent in either English or French, and perfect for this tale of boys turned into ravens: *Rabenmutter,* literally "mother raven," or "mother of ravens," which means precisely stepmother.

It seems, once again, that everyday language is quite pregnant with the sort of symbolism that Freud noticed as prevalent not only in dreams, but also in myths and fairy tales. A "sense of symbolism" seems to be a prerequisite for an appreciation of Grimms' stories, and our French critic is eminently gifted with this sense. He notices what others have missed, probably because they believe that since fairy tales are irrational, there is no need to look for meaning in them. The finale of No. 9 is a very suggestive execution of the *Rabenmutter,* who is put into a barrel filled with boiling oil and venomous serpents. From a rational point of view this is decidedly absurd, for vipers cooked in boiling oil can't do any harm (65). Bellemin-Noël's interpretation is interesting, however, for it suggests a return to death-birth in terms of penises (serpents) floating in a "mortiferous amniotic liquid. . . . It was obligatory, under Thanatos's sign, to conjugate the specificity of both sexes." With characteristic humor, Bellemin-Noël reminds us of his own oneiric bent: "This may well be a phantasm, but it is my own dear phantasm!"

The above sentence is the last one in a chapter of twenty-six pages devoted to the analysis of a tale no longer than seven pages, which is to say that Bellemin-Noël's reading is well informed and well documented. He does not label his method a psychoanalysis of the tales, but more modestly a *textanalyse.* Bellemin-Noël analyzes each text as a single unit, not only in terms of what it tells, but also in terms of what it signifies to the reader-listener's unconscious. In a felicitous turn of phrase he states that the fairy tale is a sort of prefabricated dream: *"le prêt-à porter du fantasme"* (10), an affirmation that anyone can accept, whatever his or her school of interpretation.

There is no point in paraphrasing what Bellemin-Noël writes about other tales—"The Seven Ravens" (No. 25), "The Six Swans" (No. 49), "Brier Rose" (No. 50), "Snow White" (No. 53), "Cinderella" or "Ashputtle" (No. 21), "Faithful Johannes" (No. 6), and "Hansel and Gretel" (No. 15). What I have related about his response is typical enough of his approach, which is not to say that he repeats himself. There are times when he is at his best, when he refuses to interpret, thus poking fun at himself and occasionally at another analyst of tales, the unavoidable Bruno Bettelheim. Commenting on the last two sentences of "Hansel and Gretel"—"Then all anxiety was at an end, and they lived together in perfect happiness. My tale is done, there runs a mouse, whosoever catches it may make himself a big fur cap out of it"—Bettelheim wrote: "Industry, making something good even out of unpromising material (such as by using the fur of a mouse intelligently for making a cap), is the virtue and real achievement of the school-age child who has fought through and mastered the oedipal difficulties" (165). Bellemin-Noël finds this interpretation absurd, unrelated to the text, if not revolting; so he parodies Bettleheim by writing: "Be industrious, little children, you will become worthy of the *American way of life.* . . . I prefer to think that such a statement should remain without commentary" (169).

I have focused here on my own responses to Grimms' fairy tales and on selected French scholars whose critical reception of the tales has influenced my responses. That perspective leads me to conclude with both a warning concerning reductionist interpretation and with a reflection on the role of reader response theory in the study of fairy tales. The warning can be phrased as follows. The terms of any given motif, according to the folklorists, or those of any function, according to the formalist-semioticians espousing the Proppian approach, cannot be strictly interchangeable, because this would make one fairy tale the equivalent of any other. Similarly, the interpretive grid of Freud's famous *Interpretation of Dreams,* which Bruno Bettelheim regularly and dogmatically applies to Grimms' tales, does not necessarily coincide with what the stories tell us. What one must look for in a text is something supported in its very language, or one must at least work on the basis of associations derived from the text itself. What we are looking for is the unconscious of the text, which is searched or prospected just as the earth is mined to make it yield its hidden treasures. I am not for a moment forgetting here my topic: response to Grimms' fairy tales. I am saying that these tales contain, evoke, or awaken resonances of the unconscious, what could be called in the context of this paper associative nets, or simply phantasms.

Now, in terms of the specific theories of textual responses, this reader confesses that everything he says or writes about Grimms' tales, or any other fairy-tale texts he likes, is always formulated according to a personal way of looking at texts aesthetically. For me, in Barthian terms, the reader's response is above all pleasure of the text, or no interest in the text at all. This is why my response to Grimms' texts, and to fairy tales in general, has often been determined by how texts have encouraged me or others to fantasize, to dream, trite as this may sound. Such theoretical texts as Hans Robert Jauß's *Kleine Apologie der ästhetischen Erfahrung,* which I read in French translation (*Pour une esthétique de la réception,* 1978), or Wolfgang Iser's *The Act of Reading* (1978), have helped me to understand my response. For instance, the notion of a "horizon d'attente" (Jauß 50) did help me to understand why I had to relocate Grimms' fairy tales in their sociohistorical context, without which the stories are meaningless. Similarly, the dialectic of belief-disbelief which I, as a reader, developed with respect to the Grimms' collection, is something which I had always practiced. And now in the work of Wolfgang Iser I find terms very close to my own formulation. Iser's assertion that "illusion-forming and illusion-breaking" are essential to the act of reading (127) parallels my own statement in an article on "The Aesthetics of the Fairy Tale" that the magic of fairy tales—including the Grimms'—is characterized by belief-disbelief. Perhaps that statement should conclude this improper exercise: "We could not be human beings if we were not torn between belief and disbelief in the supernatural. The best authors know how to tell a tale in which they can communicate or echo this ambivalence" (188).

Works Cited

Barchilon, Jacques. "The Aesthetics of the Fairy Tale." *La Cohérence intérieure: Études sur la littérature française du XVIIe siècle presentées en hommage à Judd D. Hubert*. Ed. Jacqueline van Baelen and David L. Rubin. Paris: J. M. Place, 1977. 187–201.

Bellemin-Noël, Jean. *Les contes et leurs fantasmes*. Paris: PU de France, 1983.

Bettelheim, Bruno. *The Uses of Enchantment: The Meaning and Importance of Fairy Tales*. New York: Knopf, 1976.

Bolte, Johannes, and Georg Polívka. *Anmerkungen zu den Kinder- und Hausmärchen der Brüder Grimm*. 5 vols. Leipzig: Dieterich, 1913–32.

Bottigheimer, Ruth B. *Grimms' Bad Girls and Bold Boys: The Moral and Social Vision of the Tales*. New Haven: Yale UP, 1987.

Carter, Angela. *The Bloody Chamber*. New York: Harper, 1979.

Eliade, Mircea. *Aspects du mythe*. Paris: Gallimard, 1963.

Faivre, Antoine. *Les contes de Grimm, mythe et initiation*. Paris: Lettres Modernes, 1978.

Iser, Wolfgang. *The Act of Reading*. Baltimore: The Johns Hopkins UP, 1978.

Jauß, Hans Robert. *Pour une esthétique de la réception*. Trans. Claude Maillard. Paris: Gallimard, 1978.

Lévi-Strauss, Claude. *Anthropologie structurale*. Paris: Plon, 1958.

Lüthi, Max. *Once Upon a Time: On the Nature of Fairy Tales*. Trans. Lee Chadeayne and Paul Gottwald. New York: Ungar, 1970.

Péju, Pierre. *La petite fille dans la forêt des contes*. Paris: Laffont, 1981.

Robert, Marthe, ed. and trans. *Contes de Grimm*. 1959. Paris: Gallimard-Folio, 1976.

———. *Roman des origines et origines du roman*. Paris: B. Grasset, 1972.

Tatar, Maria. *The Hard Facts of the Grimms' Fairy Tales*. Princeton, NJ: Princeton UP, 1987.

Tonnelat, Ernest. *Les contes des Frères Grimm: Études sur la composition et style du recueil des Kinder- und Hausmärchen*. Paris: Colin, 1912.

———. *Les Frères Grimm: Leur oeuvre de jeunesse*. Paris: Colin, 1912.

Velten, Harry. "The Influence of Charles Perrault's *Contes de ma Mère L'Oie* on German Folklore." *Germanic Review* 1 (1930): 4–18.

Vierne, Simone. *Rite, roman, initiation*. Grenoble: PU de Grenoble, 1973.

Zipes, Jack. *The Brothers Grimm: From Enchanted Forests to the Modern World*. New York: Routledge, 1988.

The Brothers Grimm
and Sister Jane

Jane Yolen

MY FIRST TASTE of fairy tales was in the collected color fairy books of Andrew Lang. Bowdlerized and tarted up as they were, the stories in those books still mesmerized me. Though I was a New York City child, I rode across the steppes of Russia, swam in the cold Scandinavian rivers, ran down African forest paths, hunted in the haunted Celtic woods with the heroes of the stories I read. I became in turn the girl on the back of a great white bear riding east of the sun and west of the moon, the Hoodie-crow's lovely wife, the farmer's woman stolen away by the fairies.

Like an addict, I went from the Lang samplers to the stronger stuff. The local librarians got used to me pulling out dusty collections from the shelves: the Afanas'ev Russian stories, Asbjørnsen and Moe's Norwegian tales, Yeats's Irish fairy lore, the *Thousand and One Nights*. (It was years before I learned it was the expurgated version.) And—of course—the Brothers Grimm.

By the time I was ten, a tomboy by day and a reader by night under the covers, I had devoured whole cultures. To the outsider, I must have seemed omniverous in my reading, catholic in my taste. But there were three stories in the Grimm collection that were my favorites. Though I could not have known it at the time, they were *life myths* to me. As it says in one of the early Gnostic gospels, *The Gospel According to Thomas:* "Whoever drinks from my mouth shall become as I am and I myself will become he, and the hidden things shall be revealed to him." If *that* is not a fairy-tale transformative curse—or blessing—I have misspent my youth! In loving these three particular stories, I became them. They were my meat and I theirs, a literary eucharist.

The three were: "Faithful John" (No. 6), "Brother and Sister" (No. 11), and "The Three Little Men in the Woods (No. 13).

It is an odd trio I adopted. They are certainly not the most popular stories in the Grimm canon. Disney has not touched them. Nor are they found in picture-book format for the youngest readers. One must search them out within the body of the Grimm tales, a task for the true child bibliophile. Yet though these were not the popular and often reprinted stories, each spoke to me in a way that knifed clear to the soul. Like Yeats's description of the class of people who loved the folk tales, the peasants who "have steeped everything in the heart; to whom everything was a symbol" (xii), I was a breather-in of stories. Those three tales, though I did not understand it at the time, were to be accurate forecasters of my adult concerns.

The first of the trio, "Faithful John," is the story of a servant to the king who promises the dying monarch that he will be equally faithful to the prince "even if it should cost me my life" (43). And of course, as such stories go, John is forced to be as good as his word. He accompanies his young master on his bridal trip and overhears three ravens prophesying what dire things await the bridal pair. Furthermore, the ravens state that anyone foolish enough to explain it to the king would immediately be turned to stone. Naturally, Faithful John saves the royal couple three times and, when ordered to explain his actions, does so and becomes stone. Only when the king and queen willingly sacrifice their own children and use the innocents' blood to return the stone to life does the tale end happily. Happily for the children, too, for they are magically restored as well.

The story is full of magic, sacrifice, and reward, all the wonderful accoutrements of a fairy tale. It is satisfyingly rounded, wasting little time between the opening, in which the dying king accepts Faithful John's pledge, to the conclusion in which "They dwelt together in much happiness until their death'' (51). An economical tale between two dyings, a critic might carp. But oh, as a child, how I loved that tale.

The faithful servant—tale type 516—was well known for centuries before the Grimms' particular version was recorded, travelling from India both orally and in the eleventh-century *Ocean of Story* collection. Some scholars point out a connection as well with the French romance *Amis and Amiloun,* which contains both the stone and the disenchantment by means of innocent children's blood. (For a fuller discussion of this see Stith Thompson's *The Folktale* 111–12.) But all that mattered to me as a child was the driving force behind that story: that faithfulness, even unto a quasi-death, would be rewarded in the end.

By the time I was an adult, only vaguely remembering the outlines of the story, I had become a peace marcher, a stander-on-line for causes. I was—in essence—a Faithful John, willing to go to jail or even to be turned to stone as the possible consequence of my actions. My stories, too, had more than a casual reference to the old tale. *Dove Isabeau* is a picture-book fairy tale about a prince who is turned to stone because of his willingness to save his own true love. He does what must be done—knowing full well that stone is his doom, that he will, quite literally, become his own monument. He is saved in the very end by a drop of blood from an innocent girl. *Friend,* a biography of my hero, that great stander-up-to-power George Fox, the first Quaker, was another offshoot of the "Faithful John" story. And "The Hundredth Dove" is a fairy tale about a faithful servant to his king who even wears the motto "Servo"—*I serve*—over his breast until he is forced to serve his king in an ignoble and terrible fashion. That was a story fueled by the Watergate hearings, but its antecedent is, unquestionably, Grimm story No. 6.

The second tale that imprinted itself on my consciousness was "Brother and Sister," an odd tale in the Grimm collection because it has always seemed unfinished to me, or strangely conglomerate, as if two stories had been badly or inappropriately stitched together.

A brother and sister who are abused by their stepmother "go forth together into the wide world" (67) and become lost in a forest whose very brooks have been bewitched by their sorcerous foe. Dying of thirst, they go from one stream to another, not daring to drink, for the first two announce, "Who drinks of me will be a tiger" and "Who drinks of me will be a wolf" (68). (Does this sound remarkably like the *Gospel According to Thomas* quotation with which I began this essay?)

At last, the brother cannot stand it any longer and drinks from a stream that promises he will become a deer. His sister ties her golden garter around his neck and leads him even further into the woods where they discover an empty cottage. There they live until a king comes upon them, falls in love with the girl, and brings them both back to the palace. Of course the wicked stepmother substitutes her own ugly daughter for the queen at the moment of childbirth, and the story finishes with the rightful queen restored, the false queen torn to pieces by wild beasts in the very woods her mother had enchanted, and the witch burnt at the stake. The deer—at last—is turned back into a man.

It was the relationship between the brother and sister that first compelled me. As an older sister to an adored younger brother, I considered myself a twin to the heroine of the tale. As she is not named in the story, I named her—Jane.

Tale type 450, called after the story "Little Brother, Little Sister," it is the prototype story of family loyalty that has been found in many different cultures. Family loyalty was prized in our house.

When I became a writer, I used the tale very consciously in my own story "Brother Hart," though that particular tale is more a romance than a fairy story, with a bittersweet ending. It is a story of jealousy and possessiveness, created at the height of feminist rage and the ongoing discussions about a woman's place in a loving relationship. Not just a recasting of an old, familiar story, it is a tale that could only have been written in the mid-twentieth century. I also used the transformation motif in a variety of other stories, all harkening back to "Brother and Sister." "The Promise," in which a boy transformed into a fish by a sorcerer is saved by his own true love; "The Catbride," in which a cat becomes a human girl in order to be married; "The White Seal Maid," in which a seal becomes a woman and bears seven sons to a fisherman to revive her dying tribe; and the transfigured brother and sister in the "Wild Goose and Gander" section of my fairy-tale novel *The Magic Three of Solatia* are just a few of them.

The third—and in some ways the oddest—of my life stories was the relatively unknown "The Three Little Men in the Woods." It begins with a widow and widower marrying and the stepmother offering preferment to her own ugly daughter. The beautiful stepdaughter is sent out into the woods in the middle of winter in a paper frock to gather strawberries, a traditional "impossible task." Since she is as good as she is beautiful, she treats the three little men she meets in the woods politely and shares her meagre dinner—a piece of hard bread—with them, thus winning their approval. They wish that she grow more beautiful every day, that whenever she speaks gold should fall from her lips, and that she marry a king. When she returns home with strawberries found miraculously in the snow, speaking a fortune at every utterance, the stepmother packs her own daughter off for the same trip. Of course she is swathed in furs and carries along a bread-and-butter cake which she neglects to share with the little men, whom she snubs. Naturally she is cursed: that she grow uglier every day, that toads spring from her mouth, and that she die a miserable death. As the adventure proceeds, both the blessings and the curses come true.

Similar to the more popular Grimms' "Frau Holle" or "Mother Holle" (No. 24), the tale at its core contains the well-known motif "Kind and unkind" daughter (Q2). Other Grimm stories also revolve around Q2: "Bearskin" (No. 101) and "The Water of Life" (No. 97; unkind sons in this case). But it was the idea of the gold pouring out of the good girl's mouth, the toads from the bad's, that riveted me. It was—though I did not know it at the time—a metaphor for the life I was to choose.

I was to use that toad image in *Sleeping Ugly,* a parody of several fairy tales, in which the nasty Princess Miserella is cursed, for a moment, to speak in toads until the homely but goodhearted Plain Jane asks for a reprieve. I also used the image in the following poem, part of a series of fairy-tale poems I wrote in the mid and late 1980s:

Toads

Sure, I called her *stupid cow*
and *witch,*
but only under my breath.
And I took an extra long lunch
last Friday,
and quit right at five
every day this week,
slapping my desk top down
with a noise
like the snap of gum.
She could've fired me right then.
Or docked my check.
Or put a pink slip
in my envelope

with that happy face
she draws on all her notes.
But not her.
Witch!
This morning
at the coffee shop,
when I went to order
a Danish and a decaf to go,
instead of words,
this great gray toad
the size of a bran muffin
dropped out between my lips
onto the formica.
It looked up at me,
its dark eyes sorrowful,
its back marked
with Revlon's Lady Love
the shape of my kiss.
Tell me,
do you think
I should apologize?
Do you think I should let
the shop steward know?

I also used the idea of something unnatural coming from a girl's mouth in the story "Silent Bianca." Bianca speaks in slivers of ice, and anyone who wants to know what she is saying has to gather the slivers and warm them by the hearthfire until the slivers melt and the room is filled with the sounds of Bianca's voice.

Every author hopes that the words pouring from the pen—or typewriter, word processor, or number 2 pencil, all mouth substitutes—are golden, indeed. Golden means the words are precious, important, powerful. Golden means that the author can make a good living. Golden suggests permanence and worth. However, I—and most writers I know—suspect that when we open our mouths we usually spit out toads, as big as bran muffins, onto the plates of our eager readers. For that nightmare—for that metaphor—we have the Brothers Grimm to thank.

Works Cited

Grimm, Brothers. *The Complete Grimm's Fairy Tales.* Trans. Margaret Hunt. Rev. James Stern. 1944. New York: Pantheon Books, 1972.

Thompson, Stith. *The Folktale.* 1946. Berkeley: U of California P, 1977.

Yeats, William Butler. *Irish Fairy and Folk Tales.* New York: Random, n.d.

Yolen, Jane. "Brother Hart." *Dream Weaver* 10–20.

———. "The Catbride." *Dream Weaver* 43–47.

———. *Dove Isabeau.* San Diego: Harcourt, 1989.

———. *Dream Weaver.* 1979. New York: Philomel Books, 1989.

———. *Friend: The Story of George Fox and the Quakers.* New York: Seabury Press, 1972.

———. *The Hundredth Dove and Other Tales.* New York: Crowell, 1977.

———. "The Hundredth Dove." *Hundredth Dove* 1–9.

———. *The Magic Three of Solatia.* New York: Crowell, 1974.

———. "The Promise." *Hundredth Dove* 39–50.

———. "Silent Bianca." *The Girl Who Cried Flowers and Other Tales.* New York: Crowell, 1974. 45–55.

———. *Sleeping Ugly.* New York: Coward, 1981.

———. "Toads." *Isaac Asimov's Science Fiction Magazine* June 1989: 145.

———. "The White Seal Maid." *Hundredth Dove* 29–37.

Grimms' Remembered

Margaret Atwood

W HEN I WAS growing up in the 1940s, my family spent over half the year in the forest lands of Northern Quebec, where my father ran a forest insect research station. We did not live in a small town or even a village, although we could see the covered bridges and white church spire of a tiny French-speaking hamlet a mile away by water. Thus my brother and I did not have many other children to play with. We could not go to the Saturday afternoon matinee so fondly remembered by some people my age, nor could we listen to the radio: although there was a radio, reception was so bad in those remote areas that the radio was turned on only for the weather, and for news of the War. There were no art galleries, special classes or plays, and television had not yet been invented. Books were it.

Some of these books were comic books—though I'm not sure how we came by them—and certainly we read the colored Saturday funnies whenever they fell into our clutches, which was not all that often. We wrote comic books, too, for each other, presumably because of the short supply. But comic books were kids' culture, and frowned on by grown-ups, like Popsicles and picking your nose. The official reading was dished out by our mother, who read to us, and usually to anyone else in the vicinity, children and grown-ups alike, as she was a good reader. We went through the entire works of Beatrix Potter, so many times that we could recite them off by heart; later we hit *Alice in Wonderland, Robinson Crusoe, Swiss Family Robinson,* and many other standard children's classics. But the book I remember the best from that time—and the one that has made the most appearances, concealed or otherwise, in my own work—was acquired as a sort of mistake.

It was a book of *Grimms' Fairy Tales,* which my parents ordered by mail. But when it arrived, it was not quite what they had been expecting. Instead of having pretty illustrations of princesses with long golden hair, it had peasant-style line drawings, primitively colored and, well, odd-looking. Worse than that, it was complete—every bit of Grimms' was there—and even worse, it was—at a time when experts were telling parents that such things as red-hot shoes, barrels full of nails, and heads that came off were bad for their kiddies' psyches—unexpurgated. Every bloodstained axe, wicked witch, and dead horse was right there where the Brothers Grimm had set them down, ready to be discovered by us.

Our parents weren't sure they should let us have this potentially frightening book, but we got hold of it anyway, and we took to it; possibly because the drawings looked more like ours than most drawings in books did, possibly because, being war babies, we were more hardened to the idea of slaughter than we were expected to be. Bruno Bettelheim had not yet appeared to tell the grown-ups that dire adventures followed by happy endings were, for various complicated reasons, good for you, so I expect my parents gnawed their nails while their adored children read about pieces of bodies falling down the chimney, Godfather Death, and other horrors. None of this seems to have given me nightmares, nor do I remember confusing it with the "real" world, the world of automobiles, bubble gum, and having to eat your cooked carrots. But I expect it was all a little more like the secret insides of our heads than anyone then would have cared to admit.

Because I knew and continue to know these stories so well, I'm always a little astonished when I hear *Grimms' Fairy Tales* denounced as sexist. Racist, yes. There was more than a dollop of anti-Semitism. But sexist? It seems to me that various traits were quite evenly spread. There were wicked wizards as well as wicked witches, stupid women as well as stupid men, slovenly husbands as well as slovenly wives. After all, these stories were not originally intended for children at all, but were for the after-sunset entertainment of the entire household in preliterate days, and many of the classic storytellers by whom the stories were passed down, and from whom they were collected, were women; nor did they neglect their constituency. When people say "sexist fairy tales," they probably mean the anthologies that concentrate on "The Sleeping Beauty," "Cinderella," and "Little Red Riding Hood" and leave out everything else. But in "my" version, there are a good many forgetful or imprisoned princes who have to be rescued by the clever, brave, and resourceful princess, who is just as willing to undergo hardship and risk her neck as are the princes engaged in dragon slaying and tower climbing. Not only that, they're usually better at spells.

And where else could I have gotten the idea, so early in life, that words can change you?

"Cut It Down, and You Will Find Something at the Roots"

Trina Schart Hyman

M Y PARENTS ARE both of German ancestry, and so I was brought up on Struwwelpeter and Grimms' fairy tales. They are the first, and indeed the only, stories I remember from my earliest childhood. For me they were more than just bedtime stories— they were the Word, the Light, a whole way of approaching most things in life. And later on, they formed an important aspect of my career.

During the first five years of my life, the most influential piece of literature ever to embed itself in my tiny mind or to inflame my over-fertile imagination was the Grimms' version of "Little Red Riding Hood." I so strongly identified with that less-than-clever trusting little twit of a heroine, and was so fascinated by her encounter with the wolf and her adventures in the forest and at Grandmother's house, that I became literally enchanted by the tale. I was so obsessed with it that the fine and wavering line between story and real life became invisible to me.

Note: The title of this essay is taken from Grimms' tale "The Golden Goose."

I became my own 1940s version of Little Red Riding Hood. My mother sewed me a little red cape with a hood, and I wore it every day for almost a year—even through the sweltering Philadelphia summer. Each day had to begin with packing an old Easter basket with goodies to take to Grandmother's house. My only grandmother lived three hundred miles away in Rhode Island, and I was not allowed to cross the street or even to leave the yard by myself; but imagination is a wonderful thing, and this Little Red Riding Hood had daily confrontations with the "wolf" (my dog Tippy) and close brushes with death-by-devouring in the deep black forest of my parents' suburban back yard.

One of Little Red Riding Hood's other preoccupations besides the wolf at this time was drawing pictures. On rainy days when the black forest was too wet, or in the evening when it was far too dark and dangerous, she used to draw endless self-portraits in the red cape, pictures of the wolf, versions of Grandma's house, the forest, and combinations thereof, sometimes with an angel or two thrown in for good measure. It was my first-ever serious job of illustrating.

When I was seven, my parents gave me the most wonderful Christmas present. It was a slipcased two-volume edition of *all* the Grimms' fairy tales and Hans Christian Andersen's tales, too. "Little Red Riding Hood," "Hansel and Gretel," "Cinderella," and "Snow White"—my "baby" favorites—quickly took a back seat as I discovered and inhaled more exciting, intricate, and mysterious fare: "Iron Hans," "The Robber Bridegroom," "The Six Servants," "The White Snake," and "The Seven Ravens."

I read the Andersen tales, too, but I never liked them as much. I thought it was because they made me uncomfortable and a little sad, but that didn't seem logical. Andersen's stories were longer (which meant better, because they wouldn't end as soon), more complex, full of great descriptions, and far more sorrowfully dramatic and tragic— all qualities I valued highly in any story. Now I realize Andersen's whole point of view was the turn-off. His stories are very judgmental, I think, and full of a strict, harsh morality. All that stuff about God, and Hell, and sinfulness! His heroines always wind up going to the bosom of God (if they're good), or else they're praying or being saved from Hell by someone else's prayers. Andersen was a sad, troubled man, and I suppose this comes through in his writing. As a child I felt it very strongly. Although "The Snow Queen" was, and still is, one of my most favorite stories, as a child I read Mr. Andersen's book only when I was feeling rather brave.

The Grimms' tales, on the other hand, I turned to for comfort, inspiration, and just plain enjoyment. There is very little mention of God or the devil in these stories. People more usually go to the sun, or the moon, or the winds for advice. Or to the animals—birds are great omen-bringers and advice-givers. Nature is full of power. Morality—in the form of "good" or "evil"—is not so clearly drawn in Grimm and almost never pointed out. Heroes and heroines often pull some pretty rotten, nasty, or self-serving tricks in order to get what they want.

Things are not always what they seem, either. A perfectly lovely princess can suddenly turn into a nasty bitch, a frightening and violent ogre can be a king in disguise or at least a good ol' boy in unexpected ways. Stupidity can be rewarded, and the purest of motives can turn the world upside down.

To me, as a child, this was satisfying and true. To me, as an adult, it is still satisfying and true. Chance and coincidence can turn any chain of events around, unexpected people can bestow great gifts, and beautiful maidens can turn vindictive in the wink of an eye; brothers usually want to kill each other, and even a fierce giant will always listen to his mother. Nature is mysterious and magical, and the cheerful and merry folk usually do survive. Ravens and stones speak truly. Men usually speak falsely.

Forty-three years later, those two books are still in my library. The Andersen is shabby around the corner but still (as book dealers say) in mint condition. The Grimm is a mess—worn through and through. Pages are stained, paragraphs are marked in pencil. The back is broken through years of use and love. And it still falls open automatically to the last page of "Little Red Riding Hood" and the first page of "The King of the Golden Mountain."

All this past history is to bring me to the point of the story: This German-American who happened to be born an artist has an intense and deep relationship with the tales of the Brothers Grimm. That little girl in her home-sewn Red Riding Hood cape wasn't drawing pictures entirely for the fun of it. Those drawings were a totem and a charm; they were a personal kind of magic. They were in fact a religious act.

Little Red Riding Hood has never stopped drawing pictures. I eventually quit the infatuation with my alter ego and took on other characters to make sense of real life, of course. But given the overfertile

295

imagination and the gift for role-playing fueled by fiction, it was natural that this artist should become an illustrator of children's books.

Many years and far too many mediocre books later, Emilie McCleod of Atlantic, Little Brown asked me to do a full-color picture-book version of *Snow White and the Seven Dwarfs*.

All of it came back from my Red Riding Hood Days, everything I had ever believed about those stories. Best of all, the story spoke to me as no story had ever done before. I had recently gone through one of those life experiences that involve coincidences, jealousies, a lot of fierce emotions, treachery, rebirths—all the emotional underpinnings of "Snow White." I put it all into that book. The story was so secure and fundamental in my mind, unleashed from memories of childhood, that I didn't even have to think about it. I knew them all; I knew exactly what they were thinking, what made them tick, exactly who they had to be. I knew what they ate for breakfast, how they brushed their teeth, even what kind of underwear they wore.

I knew how the queen was slipping into madness, and how she hated Snow White's youth. This woman wasn't evil—she was simply a complex personality whose only power was her beauty. She didn't think about the girl as a person. She hated only what Snow White symbolized, which was youth and the power and beauty of youth. And Snow White was just an innocent kid who felt threatened and ran away from home.

The dwarfs were more complicated and more fun to speculate about. In the story, they're not given any particular characters, so I felt happily free to create these seven little men from six people I knew well—and I threw myself in, too, for good measure. (I don't use models for my illustrations in the time-honored way. That is, I don't set live people in a pose and draw from them. I don't use photographs, either. All I usually need to know about drawing a human figure is in my hand and in my head. And the people in *Snow White* had been in my head for a long, long time. Now, at last, they could come out through my hand.)

I put my eleven-year-old daughter (albeit rather idealized and prettified) in the title role. For the queen, I used my longtime friend and ex-companion of seven years. It's an astonishingly accurate portrait—she really was, and is, that beautiful; and although not quite that crazy, she projects an intensity that borders on spooky. The dwarfs include my next-door neighbor, my father, my ex-husband, and Konrad Lorenz (whom I didn't know personally, but always wanted to). The prince is

Fig. 4. Trina Schart Hyman, *Snow White* (Boston: Little, Brown and Co., 1974). Illustration © 1974 by Trina Schart Hyman.

Jane Yolen's husband. He's a prince of a fellow, to be sure, but more importantly his looks convey maturity, character, and strength as well as tenderness—all the qualities that I wanted for Snow White's future husband. I figured the poor kid deserved as much stability and security as she could get, considering all she'd been through (Fig. 4).

I worked on the book steadily for almost a year, and it was one of the most exhausting, exhilarating, cathartic, and intensely rewarding jobs I have ever done. I knew I had taken a giant leap forward artistically and professionally, and I felt I had done the old story as much justice as I possibly could. Unfortunately, the book was published barely a year after the Randall Jarrell–Nancy Ekholm Burkert version of *Snow White*, and most reviewers were less than enthusiastic about the Hyman version. Nancy Burkert's cool, classical, dreamily objective illustrations could not have been more different from my own emotional, highly dramatic, subjective handling of the story. (We are, by the way,

297

great admirers of each other's work.) It seemed then, as now, that many reviewers, critics, and folklorists definitely prefer the cool and classical approach. To this point of view I could reply with a whole other (and much longer) essay, but what the hell. My editor minded all this much more than I did. To me, the book was a success, and I wouldn't do it much differently if I had to do it all over again tomorrow.

I began work on *The Sleeping Beauty* in 1975, almost immediately after *Snow White*'s publication. This time, I decided to retell the story myself as well as illustrate it. Although I have never been comfortable with the writing process, I had my well-worn old copy of *Grimms' Fairy Tales* to guide and comfort me. The pictures, and the whole mood of the book, were intentionally more lighthearted, romantic, and softer than in *Snow White*. I had great fun casting all my friends as the twelve good fairies and Michael Patrick Hearn as the thirteenth fairy. As the model for Briar Rose, I used my daughter's best friend Annie, who was fifteen years old and just as lovely, good-hearted, wise, and merry as any fairy-tale princess could be. As the book was going on press, Annie was killed in an automobile accident. She had just turned sixteen. I still cannot let myself think too much about that coincidence or examine too closely the parallels between the fairy tale and real life. It was five years before I could think about illustrating another Grimms' tale.

Holiday House, my publisher then, was hot for me to do "Cinderella." But that's always been one of my least favorite fairy tales—as far as I can tell, it's all about clothes and girls being mean to each other—and I also knew that another and highly respected illustrator was already at work on that story. So we compromised on "Rapunzel." Once again, the emotional truth and power of the Grimms' tale took a firm grip on my imagination.

To me, the key figure in the story is Mother Gothel, the witch. She cares for the girl-child like a mother and then, at the onset of puberty, locks her up in a tower. What strange things love makes us do! As a model for the witch, I used my dear friend and neighbor, who at seventy-six was one of the most attractive and enchanting women I have ever known; she could indeed be terrifying as well as kind. The prince is Barbara Rogasky, my collaborator and reteller of the story.

The previous year I had fallen in love with the work of the Russian illustrator Ivan Bilibin, and I borrowed freely from his wonderfully funky, uninhibited page design ideas and his beautiful muted color. Despite this Russian influence, I was careful to include plenty of visual stuff that had the feel of other Grimm stories—the witch's pet ravens, the interior of the peasant couple's cottage, and the misty, mysterious, dark piney forests through which so many Grimm characters must find their own path. As a result of this, I think it is the most Germanic—the most "Grimm" in feeling—of all my books.

When my editor at Holiday House wanted to follow *Rapunzel* with the TSH version of "Little Red Riding Hood," I literally recoiled in terror. I simply could not imagine myself daring to retell and to illustrate this most sacred and holy of childhood stories. A totally superstitious and primitive fear prevented me from even thinking about it rationally. After all, wasn't this my own autobiography? Wasn't that little girl in the red cape still me? If illustrating the Sleeping Beauty had somehow killed Annie, wasn't I—or anyway the child still within me—in mortal danger if I dared to illustrate Little Red Riding Hood? Well, of course I decided to do it anyway; all my editor had to say was "Okay. But if you don't do it, you know that some other illustrator will." Fighting words!

Retelling "Little Red" was easy. All I had to do was say "by heart" the Grimm version that had been embedded in my mind so long before. Casting the characters was even easier. Little Red was, of course, myself at age four. Her mother was my mom, and her grandmother my own Rhode Island grandmother. I modelled the huntsman after the Yankee farmer who has been my friend and next-door neighbor for twenty years. I knew a man across the river in Vermont who had timber wolves for pets, so I used real wolves as models for that wicked old trickster.

In a moment of sheer inspiration, I decided to set the story a century ago here in the hills and forests of rural New England, instead of in the mountains of Bavaria. After all, this was an autobiography of sorts; although I may have sauerbraten in my genes, I have never actually seen the Black Forest and I am a New Englander by choice. Strangely enough, not one reviewer caught it; they all said things like "set in the forests of Germany."

I used my own kitchen with its woodstove, my favorite cats past and present, and all the familiar ferny paths of the woods near my home. To frame the illustrations, I used the fabric patterns of all the dresses I could remember from my childhood.

I have never had so much fun working on a picture book. It was automatic writing drawn from a wellspring of memory and faith. And if

Little Red has suffered any mortal wounds from it, she has never let me know. (Although quite a few critics accused Grandmother of alcoholism because of the bottle of wine in Little Red's basket.)

Two years later, Barbara Rogasky and I decided that an interesting followup to *Red Riding Hood* would be *The Water of Life,* one of the lesser-known and more fascinating of the Grimms' tales. It seemed right for slightly older kids, and might appeal to boys for a change. It turned out to be an extraordinarily difficult book to do in more ways than one. My only sister was dying of leukemia during the year and a half I was working on the illustrations, and I remember thinking as I worked, "If the youngest son can only find the water of life . . . if the king can only discover the truth about his sons . . . if I can make this as perfect and as true and as beautiful as I possibly can, then my sister will live." Alas, she did not live, and to this day I can't look at the book without a feeling of failure even though I know that the pictures are as true and beautiful as I could make them. I should have let the world of Grimm remind me that although the power of faith and charms can work magic, the forces of nature are more powerful still.

Charting my own progress as an artist and illustrator through Grimms' fairy tales is interesting, at least to me. Trying to imagine the effect these stories have had on my personal life and the mishmash of psychological and emotional intricacies we lamely call the creative process defeats me utterly. Now, as for Struwwelpeter. . . . Well, another day.

Ashputtle:
or, The Mother's Ghost

Angela Carter

A BURNED CHILD lived in the ashes. No, not really burned—
more charred, a little bit charred, like a stick half-burned and
picked off the fire. She looked like charcoal and ashes because
she lived in the ashes since her mother died and the hot ashes burned
her so she was scabbed and scarred. The burned child lived on the
hearth, covered in ashes, as if she were still mourning.

After her mother died and was buried, her father forgot the mother
and forgot the child and married the woman who used to rake the ashes
and that was why the child lived in the unraked ashes and there was
nobody to brush her hair so it stuck out like a mat nor to wipe the dirt
off her scabbed face and she had no heart to do it for herself but she
raked the ashes and slept beside the little cat and got the burned bits
from the bottom of the pot to eat, scraping them out, squatting on the
floor, by herself in front of the fire, not as if she were human, because
she was still mourning.

Her mother was dead and buried but still felt perfect exquisite pain of love when she looked up through the earth and saw the burned child covered in ashes.

"Milk the cow, burned child, and bring back all the milk," said the stepmother, who used to rake the ashes and milk the cow once upon a time, but now the burned child did all that.

The ghost of the mother went into the cow.

"Drink milk, grow fat," said the mother's ghost.

The burned child pulled on the udder and drank enough milk before she took the bucket back and nobody saw and time passed and she grew fat, she grew breasts, she grew up.

There was a man the stepmother wanted and she asked him into the kitchen to give him his dinner but she let the burned child cook it although the stepmother did all the cooking, once upon a time. After the burned child cooked the dinner the stepmother sent her off to milk the cow.

"I want that man for myself," said the burned child to the cow.

The cow let down more milk, and more, and more, enough for the girl to have a drink and wash her face and wash her hands. When she washed her face, she washed the scabs off and now she was not burned at all, but the cow was empty.

"Give your own milk, next time," said the ghost of the mother inside the cow. "I'm dry."

The little cat came by. The ghost of the mother went into the cat.

"Your hair wants doing," said the cat. "Lie down."

The little cat unpicked her raggy lugs with its clever paws until the burned child's hair hung down nice but it had been so snagged and tangled that the cat's claws were all pulled out before it was finished.

"Comb your own hair, next time," said the cat. "I can't do it again."

The burned child was clean and combed but stark naked.

There was a bird sitting in the apple tree. The ghost of the mother left the cow and went into the bird. The bird struck its own breast with its beak. Blood poured down onto the burned child under the tree. It ran over her shoulders and covered her front and covered her back. She shouted out when it ran down her legs. When the bird had no more blood, the burned child wore a red silk dress.

"Make your own dress, next time," said the bird. "There's no blood left."

The burned child went into the kitchen to show herself to the man. She was not burned any more, but lovely. The man left off looking at the stepmother and looked at the girl.

"Come home with me and let your stepmother rake the ashes," he said to her and off they went. He gave her a house and money. She did all right.

"Now I can go to sleep," said the mother's ghost. "Everything is all right, now."

Notes on Contributors

BRIAN ALDERSON is Children's Books Editor for the London *Times* and also works as a freelance journalist and lecturer with a special interest in children's literature. After working in the English book trade in the 1950s, he became a lecturer in children's literature at the School of Librarianship at the Polytechnic of North London. In 1967 he translated Bettina Hürlimann's *Three Centuries of Children's Books in Europe*, and his *Popular Folk Tales* from Grimm appeared in 1978. Since then he has worked on translations of early versions of the stories to be published by Cambridge University Press; and he has been commissioned to prepare an extensive annotated translation for the Oxford University Press World's Classics series.

MARGARET ATWOOD is the author of twenty volumes of poetry, fiction, and nonfiction, including *The Handmaid's Tale* (1986) and *Bluebeard's Egg* (1983). Her works have been published in at least fifteen countries. She is involved in the Canadian Centre (English speaking) of International P.E.N. and is active on environmental issues. Born in Ottawa in 1939, Margaret Atwood currently lives in Toronto with novelist Graeme Gibson and their daughter Jess. Her most recent work is *Wilderness Tips* (1991).

JACQUES BARCHILON is Professor of French Literature at the University of Colorado at Boulder. He is the author of seven books and editions, and many articles. His scholarship is mainly devoted to Charles Perrault and the French fairy tale. He is also the editor of a multilingual international journal, *Merveilles & contes,* which is devoted to the promotion of serious scholarship on the folk and fairy tale. Among his publications are *Pensées chrétiennes* of Charles Perrault (1987), a critical biography *Charles Perrault* (1981), and *Le conte merveilleux français* (1975).

RUTH B. BOTTIGHEIMER teaches at the State University of New York at Stony Brook. She is the author of *Grimms' Bad Girls and Bold Boys: The Moral and Social Vision of the Tales* (1987) and editor of *Fairy Tales and Society: Illusion, Allusion, and Paradigm* (1986). She has also published articles on children's literature, illustrations, folk narrative, psychological interpretations of fairy tales, German literature, and social history, and has acted as script adviser for the fairy-tale films *Soldier Jack* and *Ashpet* (Davenport Films).

ANGELA CARTER (d. 1992) was a novelist and author of short stories. Her books include *The Bloody Chamber* (1979), which consists of stories based upon traditional fairy tales, and a translation of tales by Charles Perrault (1984). She taught writing at Brown University, Providence, Rhode Island, and the Iowa Writers' Workshop, among other places. Her most recent novel is *Wise Children* (1991).

DONALD HAASE is Associate Professor and Chair of the Department of German and Slavic Languages and Literatures at Wayne State University. He has published articles and essays on Grimms' tales, fairy-tale movies, the proverb, and the reception of the fairy tale by German exile writers. He has twice directed Summer Seminars on the Brothers Grimm for the National Endowment for the Humanities. He is currently compiling an annotated bibliography of scholarship on Grimms' tales to be published in Garland Publications' Folklore series.

TRINA SCHART HYMAN was born in Philadelphia, Pennsylvania, and knew at an early age that she wanted to become an artist. She began formal art training while still in high school and continued her studies at the Philadelphia College of Art, the Boston Museum School, and Konstfackskolan in Stockholm, Sweden. She has illustrated over one hundred thirty books for children and was the first art director for *Cricket* magazine. In 1982 her *Rapunzel* was selected an ALA Notable Book, in 1984 her edition of *Little Red Riding Hood* was a Caldecott Honor Book, and in 1985 she received the Caldecott Medal for *Saint George and the Dragon*.

SHAWN JARVIS has been conducting extensive archival research on fairy tales by nineteenth-century German women, especially Gisela von Arnim. In an effort to make texts by Arnim more generally available, she has edited the first complete edition of *Das Leben der Hochgräfin Gritta von Rattenzuhausbeiuns* (1986); a facsimile edition of Arnim's *Märchenbriefe an Achim* (1991); and a third volume of fairy tales and illustrations from the *Kaffeterkreis* by Gisela, Armgart von Arnim, and Herman Grimm (in preparation). She is currently an Assistant Professor of German at St. Cloud State University, St. Cloud, Minnesota.

INES KÖHLER-ZÜLCH studied Slavic, Germanic, and Romance languages and literatures in Marburg and Hamburg. Her dissertation was devoted to the nineteenth-century Bulgarian *Alexanderroman,* especially in the context of the Rumanian and Greek traditions. Her various publications are in the field of folkloristic narrative research. She is one of the editors of the *Enzyklopädie des Märchens* in Göttingen.

WOLFGANG MIEDER is Professor of German and Folklore, as well as Chairperson of the Department of German and Russian at the University of Vermont (Burlington). He is a Fellow of the American Folklore Society and editor of *Proverbium: Yearbook of International Proverb Scholarship*. He is the author of numerous articles and almost fifty books on proverbs, fairy tales, legends, folk songs, art, literature, and other subjects. Among his English books are *The Wisdom of Many: Essays on the Proverb* (with Alan Dundes, 1981), *International Proverb Scholarship: An Annotated Bibliography* (1982), *Disenchantments: An Anthology of Modern Fairy Tale Poetry* (1985), *Encyclopedia of World Proverbs* (1986), *Tradition and Innovation in Folk Literature* (1987), and *American Proverbs: A Study of Texts and Contexts* (1989).

SIEGFRIED NEUMANN studied in Rostock and received his doctorate in ethnology and German from the Humboldt University at Berlin in

1961. He was a scholar at the German Academy of Sciences in Berlin and is now leading the Institute for Ethnology (Wossidlo-Archiv) in Rostock. He has written and edited more than a dozen books and numerous articles in German, Polish, Bulgarian, Italian, French, and English on the history of German folklore and on subjects relating to proverbs and to folk narratives such as fairy tales, humorous tales, saint's legends, modern legends, and *Alltagserzählungen*.

RICHARD PERKINS received his doctorate in philosophy from the State University of New York at Buffalo. He currently teaches at the Bennett Park Montessori Center in the Buffalo Public Schools and directs the Western New York Center for Reflective Education, an Institute for the Advancement of Philosophy for Children affiliate center. He writes extensively on Nietzsche. His articles have appeared in journals devoted to philosophy, Germanic studies, comparative literature, and Nietzsche, as well as in symposium and *Festschrift* collections. His book, *Zarathustra's Three Metamorphoses: Nietzsche as Parodist, Syncretist, and Alchemist,* is an interpretive study dealing with the root metaphor underlying *Also sprach Zarathustra.*

KAY STONE is both a folklorist and a professional storyteller whose interests center on the *Märchen*. She has been teaching folklore and related subjects at the University of Winnipeg since 1972 and has performed for both adults and children since 1974. Her numerous articles in both academic and nonacademic publications have examined the popular fairy tales and their heroines, the translation of these tales into other media (notably the films of Walt Disney), and the contemporary use of the *Märchen* by urban professional storytellers.

MARIA TATAR teaches German literature at Harvard University. She is the author of *Spellbound: Studies on Mesmerism and Literature* (1978), *The Hard Facts of the Grimms' Fairy Tales* (1987), and *Off with Their Heads: Fairy Tales and the Literary Culture of Childhood* (1992).

JANE YOLEN, who is known as "the Hans Christian Andersen of America," has authored over one hundred books, many of them collections of her literary fairy tales. Her books have won prizes such as the Caldecott Medal, the Sydney J. Taylor Award, the World Fantasy Award, the Christopher Medal, the Mythopoeic Society Award, and others. Past president of the Science Fiction Writers of America, and a seventeen-year member of the Board of Directors of the Society of Children's Book Writers, Ms. Yolen is also on the editorial board of a number of scholarly journals in both the children's book field and the newly burgeoning field of storytelling. She is editor-in-chief of Jane Yolen Books, an imprint of Harcourt, Brace, Jovanovich, wife of Dr. David W. Stemple, and mother of three grown children.

JACK ZIPES is Professor of German at the University of Minnesota and has previously held professorships at New York University, the University of Munich, the University of Berlin, the University of Frankfurt, the University of Wisconsin-Milwaukee, and the University of Florida. His major publications include *Breaking the Magic Spell: Radical Theories of Folk and Fairy Tales* (1979), *Fairy Tales and the Art of Subversion* (1983), *The Trials and Tribulations of Little Red Riding Hood* (1983), *Don't Bet on the Prince: Contemporary Feminist Fairy Tales in North America and England* (1986), and *The Brothers Grimm: From Enchanted Forests to the Modern World* (1988). In addition, he has published a translation of *The Complete Fairy Tales of the Brothers Grimm* (1987) and *Spells of Enchantment* (1991), an anthology of literary fairy tales. He also co-edits *New German Critique,* an interdisciplinary journal of German studies, and has written numerous articles for various journals in the United States, Great Britain, Germany, Canada, and France.

Index

Individual titles of Grimms' fairy tales are indexed under the titles used in *The Complete Fairy Tales of the Brothers Grimm*, trans. Jack Zipes (New York: Bantam, 1987), as well as under common variations used in the essays.

309